ILLUSTRATIONS
OF POLITICAL ECONOMY

broadview editions
series editor: L.W. Conolly

ILLUSTRATIONS
OF POLITICAL ECONOMY

Selected Tales

Harriet Martineau

edited by Deborah Anna Logan

broadview editions

Library and Archives Canada Cataloguing in Publication

Martineau, Harriet, 1802–1876.

Illustrations of political economy : selected tales / Harriet Martineau ; edited by Deborah Anna Logan.

(Broadview editions)
Includes bibliographical references.
ISBN 1-55111-441-0

1. Didactic fiction, English. I. Logan, Deborah Anna, 1951- . II. Title. III. Series.

PR4984.M5I44 2004   823′.8   C2004-904978-X

Broadview Editions

The Broadview Editions series represents the ever-changing canon of literature in English by bringing together texts long regarded as classics with valuable lesser-known works.

Broadview Press Ltd. is an independent, international publishing house, incorporated in 1985. Broadview believes in shared ownership, both with its employees and with the general public; since the year 2000 Broadview shares have traded publicly on the Toronto Venture Exchange under the symbol BDP.

We welcome comments and suggestions regarding any aspect of our publications — please feel free to contact us at the addresses below or at broadview@broadviewpress.com.

North America
Post Office Box 1243, Peterborough, Ontario, Canada K9J 7H5
3576 California Road, Orchard Park, NY, USA 14127
Tel: (705) 743-8990; Fax: (705) 743-8353;
e-mail: customerservice@broadviewpress.com

UK, Ireland, and continental Europe
NBN Plymbridge, Estover Road, Plymouth PL6 7PY UK
Tel: 44 (0) 1752 202301   Fax: 44 (0) 1752 202331
Fax Order Line: 44 (0) 1752 202333
Customer Service: cservs@nbnplymbridge.com Orders: orders@nbnplymbridge.com

Australia and New Zealand
UNIREPS, University of New South Wales
Sydney, NSW, 2052
Tel: 61 2 9664 0999; Fax: 61 2 9664 5420
email: info.press@unsw.edu.au

www.broadviewpress.com

Advisory editor for this volume: Professor Eugene Benson

Typesetting and assembly: True to Type Inc., Mississauga, Canada.

PRINTED IN CANADA

Contents

Acknowledgements

I am grateful to Western Kentucky University for its generous support of my research on Harriet Martineau over the past few years. Funding for research travel and conference presentations was provided by the Graduate Studies Committee, the Potter College Travel Committee, and the travel committee of the Department of English, as well as by the Willson Wood Fellowship awarded to me by the English Department. For their editorial assistance on this project, I thank Karen White, Ben Crace, and Natalie Rich. Special thanks are due to Tony Rafalowski, the Willson Wood Graduate Fellow (2002-03), who worked with me on this and other Martineau projects. This book was improved in every way by their scrupulous attention to detail in the editing and proofreading processes. At Broadview Press, I thank Julia Gaunce for her enthusiasm for, and support of, this project, and for her insight into the significance of Harriet Martineau's contributions to the histories of literature, culture, and the social sciences. I dedicate this volume with love and thanks to my son, Zachary, whose optimism and compassion, encouragement and patience are to me a daily inspiration.

Introduction

1. Revolution and Reform

> Since the Reform Act of 1832 the most important social issue has
> been the condition of the working classes, who form the vast
> majority of the English people...What is to become of these prop-
> erty-less millions who own nothing and consume today what they
> earned yesterday? What fate is in store for the workers who by
> their inventions and labour have laid the foundations of England's
> greatness? What is to be the future of those now daily becoming
> more and more aware of their power and pressing more and more
> strongly for their share of the social advantages of the new era?
> (Engels 25)

Harriet Martineau (1802-76) began publishing monthly numbers of
her *Illustrations of Political Economy* in 1832, the same year Parliament
passed the First Reform Bill. Martineau's series enjoyed immediate
popular success, signifying the timeliness of the topic and the public's readiness to understand and utilize political economy theory as
a tool for social reform. The Reform Bill, on the other hand, was
notoriously controversial, enduring endless debate and repeated
rejections before its final passage. Even then, opponents complained
that the English way of life was doomed, while proponents complained that the Bill had not gone far enough. Together, these events
reflect the social unrest that had been gathering momentum for
decades prior to 1832 and that would continue to increase for many
more decades as England struggled to come to terms with the social
costs of industrialization. That Frederick Engels situates the problems of Britain's working classes after, rather than before, the 1832
Reform Bill overlooks the suffering they endured since the very
inception of the Industrial Revolution. Martineau's *Illustrations of
Political Economy* responds to that suffering, demonstrating compassion for people of any class whose quality of life was compromised
by, rather than enhanced by, the cultural progress and social evolution industrialism promised.

   In 1833, Harriet Martineau argued that the social problems created by industrialism, problems the science of political economy
attempted to explain, were appropriate topics for literature. Of the
reigning genre of the period, the novel, she wrote:

We must have, in a new novelist, the graver themes...which the present condition of society suggests. We have had enough of ambitious intrigues; why not now take the magnificent subject, the birth of political principle, whose advent has been heralded so long? What can afford finer moral scenery than the transition state in which society now is! Where are nobler heroes to be found than those who sustain society in the struggle; and what catastrophe so grand as the downfall of bad institutions, and the issues of a process of renovation? ("Achievements" 454)

Her remarks herald a pivotal moment in literary and political history in which these two avenues of social inquiry dovetailed to promote the interests of the "spirit of the age" in an unprecedented, and perhaps still unparalleled, union. The general mood of reform marking the 1820s and 1830s was fueled by a proliferation of political tracts, treatises, self-help and self-improvement literature aimed at facilitating working-class autonomy, economic independence, and institutional change. Martineau's radicalism in presenting reform issues—the "magnificent subject"—as suitable material for literature, in citing reformers as the "noble" heroes of the new era, and in encouraging the "downfall of bad institutions" to promote the moral "renovation" of society should not be underestimated: it certainly was not by the ruling class, who regarded the period's invigorating spirit of reform as a direct threat to its way of life.[1]

As the world's first industrialized nation, England endured the growing pains necessary for the shift from a rural, agrarian culture to an urban, industrial society. "The steam-engine had 'drawn together the population into dense masses'," writes E.P. Thompson, creating "new social relationships, institutions, and cultural modes....It is as if the English nation entered a crucible in the 1790s and emerged after the [Napoleonic] Wars in a different form" (208-09). Harriet Martineau's intellectual development was shaped during the turbulent first two decades of the century; her apprenticeship as a writer occurred during the 1820s, when political and social ferment inten-

---

1 Herbert Tucker notes that the 1830s yielded progressive social reforms
   but little imaginative literature: "The paradox of the 1830s has often been
   described in terms of the striking contrast between the richness of their
   political history...and the apparent barrenness of the cultural scene" (5).
   Martineau recognized the need for a genre appropriate to the concerns
   of the time; clearly, the *Illustrations of Political Economy* negates the charge
   of either cultural or literary "barrenness."

sified, leading to the parliamentary debates resulting in the 1832 Reform Bill. It was Martineau's sharp awareness of the significance of current events in the broader scheme of history and her keen sense of timing that prompted her to write the *Illustrations of Political Economy*—a series best regarded as secular "tracts for the times."

Whereas the cultural revolutions marking the period were primarily political in orientation, the revolution shaping British society, the Industrial Revolution, made the country's social problems unique among nations throughout the world.[1] Yet, the cultural impact of industry made technological progress a highly politicized issue. Industrialization facilitated radical shifts in Britain's class structure and highlighted the need to adapt protective legislation for the thus far unrepresented masses—especially the increasingly powerful middle class—as England entered the early modern age. In the early decades of the nineteenth century, the term "masses" included the middle- and lower-classes, anyone not born into wealth and position but having to work for a living, and anyone excluded from the franchise. Both the 1832 and the 1867 reform bills extended the franchise, but even then only property owners were permitted to vote, thus excluding, on material grounds, those most in need of shifting the balance of political power in their favor. By the 1830s, the most direct beneficiaries of industrial prosperity, the middle classes, were no longer part of the masses but were well on their way to becoming the new ruling class.

Throughout the first half of the nineteenth century, fears that the bloody revolution in France would be replicated by an uprising of Britain's disenfranchised lower classes underpinned and shaped public discourse as politicians and reformists debated the benefits and pitfalls of *laissez-faire* government. The argument at the center of reform discourse, a *laissez-faire* or "let alone" political system, is one in which government intervention in private sector economy is minimal or, ideally, absent altogether. In practice, such a system enabled the ruling class to maintain its position while preventing the lower orders from achieving economic ascendancy or social progress of any kind; such blatant social imbalance was unacceptable to the masses,

---

1 "The phrase *Industrial Revolution*," notes Raymond Williams, "is modelled explicitly on an analogy with the French Revolution" (xiv) and its precursor, the American Revolution. Although by different means, society in America, France, and England changed radically, each producing a new cultural and national identity. The terms "industry" and "democracy" indicate social revolutions on all fronts, from political to economic.

who demanded a more equitable distribution of opportunities in increasingly insistent tones. Of those in a position to debate the issue, some argued that government non-intervention was the only prevention for social revolution; others maintained that legislative reform alone would quell the potential for an uprising. It was the latter option which won the debate, with the period's reform measures wresting some political and economic power from the ruling classes, to be distributed more equitably among the middle classes and—although much later in the century and to a far less degree—to the lower classes.

Although Harriet Martineau's ideology has been termed *laissez-faire* (and she does advocate non-intervention wherever feasible), her long and illustrious career as the period's premier woman social-reform writer, whose work is distinguished by her uncompromising ideals concerning social justice and by her criticisms of inequitable social policies, complicates the claim that she advocated a "do-nothing" government. Further, her writing exerted considerable influence in parliamentary and industrial circles, even as she resisted party affiliations.[1] The conflict Martineau experienced on this point was typical of the period: many agreed that government intervention in the affairs of business and economy in the private sector was undesirable. However, because self-interest was the predominant motivation, making voluntary self-regulation notoriously unreliable, legislation proved to be necessary in order to protect the interests of the new ruling class, while the more pressing subsistence concerns of the lower classes lagged behind. Richard Altick notes the intensification of class animosity once the working-classes realized that the 1832 Bill "for which the masses had entertained such high hopes was an instrument to solidify middle-class control of the nation" (193).[2] Some considera-

---

1 Gillian Thomas synthesizes the ideas of *laissez-faire*, legislative intervention, and social problem writing with education and reconciles Martineau's apparent self-contradiction by emphasizing that her interest was less in legislative than in social intervention (*Harriet Martineau*).

2 E.P. Thompson notes: "A witness before the parliamentary committee enquiring into the hand-loom weavers (1835) was asked to state the view of his fellows on the Reform Bill: Q. Are the working classes better satisfied with the institutions of the country since the change has taken place? A. I do not think they are. They viewed the Reform Bill as a measure calculated to join the middle and upper classes to Government, and leave them in the hands of Government as a sort of machine to work according to the pleasure of Government" (915).

tion of the social and political climate of the late eighteenth and early nineteenth centuries, and of the thinkers and writers that shaped not only public discourse but also Martineau's intellectual development, dramatizes how her "coming of age" as a reform writer aptly reflects the spirit of the age whose spokeswoman she was destined to become.

2. The Spirit of the Age

These Chartisms, Radicalisms, Reform Bill, Tithe Bill, and infinite other discrepancy, and acrid argument and jargon that there is yet to be, are *our* French Revolution: God grant that we, with our better methods, may be able to transact it by argument alone.
—Thomas Carlyle[1]

The following overview of the events and influences shaping the reform era highlights the primary intellectual trends that established the socio-political climate necessary for the enthusiastic reception of Martineau's *Illustrations of Political Economy*. The period surrounding the series' publication, fancifully characterized by Joseph Kestner as "the collectivist twenties, the radical thirties, the hungry forties, the becalmed fifties, and the equilibrated sixties" (16), has a history dating back to the American Revolution in 1776 and heralds the subsequent spread of democracy across Europe. A survey of the issues debated by prominent thinkers and writers of the period—ideas which Martineau, as a radical Dissenter and intellectual liberal, was well acquainted with—reveals that an essential site for social change concerned a reordering of ancient class hierarchies.

The eighteenth century's Age of Reason, with its—to modern perspectives—startling complacency about the inviolability of existing class structures, erupted into an era of revolutions that continues to reverberate in the postmodern world. Two of the most symbolic influences that were to shape nineteenth-century British culture occurred in the same year: the American Revolution and the publication of Adam Smith's *An Inquiry into the Nature and Causes of the Wealth of Nations*.[2] With its infamous "shot heard round the world,"

---

1   *Works of Thomas Carlyle* (vol. 6, 137). Thomas Carlyle (1795-1881), British philosopher, historian, and social critic. He is the author of *Sartor Resartus* (1833-34) and *Past and Present* (1843).

2   Adam Smith (1723-90), political economist. His best-known work is *An Inquiry into the Nature and Causes of the Wealth of Nations* (2 vols., 1776; 3 vols., 1784).

the Revolution alerted the ruling classes of Europe to the genuine threat posed to their interests by the unrepresented masses, a class far too numerous to be ignored. As the theoretical counterpart to the war in America, it is a remarkable coincidence, and certainly no accident, that Adam Smith's formulation of an ideology destined to be instrumental in the transformation of political, economic, and class relations was published in the same year.[1] Reacting against eighteenth-century attitudes towards aristocratic privilege, Smith promoted a *laissez-faire* ideology in which the marketplace would be primarily self-regulatory and government intervention minimal. The potential benefit of *laissez-faire* was that it permitted the non-aristocratic classes, who were politically unrepresented, to participate in the marketplace despite their lack of aristocratic privilege. But the drawbacks of *laissez-faire* were more obvious to those of the lower classes: that is, that the interests of the politically unrepresented were hardly on a par with those of the ruling classes, and these interests could not hope to progress without government intervention, a dynamic just barely initiated by the 1832 Reform Bill. An affront to aristocratic tradition at the time, *The Wealth of Nations* foregrounds the idea that, while voluntary self-regulation is desirable, it is unrealistic until a more equitable balance is achieved among the classes, institutionally and politically, economically and materially.

A concurrent influence was Jeremy Bentham's utilitarianism, a theory arguing first, that pain and pleasure (self-interest) are what govern human conduct and second, that social progress should be measured according to that which ensures the greatest happiness for the greatest number of people.[2] Offering two more remarkable instances of timing, Bentham's ideas were published, first as *Fragment on Government* in 1776 and then as *Introduction to Principles of Morals and Legislation* in 1789. Of Bentham, Martineau writes: "[N]o man was more acute in exposing legislative faults, and proposing the true principles

---

1   The new science of political economy developed in reaction not only to political revolutions but also to industrial culture. Maxine Berg writes, "It was no mere coincidence that industrialisation and the emergence of political economy occurred at virtually the same time. Political economy became a distinct discipline from the 1790s" (17).

2   Jeremy Bentham (1748-1832) promoted the theory of utilitarianism and advocated prison reform and civil rights. Bentham applied the idea of the Panopticon, originally developed for use in factories, to prisons. Panopticon is an architectural arrangement in which all parts of an interior are visible from a central surveillance point.

on which remedy should proceed; and to him we owe, primarily, a large proportion of the legislative and social reforms of the half-century" (*History* 1:449-50). But Martineau's enduring interest is in testing theory by measuring its practical application, and in this she finds Bentham wanting: "His Utilitarian Philosophy will not stand by itself, though it has been a valuable check on the selfishness of power, and an inestimable assertion of the rights of the depressed." Investigating the intersection of principle and practice provides the essential motivation underpinning all of Martineau's social problem writing.

Taking inspiration from the American example, in which the formidable power of the British Empire was successfully overthrown by the "citizen soldiery" of rebellious colonials, the French launched their own revolution in 1789, this one more deliberately aimed at transforming class hierarchies. Britain watched warily as this second instance of a radical uprising unfolded, uneasy lest the spectacle of rebellion against ruling class tyranny might give its own restive populace similar ideas. As the democratic ideals of the French Revolution gave way to the bloody Reign of Terror and were further perverted by Napoleon's expansionist policies, Britain's anxiety about events across the channel proved to be justified.[1]

Two avenues through which those fears were expressed were religious and political persecution. In 1791, Joseph Priestley, a chemist, Necessarian, Jacobin, and Unitarian Dissenter,[2] had his Birmingham home and laboratory destroyed by a "Church and King" mob. The incident reveals the prevailing mood of fear and lawlessness, the lat-

---

1   Georg Lukacs stresses the impact of the French Revolution on the formation of the modern novel: "the history writing of the Enlightenment was...an ideological preparation for the French Revolution" (20), just as eighteenth-century British society fostered "the economic and social preconditions for the Industrial Revolution" (21). Lukacs argues that the French Revolution "for the first time made history a *mass experience*" (23), generating the cultural energy needed to establish the democratic era. Social *evolution* thus depends on social *revolution*.

2   Joseph Priestley (1733-1804), theologian and scientist, was the first to isolate the element oxygen. Necessarianism is the doctrine of determinism, the belief that events are not a result of individual will but are predetermined. A Jacobin is sympathetic to the ideals of the French Revolution. Unitarianism is a sect advocating social reform and dissenting from or rejecting the doctrines of the Church of England. Dissenters were punished for their radicalism by the Test and Corporation Acts (enacted seventeenth century, repealed 1828), which prohibited their participation in public office or other positions of influence.

ter sanctioned in the name of suppressing any religious or political dissent threatening the social fabric. Martineau acknowledged her intellectual debt to the exiled Priestley by making a pilgrimage to his Pennsylvania home when she visited America and by devoting an entire chapter to him in *Retrospect of Western Travel*. Priestley, she writes, was a "single-minded martyr," who stood by his convictions despite their unpopularity (*Retrospect* 110). Similar examples of political paranoia include the near arrest of William Wordsworth and Samuel Taylor Coleridge by an eaves-dropper whose suspicions were aroused by their discussion about the philosopher Spinoza (heard as "Spy Nozy"). And William Blake's objection to a British soldier tramping through his garden resulted in his trial for sedition; although acquitted, his brush with bureaucratic tyranny scarred him permanently.

In such a social climate, it is hardly surprising that political activist Tom Paine,[1] who had been instrumental in the American conflict, was exiled from Britain in 1793, his *Rights of Man* banned as seditious libel. Paine's exposure of what E.P. Thompson terms "the inertia of class interests" (98) demonstrates the logical progression linking Adam Smith's political economy theories with the practical social justice Paine advocates, both fueled by the pervasive urge toward democracy. Thompson notes that the *Rights of Man* and the *Wealth of Nations* "supplement and nourish each other," and that "nineteenth-century working-class Radicalism took its cast from Paine" (105). Martineau admired the man as well as his writing: "O Tom Paine! How beautiful!" she wrote to publisher William Fox. "That is the style I should like to write. If I could send you a paper in his manner, how happy I should be!"[2] She also admired radical philosopher William Godwin, whose novel *Caleb Williams* (1794) articulated his views on social injustice and shifting class relations, providing a suggestive model for the didactic fiction that was to earn Martineau her earliest fame. Prior to her departure for America in 1834, Godwin took Martineau on a tour of Parliament, whose buildings were burned several months later, an event dramatizing the shift in the balance of power from crown and peerage to the House of Commons and middle-classes initiated in 1832.

---

1 Thomas Paine (1737-1809), British writer and social and political activist. Paine contributed to the American and French revolutions and is best known for "Common Sense" (1776) and *The Rights of Man* (1791-92).
2 Martineau to William Fox, April 1832 (Bancroft Library, University of California at Berkeley, 2:33).

One of the most insightful voices in social discourse was that of Thomas Malthus,[1] whose *An Essay on the Principle of Population* (1798) exerted profound influence over reform debates. Reverend Malthus posited that a large part of the deprivations suffered by the lower classes stemmed from too few resources for too many people. In the absence of protective legislation designed to ameliorate the economic problems of the poor, Malthus's solution—that the lower class control the balance between resources and people by exercising the "preventive check" of sexual abstinence (voluntary celibacy and delayed marriages)—was destined to become one of the most controversial ideas of the time. Despite its elegant simplicity, Malthusian theory raised complex issues, including the perpetuation of ruling-class ascendancy and lower-class oppression by placing (or seeming to place) the solution for an inequitable economy solely on the latter. But Malthus' intended purpose was simply that "domestic virtue and happiness should be placed within the reach of all" (*Autobiography* [hereafter *AB*] 1:209). Martineau adds, "It was my business...to exemplify Malthus's doctrine....It was that doctrine 'pure and simple,' as it came from his virtuous and benevolent mind, that I presented; and the presentment was accompanied by an earnest advocacy of the remedies which the great natural laws of Society put into our power" (*AB* 1:210-11). She concludes that Malthus, like other social pariahs of the period, "did more for social ease and virtue than perhaps any other man of his time, [yet he] was the 'best-abused man' of the age." Loyal to her friend and mentor, Martineau remained sanguine about earning herself the epithet, "that Malthusian woman," with which she was associated for the rest of her life.[2]

By the end of the eighteenth century, bureaucratic concerns about increasing social unrest resulted in legislation—not to protect the masses, but more fully to protect the ruling class against the threats

---

1   Reverend Thomas Malthus (1766-1834), political economist best known for his *Essay on the Principle of Population* (1798). Malthus held the Professor of Political Economy chair at Haileybury College, where Martineau visited him on several occasions.

2   See also *AB* 1:327-29 for an account of the friendship between Martineau and Malthus. After reading her political economy tales, Malthus requested a meeting with her, eager to meet the writer who "had represented his views precisely as he could have wished" (1:327). For Martineau, the "great natural laws of Society" are those which guide social evolution and are articulated by political economy theories.

represented by the poor. The Combination Acts of 1799-1800 made workers' organizing illegal; even social gatherings of a few people were forbidden as potentially subversive. But the ploy backfired, resulting not in the elimination of "combining" but in the retreat of such organizations "into an illegal world in which secrecy and hostility to the authorities were intrinsic to their very existence" (Thompson 550). Forced underground, alliances among workers continued to strengthen, while polarization from hegemonic institutions increased the cultural alienation between the "two nations" (rich and poor) that Thomas Carlyle, Benjamin Disraeli, and Frederick Engels found so striking in subsequent decades.

The stamp tax or "tax on knowledge," which made the mainstream press prohibitively expensive for the masses, patently served the interests of the ruling class and promoted its ideology. But the alternative press was also vitally active at this time, disseminating newspapers, periodicals, pamphlets, and broadsides attesting to the burgeoning energy of the reform counter-culture. One of the most influential periodicals of the alternative press was William Cobbett's *Political Register*, begun in 1801. A political radical and reformer, Cobbett voiced an idea essential to the period's reform discourse by asserting that, as a solution for the poor, charity should be avoided as it promotes *interference* (thus compromising the principle of *laissez-faire*) on the one hand while fostering *dependence* on the other by depriving the poor of agency and autonomy. Martineau similarly juxtaposes patronizing interference with passive dependence, advocating self-help and self-sufficiency as the necessary pre-requisites for social progress. Simply put, teaching the poor how to "do" for themselves empowers them and subverts their oppression by the ruling class, an oppression insidiously perpetuated by charitable schemes, however benevolently intended.[1]

A more graphic demonstration of the failure of the Combination Acts to suppress workers' organizing was demonstrated by the Luddite crisis of 1811-13. The Luddites (named after Ned Ludd, leader of the first such outbreak) were associated primarily with frame-

---

1 Martineau's philosophical orientation was based on Necessarianism, "which taught the need for the utmost exertion on the part of each individual to bring himself or herself into line with the natural laws of the universe...for every result there was a cause, and...knowledge of these causes put the individual's fate in his own hands" (Polkinghorn 1998, 19). This insight underlies the didacticism distasteful to modern readers, who prefer a clearer distinction between fiction and nonfiction.

breaking, that is, the destruction of the industrial machinery workers believed deprived them of their livelihoods and drove them further into poverty. Luddite violence targeted not only machines but also the factories and homes of the mill owners, and even industrialists themselves. Although Martineau was committed to empowering the poor, she deplored violence and, in her assessment of Luddism, she added her voice to those condemning organization and solidarity among the working classes: "There never before was such an organized system of havoc resorted to by men who were at once grossly ignorant and preeminently crafty" (*History* 2:54). While she acknowledges that industrialization created permanent and irrevocable changes, particularly to the economic and social well-being of the working poor, she insists that neither combining nor frame-breaking is a viable solution. The answer does not lie, she asserts, in attempting to thwart progress—a futile endeavor at best—but in finding alternative employments for those who have lost their livelihoods to the new technology: "The ignorance which has more or less prevailed at all times on the subject of machinery—coupled with the want of employment produced by the depression of every branch of industry—was the cause that, undeterred by the terrible penalties of the law, the Luddites still pursued the course which had wellnigh...converted temporary into permanent ruin" (2:55). An 1812 law that made machine breaking punishable by death succeeded in driving the movement underground, although sporadic outbreaks of Luddism continued for years. But the measure addressed only the symptoms, not the underlying problems, of industrialization; and social unrest and the need for constructive reform persisted, requiring more permanent measures to ensure against the threat of social upheaval.

A comparatively peaceful counter-culture movement of the period was Owenite socialism, named after businessman Robert Owen,[1] which emphasized cooperation over competition within the capitalist paradigm. Seeking to humanize the dehumanization of industrialism, Owen urged that kindness and compassion replace

---

1   Robert Owen (1771-1858), businessman and socialist thinker who established several utopian communities, in England and America, to demonstrate his theories. Owen stressed cooperative relations in industry, government, and society, and emphasized a compassionate and nurturing approach to child-rearing, including education, that anticipated the child-labor law reform movement. While Martineau admired Owen's social theories, she argued that he was too idealistic and impractical to successfully implement his theories.

brutality and exploitation; he established schools in his mills to encourage literacy among the workers and limited children's work hours, anticipating the Factory Acts (1833) for the protection of child laborers. Owen published his alternative vision of social relations in *A New View of Society* (1813) and applied his ideas in his mills at New Lanark as well as in his utopian community at New Harmony, Ohio. Although Owenism was destined to fail because, as Martineau later claimed, its founder's vision was undermined by his lack of practicality, Owen's ideas profoundly impacted early nineteenth-century British society. Owen called on Martineau during her London years, but he was unable to convince her to promote his doctrine in her fiction. In her view, Owen's wisdom was overshadowed by his "absurdity," and his social vision by his "eccentricity," although she concedes that the reform movement owed much to his efforts to create alternative social frameworks.[1]

The end of the Napoleonic wars launched an intensification of reform movements. The year 1815 marked Napoleon's defeat at Waterloo, initiating a period E.P. Thompson terms "the heroic age of popular Radicalism" (660). The Corn Laws (1815), a protective tariff which taxed imported grain in order to enhance the domestic market, benefited the land-holding aristocracy but further exacerbated the sufferings of the poor. Those who could not afford the high-priced domestic product had no alternative but to starve, a dynamic dramatized by Martineau in "Sowers not Reapers." The struggles of the lower classes highlighted the tragic anomaly of suffering among the masses in the foremost industrialized, technologically advanced, and progressive country in the world. Martineau advocated Corn Law repeal and was an outspoken critic of protectionism (tariffs obstructing competitive foreign trade), to her mind the most insidious form of government interference in private economic affairs.

Several popular uprisings in 1816 resulted in the suspension of Habeas Corpus and the passage of the Seditious Meetings Act. But as history repeatedly proved, suppression only caused discontent to ferment, and 1817 was marked by more uprisings of working-class petitioners whose purpose was to air their grievances, not to commit violence. Their method of protest was simply to gather together and walk, perhaps to a site where relevant meetings effecting their well-being were being held, their non-violent protest being limited to a

---

1 See *AB* 1:231-33 and Martineau's obituary of Owen in London's *Daily News*, November 19, 1858.

show of numbers. These workers' marches appealed, peaceably, to the need for reform, but the perceived threat of potential violence provoked fear and swift bureaucratic retribution. For example, the Pentridge Rising garnered a few hundred participants who were quickly put down and dispersed by troops; several of the leaders were charged with treason and hung. Also in 1817, David Ricardo's[1] *On the Principles of Political Economy and Taxation* was published. Along with his theory of rents, Ricardo promoted free trade and formulated the wages-fund doctrine, the latter positing that the amount of workers' wages, like manufacturers' profits, depended on economic fluctuations in the marketplace. Martineau incorporated Ricardo's theories in "Ella of Garveloch" and "A Manchester Strike."

Marking the end of "the heroic age of popular Radicalism" was the tragic 1819 Peterloo Massacre, in which a peaceful, unarmed protest by the poor and working classes (numbering about 60,000) was aggressively put down by armed forces, leaving eleven protesters dead and four hundred injured. The event had various implications: that civil discontent was not to be suppressed or ignored; that social protest, even if nonviolent, posed a threat that could and would be halted with bureaucratic force; and that public sympathy was increasingly shifting away from the privileged and toward the poor. Percy Shelley's "The Mask of Anarchy" captures the growing spirit of public outrage against government excesses and displays of force against those powerless to defend themselves, people simply seeking social justice. Comparing the national mood surrounding the Peterloo Massacre with that of the First Reform Bill, E.P. Thompson observes: "1819 was a rehearsal for 1832. In both years a revolution was possible....And in 1819 the reformers appeared more powerful than they had ever been before *because* they came forward in the role of constitutionalists. They laid claim to rights" (737). This demand for social justice reflects the human rights ethic underpinning democratic ideology.

With influences such as these shaping her intellectual growth, Martineau first began to conceive of herself as a writer in the decade that witnessed the greatest intensification of reform agitation. The 1820s were marked by an accelerated use of the radical (unstamped) press to spread reform propaganda, particularly through the dissemination of pamphlets among the increasingly literate lower classes.

---

1   David Ricardo (1772-1823), political economist best known for his theories on rent. He also wrote various treatises on currency and economic policies.

James Mill's[1] *Elements of Political Economy* (1821) outlined four basic categories of investigation—production, distribution, interchange, and consumption—and provided the framework through which Martineau organized her own series. Although Mill had initially tried to dissuade William and Charles Fox from publishing the *Illustrations*, arguing that fiction was not a suitable medium for political economy, he later apologized to Martineau and acknowledged the irrefutable success of her series (*AB* 2:1). Also notable at this time is Martineau's first appearance in print, when her article "Female Writers on Practical Divinity" (1822) was published in the Unitarian periodical, *Monthly Repository*. The modest success and warm reception of her first literary effort encouraged her to continue writing and publishing throughout the decade, an apprenticeship that was to prepare her for the greatest professional undertaking of her life.

The repeal of the Combination Laws in 1824 paved the way for a proliferation of trade union activity, fostering the various movements that culminated in Chartism in the 1830s and 1840s.[2] Martineau's earliest contribution to manufacturing discourse was the 1827 tale, *The Rioters; or, a Tale of Bad Times*, a story in which she denounces working class combining even as she encourages self-empowerment in that class—a perspective that, to modern readers, seems a contradiction in terms. Also repealed were the Test and Corporation Acts (1828), which exerted control over Dissenters (any who rejected the Church of England's supremacy) by prohibiting their participation in any official or public capacity. Martineau's second tale on the manufacturing milieu, *The Turn-Out; or, Patience the Best Policy*, was published in 1829, the year Parliament passed the

---

1 James Mill (1773-1836), Utilitarian philosopher and writer. Mill's best-known works include *History of India* (1818) and *Elements of Political Economy* (1821). Mill served on the board of the East India Company, as did his son John Stuart Mill.

2 Martineau dates Chartist organizing from 1835, noting: "as it is living so long after the announcement that it was dead, so was it living long before it was declared to be born" (*History* 4:554). The movement originated with those "who saw that the Reform Bill was, if not a failure in itself, a failure in regard to the popular expectation from it. A vast proportion of the people—the very part of the nation whose representation was most important to the welfare of the State,—were not represented at all" (4:555). With the increase in Chartist activism in the 1840s, Martineau's *The Rioters* (1827) was reissued in 1842, illustrating its continued relevance to the concerns of the time.

Catholic Emancipation Bill. This legislation proved to be a significant indicator that the further-reaching parliamentary reform promised by the 1832 bill was inevitable.

As a response to the social problems of industrialization and the political and economic inequities of Britain's class structure, the science of political economy had continued to develop in the half-century since Adam Smith's *Wealth of Nations,* culminating in John McCulloch's[1] 1830 treatise, *The Principles of Political Economy.* Distinct from the male theorists who articulated social issues and shaped public policy with varying degrees of success (in terms of applicability), Martineau's contribution to this discourse is distinguished by her desire to make it accessible to a wider audience than the intellectually elite and to model more practical solutions to social problems than the theorists offered. Recalling Wordsworth's aim in *Lyrical Ballads* to write in the "real language of real men" (*Preface*), Martineau's series succeeded in popularizing political economy, aptly reflecting the general urge toward the democratization of social, economic, and political resources, an ideology that shook British complacency in 1832, no less than in 1776.

By 1829, Thomas Carlyle observed that the spirit of the age was no longer revolutionary but mechanical. In *Signs of the Times*, he observed: "Were we required to characterize this age of ours by any single epithet, we should be tempted to call it, not an Heroical, Devotional, Philosophical, or Moral Age, but, above all others, the Mechanical Age. It is the Age of Machinery, in every outward and inward sense of that word."[2] But Carlyle was only partially correct, for ruling class fears that social and political revolution might occur on British soil were at no time more justified than at the beginning of the 1830s, when the social problems engendered by industrialism were most acute, when reform agitation could no longer be suppressed or ignored, and when *laissez-fairism* was no longer a viable response to accelerating social unrest. With the national mood pushed to the extreme by a cholera epidemic,[3] reform measures were introduced in Parliament in the hope that social revolution could be

---

1 John Ramsay McCulloch (1789-1864), statistician and political economist.

2 *Works of Thomas Carlyle* (vol. 22, 233).

3 Writing of the cholera epidemic in *History of the Peace*, Martineau observed that "the awakening of society in England to the duty of care of the public health must date from the visitation of the cholera in 1831-32" (3:313). See also *AB* 1:409.

averted by giving the people what they wanted and needed, before they took it by force.

"The year 1831 opened gloomily," wrote Martineau, punctuated by rick-burning, machine-breaking, the murders of factory owners, and trade union agitation. "The ignorant and misled among the peasantry and artisans looked upon the French and other revolutions as showing that men had only to take affairs into their own hands, in order to obtain whatever they wanted" (*History* 3:250). She defines the confrontation as that between the "anti-reforming aristocracy" seeking to preserve its interests and the "large masses of malcontents....who are always eager for change, because they may gain, and cannot lose" (3:251).[1] Despite the harshness of the term "malcontents," the essential point in this passage is that the masses are in a state of agitation because they *have* nothing and so have nothing to lose by fighting for social justice. The ruling classes, in contrast, had everything to lose and thus had an enormous stake in maintaining the power imbalance that secured them privilege at the expense of the masses, a dramatic illustration of utilitarianism gone awry.

But by this time reform was inevitable: "there was enough unrest, enough violence, enough organization, and enough remembering to make men think first of the possibility of revolution and how to avoid it by reform—a reform whose revolutionary quality only later generations could discover" (Webb 1980, 203). The year 1832 marks the passage of the First Reform Bill and the publication of the first number of Martineau's *Illustrations of Political Economy*, making available for the first time in history an investigation of the social, political, and economic forces controlling the lives of the masses in a popular form. A new era was ushered into British culture and society, anticipated by the spread of democracy from America and France, prompted by the growing pains of the world's first industrialized society, and impelled by the pull of the modern age, towards which Britain was now rushing with an inevitability that was both frightening and exhilarating. Prior to 1776, Adam Smith had urged Parliament to give America the political representation it sought in order to prevent losing the colonies altogether, and his warning was ignored. But in 1831, Parliament did listen to Thomas Macaulay when he advised, "Reform, that you may preserve." Illustrating the complex relations and democratic underpinnings shared by the polit-

---

1 For Martineau's full account of the reform bill controversy, parliamentary debates, and the bill's final passage, see *History of the Peace* 3:250-309.

ical, industrial, and social revolutions of the period, the 1832 Bill "moved the country peacefully and without Continental style convulsions toward democracy" (Tucker 7). Thomas Carlyle's fervent hope that England will navigate its revolution "by argument alone" rather than by bloody uprisings found realization through ruling class concessions to middle class demands in 1832.

In view of critics' complaints that the First Reform Bill realized little of its potential, its passage is more usefully regarded as a beginning, not an end in itself, and in that it was a resounding success. The events of 1832 initiated a process of reform which, once begun, could never be turned back. During the three years in which Martineau wrote and published her series, several events illustrated the accelerating momentum of reform. The Factory Act of 1833 raised the age of employment in textile factories and limited the working hours of all children; although not the first of its kind, the Act was the first to provide precise measures to ensure that the law was enforced. In 1834, the Tolpuddle Martyrs, a group of Dorset farm workers charged with combining, were tried and transported. Demonstrating continued fear and persecution of trade unionism, the men were sentenced to seven years, despite the circulation of a popular petition which garnered half a million signatures urging their acquittal. That they were released only two years later demonstrates that public opinion about unionization had shifted, indicated most tellingly by the convicted men's designation as martyrs.

Generating nearly as much controversy as the Reform Bill, the 1834 Poor Law Amendment Act (also called the New Poor Law) transferred responsibility for the poor from local parishes to more centralized unions called workhouses. In order to distinguish between the deserving and the undeserving poor, the workhouse regime was designed to be so punitive that few people were inclined to enter, even in the direst of circumstances. But rather than forcing the poor to be self-sufficient, the Act further exacerbated the problems of this class.[1] Also in 1834, Martineau published *The Tendency of Strikes and Sticks to Produce Low Wages*, which argues against combinations and trade unions, proposing instead that workers unite *with*, not *against*, management to promote a relationship based on mutual interests. In her view, because workers and management share the same goal—profit—the interests of both are better served through

---

1 See *AB* 1:221-25 and *History of the Peace* 4:313-332 for Martineau's accounts of the New Poor Law.

cooperation than through confrontation. Although a laudable perspective, Martineau's thinking on this point was unrealistic, as the employer/employee relationship is by definition inequitable.

The rise of the Chartist movement in the mid-1830s represented the culmination of decades of reform agitation; social discontent was methodically articulated in the list of demands drawn up by the Chartists, a movement notable for being the first successful attempt at workers' organizing. Part of its success is due to the dissemination of Chartist ideology through pamphlets and the popular press, a mode pioneered by activists like Richard Carlile.[1] As reformers, the Chartists were prepared to operate "Peaceably if we may, forcibly if we must" (Thompson 683). However, despite the energy generated by this early workers' movement, the Chartist movement was short-lived, serving (like the 1832 bill) more as a means to an end than an end in itself. "Chartism marked the end of an old world, not the beginning of a new" (Webb 1980, 251), yet it represented a significant "sign of the times" in an age marked by the spirit of reform no less than by the machine. Martineau's earlier promotion of "the graver themes...which the present condition of society suggests" reflects an environment in which chronic social problems were magnified with each level of technological progress gained.

Harriet Martineau's career, a half-century long, is distinguished by her shrewd sense of timing at several pivotal moments in nineteenth-century history. Her studies and intellectual preparation, and her Unitarian upbringing, combined with society's urge toward reform, led her to conceive of the idea to illustrate the theories of political economy through didactic fiction designed both to entertain and instruct. Her belief in the efficacy of the project, her passion for social justice, and her commitment to working for reform compelled her to persist in finding a publisher, despite being discouraged by indifference at seemingly every step of the way. This overview of intellectual currents highlights the factors that molded Martineau's thinking about the science of political economy and about how to

---

1 E.P. Thompson notes, "Where Daniel Eaton served imprisonment for publishing Paine, Richard Carlile and his shopmen served a total of more than 200 years imprisonment for similar crimes" (210). One contemporary complained, "The writings of Carlile and ... other infidels are more read than the Bible or any other book" (467). Carlile advocated "tyrannicide," viewing the killing of those tyrannizing over the masses as justifiable; he was repeatedly imprisoned for his radical activities, both spoken and printed. See Thompson 838–44.

transform its rarified theories into practical tools for social reform. But Martineau's ideology is as eclectic as her sources, and she resists using her series as a platform to promote the agenda of any one theorist or political party. Consistent with her resistance to dogma of any kind, she prefers simply to illustrate the "beauty" and variability of the science that was to launch her career as one of the most prominent and prolific of the century's social problem writers.

3. The Illustrations of Political Economy

> If a period ever existed, when public peace was secured by refusing knowledge to the population, that epoch has lapsed. The policy of governments may have been little able to bear the scrutiny of the people. This may be the reason why the fountains of English literature have been sealed—and the works of our reformers, our patriots, and our confessors [...] *have not been made accessible and familiar to the poor.*
> –James Kay-Shuttleworth (94)

Born and raised in Norwich, Martineau was descended from exiled French Huguenots, and her earliest influences as the daughter of a fabric manufacturer in a family of Unitarian dissenters constructed a unique combination of political conservatism, religious radicalism, and intellectual liberalism. In light of her literary career as a political commentator and social reform writer, Martineau's assertion that her first "political interest" occurred at the precocious age of four is highly suggestive. As a child, she grieved over the death of Admiral Nelson and worried that Napoleon Bonaparte might land on the Norwich coast. She also exhibited an early sensitivity towards the class disparities evident even in the Martineau household: "my passion for justice was cruelly crossed...by the imposition of passive obedience and silence on servants and tradespeople" (*AB* 1:24).

Characteristically, the child Martineau found a way to bridge her dual interests of politics and social justice by keeping the family servants informed of "Boney's" latest escapade, determined that they be aware of the greater social and political forces affecting their lives. Later, as an adult in charge of her own household, Martineau was more interested in teaching her servants how to learn for themselves, calling them about her with the latest newspapers, maps, and a globe "with the dominant desire to give these intelligent girls an interest in the interests of freedom, and a clear knowledge of the position and duties of England" (*AB* 1:79). Her own political thinking as an adult was shaped by the "Waterloo slaughter," the "grand days" of William Cobbett, and the "spy-systems and conspiracies" of Castlereagh and Sidmouth, events that had dominated the news during her childhood years (1:80).[1]

Martineau's literary influences were no less idiosyncratic. Upon discovering Milton's *Paradise Lost* at age seven, she asserts, "my mental destiny was fixed for the next seven years" (*AB* 1:42). At age eleven she studied Cicero, Virgil, and Horace, rhetoric, composition, and arithmetic. At fourteen she studied Shakespeare and political economy, and by fifteen she had thoroughly absorbed the theories of Thomas Malthus. At nineteen, her philosophical interests included the writings of John Locke, David Hartley, Dugald Stewart, and Joseph Priestley. In a letter to American acquaintance Louisa Gilman, Martineau recalled that during girlhood she arose at 5 a.m. to read, sew, write and study: she taught herself Italian and French, translated Tacitus and Petrarch, learned Wordsworth "by the bushel," read philosophy, and "puzzled out metaphysical questions in my own mind, all day long."[2] Summing up her early intellectual influences, she observes, "I was all the while becoming a political economist without knowing it, and, at the same time, a sort of walking Concordance of Milton and Shakespere [sic]" (*AB* 1:71-72). Although she had only about two years of formal schooling, the breadth of her independent study and reading during these formative years, activities encouraged by her family (as long as she kept up with her sewing basket), attests to an exposure to historical and contemporary ideas of a degree seldom enjoyed even by most boys, much less girls, in nineteenth-century Britain.

The seeds of Martineau's acute awareness of gender disparities were also sown during her youth. While admitting that "the strongest passion I have ever entertained was in regard to my youngest brother," James, she also asserts that "Brothers are to sisters what sisters can

---

1 Robert Stewart, Viscount Castlereagh (1769-1822), 2nd Marquis of Londonderry, a British Foreign Secretary. Henry Addington, Viscount Sidmouth (1757-1844), Home Secretary. Thompson notes that Castlereagh and Sidmouth "were seen as men intent upon displacing constitutional rights by despotic 'continental' rule" (737). In 1819, Percy Shelley wrote "To Sidmouth and Castlereagh":—"Two vipers tangled into one." The Battle of Waterloo marked the end of 22 years of war between England and France when the Duke of Wellington defeated Napoleon, driving him into permanent exile.

2 Harriet Martineau to Louisa Gilman, Norwich Record Office, November 10, 1834.

never be to brothers as objects of engrossing and devoted affection" (*AB* 1:99). Though far superior in intellectual vigor to her brother, Martineau was forced by social custom to stay at home with her needlework while James went off to university. To assuage her distress over the separation, she began to write, to publish, and to distinguish herself with a literary career that was to span half a century. Following the deaths of her father and her fiancé, with the failure of the family business making her economic self-sufficiency necessary, Martineau was freed from the middle-class constraints hampering women to devote herself fully to a literary career. Raymond Williams notes that the expansion of commercial publishing during this time made the novel a primary commodity: "its main history as a literary form follows...precisely the growth of these new conditions" of industrialized society (35). It was at this point that Martineau entered the literary arena, introducing a short-lived but immensely influential literary hybrid that provided an essential stage in the development of literary and social history.

In her series, Martineau presents political economy theories in two ways: dramatized through such literary devices as character and plot, and in the "Summary of Principles Illustrated in this Tale" with which each story concludes. The dual methodology is designed to appeal both to those who read for entertainment (fiction) and those who read for instruction (theory). Literary influences that inspired Martineau include Hannah More and Jane Marcet. More's popular *Cheap Repository Tracts* (1795-98) aimed to instruct the laboring classes about moral and political issues, exemplifying the growing interest in teaching the poor how to help themselves. A more direct influence was Jane Marcet's *Conversations on Political Economy* (1816), which was geared toward young readers and dramatized political economy theories through the sort of expository conversations Martineau employs in her own series. She first read Marcet's book in 1827, "chiefly to see what Political Economy precisely was," and was surprised to learn that "I had been teaching it unawares, in my stories about Machinery and Wages....I had been writing Political Economy without knowing it" (*AB* 1:138; 233). Aided by an array of social, political, and literary influences, Martineau in her *Illustrations* forged an entirely new genre whose innovativeness was peculiarly suited to society's needs in 1832. But its perfect timeliness also accounts for its eventual redundancy as the paths of political economy and fiction diverged and the novel came to be defined according to entertainment values, reform to be defined according to socio-political ideologies, and political economy to be defined by scientific standards.

But even timeliness does not ensure a smooth publishing course, and Martineau was repeatedly frustrated in her attempts to secure a publishing commitment. The response she received most often was that the cholera epidemic and the reform bill controversy rendered new publishing ventures risky business, particularly those involving an unknown woman writer with such an unlikely (because untried) proposal. In desperation, she announced to her family, "You know what a man of business would do in my case....Go up to town by the next mail, and see what is to be done" (*AB* 1:164). She does go to London, as a *woman* of business, and secures a commitment from reluctant publisher Charles Fox (having been advised against the project by James Mill), who offered to publish the work provided she raise five-hundred subscriptions prior to publication. Highly discouraged by this unusually severe arrangement, Martineau set to work writing while raising subscriptions. "I tell you this," she proclaimed defiantly to Fox, "the people want this book, and they *shall* have it" (*AB* 1:170). At her lowest point, after Fox amended their arrangement by stipulating that the first number must sell a thousand copies in the first fortnight or their agreement was canceled, she rather faintly asserted, "My book will do yet."

During this difficult time, she was encouraged in her endeavor by some, while others suggested she return to her needle, the only respectable occupation for a woman forced into the ignominy of having to work for her living. At her mother's suggestion—which Martineau asserts had "much to do with the immediate success of the book"—she sent copies of her series' prospectus to every member of Parliament, both Lords and Commons: "There was nothing of puffery in this....It was merely informing our legislators that a book was coming out on their particular class of subjects" (*AB* 1:175). The strategy served to introduce her to influential policy makers, thus cementing her professional credibility and the links with lofty political circles that characterized much of her career. Martineau's faith in the efficacy of her series proved to be prophetic: within ten days of publication, the book's phenomenal popularity assured the continued success of the project. She became an overnight celebrity, and her fame as the author of the *Illustrations of Political Economy* earned her financial stability and international acclaim. No period of her life offered "a more intimate connexion with the formation of character" than that which culminated in the *Illustrations'* publication: "I had now, by thirty years of age, ascertained my career, found occupation, and achieved independence; and thus the rest of my life was provided with its duties and interests. Any one to whom that happens by thirty years of age may be satisfied; and I was so" (*AB* 1:181).

Each *Illustrations* tale is designed to dramatize certain economic principles, such as population theory or wages fund theory. After studying the appropriate texts of classical political economy, Martineau listed the essential tenets of those theories that eventually comprised the "Summary of Principles" concluding each tale and guiding her fictional narrative. She then chose the geographical and social contexts, and outlined the character types and plot devices, which would best dramatize these principles; after paging her paper, her writing "went off," as she claims, "like a letter" (*AB* 1:195). Martineau's gifts as a writer include a remarkable facility for, and ease in, composing, an enviable self-confidence, and a consummate knowledge of her craft that precluded drafting, revising, or rewriting. Her union of literature with political economy challenges the idea that the purpose of fiction is for entertainment only and offers an alternative to the theoretical texts intellectually prohibitive to minimally educated readers. Thus does the *Illustrations of Political Economy* participate in the "democratization" of knowledge encouraged by the Romantic writers, in turn establishing the foundation for the reform literature of the 1830s and paralleling the rise in literacy among the masses.

An essential factor contributing to the spirit of the age was the rise of scientific inquiry as a viable standard of measure, true of both the "hard" and the "soft" sciences. Empirical observation, aided by continual improvements in technology, instrumentation, and methodology, dovetailed with the reform and self-help movements. Commenting that the 1832 bill marked the official shift away from *laissez-fairism*, Joseph Kestner notes that "The rise of statistical analysis implied the existence of government intervention on a new scale" (50). The collection of official statistics for legislative purposes offered a primary source through which to promote reforms, and it is a significant mark of the esteem in which Martineau was held that Parliamentary members and other institutional sources provided her with "Blue Books," or official parliamentary statistics, to assist in her writing. Access to Blue Books was not offered to the general public until later in the decade.[1]

---

1   Urging immediate utilization of statistical information on the plights of hand-loom weavers, Sir John Maxwell argued that Blue Books demonstrate that Parliament "is omnipotent to save"—by taking action—"as well as to destroy"—by failing to take action (preface). Statistical analysis provided an essential method by which to measure the effects of industrialization on society.

Martineau's influence was aggressively courted to earn her support of various social reform measures, another factor complicating the claim that she endorsed *laissez-faire* ideology; but she was democratic in her use of this influence, steadfastly refusing to align with any political agenda and promoting only those causes she felt would yield the greatest good for the greatest number.[1]

In her 1832 article, "On the Duty of Studying Political Economy," Martineau argued that "the people must begin by informing themselves, if they wish for a better state of things....[They] must become practically acquainted with the principles of political economy, before they can expect to have their interests properly taken care of by the government....[I]t concerns the people to understand their own interests,—i.e. to learn political economy....[W]e hold it as a positive obligation on every member of society who studies and reflects at all, to inform himself of its leading principles" (26). Similarly, the *Illustrations'* preface, written the same year, aims to conduct an "inquiry into the principles which regulate the production and distribution of the necessaries and comforts of life in society" (iii). Her purpose is to determine why "the mass of the people"—those whom Political Economy "most concerns"—do not enjoy economic parity and to explore why it is that the few are "pampered above-stairs while others"—the masses—"are starving below" (v). Political economy effects every member of society, she argues; and economic parity cannot be achieved until people make it their business to comprehend the forces aligned against them and until "the errors of our national management are traced to their source" (vi). She concludes, forcefully, that "It is the *duty of the people* [emphasis added] to do this" in order to facilitate interactions between the ruling class and the ruled that will lead to a more equitable society.

What Thomas Carlyle called "the dismal science" of political economy, Harriet Martineau termed the "utility and beauty" of a "few grand principles, which, if generally understood, would gradually remove all the obstructions, and remedy the distresses, and equalize the lot of the population" (Preface ix).[2] Although she pays

---

1 Periodically, Martineau was offered a government pension in acknowledgment of the public service her writing performed. Even when faced with illness and financial loss, she refused the offers, arguing that to accept would imply her alignment with party politics and compromise her literary credibility, particularly as a journalist.

2 Beauty is not an abstract aesthetic concept to Martineau but one measurable through considerations of utility: "Enough has been said...to prove

homage to Adam Smith's *Wealth of Nations*, she outlines her approach to political economy as more practical in its design to provide "pictures" to dramatize abstract theory. Smith's book is "marvellous when all the circumstances are considered, but [...] not fitted nor designed to teach the science to the great mass of the people" (x). Her series bridged the gap between theory and practice—and, by extension, between ruling class intellectuals and the newly literate laboring classes—through entertaining narratives. What she accomplishes is the popularization of political economy—viewed by some as a derogatory term, and by others as the reason for her phenomenal success.[1] She purports to "convey the leading truths of Political Economy" (xii) through dramatizing its effects on people's lives, asserting that "example is better than precept" (xiii). Her explicit aims are to teach, to address the concerns of all classes, and to ensure that political economy be clearly understood by everyone.

For Martineau, political economy was not, therefore, a sterile intellectual pursuit. "The utility and beauty of the science" (viii) resides in its practical application to everyday life and to human relationships and social interactions. Physical and material comfort will ensure both individual "virtue" and broader social progress, contributing to the progressive evolution of society. Martineau's idea of virtue reflects the utilitarian concept of "duty" in which individuals have a responsibility to find and perform their proper work not only for their own well-being but for the greater social good. Economics is a science, and it is for Martineau a *moral* science in that understanding its principles will promote culture-wide material contentment and thus, social stability.

Martineau's aim to educate readers through demonstrating the complex concepts of political economy—"we want its picture ...illustrations of those truths" (Preface xi)—reflects a method of instructing traditionally held to be particularly expedient when addressing the uneducated classes. However, she does not dedicate

---

the *utility* of the study of political economy. Much...might also be said of its *beauty*.... notwithstanding all that is said of its dryness and dulness, and its concentration in matter of fact, we see great attractiveness and much elegance in it" ("On the Duty" 31).

1   "Popularizing" was a derogatory term associated with women writers, who fell into disfavor as a result of the academic "masculinization" of political economy and other disciplines from which women were primarily excluded—as students, as teachers, and as theorists—until well into the twentieth century.

the series to any one class but to those of every class, sex, and race, "appealing to the total population of the empire" (xv). Insofar as literature reflects reigning social mores and anticipates cultural tendencies, Martineau's *Illustrations of Political Economy* foregrounds the move toward democracy that was already transforming the British Empire through both cultural and counter-cultural modes.

4. Those "remarkable little books": Victorian Reception History

> Authorship has never been with me a matter of choice. I have not done it for amusement, or for money, or for fame, or for any reason but because I could not help it. Things were pressing to be said; and there was more or less evidence that I was the person to say them.—Harriet Martineau (*AB* 1:188).

Offering a dramatic contrast with the difficult period prior to the *Illustrations*' publication, the popular success of the series was immediate. While Fox struggled to keep up with the demand for more copies, Martineau was amused to find herself stared at unabashedly in the streets: "I became the fashion," she notes with some chagrin (*AB* 1:185). With a clear sense of purpose, she moved to London for greater accessibility to the resources necessary to accomplish her writing. Immediate public enthusiasm for her project was seemingly universal: "The entire periodical press, daily, weekly, and, as soon as possible, monthly, came out in my favour," she wrote excitedly, "and I was overwhelmed with newspapers and letters, containing every sort of flattery" (*AB* 1:178). But although a celebrity, Martineau steadfastly resisted the temptations of "Literary Lionism," preferring to remain focused on her social mission than to be the toast of London society.[1]

The *Illustrations* was written and published serially, one volume a month, totaling twenty-five numbers. According to Louis Cazamian, each number sold approximately 10,000 copies, with a readership C. Fox estimated at about 144,000.[2] "The first day of each month is marked by no publication of more importance than Miss Martineau's *Illustrations of Political Economy*," wrote the *Spectator*. "Each succeeding Number increases our admiration for the writer's abilities, and our gratitude for the useful direction in which they are exerted" (Sept. 8,

---

1 See *Autobiography* 1:271-95 for her views on "Literary Lionism."
2 See R.K. Webb, *Harriet Martineau: A Radical Victorian* (New York: Columbia UP, 1960) 113.

1832: 853). Distributed in America as well as throughout Europe, the series was translated into Dutch, German, Spanish, French, and Russian. It was purchased by the courts of Russia and Austria, and France adapted the series for use in public schools.[1]

Among her readers were Princess Victoria, Samuel Taylor Coleridge, Florence Nightingale, Richard Cobden, and Prime Minister Robert Peel. Martineau's timeliness is evidenced both by the *Illustrations'* popular success and by the serious attention it garnered from members of Parliament, who saw in her a reform writer perfectly suited to the concerns of the period. Lord Chancellor Brougham, for example, personally sought out Martineau in her humble walk-up flat, offering her Blue Books to assist in her work and enlisting her services for the Society for the Diffusion of Useful Knowledge (SDUK).[2] Lord Althorp, Chancellor of the Exchequer, requested that she write on tax reform, while Oxford professor of political economy Nassau Senior[3] was another distinguished caller. Victorian biographer Florence Fenwick Miller captures the remarkable phenomenon of Martineau's success in terms of gender and class: "she afforded the first instance on record of a woman who was not born to sovereign station affecting practical legislation otherwise than through a man" (88). The very success she enjoyed indicates the degree to which gender and class reform had already permeated British society.

---

1 Demonstrating the significance of popularizing, Gillian Thomas notes that "the populist nature of her conservatism offended her early supporters. Mrs. Marcet....was distressed when Martineau offended the French king by 'writing about Egalite.'....The Russian czar and Austrian emperor both ordered all copies of the series to be burned and Martineau was prohibited from entering either Russia or the Austrian Empire" (12). Martineau remained as unmoved by such political posturing as by "literary lionism," claiming simply that she had written the series to inform the people.

2 While writing the *Illustrations of Political Economy* (25 parts, 1832-34), Martineau also wrote two series for the SDUK: *Poor Laws and Paupers Illustrated* (4 parts, 1833-34) and *Illustrations of Taxation* (5 parts, 1834). She later became disillusioned with what Thompson calls "Half-hearted or equivocal reformers like Brougham" (661). Publications sponsored by the SDUK provided a primary source for the popularization of political economy among the masses. See also Martineau's *History of England* (3:194-97).

3 Nassau William Senior (1790-1864), political economist and advocate of poor law reform. He wrote various treatises on precious metals, population, wages, paper money, and tithes.

Along with breaking through gender and class boundaries, the *Illustrations* marks a shift away from the rarified realms of academia and toward popular culture. The concept of popularization, of translating theory into a practical form relevant and useful to ordinary people, is central to understanding the enthusiastic reception the series enjoyed. A contemporary review by Edward Bulwer entitled "On Moral Fictions" highlights the gap between the theory and practice of political economy that had traditionally minimized its usefulness: "There may be often truths known to the few which it is almost originality to popularize to the many. For next to inventing a truth, is the merit of making it generally known....Miss Martineau, in the excellent fictions she has given to the world, has performed this noble undertaking, and accomplished this lesser species of inspiration" (147). Modern critics credit popularizers with exerting even more influence over society than the original theories or theorists: "It was not the scientific economic theories themselves that had an impact on policy, but the translation of the theories into a 'popular mythology' that was critical," writes W.D. Sockwell. Popularizers often "play a more important role in the formulation and acceptance of policy than the original thinkers" (99).

Quick to detect the social significance of the *Illustrations*, the *Spectator* critic asserts, "She will prove herself one of the benefactors of her species" (February 4, 1832: 112) through her efforts to make theory accessible and practical in its application. Too often, the writer posits, "It unluckily happens, that persons who are best qualified to make discoveries in science, are often least prepared to propagate them. Invention and communication are very distinct offices of the human mind." The reviewer regrets that the usefulness of political economy has been limited to university professors, kept "locked up in the strong boxes of Mill and M'Culloch" rather than "a part of the ordinary information of a useful and respectable citizen." But because Martineau's series subverts that intellectual elitism, these small, affordably priced volumes "ought to be universally circulated; and every philanthropist who may contribute to their spreading, may rely upon being engaged in a task of unmixed good" (115).[1]

---

1 Martineau specified that the volumes be small so that they might fit in the lunch boxes and pockets of "the workies." Periodically throughout her career, she requested specific sales prices for her books, in order to ensure that cost not be an obstacle in disseminating information relevant to the working class.

For some readers, like American abolitionist Maria Weston Chapman, the success of Martineau's series represented an achievement for all women who braved the insults and sneers of society by committing their lives to social activism in the public realm. "In this new literature of the people Miss Martineau takes a high rank," she wrote. "Inspired with the finest affections of a woman, and taking her stand on all in human nature and the counsels of God which her affections reveal, her clear understanding gives her a wide and true view of social relations and duties" (179). But among some of Martineau's contemporaries, it was the series' literary value that was of more interest than its political economy. For Florence Fenwick Miller, the tales are "inevitably damaged, as works of art, by the fact that they were written to convey definite lessons" (81); Martineau's literary creativity is "fettered" by writing "novels with a purpose" rather than for art or entertainment.

Similarly, Mary Russell Mitford rejects the combination of political economy and literature altogether, claiming that "The only things of hers I ever liked were her political economy stories, which I used to read, skipping the political economy" (Courtney 236). With startling foresight, she predicts that "Fifty years hence she will be heard of as one of the curiosities of our age, but she will not be read." Victorian critic Daniel Maclise disagrees: "As felicitous illustrations of important truths they are of great and enduring value; and they will doubtless continue to be read for their interest as works of fiction and admired for the ingenuity which the writer has shown" (207). Going beyond considerations of the staying power of the literature, publisher Charles Knight situates the importance of the *Illustrations* in the broader context of literary history, particularly as that concerns the development of the novel genre. Knight argues that "these remarkable little books...led the way in the growing tendency of all novel-writing to extend the area of its search for materials upon which to build a story, and to keep in view the characteristic relations of rich and poor, of educated and uneducated, of virtuous and vicious, in our complicated state of society" (Cazamian 59). Such varied responses suggest that Martineau's sense of timing was not limited solely to the culture's readiness for the proliferation of political economy. Other factors include the rise of a new morality based on social justice and human rights, the example of women's social progress modeled by the achievements of women like Harriet Martineau, and the impact of democratic ideology on the developing history of the novel genre.

Although to modern perspectives the link between political economy and social morality seems forced, reviewer Josiah Conder sees a clear correlation between the two: "These 'Illustrations' sufficiently prove that, with purely economical inquiries, collateral questions of a strictly moral or political nature are indissolubly connected and interwoven" (62). Similarly, Edward Bulwer Lytton's review, "On Moral Fictions," claims that the *Illustrations'* strength is its ability to convey moral truths; a weakness is the lofty language voiced by Martineau's lower class characters, pinpointing the incongruity of theoretical expository conversations among people of this class. However, the critic attributes this to the "nature of the work," in which the author's lofty aims exceed the limits afforded by the confining structure of these short tales. Otherwise, "A remarkable excellence...is the beauty of her descriptions" (150) of scenery, events, and people. Such assessments highlight the originality of the series' eclectic structure as well as the sometimes conflicting interests of its dual aims to entertain and instruct.

John Stuart Mill's[1] review of what he rather patronizingly terms "Miss Martineau's little work" is favorable but lukewarm: "As an exposition of the leading principles of what now constitutes the science [political economy], it possesses considerable merit" (321). Mill objects to her "unqualified condemnation of the principle of the poor-laws," in which she condemns private charity and public welfare schemes as deterrents to lower-class self-sufficiency. Unlike his father, Mill seems unable or unwilling to concede the immense public service performed by these "little books," whose successful popularization of political economy better reflects the spirit of the era than the dry theoretical texts on which they are based. Interestingly, Mill apparently acknowledges Martineau and Marcet in *The Subjection of Women*, but he does not articulate their names: "Two women, since political economy has been made a science, have known enough of it to write usefully on the subject: of how many of the innumerable men who have written on it during the same time, is it possible with truth to say more?" (70). In the context of Mill's discussion of the cultural contributions of women, his omission of their names is curious indeed.

The most ludicrous critical attacks on Martineau were those that

---

1   John Stuart Mill (1806-73), social philosopher, writer on political economy and women's political and social rights; he was the son of James Mill. He is best known for "On Liberty" (1859), "Utilitarianism" (1863), "Auguste Comte and Positivism" (1865), *The Subjection of Women* (1865), and numerous writings on political economy.

refused to engage with her as a writer, focusing instead on her disability, deafness, and on speculations about her appearance. As a single woman or spinster, she was assumed to have become a writer only by default, since her plainness prevented her from attracting a spouse. In lieu of literary analysis, the *Poor Man's Guardian* terms Martineau an "anti-propagation lady, a single sight of whom would repel all fears of surplus population, her aspect being as repulsive as her doctrines" (220). Similarly, William Maginn "ungallantly hints that no one who inspects her portrait can wonder at her celibate proclivities, or is likely to attempt the seduction of the 'fair philosopher' from her doctrines on the population question" (quoted in Maclise 211). Maginn is quoted elsewhere as observing, "[We] think that a lady ought to be treated, even by reviewers, with the utmost deference, *except she writes politics, which is an enormity equal to wearing breeches*" (qtd. in Marks, 32; emphasis added). The focus on women's appearance and concern with their usurpation of the male dominated field of political economy is characteristic of the "old boy network," invested as it is in confining academic disciplines to the rarified realms of universities, from which many men but all women were excluded. Martineau's refusal to employ a male or gender-neutral pseudonym further targeted her for this sort of sophomoric venting presented as literary criticism.

But some reviewers appreciated Martineau's aim to adapt the novel genre to the changing times. The *Tatler* cites the series' didacticism as, far from a weakness, its strength, in that it "may put to shame all the disgusting details of sickly sentimentality, wherewith our novels and romances abound *usque ad nauseam*" (Review of "Life in the Wilds" 269). Written a generation after the *Illustrations of Political Economy* and demonstrating the period's continuing preoccupation with social reform fiction, "Novels with a Purpose" revisits the central question employed to measure the influence of social problem writing. Noting novelists' pervasive influence over culture, the writer asks: "Can this influence be turned to any direct and deliberate account? Is it given to the novelist to accomplish any definite social object, to solve, or even help towards the solution of any vexed social question?" (28). Further, does purposeful writing compromise the creative muse? Applied to Martineau's *Illustrations*, such questions highlight a primary criticism of the series—that its perfect timeliness accounts both for its immediate success and for its lack of staying power or long-term relevance, the standard traditionally employed to measure literary worth. But the *Illustrations* requires a different sort of measure, as it is not a novel in the modern, generic sense of the term but a pivotal stage in the development of literary, economic, and social history.

In his retrospective of Martineau's life and contributions following her death, Daniel Maclise asserts that "she has earned our respect and gratitude for a long and consistent life of labour, whose sole object was the improvement and benefit of [her] generation....Nothing is more remarkable in the character of Miss Martineau than the decision with which she formed opinions, and the courage with which she expressed them. At her day, this was a matter of greater singularity and difficulty than at the present one; and the amount of suspicion, ridicule, misconception, and dislike which it engendered was correspondingly greater" (206; 211).

Maclise thus acknowledges the challenges and obstacles, and the social prejudice and critical resistance, Martineau faced in the early 1830s. That circumstances were vastly improved for women in all aspects of life and society by the time of her death in 1876 is due in no small part to Martineau herself, whose work as a writer in the public realm and whose personal example established a foundation for the next generation of women activists and reformers, now called "first wave" feminists.

5. Twentieth-century Criticism: the Illustrations' role in the history of the novel

Although Martineau's presence in literary history was rather tenuous throughout the first half of the twentieth century, it never completely disappeared, and biographies and studies of her life and work surfaced periodically. R.K. Webb's comprehensive *Harriet Martineau. A Radical Victorian* (1960) sparked a revival of interest in Martineau that flowered in the 1980s and continues to grow today. Distinct from nineteenth-century critics, modern critics—oriented as they are by specific disciplinary perspectives—focus on her impact on such fields as literature, sociology, philosophy, history, and journalism. But Martineau remains resistant to tidy categorization of the sort required by traditional academia, and any attempt to claim her as exclusively a sociologist or a novelist results in presenting only one aspect of her remarkably eclectic intellectual interests and literary expertise. The most significant contribution of modern Martineau criticism is in its serious critical analyses of her writing, viewed in the context of her time, through the methodology of relevant academic disciplines, and through the broader perspectives permitted by postmodern interdisciplinary studies.

An early twentieth-century assessment of the *Illustrations*' impact on novel and social history is Louis Cazamian's *The Social Novel in England* (1903). Cazamian explores "the relation between literary and social evolution" (1), noting that the development of didactic literature coincided with the rise of the middle-classes and with the "submission of Parliament to public opinion" (5) in 1832. He juxtaposes "utilitarian individualism" with "compassionate interventionism," claiming that "England between 1830 and 1850 reduces simply to this classic opposition, which has certain national qualities, and constitutes a decisive moment in the psychological history of the nation" (13). Ambivalently, Cazamian charges that Martineau represents "the negative aspect of individualism" and that the *Illustrations* are "the sharp chilling response of dogmatic learning to popular aspirations" (50). Alternatively, as a "species of intellectual philanthropy" (51) the *Illustrations*' focus on social reform encapsulates the defining qualities of the period, "of which their author was representative" (54). Cazamian credits Martineau's work with influencing the novels of Charles Dickens, Benjamin Disraeli, Elizabeth Gaskell, and Charles Kingsley, writers prominent during the "hungry forties" when social suffering had reached disastrous proportions. Similarly, of Dickens' literary debt to Martineau, Ivanka Kovacevic observes that she "was the first to concentrate on the conflict between capital and labour in industry....she preceded him by a whole generation in her treatment of the industrial theme" (110).

To Cazamian's list of literary influences, Monica Fryckstedt adds Frances Trollope, Charlotte Elizabeth Tonna, and Elizabeth Stone as direct descendants of Martineau's work in the *Illustrations* (12-13; 16). All of these writers wrote "industrial fiction" that focused on the plights of factory workers and their vexed relations with manufacturers. A more impressive legacy is Martineau's influence on one of the best-selling novels of all time: Harriet Beecher Stowe's *Uncle Tom's Cabin* (1852) which, along with her *Dred: a Tale of the Great Dismal Swamp* (1856), pays homage to Martineau's antislavery *Illustrations* tale, "Demerara" (1832). Claire Midgley attributes this intellectual debt to Martineau's "view of labour as a measure of value" and her presentation of "classic economic doctrine through a didactic tale" (97). The decades-long influence Martineau exerted over not only the social problem genre but over some of the most popular and prominent writers of the period results naturally from the needs of the time and the receptiveness of a new reading audience.

Valerie Sanders's analysis extends Martineau's influence to Charlotte Brontë and George Eliot, whose novels have long been staples in the English literature canon. Sanders notes that Martineau was both timely and trend-setting: "Her tales discussed all the most topical questions that were agitating the country in the 1830s, at least ten years before the major Victorian novelists began to consider them....Her lasting significance rests on her advancement of new ideas, her exploration of new areas for the novel to claim as its legitimate territory, and her embodiment of the leading doubts and convictions of the age" (195). The *Illustrations* anticipates the trend toward realism in literature, popular from the mid- to late-century: "Her popularity as a writer of fiction owes much to her ability to translate great events into human terms, to show how a particular piece of legislation, or specific social abuse, might be an integral part of a man's or woman's daily life" (108). Similarly, Vineta Colby terms Martineau's ability to illustrate abstract theories the "fiction of domestic realism" (224); she finds much to admire in her writing style, praising its "crisp, natural prose making no claims to high literature. She writes engaging passages of description, dialogue, and characterization even in the chilly depths of exposition on political economy" (221). But Colby agrees with those critics who objected to the incongruousness of the expository conversations, particularly involving lower-class characters, designed to convey economic theory: "Her characters evolve from personified economic abstractions into human beings...Dialogue, when it is not devoted to expository speeches on economic theory, is natural and dramatic" (223).

The *Illustrations'* influence extended from literary to social circles, incorporating the broader class issues challenging the period. R.K. Webb emphasizes Martineau's radicalism in the series, suggesting that her challenge to the ruling classes was even more striking than her aim to enlighten the middle and working classes. Countering the suggestion that Martineau's primary accomplishment was merely to justify and reinforce the status quo of inequitable social relations, Webb notes that some tales were "aimed at higher game than working men"—for example, "Demerara" (slave owners), "Berkeley the Banker" (financiers), "The Loom and the Lugger" (manufacturers), and "Cinnamon and Pearls" (imperialists). Webb distinguishes Martineau's accomplishments from those of her predecessors, particularly Jane Marcet: "If the series were directed solely to the task of convincing the lower classes of the inevitability of the bourgeois industrial order and social morality, if its effect were intended to be entirely conservative, preponderant attention would hardly have been given to the present abuses of the system, and something more on the hygienic order of Mrs. Marcet's fairy tales would have resulted.

In the coupled purpose of the series, the radical outweighs the conservative" (1960: 118). Webb concludes that Martineau's shrewd sense of timing, her topic and its treatment, and her unique gift for "popularizing" account for her extraordinary success: "By a lucky hit, Miss Martineau took the tide at its height, when the world was all agog for political economy" (Webb 1960, 124).

Along with literary and social reform are considerations of the series' impact on the evolving discipline of political economy. Noting with interest that the two "best selling English economists of the first half of the nineteenth century" were women—Marcet and Martineau, J.R. Shackleton objects to the fashion of denigrating both as lightweight popularizers, charging that Martineau's reputation has been "deliberately undermined by hostile critics in her lifetime and since" (1990: 283, 290). Yet she demonstrated impressive foresight by viewing political economy "as a subject which it was crucial to disseminate as widely as possible, for its lessons were vital to the well-being of the working classes whose demands were increasingly pressing on the consciousness—and the conscience—of the middle classes to which she belonged" (291). The emphasis on education and on disseminating information that would enable social evolution highlights an unlikely set of factors underpinning the success of the series. For example, perhaps because she was herself an informally educated woman, Martineau aims to educate "my great pupil, the public."[1] She studies classical political economy on her own, assimilates its organizing precepts, synthesizes its theories through practical application, and recasts it in an accessible form. Thus did an informally educated woman usurp and refashion the province of men who, in a sense, retaliated by minimizing or eliminating altogether her contributions to the discipline.

But if Martineau's reputation waned in the academy, observes Willie Henderson, "In terms of intellectual history [she merits] a distinguished position in her own right" (383). Emphasizing the significance of popularizing, Henderson argues that Martineau's contributions to political economy are "most significant, having made a tremendous impact on the popular discussion" of the discipline. Henderson associates Martineau's brand of popularizing with educa-

---

1 Martineau wrote to an unknown recipient: "I am anxious to see all that I can lay hold of with any reliance, for the sake of my *great pupil*, the public. [...] I am very greedy of effectual help, and make few apologies for the trouble I give, as it is for a public object" (14 September 1833, University College, London).

tion: her concern is to *illustrate* political economy, "and the execution of the project, marks her as a brilliant economics educator...her work struck a chord with those frustrated by the abstract nature of existing economic thinking" (385). Martineau "proved that she understood the needs of the British reading public better than James Mill, [publisher Charles] Fox, and numerous Members of Parliament" (389). She had tapped into the mood of the times, "a mood that the academic political economists had failed, with their disputes within the Political Economy Club, to capture or to inform" (396). Since Martineau's writing was compared with that of other women writers (associated primarily with domestic fiction) rather than to that of the political economists, most critics missed "the educational force and impact of the tales" (399). Simon Dentith agrees that the tales require a means of assessment more appropriate to political economy than to literature: "though discursively comparable to those of the novel, [the tales] are untypical of the novel because they spring so exclusively from Political Economy" (192). Although Martineau never claimed to be a political economist, she was committed to her mission as an educator who made bold, cross-disciplinary links in order to broaden the limitations of discourse, to shake readers' complacency, and to promote social change.

Bette Polkinghorn also regards education as Martineau's primary agenda, calling the *Illustrations* "a successful experiment in adult education" (1998: 26), while Vineta Colby links this theme with timeliness: "In their time these tales answered a need—not only the general demand for self-education and self-improvement...but also a more specific and urgent demand for popular education in political and economic subjects" (V. Colby 216). Critic Robert Colby associates this quality of timeliness with the period's valuation of utilitarian ideology, and both with the development of the novel: novelists aimed "to demonstrate the utility of the novel and its relation to reality" (11). As a medium for enabling self-improvement, novels—and the writers who wrote them—enjoyed greater respect and popularity as the genre evolved. Finally, Richard Altick brings this discussion of literature, social science, self-improvement, utilitarianism, and education back to bear on the impact of democracy on British culture by claiming that "The history of the mass reading audience is, in fact, the history of English democracy" (3). The social agitation resulting in dramatic shifts in political power after 1832 was effectually channeled, Altick argues, through the growth of the popular press. Such a perspective emphasizes the significance of Martineau's contributions, which link reform-era agitation with mid-Victorian social stability by facilitating an intellectual revolution rather than a "Reign of Terror."

The period's concern with *morality* expressed by some of Martineau's contemporaries makes more sense to modern readers when regarded in light of her contributions to the social sciences disciplines. Situating the *Illustrations* in the early development of social science, Shelagh Hunter terms Martineau "a pioneer quite beyond her own or any contemporary imagination" (40). By insisting that "Imagination and poetry are appropriate tools in the dissemination of political science because it is a moral science," Hunter emphasizes the *Illustrations*' synthesis of literary devices with social theory, the point to which critics have most frequently objected. "As tools of the moralist," Hunter concludes, imagination and poetry "belong to the social applications of abstract theory, that part of the science which will contribute to the betterment of humankind. The stories are not a substitute for the hard data of a science, but illustrations of the working of the principles in social life" (51).

Martineau's instinctive understanding of the importance of objectivity to her work—a fundamental tenet of modern sociology—is another significant quality distinguishing the *Illustrations.* Claudia Orazem views this factor as essential to the endeavor of popularizing a topic bound to arouse ambivalence in some readers: "In order to make Political Economy acceptable to a wide public, it had to appear nonideological and politically neutral" (99). Her political economy was "strictly scientific and...value-neutral...the product of a process of strictly logical reasoning of the highest intellectual standards" (100). Orazem notes that while Martineau did not fully promote the agendas of any of the political economists whose theories she employed, she did "introduce some new interpretations of accepted principles." This assessment counters the idea, promoted even by Martineau herself, that she could boast of no creative or inventive genius, being only a popularizer of others' ideas. Yet as this survey of the series' reception history indicates, Martineau's ability to provoke such lively responses through her writing establishes her as a cultural force whose influence extended far beyond the Reform Bill era and far beyond her native England. Contemporary responses and modern critical analyses, along with considerations of the *Illustrations*' impact on various disciplines (from humanities to social sciences) and on social and public policy reform attest to the continued relevance of the series. More a pioneer than simply the right person in the right place at the right time, Martineau's success was not only a "lucky hit" benefiting women, the poor, and democratic ideology: it symbolized, like the Reform Bill itself, the beginning of the modern era.

6. Conclusion: the Illustrations' relevance to the 21st Century

> I believe that I may so write on subjects of universal concern as to inform some minds and stir up others...of posthumous fame I have not the slightest expectation or desire. To be useful in my day and generation is enough for me.—Harriet Martineau (Pichanik 31)

This survey of nineteenth- and twentieth-century criticism demonstrates that the *Illustrations* evoked lively responses and continue to do so today. Yet such critical energy raises the inevitable question, why did the series, which was so enormously influential on the people, issues, genres, and disciplines of the time, disappear from literary history for a century-and-a-half? More to the point, why did Harriet Martineau, who enjoyed nearly a forty-year career following the publication of the *Illustrations*, herself slip into obscurity in the annals of Victorian social history? One way to account for the virtual disappearance of Martineau and her works concerns the strict codification of academic disciplines occurring after the heyday of her career. As an intellectual woman excluded from a university education by virtue of her sex, Martineau, in her critical analyses, was similarly excluded from the academy by the sorts of scholars whose work she had made accessible to the mass reading audience.

As an informally educated woman, Martineau had more than the "jealousy of men" to contend with. For example, because she wrote in a wide variety of genres and disciplines, her work was difficult to categorize; her reputation never found a secure home in either literature, history, journalism, political economy, philosophy, or sociology, although she made significant, sometimes ground-breaking, contributions to all those fields. But in terms of efforts to dismiss Martineau's role as "national instructress" as "irrelevant," pedagogical trends have shifted recently in ways that have permitted re-evaluations of the contributions of women writers, particularly women writers of "serious" nonfiction. In particular, interdisciplinary curriculums, like women's studies, cultural studies, and Victorian studies, have provided an appropriate and relevant platform for assessing the work of women writers who have long been excluded from the rigors of academic study. That Martineau's reputation now enjoys a remarkable resurgence of scholarly interest is demonstrated by the proliferation of critical analyses and especially by the availability of reprint editions, such as this volume, of her work. Whereas during her life Martineau's career was characterized by timeliness, scholarly interest in the woman and her work over a century later illustrates that, in another sense, Harriet Martineau is an idea whose time has come round—once again.

With its unique blend of fiction and social theory, the *Illustrations of Political Economy* offers an ideal venue through which contemporary students and scholars can study reform-era literature written from interdisciplinary and cross-cultural perspectives. This edition of selected *Illustrations* tales also participates in contemporary interest in recuperating the literary history of women writers in general and of Harriet Martineau in particular. Because she was so keenly attuned to the pulse of the Victorian era—an age dichotomized by social upheaval and the urge toward stabilization, by desperate poverty and unprecedented prosperity, and by imperialist expansion and democratic ideals—she repeatedly proved herself to be one of the most representative voices of the period. Yet Martineau is also strikingly relevant to the post-modern age, evidenced by the compassion, sensitivity, and insight she brings to topics like race and slavery, gender and sexuality, and class stratification and economic inequities. Her contributions to a "literature of the people" participates in the democratization of literature and other academic disciplines that characterizes the nineteenth century while anticipating such post-modern interests as race, class, and gender, colonialism and post-colonialism, and imperialism.

The following tales have been chosen for their literary quality as well as for their demonstration of key issues of interest to the period. "Weal and Woe in Garveloch" earned notoriety for addressing such topics as sexual abstinence and delayed marriages, over-population and the lack of birth control options, infanticide, and Malthusian population theories. Martineau rejects the claim that respectable women do not discuss such issues, demonstrating instead that women must look out for their own interests, and not rely on men to do that for them. "A Manchester Strike," one of the earliest "industrial tales," studies the impact of industrialization and the factory milieu on the working poor and on the rising middle-class manufacturers. Inadequate wages, work-related illness and death, strikes and strike breakers, union organizing, and fluctuations in the market economy—these are themes introduced by Martineau to be endlessly rehearsed by subsequent writers throughout the century.

"Cousin Marshall" illustrates the inadequacies of the out-moded Elizabethan poor law system in industrial society and dramatizes the need for poor law reform. Punitive treatment of the poor, workhouse abuses and exploitation, charity and lack of incentive, and a desperate need for solutions for the growing pauper population are themes that anticipate the passage of the New Poor Law in 1834. Finally, "Sowers not Reapers" highlights the social problems engendered by the combination of famine and drought, poverty and alcoholism, while dramatizing the effects of the controversial Corn Laws on the working poor. This early anti-corn-law tale presupposes the repeal of the laws in 1846, when the shift in the socio-political power balance initiated by the 1832 Reform Bill was most fully and satisfactorily realized.

Works Cited

Altick, Richard D. *The English Common Reader. A Social History of the Mass Reading Public 1800-1900.* Chicago: U of Chicago P, 1957.

Anon., "On the Review Entitled, 'Miss Martineau's Monthly Novels,' in the last Quarterly." *The Monthly Repository* 7 (1833): 314-23.

Bates, W. "Miss Harriet Martineau From The Maclise Portrait Gallery." 1883: 206-12.

Berg, Maxine. *The Machinery Question and the Making of Political Economy.* Cambridge: Cambridge UP, 1980.

Bulwer, Edward Lytton. "On Moral Fictions. Miss Martineau's *Illustrations of Political Economy.*" *The New Monthly Magazine and Literary Journal* 37 (1833): 146-51.

Carlyle, Thomas. "Signs of the Times." *The Centenary Edition. The Works of Thomas Carlyle.* London: Chapman and Hall, 1896-99.

Cazamian, Louis. *The Social Novel in England 1830-1850. Dickens, Disraeli, Mrs. Gaskell, Kingsley.* Trans. Martin Fido. London and Boston: Routledge & Kegan Paul, 1973.

Chapman, Maria Weston. *Memorials of Harriet Martineau.* Boston: J.R. Osgood, 1877.

Colby, Robert A. *Fiction With a Purpose. Major and Minor Nineteenth-Century Novels.* Bloomington and London: Indiana UP, 1967.

Colby, Vineta. *Yesterday's Woman: Domestic Realism in the English Novel.* Princeton: Princeton UP, 1974.

Conder, Josiah. "Illustrations of Political Economy." *Eclectic Review* 8 (1832): 44-72.

Courtney, Janet. *The Adventurous Thirties. A Chapter in the Women's Movement.* London: Oxford UP, 1933.

Dentith, Simon. "Political Economy, Fiction and the Language of Practical Ideology in Nineteenth-Century England." *Social History* 8 (1983): 183-99.

Engels, Frederick. *The Condition of the Working Class in England.* Trans. and eds. Henderson, W.O. and W.H. Chaloner. Oxford: Oxford UP, 1958.

Fryckstedt, Monica Correa. "The Early Industrial Novel: *Mary Barton* and its Predecessors." *The John Rylands University Library Bulletin* 63 (1980): 11-30.

Henderson, Willie. "Harriet Martineau or 'When political economy was popular'." *History of Education* 21:4 (1992): 383-403.

Hunter, Shelagh. *Harriet Martineau. The Poetics of Moralism.* Aldershot: Scolar Press, 1995.

Kadish, Alon, ed. *The Corn Laws. The Formation of Popular Economics in Britain.* Vol. 6. London: William Pickering, 1996.

Kay-Shuttleworth, James Phillips. *The Moral and Physical Condition of the Working Classes Employed in the Cotton Manufacture in Manchester.* London: James Ridgeway, 1832.

Kestner, Joseph. *Protest and Reform. The British Social Narrative by Women 1827-1867.* Madison: U of Wisconsin P, 1985.

Kovacevic, Ivanka. *Fact into Fiction.* University of Belgrade: Leicester UP, 1975.

Lukacs, Georg. *The Historical Novel.* Trans. Hannah and Stanley Mitchell. Lincoln and London: U of Nebraska P, 1962.

Marks, Patricia. "Harriet Martineau: *Fraser's* 'Maid of [Dis]Honour'" *Victorian Periodicals Review* 19 (1986): 28-34.

Martineau, Harriet. "Achievements of the Genius of Scott." *Tait's Edinburgh Magazine* 2 (1833): 445-60.

___. *Harriet Martineau's Autobiography.* 2 vols. London: Virago, 1983.

___. *History of the Peace. being a History of England from 1816 to 1854.* Boston: Walker, Wise, and Company, 1864.

___. *Illustrations of Political Economy.* 9 vols. London: Charles Fox, 1823-34.

___. "On the Duty of Studying Political Economy." *Monthly Repository* 6 (1832): 24-34.

___. *Retrospect of Western Travel.* London: Saunders and Otley, 1838.

Maxwell, Sir John. "Manual Labour, versus Machinery." London: Cochrane and M'Crone, 1834.

Midgley, Clare. *Women Against Slavery: The British Campaigns, 1780-1870.* London: Routledge, 1992.

Mill, J.S. "Miss Martineau's Summary of Political Economy. *Illustrations of Political Economy* No. XXV, 'The Moral of Many Fables'." *Monthly Repository* 8 (May 1834): 318-22.

___. *The Subjection of Women.* Arlington Heights, IL.: Harlan Davidson, Inc., 1980.

Miller, Florence Fenwick. *Harriet Martineau.* London: W.H. Allen, 1884.

"Novels with a Purpose." *Westminster Review* 82 (1864): 24-49.

Orazem, Claudia. *Political Economy and Fiction in the Early Works of Harriet Martineau.* Frankfort: Peter Lang, 1999.

Pickanik, Valerie Kossew. *Harriet Martineau. The Woman and Her Work, 1802-76.* Ann Arbor: U of Michigan P, 1980.

Polkinghorn, Bette, and Dorothy Lampen Thomson. *Adam Smith's Daughters: Eight Prominent Women Economists from the Eighteenth Century to the Present.* Northampton, MA: Edward Elgar, 1998.

Review of "Cousin Marshall." *Spectator* (Sept. 8, 1832): 853-55.

Review of *Illustrations of Political Economy. Poor Man's Guardian* 167 (1834): 220.

Review of "Life in the Wilds." *The Spectator* (Feb. 4, 1832): 112-15.

Review of "Life in the Wilds." *The Tatler* (March 20, 1832): 269-70.

Rivlin, Joseph. "Harriet Martineau. A Bibliography of her Separately Printed Books." *Bulletin of the New York Public Library* 50:2 (May 1946).

Sanders, Valerie. *Reason over Passion.* Sussex: Harvester Press, 1986.

Shackleton, J.R. "Jane Marcet and Harriet Martineau: Pioneers of Economics Education." *History of Education* 19:4 (1990): 283-97.

Sockwell, W.D. *Popularizing Classical Economics: Henry Brougham and William Ellis.* New York: St. Martin's Press, 1994.

Thomas, Gillian. *Harriet Martineau.* Boston: Twayne Publishers, 1985.

Thompson, E.P. *The Making of the English Working Class.* London and New York: Penguin, 1991.

Thompson, Noel W. *The People's Science. The Popular Political Economy of Exploitation and Crisis 1816-34.* Cambridge: Cambridge UP, 1984.

Tucker, Herbert F., ed. *A Companion to Victorian Literature & Culture.* Oxford: Blackwell Publishers Ltd., 1999.

Webb, R.K. *Harriet Martineau. A Radical Victorian.* New York: Columbia UP, 1960.

___. *Modern England from the Eighteenth Century to the Present.* 2nd ed. New York: Harper and Row Publishers, 1980.

Williams, Raymond. *Culture and Society: 1780-1950.* New York: Columbia UP, 1983.

Wordsworth, William. Preface to *Lyrical Ballads.* 2nd ed. London: Longman and Rees, 1800.

Harriet Martineau: A Brief Chronology

1802 Born in Norwich, June 12.

1814 Onset of deafness.

1822 First appearance in print: "Female Writers of Practical Divinity," *Monthly Repository*.

1827 "The Rioters," first industrial tale.

1832-34 *Illustrations of Political Economy* (25 tales). Moves to London.

1833-34 *Poor Laws and Paupers Illustrated* (4 tales).

1834 *Illustrations of Taxation* (5 tales).

1834-36 Travels throughout America.

1837 *Society in America.*

1838 *How to Observe Morals and Manners* and *Retrospect of Western Travel.*

1839 *Deerbrook* (novel).

1839-44 Invalided at Tynemouth.

1841 *The Playfellow* (4 tales) and *The Hour and the Man* (historical romance).

1844 *Life in the Sickroom.*

1845 Moves to Ambleside in the Lake District; builds her home, The Knoll.

1845-46 *Forest and Game Law Tales* (3 volumes).

1846-47 Travels throughout the Middle East.

1848 *Eastern Life, Present and Past.*

1849-50 *History of England during the Thirty Years' Peace.*

1851 *History of England A.D. 1800-1815.*

1852 Travels to Ireland. *Letters from Ireland.*

1852-66 Writes regularly for London's *Daily News*.

1853 Translates and condenses Auguste Comte's *The Positive Philosophy.*

1855 Writes the *Autobiography*; distributed posthumously in 1877.

1855-76 Illness and old age.

1857 *British Rule in India.*

1858 *Suggestions toward the Future Government of India.*

1869 *Biographical Sketches.*

1876 Dies June 27. Self-authored obituary published in the *Daily News*.

A Note on the Text

Each of the twenty-five numbers of the first edition of the *Illustrations of Political Economy* was published individually by Charles Fox (London) between 1832 and 1834. The text of the *Illustrations* tales reprinted here is taken from the nine-volume edition of the twenty-five parts, published by Fox in 1834. Joseph B. Rivlin's "Harriet Martineau. A Bibliography of Her Separately Printed Books" provides a comprehensive account of printings and editions of the series (pages 789-849), compiled for the *Bulletin of the New York Public Library* (volume 50, number 5, May 1946). Martineau never revised the original tales for reprinting: "I alternately admired and despised what I wrote," she notes in the *Autobiography*; but she admits that, "when I saw it in print, I was surprised to see how well it looked. After an interval of above twenty years, I have not courage to look at a single number" (1:258). With a few notable exceptions, she turned almost exclusively to nonfiction political and social reform writing after 1834.

Martineau's original notes have been retained in the text and are identified by asterisks. Where necessary, editorial explanations of Martineau's notes are included in square brackets immediately following the note.

Illustrations of Political Economy
Selected Tales

Weal and Woe in Garveloch

[The fifth entry in the *Illustrations of Political Economy* is "Ella of Garveloch," followed by a sequel, "Weal and Woe in Garveloch." The first tale is notable for its strong and memorable characterization of a Scots fisherwoman, Ella, one of Martineau's best-drawn characters. Life in this Scottish fishing village is difficult and strenuous, and Ella faces more challenges than most: she is young and inexperienced, poor and without resources, and resented by a jealous overseer. As the head of her family of orphaned brothers, including the simple-minded Archie who requires constant supervision, Ella proves herself equal to the task: by negotiating directly with the "Laird," an absentee landlord who is scandalized by her rough, unladylike appearance[1] but impressed by her character and determination; by setting herself and her brothers to work fishing and farming, quickly establishing economic self-sufficiency; and by boldly negotiating with rough fishermen who resist doing business with a woman. The men in this patriarchal fishing village resent Ella's forthright honesty and seemingly limitless capacity for hard work, but she is undeterred in her aim to provide for her family. The story concludes with Ella's marriage to her fiancé, Angus, on his return from overseas. Ella is a compelling feminist prototype, and the narrative was reputed to be one of Princess Victoria's favorites. The tale illustrates David Ricardo's theories on rent and introduces the Malthusian theme more fully addressed in the sequel. Both tales feature families hard-pressed to maintain primary subsistence levels, raising the *moral* question of child-bearing without adequate provision for child-rearing in the face of such unforeseen difficulties as natural disasters or marketplace fluctuations.

The tale printed here, "Weal and Woe in Garveloch," continues the story years later, when Ella and Angus live in their own house with their brood of nine children. The Garveloch community has enjoyed economic prosperity for some time, best seen in the increase in population, in the assumption that prosperity is permanent, and in the general failure to save against hard times. Economic collapse results from a combination of factors—war and poor crops, followed by

---

1 Aptly dramatizing the darker side of Malthusian theory and attesting to the ongoing issue of hunger, Ella's prematurely aged appearance is explained in the sequel as due in part to an extended period of malnutrition she had endured earlier in life, a period of nutritional lack that completed the ruin of her father's health.

famine and disease—all testing people's strength of character as they attempt to cope. Ella is a model of frugality and thrift, but less careful people find themselves cast adrift with few resources and less prospects; others, like the young widow Katie Cuthbert and her children, are simply caught in a situation not entirely of their own making. Although some relief is promised to Katie through marriage to Ella's brother, Ronald, the marriage never materializes. Instead, Ronald demonstrates exemplary "morality" by choosing to remain single and celibate rather than to marry and add more children to an already over-burdened economy. Highlighting the period's lack of practical birth-control options, the "preventive check" of voluntary self-restraint is offered as the moral solution to an economic problem. This tale provoked notoriety for its frank discussions between Ella and Katie about "preventive checks" to population growth—including sexual abstinence, delayed marriages, and infanticide—as they ponder whether war, famine, and disease are Providential warnings against taking too literally the Biblical precept to "be fruitful and multiply."

As a student of Thomas Malthus's population and economic theories, Martineau believed that indiscriminate child-bearing was the primary factor contributing to the perpetuation of poverty among the lower classes.[1] Of course, she understood that the economic forces governing this level of society were largely beyond its control, and educating the public about those complex forces provides the impetus behind the writing of the *Illustrations*. But some factors dictating the economic quality of life *can* be controlled by people of any class, and managing one's family size is one of them. Although she simply suggests that abstinence could easily improve the economic status of the poor, she was as praised by some for addressing this difficult topic as she was condemned by others for what was regarded a direct affront to the period's revered maternal ideology. Written at a time when any woman who was not producing babies regularly was a social anomaly—like Harriet Martineau, for instance—, the promotion of "preventive checks" as a primary tenet for social reform was daring indeed.]

---

1 Critics of Malthusian theory question its class-bias seen through its focus on the poor, while seeming to sanction prolific child-bearing among the rich. Yet if the issue is adequate subsistence for offspring, this is a problem for the poor though not for the rich, who (theoretically) can have as many children as they can support. Taken to its logical extreme, only the rich should reproduce; for the poor to do so indiscriminately evidences their "immorality" in breaking the "natural" laws of political economy.

Chapter I: Times are Changed

About ten years before the period at which our story opens, the laird of Garveloch had transferred his property in that and the neighbouring isles to a large Fishing Company.[1] The terms of the bargain were advantageous to both parties. The laird was to receive, in addition to the annual rent which his island-tenants had been accustomed to pay, and which did not amount to more than sixty guineas a year all together, a sum of several hundred pounds in consideration of the improvements to be effected on the property.[2] As there was little prospect of such improvements being effected, to the extent of some hundreds of pounds, by himself or his poor tenants, the transaction was evidently a profitable one to him; while the Company reasonably expected that the changes they were about to introduce would much more than repay their advance—an expectation which was not disappointed.

Among the numerous fishing stations established by this opulent Company, there was one in Islay.[3] A warehouse was erected, where salt for curing the fish, hemp for making nets, timber for boat-building, staves for cooperage,[4] and all materials necessary for the apparatus of an extensive fishery, were stored.

A curing-house, a building-yard, and a cooperage were at hand; a pier, around which there was a perpetual traffic of boats, stretched out into the sea. A little town had risen round these buildings, where but a few years before there had been only a congregation of sea-fowl. Where their discordant cries alone had been heard, there now prevailed a mingling of sounds, not more musical to the ear perhaps, but by far more agreeable to the heart. The calls of the boatmen, the hammer of the cooper, the saw of the boat-builder, the hum from the curing-house, where women and girls were employed in gutting, salting, and packing the herrings, and drying the cod, the shouts and laughter of innumerable children at play among the rocks,—all these together formed such a contrast to the desolation which pre-

---

1 Laird is the Scots form of the word "Lord." Garveloch is an island off the west coast of Scotland, in the Hebrides.
2 A guinea is a monetary unit that equalled one pound, one shilling. Although guineas have not been minted since 1813, the term remains in use for the pricing of merchandise.
3 Islay is an island off the west coast of Scotland.
4 A cooperage is a business that produces casks or barrels which, in Garveloch, were used for storing cured fish.

vailed ten years before, that the stranger who returned after a long absence scarcely knew the place to be the same.

Nor was the change less remarkable in others of the islands. Rows of dwellings stretched along many a favourable line of beach, and huts peeped out of a cove here and there, where no trace of man had been formerly seen, but an occasional kelping [seaweed] fire. On Garveloch a fishing village had arisen where the dwelling of Angus and Ella had for some years stood alone. The field which they had cultivated from the year of their marriage till the establishment of the Fishing Company, was now covered with cottages; and a row of huts, most of them with a patch of ground behind, stretched from the bar on the one hand, to the promontory which had been Ronald's on the other. Angus and Ella lived in the old house; but it was so much enlarged and improved as to look like a new one: it was the best in the village; and it was made so for comfort, not for show. There were nine children to be housed; and both their parents knew enough of comfort to see the necessity of providing room and ventilation if they wished to keep their large family in health and good habits. They had worked hard, and on the whole successfully; and though the perpetual calls upon them prevented their laying by much in the form of money, they had been able to provide their dwelling with more convenient furniture, and their children with more decent clothing, than was usually thought necessary in the society of which they formed a part.

Angus's vessel had yielded him all the profit he had expected, and more. Before the Company was established, he had usually had business enough committed to him to make it answer to cross the Sound twice a week; and since the fishing station had been opened in Islay, he had made a double use of the Flora, as his boat was now called. The possession of a decked vessel had enabled him to share the herring bounty; and he now gave his principal attention to the fishery, only following the coasting trade in spring and autumn,—the intervals of the herring seasons.

As they possessed so great a treasure in this boat, now of the rank of a herring-buss,[1] Angus and Ella thought they could afford to give the old boat to Fergus for a wedding present, and thus enable him to fish for cod on his own account, instead of being a hired fisherman on board one of the Company's vessels. Those who had only open

---

1   A herring-buss was a small fishing boat, averaging 50 feet long, with three masts; they were popular in the 17th-18th centuries.

boats were excluded from the herring fishery by the bounty, which was granted to the produce of decked vessels only, and which therefore gave an advantage to such produce in the market which could not be contested; but there was a fair sale for cod, however caught; and now that a market was always open at hand, the possession of a boat seemed to Fergus to afford a prospect of a certain and sufficient maintenance. He married at one-and-twenty, a year after the opening of the station in Islay, and in consequence of it; for he fell in love with a girl who had come with her family to settle at the station as fishers. Janet was young and giddy, and quite willing to leave her father, who was only a hired fisherman, for a husband who had a boat of his own; and, after a short courtship, the young folks settled down in a cottage within a stone's throw of Angus's house. They had made a shift to get on till now, though their family increased every year; and as they had never suffered actual want, they began to think they never should, and to smile at some of Ronald's wise sayings. Fergus declared that, if one or two seasons of extraordinary plenty would come, so as to enable him to get a new boat, he should have no anxiety remaining. He had been anxious when he had only one child to feed; and he was apt to be anxious at times now that he had five: but if he was but sure of being able to continue his fishing, he would trust that Providence would feed them as they had hitherto been fed. But if these rare seasons should not come, Ronald observed, what was to be done? For the boat was wearing out fast. It must be patched and mended to the last, Fergus replied, and he must still hope for extraordinary profits some happy year. He said nothing, though he probably thought much, of the consequences of a season of failure.

Ronald was free from all cares of this kind, though he had had his share of trouble in other ways. He was a single man and engaged in a good business, and therefore well provided for as to external comfort. He was a cooper at the station in Islay, and as casks were wanted as long as fish were caught, he had reason to suppose himself supplied with employment as long as the establishment should be kept up. He was truly happy to be able to afford assistance to her who had carefully tended his youth, and received Ella's eldest boy with the intention of teaching him his trade. The trouble from which we have mentioned that Ronald suffered arose from disappointment in an attachment he had formed and long cherished. He had loved a maiden who came in the train of the company, but his friend Cuthbert had won her, and after having made her happy for a few short years, had been taken from her by an accident at sea, leaving her with four children, and no possessions but such as his industry had earned. The widow Cuthbert lived in Garveloch, and supported her little family by net-making. She was respected by all her neighbours, and loved as much as ever by Ronald, who, however, conducted himself towards her as the widow of his friend, rather than as the object of his early and long attachment.

The widow Cuthbert was regarded as the lady of the island, though she was no richer, no better dressed, and, for all her neighbours knew, no better born than any around her. She was better educated; and this was her title to distinction. No one else, except Angus, had seen so much of the world; and even he could not make a better use of what he had learned. There was a sober truth in the judgments she formed of people and of circumstances, which was all the more impressive from the modesty with which she held her opinions, and the gentleness with which she declared them. Those opinions were respected by all, from the highest to the lowest,—from Ella down to Meg Murdoch. Her management of her little family was watched by all who cared for the welfare of their children, and her skill and industry in her occupation were marvelled at by those who did not attempt to imitate her.

It would have amused an attentive observer to see how a distinction of ranks was already growing up in the little society of Garveloch, where none had originally brought wealth enough to authorize such distinction. Next to the widow Cuthbert ranked the farmer and his family—the Duffs, who were looked up to from their great importance as corn-growers [grain] to the society. The produce of their fields being much in request, they had enlarged their farm, and improved it to a great extent. By means of the more ample supplies of manure afforded by the curing of so much fish, and through the help of the better implements and modes of tillage which their prosperity enabled them to use, their land produced twice as much as when they had entered upon the farm, fifteen years before. They had every inducement to go on increasing its productiveness; for corn still fell short, and supplies were brought now and then from other islands to make out till harvest. Of late, indeed, the demand had somewhat lessened, as an Irish family had set the example of growing potatoes in their patch of ground, and many of their neighbours had done the same, with the hope of saving the expense of oat and barley meal. Among these were the former tenants of the farm, the Murdochs, who, having failed in all their undertakings, now had recourse to what they supposed an easy and nearly infallible method of getting a living. They had sunk from year to year, and there was little hope of their rising again when they began to place their dependence on potato tillage. They now filled a station as much below that of Ella and her husband as Ella's had been supposed below theirs on the day of her father's funeral. Murdoch had not parted with any of his pride or jealousy as he parted with his worldly comforts. He still looked with an evil eye on Angus; and, when disposed to vent his complaints or seek counsel, went to new comers in preference to old neighbours. He was particularly intimate with the O'Rorys, who lived in a cottage next to his own, and who were of an age and in circumstances too unlike his own to come into comparison with him in any way.

Dan O'Rory was a lad of twenty, who had brought over his yet younger wife to seek employment in the Garveloch fishery, as there was none to be had at Rathmullin.[1] He had not yet been able to make interest for wages on board one of the busses, and he had no boat of his own; so he dug up and planted his potato-ground, and was content, talking of future doings, but caring little as yet whether they ever came to pass. One evil of their coming to pass, indeed, would be that there would be no longer time for talk, which Dan loved full as well as did Noreen, his wife.

One day, when Noreen was tired of her husband, and had gently turned him out of his cabin, he strolled to Murdoch's door, and lay down to bask in a July sun, his head resting on the wooden step, his fingers stuck into his hair, and his feet reposing among the fishy remains which lay as usual strewed round the door, and saluting more senses than one of the passers by. Hearing a step on the shingle, Dan half opened his eyes, and saw Murdoch approaching with a leaky barrel on his shoulder, from the seams of which the red pickle[2] was dropping down his clothes and meandering over his face.

"Them are the briny tears for which ye'll be never the worse," cried Dan. "I'd weep such tears every day, if the powers would give me leave."

"Get up, Dan, can't ye, and let me come in at my own door."

"With all the pleasure in life," said Dan, pushing the door open, and withdrawing himself as little as was necessary to let Murdoch pass.

"Eh! It's the herrings back again! O, father, what will ye do for the money? What good does the bounty do to them that can't sell

---

1   Rathmullin is a coast town in County Donegal, Ireland.
2   Red pickle refers to the brine used for pickling and preserving fish.

their fish?" resounded from the inside of the cottage in shrill tones of anger.

Murdoch swore at the bounty and the Company, and its officers, and at those who, he said, supplanted him.

"Well, but what did they say this time?" inquired his wife. "I took the largest barrel we had,—if it did not hold thirty-two gallons, there's not one in the island that does."

"They did not dispute that this time; how should they? But they say, not a cask that leaks shall be branded for the bounty."

"Never deny the leaking," said Dan, looking in from the door. "Your own head is pickled as fine as if it stood for the bounty."

Murdoch took no notice of him, but went on impatiently. "And for the rest of the complaint, I may thank you, wife, or Meg, or both of ye. There is not a fish clean gutted in the barrel; there is not one untainted with the sun; and besides, the cask is half full of salt. You women may raise the rent-money as well as you can, for I shall never do it if this is the way you help me."

Meg began to complain that the boat was so foul that the fish were tainted before they came ashore; that her mother had given her something else to do when she should have been curing the fish; that Rob had carried off the knife, so that she was obliged to gut them with her fingers; and that, as her mother would have a large barrel and her father would not catch more fish, what could be done but to fill up the cask with salt? The quarrel was beginning to run high, when Dan interfered to divert the course of the storm.

"I wonder," said he, "ye submit to be troubled with the villains that carry themselves so high. I'd leave them to catch their own fish, and keep cool and comfortable at home."

"We must live, Dan; so you talk only nonsense."

"True, neighbour; all that are not gentlemen must live. But there's nothing in life easier than to live without their help; and I'd be proud to do it, if it were only to see them standing and standing all day, and many days, to see the shoals[1] go by, and never a boat out to catch a fish for them. I'd go ten miles any day to see them stand idle, with all their sheds and cranes, and the new pier with the boats lying about it as if all the world was asleep. There would be easy work for a summer's day!"

"Easy enough for them, Dan, but hard enough for us that have not our pockets full of money like them."

---

1 A shoal is a school of fish.

"Never mind the money; where's the money that will buy such a sunshine as this?"

"If people like the sunshine as well with bare limbs and an empty stomach, Dan, I have nothing to say to them. For my part, I begin to feel the north wind chilling, now I am growing old; and I can't fish till I have had my morning meal."

"O, the morning meal is the pleasantest thing in nature when it gives one no trouble; and if you would do as I do, you would have one every day in the year, without giving a triumph to them villains. Just bestir yourself to plant your potatoes, and then you are provided without more words. O, people should go to old Ireland to learn how to live!"

"I thought Ireland had been a bad place to live in."

"Devil a bit, neighbour. It is the cheerfullest, brightest land the saints reign over,—glory to them for it!"

"Then what brought you here?"

"Just somebody told Noreen's father that one might fish guineas in these seas; so he had us married, and sent us over; but, as I tell Noreen, there is less gold here than at Rathmullin, seeing that the sun shines one half less. But we make ourselves content, as they do in Ireland; and that a man may do all the world over—let alone a woman that has a gentle cratur like me for a husband."

"But how would you have me make myself content, when I can't sell my fish either fresh or salted? I thought you had had more feeling for your neighbours, Dan."

"I! God help me, I'm as tinder-hearted as a lord's lady. It is because I am so tinder-hearted that I would have nobody bother themselves. Just give a man a cabin, and a bit of ground, and a spade, and a girl for a wife to crown all, and why should he trouble himself till the stars fall out of the sky?"

"And is that the way you do in Ireland?"

"Just so; and that is why Ireland is better than any other land."

"But I have more to provide for than my wife," said Murdoch, casting a look towards his little field.

"Make Rob dig it for you the first year," said Dan; "and if there is potatoes enough, well and good; and if not, go fish for what is wanting, or let Rob get a potato-ground for himself."

"But we shall want clothes, and money for rent."

"Tell the Company you'll work out the rent, or sell your boat for it, or beseech the saints that love to help. Any way better than bother yourself."

"Anything rather than bother myself," repeated Murdoch to himself, under the united provocations of heat, fatigue, disappointment, and jealousy. "I'll be free of them all, and never trouble myself to offer another fish to any man breathing. I can get fowl to help out our potatoes, and then we shall do well enough."

At this moment he saw farmer Duff approaching, and gave the hint to Dan, that he should observe how the farmer would behave when it should appear that he was to have no more custom from either family.

Duff declined the seat offered him by Murdoch's wife, as his first desire was to get to windward of that which strewed the ground where Meg had been curing fish. He asked Murdoch to walk a little way with him; but as Murdoch declined, Duff took the liberty of closing the door, and attempting to open the shutter which occupied the unglazed window.

"I live on the height, you know," said he, "and out of the way of your kind of business, so that I may seem to you over nice; but I was going to offer to relieve you of this litter. I have been round the village to engage for all the offal[1] of the season, and I will take up yours at the same price with the rest."

"I can't spare it, farmer."

"Well, just as you please; but I really hope you are going to remove it directly, for your health's sake."

"I trust my health will serve me to sow and gather many a crop that shall cost me less than your oatmeal, and be more wholesome than the pickles in yonder barrel. I have done with herrings for ever. Do you know any one that wants a boat, farmer?"

"More than you have boats to sell. There's Dan, for one. Dan, you mean to be a fisherman?"

"Perhaps I may, if the station offers me a place in a buss without any trouble; but I could not bother myself with a boat. Murdoch and I are content to be easy with our potatoes, no offence to you, I hope."

"None whatever. The only offence in the case is the offence of a wet season, if such a one should come;—where will the offence be then?"

"After a wet season comes a dry," said Dan; "and the powers will preserve us to witness it."

"Let me see your boat," said Duff. "Your relation Fergus was

---

1 Offal is refuse or garbage—here, referring to fish remains that were used to enrich the soil for crop-growing.

looking at his this morning as if he thought it would bear little more patching."

"Mine is nearly as old as his, but it will last a few fair seasons, yet, I expect. I will make him the offer of it."

Duff was going there now; and having no more time to spare, Murdoch and he set off together, leaving Dan to bask as before, or to vary his amusements by watching the flow of the tide.

As they went, they looked in on Ella, with whom Duff wished to negotiate as with Murdoch. Ella was in the shed built for a curing-house, surrounded by her children, three or four of whom were assisting her in her employment of salting and packing herrings, and the rest amusing themselves with playing hide and seek among the barrels.

"What a store of new barrels!" exclaimed Murdoch: "You must lose much by the old ones."

"Not at all," replied Ella: "they serve for our coasting trade when they will no longer do for the Company. If we often got such a cask as this," pointing to one beside her, "we should seldom have to buy. Kenneth made that."

"Your boy Kenneth!" exclaimed Murdoch. "Impossible!"

"He has been well taught by his uncle," said Duff, "and has good materials. See, the staves are half an inch thick, and even throughout, and the flags laid between the seams at both ends, and the hoops as regular and well fastened as Ronald himself could have made them."

"You will only waste such a barrel," said Murdoch, "if you let the children touch the fish. My Meg has wasted tons of fish and bushels of salt."

Little Annie, who was sprinkling the salt at this moment, turned very red, and looked at her mother as petitioning for a defence. Ella smiled as she invited Murdoch to look and see how evenly the fish were packed, and told him that there was a trial of skill among the children this day, and that it was to be determined, when her husband came home, whether Annie's salting was worthy of Kenneth's barrel.

"Kenneth is not to see till all is done," said Annie; "he is helping uncle Fergus to mend his boat, and uncle Fergus says he will make it last much longer than any body else could do but uncle Ronald."

"Ronald sent him this very morning, when he was most wanted," said Ella. "His father should have seen the landing. He brought me this barrel as a present, and he himself thought of bringing his tools and some staves in case Fergus's boat wanted mending, which it did sadly. You will excuse our going on with our work, neighbours, for you know it will not do to lose time in this weather: but the little ones will get you all you want if you will step within. Go, my little maids, and set out the bannocks[1] and the cheese, and I will bring the whisky."

Duff could not stay, however, longer than to settle when to send his pony and panniers[2] for the offal.

"Surely that cannot be little Kenneth!" exclaimed Murdoch, when, guided by the echo of hammering among the rocks, they came in sight of a fine tall lad repairing a boat. "Yes, it is Kenneth, so like his father, and just as handsome!"

Kenneth looked modestly happy when his uncle declared that he did not want to purchase Murdoch's boat, as he believed his own would be the best of the two by the time Kenneth went back to Islay.

Murdoch wondered why his children gave nothing but trouble while they were young, and did little but damage now that they were grown up, while other people made a profit of theirs. He took a poor price, paid in produce, from a cottager for his crazy boat, and went home wishing that he had sent Rob to learn something at the station, as he could teach him nothing at home.

Chapter II: Neighbourly Chat

At a late hour of this night, the young widow Cuthbert was still busy, as she had been all day, at her employment of net-making. The song with which she lulled her infant to sleep had long ceased, and she pursued her work in perfect silence by the dim light of her solitary lamp; her thoughts were alternately with the children who lay sleeping around her, and with the husband whose place of long repose was beneath the waters. As often as a little hand stirred above the coverlid, or a rosy cheek was turned upon its pillow, the anxious mother gazed and watched, and as often as the gust swept past, or a larger billow broke upon the shingle, her heart throbbed as if she was still awaiting the return of him who should never more return. She started, at length, on hearing a tap at her door.

"It is only Ella," said a voice from the outside; and the widow hastened to open the door.

---

1   Bannocks are flat griddle-cakes made of oatmeal or barley.
2   Panniers are a pair of baskets or other containers slung over both sides of a pack animal for carrying goods.

"Your husband, your husband!" she exclaimed; "no ill to him I trust. You are not in fear for him, Ella?"

"He is safe home, thank Him who guides the storms!" replied Ella: "but it is a gusty night."

"Ye look cold and your plaid[1] drips," said the widow, setting down the lamp, and applying more fuel to her smouldering fire. "What brings ye here so late, Ella?"

"Only a message from Angus about the nets, which I should have left till the morn, but that Kenneth and I saw a glimmer beneath your door, and I knew I should find you at your occupation. We press you too close for your work, Katie. It's an ill thing for sad hearts to watch so late. Better that we should do without our nets, than that you should look as you do now."

"'Tis for my bairns [children]," said Katie, "or I would not undergo it. O, Ella! I have been jealous of you these two hours past, if, as I supposed, you were on the rock looking out."

"No wonder, Katie; and yet I could have found in my heart to be jealous of Fergus's wife, and all the wives that were serving their husbands by the fireside, instead of breasting the wind, and mistaking every jet of the surge for a sail, as I have been doing since the sun went down. But I had Kenneth to while away the time with, and help to keep in the light. He showed me how they hoist the lanterns at the station, and our signals will be better managed from this night forward. O Katie, you must see Kenneth, and I must tell you all that his uncle has done for him."

"But your husband," interrupted the widow; "how long was he? and in what style did his boat come ashore? and which of you first saw him? and—"

"Now, Katie, why will ye be ever asking such questions as you know it wounds me to answer? I have told you he is home safe. He has brought such a store of fish, that, busy as the curers have been on board, there is as much left for the lassies and me to do to-morrow as we can finish before the twenty-four hours are gone. And that reminds me of the nets: Angus must have those he ordered within three days, he bids me tell you; but let us look about for some one to help you, instead of your toiling with your fingers, and harassing your spirits through the night."

"We must toil while the season lasts," replied Katie; "and as for the

---

1 A plaid is both a cross-checked pattern and a rectangular scarf worn over the shoulders or head like a shawl.

wear of spirits," she continued smiling, "that is all fancy, and must be got over. I have nothing now to tremble for—no need to listen and look out, and I must learn not to heed the storm further than to be thankful that my bairns have about them all that makes a storm harmless. If this was a time of hardship, Ella, like some that have been known here, how I might have envied some who were kept watching, not by cold or hunger, but only by having more employment than they could finish in the day!"

"It is a rich season, indeed," said Ella. "The shoals are such as Angus never saw before, for the multitude and the quality of the fish; and what is more, the crops are coming up kindly, and farmer Duff says that he reckons on the best harvest he has had since he took the farm."

"Thank God!" exclaimed Katie. "This plenty may prevent the price from rising, and nothing else could. It almost frightens me sometimes when I see the numbers that are growing up, to think how we are to get oat and barley meal for them all."

"If you had been here all the sixteen years since I first came to this bay," said Ella, "you would wonder at the change, and be thankful to see how improvements have risen as wants increased. Now trim your lamp, and go on with your business; it will be some time yet before my husband and Kenneth have finished with the boat and come for me.—Surely you make your meshes more than an inch wide;—no, the exact measure.—Well, that is one of the improvements I speak of."

"It was folly, indeed," replied Katie, "to use such nets as I used to make—nets that caught the fry and let the full grown go free. That was the quickest way to make every season worse than the last. Then there are the boats, so much safer from having pumps, so much more favourable to the fish from being cleaner, and so much better built that our fishers need not lose their time in short trips, but can push out into the deep seas, and stay many days together. All these things help to make fishing profitable."

"Besides," said Ella, "they help farming, which is of as much importance to us as the fishing. Corn from abroad is so dear, that we should be little better off than before, if farmer Duff did not grow more than Murdoch once did."

"The people in the other islands and in Lorn[1] want all they can grow as much as we," replied Katie, "for their fishery grows with

---

1 Lorn is situated in western Scotland.

ours. Meat and bannocks are as dear in all the countries round as they were here last year."

"Then we may thank farmer Duff for all the pains he has taken with the soil of his fields and the stock of his pastures. He reaps just double what he reaped fifteen years ago."

"And so he had need, for there are more than double the number of mouths to feed. Besides the strangers that have come to settle, look at the families that have grown up. Where Mr. Callum used to spend a few days now and then, there is Mary Duff's husband and her five bairns; then there are your nine, Ella—how your household is increased!"

"There lies one brother under the gray stone," said Ella, "and Ronald seeks his bannocks elsewhere; but there is Fergus's tribe as well as my own; and setting one against Murdoch's son that died, and another against his daughter that went off with the soldier, there is still more than double the number by far."

"Even supposing," added Katie, "that Murdoch's daughter does not come back upon her father with her children, which I have heard is likely. But, Ella, Duff's farm ought to yield double and double for ever, if it is to go on to feed us, for our children will marry and have their little tribes as we have. If you and I live to be like many grandmothers in these islands, we shall see our twenty or thirty grand-children, and perhaps our eighty or ninety great-grand-children."

"And then," replied Ella, "may God keep us from the poverty that weighs on such! May we never see our strong men wasting on shell-fish and weeds, and our aged people dropping cold and hungry into their deathbeds, and our young mothers tending their sickly infants, knowing that food and warmth might save them, and unable to bring them either the one or the other!"

"Do not let us think of it," said Katie, looking round upon her domestic comforts. "Providence has blessed us thus far, and let us not be too keen to foresee the evil day that man's power cannot remove."

Ella was silent. Katie proceeded,—

"Surely man cannot remove that day, Ella, though you say nothing. Let farmer Duff do all he can; let every foot of land be tilled that will nourish an ear of barley, still the day may come; and what else can man do?"

Ella made no direct reply. Presently she observed that Dan and his wife seemed not to care for the evils of such a time, since they lived by choice on the poorest food, and provided themselves with nothing that they could lose in the worst of seasons.

"They are content, always content," observed the widow; "and they say they have all that is necessary; and they wonder that we can trouble ourselves to obtain anything that is not necessary: but I tell them we do not; I think a chimney, and a window, and bedding, and decent clothes all necessary for the children."

"Unless you would have them live like pigs in a sty," observed Ella. "When God gave us the charge of these little ones, he gave us no leave that ever I heard of to expose them to sickness and hardship, and to corrupt them by letting them live like brutes. By making them helpless and quick in their feelings, he has shown as plainly as if he sent a prophet to tell us, that we are to tend them as carefully and keep them as innocent as ever our labour and forethought can help us to do. Whenever I see a little one grovelling in dirt, or pining in want, or given to vice such as it should not even have heard of, I always feel as if God's plain-spoken message had been at some time misunderstood; either that the trust has been wrongly undertaken or wrongly managed."

"I knew you thought so, Ella; and yet what can we say when parents see and mourn all this, and cannot help themselves?"

"We can only say that if both father and mother have considered and judged for the best, and worked hard, and denied themselves, no fault rests with them. Where the fault lies in such a case is a thing that Angus and I have talked over many a time. But such a case does not concern those we were speaking of—those who are content with destitution, when they might have comfort."

The widow looked on her children and sighed.

"Nay," said Ella, smiling, "there is no need for you to sigh. You might carry your bairns to Inverary, and match them with the duke's, and not a stronger, or fairer, or more innocent would you find among them all."

"May it please Providence to keep them so!"

"Why should you fear? You have comfort about you, and a prospect of abundance. Keep your tears for a darker day, if there be such in the years to come."

"Every day is dark to me now," thought the widow; but she kept down a feeling that seemed ungrateful. Ella went on, anxious to cheer her.

"I watched your little Hugh this morning, as he and my younger ones were playing on the sands, and I thought he looked as if he was made to carry his own way through the world. You should have seen him managing the dragging of the pool with the ragged net Angus gave the children. You would have thought he had been to the station to take a lesson of the superintendent, by his direction of the rest."

"Aye, I am afraid he is overbearing," replied the mother.

"Not at all; only spirited. If you keep him innocent with such a spirit as he has, he may be anything; he may be like Ronald himself, who is so fond of him. O, he is not overbearing. I saw him let go the net the moment little Bessie was frightened at your dog that jumped upon her; and he carried her through the water that was too deep for her to wade, as soon as ever she began to cry for me. Now I think of it, Ronald did take him to the station once, surely."

"Yes; not very long ago, the last time he was here; and Hugh saw the superintendent as you suppose, and has been full of imitation of all that he saw ever since."

"He may be superintendent himself some day or other, Katie. But does not he love Ronald very much?"

"Very much; as he ought to do."

"All my children do," replied Ella. "It is always a happy time when uncle Ronald comes. The same man that the officers respect above all who are under them is as much beloved by the little ones as if he were a soft-hearted girl."

"You had the making of Ronald, and I give you joy of your work," said the widow.

"Ah, Katie, that is the way you always silence me about Ronald," said Ella, smiling.

"Well, then, tell me about Fergus: he is your work too."

"You know all I can say about him," said Ella, sighing. "You know my pride in him, and that this very pride makes me the more griev-ed when I see his temper harassed and soured by care, as I feel it must go on to be, more and more. I am always in dread of a quarrel with one neighbour or another; and more than ever now, in the high fish-ing season."

"Surely he has less care now than at other times," observed the widow. "There is just now abundance for every body."

"True; but this is the time for revenge. If Fergus has carried him-self high towards any neighbour, or given the sharp words that are never forgotten, now is the time for his nets to be cut, or his boat set adrift, or what he has fished in the day carried off in the night."

"There are those in Garveloch, I know," said Katie, "who can bring themselves to do such things."

"Let us mention no names, Katie; but thus it is that men shame their race, and spurn the gifts they little deserve. To think that we cannot enjoy a plentiful season in peace and thankfulness, but that some must injure, and others complain! These are times when we should leave it to the osprey to follow a prey, and to the summer storms to murmur. Hark! There is Angus's step outside; and time it is, for it cannot be far from midnight."

The widow invited Angus in to warm himself by her now bright fire; but it was time for rest. Kenneth had gone home an hour before.

"He would find supper on the board," said Ella; "and now, Angus, you will be glad to do the same."

Katie promised the nets within three days; and as soon as she had closed the door behind her guests, sat down again for one other hour to help the fulfilment of her promise, and then slept all the better for having watched till the wind went down.

Chapter III: Kindred not Kindness

It was not very long before Ella's fears on account of her brother Fergus were in part realized, though the evil day was deferred by an arrangement offered by Angus and eagerly accepted by his brother-in-law. The herring fishery being peculiarly abundant this year, Angus wanted more help on board his vessel; and as it was expected that the cod would be plentiful in proportion, Angus might in his turn assist Fergus, when the herring shoals were past, and the cod which follow to make prey of them should become the chief object of the fishery. Fergus laboured from July to October for a certain share of the herring produce; and Angus was to go out with Fergus in all the intervals of his coasting trips during the late autumn and winter. While Fergus was on board Angus's vessel, all went well; for Angus had no enemies. He might spread his nets to dry on the beach, and his youngest child was guard enough to set over them. He never left his fish on board all night, while he was at home, thinking it wrong to put such a temptation to theft in the way of any one; but if he had, no harm would have been done out of malice to himself, as was too frequently the practice in this fishery.

Poor Fergus was not so secure, as he had found before, and was destined to find again. Like most men of hasty tempers, who are besides subject to care, he had enemies among those who did not know how to make allowance for him, and were not disposed to forgive harsh expressions which the offender was apt to forget that he had used. Dan, easy and content as he seemed to be, had the selfishness common to lazy people; and there is no more inveterate enemy to good-will than selfishness. Dan was not, like many of his countrymen, ready with his oaths and his cudgel at a moment's warning, if anything went amiss; but Dan could drawl out the most provoking things imaginable, and enjoy their effect upon an irritable person, and show that he enjoyed it; and having thus encouraged a quarrel, in which he did not give his adversary the satisfaction of bearing his share heartily, he let it drop; but had no objection to see it carried on by somebody else. He amused himself with watching what befell Fergus, and with laughing at every little distress which arose subsequent to a certain dispute which had once occurred between them. He did no harm with his own hands, but people knew that he did not object to seeing it done; and such sympathy affords great advantage to the doers of mischief. Among these was Rob Murdoch, a doer of mischief by nature as some said,—at all events by habit, and very often by express will. Rob had never felt at ease with Ella or any of the family since the day of his upsetting the boat; though there was never a look or word from any of them which could have made him uncomfortable, if his own consciousness had not. He was always ready to suppose offence, and found no difficulty in creating it where he was not liked, and only tolerated on account of long neighbourhood and distant relationship. He kept out of Ella's way, for he was mightily afraid of her. He hated Angus, having been formerly taught by his father that Angus was a traitor who intended to supplant him, and the impression remained on his stupid mind long after the cause had been removed. Ronald was out of his way entirely; and Fergus was therefore the only one exposed to his poor spite, while he was the one least able to disregard it. The time had been when Fergus would have scorned the idea of being moved by anything Rob could say; but Fergus was more easily moved than formerly, and it stung him to hear Rob predict, as he lounged on the shore, that the wind would be contrary when Fergus wished it fair; to be met on his return from an unsuccessful expedition with the news that everybody else had caught a vast deal of fish; and, above all, to see the enemy fretting the children into a passion, which was a frequent pastime of Rob's when he had nothing better to do. Out of these provocations arose quarrels; and out of quarrels, Rob's desire of revenge; a desire which he could gratify only in a small way as long as Fergus worked for his brother-in-law. Rob asked several times for the loan of Fergus's boat during the herring season; and as he made the request in his father's name, it was not refused; but when it was found that the boat received some injury each time, Fergus very reasonably desired Rob to repair the mischief as often as he caused it. Being too lazy to do this, the loan was denied to him, and then he made bold to use the boat without leave when he knew that Fergus was absent; and the exclamations of the children having brought their mother out to see what was the matter, the ill-will was not lessened by the addition of a woman's tongue. No terms were kept after the railing bout between Rob and Janet on the sands: they regarded and acted towards each other as enemies from that day forward.

Angus offered Fergus a benefit, as he called it, to finish off the season with; that is, all the fish caught in the last trip were to be Fergus's; and to the winnings of this trip he looked for the means of finally making up his rent, and of improving the clothing of the children before the winter. The signs of the weather were anxiously watched by himself and his family, the nets were carefully repaired, the casks looked to, more salt brought in from the station, and every preparation completed the evening before, when the nets and stores were carried on board, and all made ready for starting at dawn. It was a misty morning, such as would not have tempted either Janet or Ella abroad if this had been any other trip than the last of the season: but as it was, they attended their husbands down to the shore, with their children flocking about them. As it was too foggy to let them see the vessel at fifty yards distance from the beach they presently returned, walking so slowly, that before they reached home the mists had partly dispersed at the appearance of the rising sun, and opened a prospect along the shore.

"There's Rob turning the point," cried one of the little ones.

"Rob at this time of the morning? Impossible!" said Ella. "They that have no more to do than he are not stirring so early. It is he, however. Look, Janet, how he peeps at us from behind the rock! I will go and speak with him for he has no quarrel with me, and I do not forget we are cousins."

It was not so easy, however, to catch him. When he saw Ella approaching, he withdrew from sight; and when she turned the point, he was already high up among the rocks, on a path which he could not have reached without exercising more activity than was his wont.

"I believe the man thinks," said Ella to herself, "as Mr. Callum used to do, that I am a witch, for he flees me as a fowl flees the hawk. If I could but win his ear for half an hour, there might be an end of this ill-will between him and Fergus, which is a scandal to relations, and to those who, living far from war, ought to live in peace."

Where enmity once creeps in, it is difficult to preserve peace with any of the parties concerned. After having missed Rob, Ella found that Janet was offended at her having sought him; and it was with some difficulty that she brought her sister-in-law to acknowledge that a quarrel has done quite enough mischief when it separates two families, and that no advantage can arise from its involving a third.

Before many hours had elapsed, the children came running to their mother, crying—

"The boat! The boat! She is warping into the Bay. Father will be on shore presently."

"It cannot be our boat!" said Ella, turning pale, however, as she spoke. "It must be one of the station boats."

A glance showed her that it was indeed her husband's vessel coming in already, instead of three or four days hence, as she had expected. Her only way of accounting for this quick return was by supposing that some accident had happened on board. The wind was contrary, so that it must be some time before the crew could land, and Ella was not disposed to wait for tidings. She commanded her children not to go out and tell Janet, who, being busy within doors, might not know of the return; and then went down to the place where Murdoch's old boat was lying, obtained a hasty leave to use it and help to launch it, seized the oars and pushed off, and was presently alongside her husband's vessel. Fergus was already half over the side, ready to jump down to his sister, and impatient to gain the shore, while Angus in vain attempted to hold him back.

"Push off, Ella!" cried Angus. "Do not come near till I bring him to reason."

Seeing that her husband and brother were both safe, Ella repressed her anxiety to know what had happened, and by one vigorous pull shot off out of Fergus's reach. He threw himself back into the vessel, and trod the little deck like one in a towering passion.

"My husband! my brother!" cried Ella, in a tone which reached the hearts of both, "you have not quarreled?"

"O no! Nor ever shall," said Angus, laying his hand on Fergus's shoulder, "and least of all this day."

"Do you think I could fall out with Angus?" said Fergus. "No! I must be sunk indeed before I could do that. It is he who has kept me from ruin till now, and it is he who would make me think I am not ruined to-day."

Ruined!—The truth was soon told. Fergus's nets were destroyed. They had been safe the night before. This morning, when he was preparing to throw them, he found them cut almost to shreds. If he had had money to buy more, they could not be provided in time. The season was over; his benefit was lost; and with it went all hopes of making up his rent by the day it would become due, and of supplying the additions he had proposed to the comforts of his little ones.

Ella's suspicions lighted upon Rob even before she heard Fergus declare that it could be nobody else. A sudden thought having struck her, she came alongside once more, and having communicated with her husband in a tone which Fergus could not overhear, she again departed, shaping her course for Murdoch's dwelling.

Rob was lying on the beach asleep, as she expected; and beside him was Dan, also asleep. If they had been awake, they would not have seen Angus's vessel which was now behind the point to their right. Ella stepped on shore and wakened Rob, saying,

"I see you have no business of your own this bright noon, Rob; so come and take an oar with me."

Rob started up when he saw who was standing over him. He wished his tall cousin far over seas, or anywhere but at his elbow.

"Ask Dan," said he. "Dan! Here's my cousin Ella wants a trip. Take an oar with her, will ye?"

"No," replied Ella. "Let Dan finish his dream."

"Meg is stouter than I at the oar," pleaded Rob.

"It is you that I want, and that this moment," said Ella, pointing his way to the boat, towards which Rob shuffled unwillingly, like a school-boy going in search of the rod with which he is to be whipped.

Instead of giving him an oar, Ella took both; and as he sat opposite her with nothing to do, he felt very silly, and this feeling was a bad preparation for what was to follow. When they were fairly beyond the breakers, Ella rested on her oars, and, looking her companion full in the face, asked him where he had passed the previous night. Rob looked up to the sky, back to the shore, and around upon the waters, and then scratching his head, asked,

"What was that ye said, cousin Ella?"

"You heard what I said."

"Well; where should I have passed the night?"

"That is for you to answer. I ask again where you were when the moon set last night?"

Rob shuffled in his talk as well as in his gait. He told how he oftentimes spent his time on the rocks rather than bear the smell of putrid fish under his father's roof; and how Meg had foretold a bad night, and it turned out fine; and many other things that had nothing to do with Ella's question. She let him go on till, by turning the point, they came in sight of the Flora standing south-west. She directed his attention to it, saying that the Flora was her object. Rob swore a deep oath and demanded to be set on shore again, cursing himself for having come without knowing whither he was to be taken. Ella's steady eye was still upon him when she asked the reason of this sudden horror of meeting his cousins and boarding their boat: adding,

"I fancy it is not so very long since you were on board the Flora of your own accord."

Rob had sense enough to see that he only betrayed himself by showing eagerness to get back, and therefore held his peace till they approached the Flora, when he hailed Angus, requesting him to help Ella on board; and then said to his companion,

"I'll take the boat straight back with pleasure, cousin, with your thanks, I suppose, to Duncan Hogg for the use of it."

"Not yet," said Ella; "I have more to say to you. Now, Rob, tell me honestly whether you were at home all last night, and here the mischief may end; but if you will not give an account to us, you must to the magistrate at the station. If you are innocent you can have no objection to clear yourself; if you are guilty, depend upon it you will meet with more mercy from your cousins than from a stranger who comes to execute justice."

"As sure as ever anything happens, you always suspect me," muttered Rob. "What care I what happens to Fergus, or what he makes of his benefit?"

"O then, you know what has happened," observed Ella, "and yet I have not told you."

Rob, finding that he only gave new occasion of suspicion by everything he said, took refuge in sullen silence, got on board at Ella's command, and sat immovably looking at the sea as they steered for Islay, having fastened the little boat to the stern of the Flora.

Rob's courage or obstinacy failed him when the station became visible, the white house of Mr. M'Kenzie, the magistrate, appearing at some little distance above and behind the pier, the cooperage, the curing house and the village. Ella, who watched an opportunity of saving the culprit from a public exposure, was by his side the moment he showed an inclination to speak.

"If ye will only just say ye are willing to make reparation, and will never play such an unkind prank again," said she, "I will intercede with Fergus to forgive you."

"What may be the cost of the nets?"

"More than you can make up without hard work; but it may be made up; and I would fain set ye home, Rob, without having seen the magistrate's face."

Rob muttered that he did not see why he should be brought to justice more than others that did the same trick. It was but a prank; and when they were boys and no magistrate within reach, nobody talked of justice.—Ella reminded him that Mr. Callum had united all the offices of law and justice in his own person when the island was inhabited by few except themselves; but that circumstances had now changed, and relations multiplied, and that property must be protected from the player of pranks as well as from the thief.

Fergus, touched by the kindness of his brother and sister, controlled his passion, and received Rob's submission with more grace than it was tendered with, agreeing to take compensation as the offender should be able to give it, provided nets could be obtained at the station on promise of future payment.

Chapter IV: Looking Before and After

None of the party left the station without having seen the face of the magistrate. He was in the store house when Fergus went to make his application for nets.

"What makes you want so many feet of netting at once?" asked Mr. Mackenzie; "and in such a hurry too. I hope yours have not been destroyed?"

"Indeed but they have, your honour; and another such loss would destroy me."

"The law must be put in force in its utmost rigour," declared the magistrate;—whereupon Rob hastily withdrew to the cooperage, where he might be out of sight. "Scarcely a day passes," continued Mr. Mackenzie, "without information of some act of violence or another. How to you suppose this happens, Mr. Angus?"

"Through jealousy, I believe, sir. We seldom hear of thefts—"

"I beg your pardon, Mr. Angus. I have had several complaints within a few days of depredations on the fishing grounds in the lochs [lakes] where the cod are just showing themselves."

"I rather think even these thefts must arise from revenge more than from a desire of gain; for there is or ought to be no want at present through the whole extent of the fishery. Some, like my brother Fergus, are reduced to difficulty by the destruction of their implements; but in such a season as this, there can be no absolute distress for any who are willing to work."

"I scarcely know which is the most painful," replied the magistrate; "to see men snatching bread out of one another's mouths through jealousy and spite, or under the impulse of pressing want.

The worst of it is, the last usually follows the first. This enemy of your brother's, who has been injuring him now without a pretence, may plead starvation in excuse for some other act of violence hereafter."

"I trust you are mistaken, sir," replied Angus. "I trust the miseries of poverty that I have seen elsewhere are far from our shores."

"The first sign of their approach, Angus, is when men begin to fancy their interests opposed to each other,—which the interests of men in society can never be. Fair competition leads to the improvement of the state of all; but the jealousy which tempts to injure any interest whatever is the infallible token that distress is at hand. You have seen enough of the world to know this to be a general truth, Angus. Why do you dispute it in the present case?"

"Perhaps my own interest in the issue blinds me," returned Angus. "I have seen enough in other countries of what you describe to make me melancholy when I witness men pulling one another's fortunes to pieces instead of building up the prosperity of the whole by labouring together at that of every part. Whether I hear of different classes in a commercial country petitioning for impediments to be thrown in one another's way, or see (as I saw in Canada) jealous neighbours levelling one another's fences in the dark, or laying siege to them in the day-time, I feel sure that destruction is ready to step in and beggar them all, whether it be in the shape of a prohibitory duty imposed by government, or of wild cattle that come to trample down the corn on which the quarrellers depend."

"You once told us of some who united to make a road," said Ella, who had now joined her husband. "That was wiser than pulling down fences."

"Where all helped to give each other the fair advantage of a road," replied her husband, "a flourishing settlement presently arose among the fertile fields. Where the fences were levelled, there was soon no need of fences. Some who had dwelt within them lay under the sod, hunger having cut short their days, and others were gone in search of food, leaving their fields to grow into a wilderness once more."

"Theirs was indeed the lowest degree of folly that can be conceived."

"Not quite," observed Mr. Mackenzie. "I can fancy a lower, though I do not ask you to receive it as fact. This letting in of wild cattle to trample the corn took place when but few wanted to be fed, and those few had immediate resources. If, instead of this act of folly, the perpetrators had waited till hundreds and thousands were in expectation, with an appetite which the most ample harvests could not satisfy, and had set fire to the produce at the very season when it was most wanted, under the idea of vexing the holders of the land, what would you say then?"

"There is nothing to be said, sir, but that such would be an act of mere madness,—too evidently madness to be committed by more than an individual, and that individual an escaped maniac."

"The school of ignorance is the innermost court of Bedlam,"[1] replied Mr. Mackenzie; "and while there are any patients remaining in it, it is possible that corn-stacks may be burned by discontented people with the notion of revenging the wrongs of the starving. But I put it only as a possibility, you know.—Can it be, Angus, that you do not see the tendency of the acts of violence that are disturbing this very district? Do you not see distress and ruin in full prospect if they are not checked, and if, moreover, the temper of the people be not directly reversed?"

"Our resources are so improved that I would fain hope the best; and yet our numbers increase in full proportion, so that we had not need waste any of our capital."

"I think not indeed. I have been visiting every station on the coast and in the islands, and I find the same state of things everywhere,—a prosperity so unusual in these districts, that the people think their fortune secure for ever, while they are hastening, by every possible means, the approach of distress."

"I hope you find the farms and pastures improving with the fishery?" observed Angus.—"Everything depends upon the food keeping pace with the employment."

"The farms are improving to the utmost that skill and labour can make them improve. There is the powerful stimulus of an increasing demand, while there are increasing facilities of production. There is more manure, there are better implements, and more cattle; so that some farms produce actually double what they did when the fishery began."

Angus shook his head, observing that this was not enough.

"They have done their best already in the way of increase," said he. "They may be improved for some time to come, and to a great degree; but each improvement yields a less return: so that they will be further and further perpetually from again producing double in

---

1 Bedlam is the colloquial name for St. Mary of Bethlehem hospital for the insane in London.

ten years; and all this time the consumers are increasing at a much quicker rate."

"Not double in ten years surely?" said Ella.

"Certainly not; but say twenty, thirty, fifty, a hundred, any number of years you choose;—still, as the number of people doubles itself for ever, while the produce of the land does not, the people must increase faster than produce. If the corn produced corn without being wedded to the soil, the rate of increase might be the same with that of the human race. The two sacks of barley might grow out of one, and two more again out of each of those two—proceeding from one to two, four, eight, sixteen, thirty-two, sixty-four, and so on."

"If capital could be made to increase in this way, I see, Angus, that there could never be too many people in the world, or in our little world, Garveloch."

"Or if, on the other hand, human production could be kept down to the same rate with the production of our fields, we need have no fear of a deficiency of food. If the number of producers increased only in proportion to the increase of food, there would be no distress of the kind our islands were formerly afflicted with, and may be afflicted with again. But nobody thinks of establishing such a proportion; and in the meanwhile, food is yielded, though in larger quantities, in less and less proportions, while the eaters go on doubling and doubling their numbers perpetually."

"Then, to be sure, it is madness to destroy one another's means of living," cried Ella. "It seems the first duty of everybody to increase the production of food; and yet, here we are, cutting one another's nets to pieces, and driving the fish away on which we depend for our subsistence!"

"You do not wonder now," said Mr. Mackenzie, "at my grief for the ignorance of the people, and my disgust at the quarrels that have such consequences. I assure you the season is actually lost in some of the northern lochs; for, not only are some fishers left without nets or lines, but the fish have made no stay, being alarmed by tumult; and it is but too probable that they will not return."

"And all this time," continued Angus, "these very quarrellers go on marrying early, and raising large families—that is, they bring offspring into the world while they are providing as fast as possible for their future starvation."

"There is no need to do here as the Romans did," said Mr. Mackenzie, "and as many other nations have done—no need to offer bounties for the increase of population."

"I think not indeed," said Ella. "It seems a thing to be checked, rather than encouraged."

"All depends on time and circumstances, Ella. When Noah and his little tribe stepped out of the ark into a desolated world,[1] the great object was to increase the number of beings, who might gather and enjoy the fruits which the earth yielded, in an abundance overpowering to the few who were there to consume. And the case is the same with every infant nation which is not savage."

"Savages do not value or subsist upon the fruits of the earth so much as upon the beasts of the field," said Ella;—"at least so Angus told me of those who have retreated from before us in America."

"Savages care for little beyond supplying the pressing wants of the moment," replied Angus. "They make no savings; they have no capital; and their children die off as fast as poverty and disease can drive them out of the world. There is no growth of either capital or population among savages."

"Those have indeed a poor chance for life and health," said Mr. Mackenzie, "whose parents feed at the best on raw roots and berries, who sometimes keep themselves alive by swallowing grubs and worms, and at other times fast for a week together. Shrunk, deformed, and weakly themselves, their offspring are little likely to survive a scarcity, even if it were possible to rear them under the most favourable circumstances."

"It is absurd," said Angus, "to doubt the rate at which the human race increases on account of the decrease of numbers among savages. The whole question is concerning the proportion which capital and population bear to each other; and it cannot therefore be tried where no capital exists."

"I suppose," observed Ella, "that flocks and herds are the first capital which a tribe possesses in any large quantity. How do numbers increase among people who seek pasture but do not till the ground?"

"Such tribes are most numerous where pastures are fine, and weak where the natural produce of the earth is scanty. But each continues a tribe, and cannot become a nation while following a pastoral life.

---

1   Martineau refers to the biblical legend in which the patriarch Noah was instructed by God to build an ark for his family, on which he was also to house a male and female of every species, to preserve them from the flood that was to destroy the world as it was known at that time. See Genesis 5-9.

Their flocks cannot multiply beyond a certain point unless the food of the flocks is increased; and they who subsist upon the flocks cannot, in like manner, multiply beyond a certain point, unless the flocks on which they feed are multiplied."

"But they not only do not increase," observed Mr. Mackenzie, "they are lessened perpetually by one or another of the unfortunate accidents to which their condition subjects them. Pastoral tribes are particularly prone to war. Instead of keeping possession of a certain territory on which they always dwell, they rove about from one tract of country to another, leaving undefended some which they call their own;—another tribe takes possession; and then comes a struggle and a destructive war, which reduces their numbers. Many of these tribes live in a state of continual hostility, and therefore dwindle away."

"But when they begin to settle and till the ground," said Ella, "I suppose their numbers increase again."

"Yes; the Jews, after they were established in Canaan,[1] became an agricultural nation, and multiplied very rapidly. It was made, both by their laws and customs, a point of duty to marry and to marry young; and when the check of war was removed, their small territory became very thickly peopled."

"I suppose it was to repair the waste of war," said Ella, "that the bounty on population was offered among the Romans."

"Not only from this cause," replied Mr. Mackenzie, "but to repair the breaches made in other ways. In the early days of Rome, the population was too large for the capital in intervals of peace, as appears from the law of their king Romulus,[2] that no child should be exposed to die in the desert before three years of age—a proof that it had been the previous practice to expose children under that age. In after times—in the days of Roman glory—the population was apt to decrease, even in times of peace, from the faults in the distribution of property. The land had fallen into the hands of a few great proprietors, and was not tilled by free labour. Swarms of slaves were brought in from all conquered countries, and they alone were employed where free labour should have claimed a share of labour

---

1 Canaan, the Promised Land of the Jews according to a covenant made by God, situated between the Mediterranean, the Dead Sea, and Jordan. See Genesis 12:7.

2 Romulus is the legendary founder of Rome. According to the tradition, Romulus and his twin brother, Remus, the sons of the god Mars, were suckled by a wolf.

and reward; and there was therefore no subsistence for a middling and lower class of free people. Their numbers dwindled so as to alarm their rulers and give occasion to express laws for the encouragement of population. If, instead of passing laws to promote early marriages, and offering privileges to those who had a certain number of children, the Roman emperors had allowed liberty to the people they governed to labour and subsist, there would have been no complaint of a deficiency of numbers, but rather an inquiry, as there is among us, how all that are born are to be fed?"

"But do you mean, sir," said Angus, "that there were not children born to the lower classes of the Romans, or that they were born and died through want?"

"Multitudes that were born died immediately, from being exposed; and besides this, marriage was less practised during these ages of the Roman empire than among the same number of people in any other country."

"The laws were not of much use then."

"And how can we wonder, when it was actually the custom to give away corn [grain] gratis [free] to thousands upon thousands who had no means of earning it! What inducement has a man to marry, when he must either expose his children, or see them die at home, or take his chance of a gratuitous dole of food for them? The laws, if they acted at all, would not act upon these large classes, but upon those of a higher rank, who would marry if there were no law."

"If in any country," observed Ella, "there are no laws to encourage or to check marriage, it seems as if that country ought to afford a fair example of the natural increase of numbers."

"Nay," said her husband, "human laws have little influence in this case, while the natural laws which regulate the production of life and of capital are seldom suffered to act unchecked. Leave the people of any country as free as you please to marry or not as they like, still, if capital is controlled in any way, the population is controlled also."

"Where then," inquired Ella, "does capital act the most freely? Where in the world may we see an example of the natural proportions in which men and subsistence increase?"

"There has never been an age or country known," replied Mr. Mackenzie, "where at once the people have been so intelligent, their manners so pure, and their resources so abundant, as to give the principle of increase an unobstructed trial. Savage life will not do, because the people are not intelligent. Colonies will not do, because they are not free from vicious customs. An old empire will not do, because the means of subsistence are restricted."

"A new colony of free and intelligent people in a fertile country affords the nearest approach to a fair trial," observed Angus. "In some of the best settlements I saw in America, the increase of capital and of people went on at a rate that would scarcely be believed in an old country."

"And that of the people the fastest, I suppose?"

"Of course; but still capital was far a-head, though the population is gaining upon it every year. When the people first went, they found nothing but capital—all means of production and no consumers but themselves. They raised corn in the same quantity from certain fields every year. There was too much corn at first in one field for a hundred mouths; but this hundred became two, four, eight, sixteen hundred, and so on, till more and more land was tilled, the people still spreading over it, and multiplying perpetually."

"And when all is tilled and they still multiply," said Ella, "they must improve their land more and more."

"And still," said Angus, "the produce will fall behind more and more, as every improvement, every outlay of capital yields a less return. Then they will be in the condition of an old country like England, where many are but half fed, where many prudent determine not to marry, and where the imprudent must see their children pine in hunger, or waste under disease till they are ready to be carried off by the first attack of illness."

"May this never be the case in Garveloch!" cried Ella.

"The more waste of capital there is," said Mr. Mackenzie, "the sooner will that day come."

"But our islands are now in the state of a new colony, like that Angus was speaking of," said Ella. "Want must be far from us at present."

"Except that we have not a fertile soil or a good climate," replied her husband. "It is true we do not depend entirely on corn; —we had not need for our home supply can never be large. We have the resource of fish, but it is so precarious a resource, that we ought to keep some means of subsistence in reserve. If the herrings should desert us for a season or two, and the harvest fail, some of us must starve, or all be half-starved, unless we have a stock in reserve."

"Poor Fergus!" exclaimed Ella. "No wonder he was grieved and angry this morning! Five children and no capital stored up! He may well watch the seasons and tremble at the storm."

"I am sorry," observed Mr. Mackenzie, "that he will not give up the name of the offender who has injured him. It is necessary to the public safety that this wanton destruction of property should be put an end to; and I give it in charge to you, Angus, to see that full compensation is made, or that the culprit is delivered into my hands to be made an example of. If it had been generally known that I am here to administer the law, I would not have yielded this much; but as I have only just arrived, and am but beginning to make known the law, I do not insist on an information being laid this time. Henceforward I always shall; for connivance at an offence is itself an offence."

Chapter V: More Haste than Good Speed

Fergus meanwhile was consulting Ronald as to the best mode in which Rob's labour could be applied towards repairing the damage he had caused. He was too stupid and awkward to be entrusted with any occupation in which he would not be overlooked by some more competent person; and Ronald knew, though he did not say so, that there would be perpetual danger of a quarrel if Rob became Fergus's assistant in fishing. Ronald, therefore, kindly offered to give Rob some inferior employment about the cooperage, providing for his support out of his wages, and paying the rest over to Fergus till the whole debt should be cleared. Rob, to whom all labour was disagreeable alike, sulkily consented, and swore at himself and everybody else when he saw the Flora clear out from the little harbour, and leave him behind to repair by the labour of weeks and months the mischief he had done in two short hours. He had not only the cost of the nets to pay, but the amount which Fergus would have cleared by the benefit he was now prevented from taking.

While he was involuntarily saving during this winter, his neighbours in Garveloch were going on as variously as might be expected from the difference in their knowledge, in their desires, and in their habits. The Company was prosperous in a very high degree, and so, therefore, might their labourers of every rank have been; but in this society, as in all, some were wise and some were foolish; some provided for a time of darkness, and some did not.

None were more provident than Angus and Ella, or provident in a wiser manner. Seeing so clearly as they did the importance of an increase of capital in a society which was adding to its numbers every day, they reflected and consulted much on the modes and rates of increase of capital differently applied, and saw that the interest of the Company, and of every individual employed by it, was one and the same. Since capital grows from savings only, there seemed no hope that that of the Company should keep pace with the demands upon it; but something might be done by increasing the value of the capital,—by making it secure, by lessening the attendant expenses, by using every possible method of making production easy and rapid. If all the corn that was raised in the islands had been used for seed-corn, instead of nine-tenths of it being eaten; if all the fish had been turned into its market-price on the spot, without any expense of curing, packing, and conveying, this capital would still have doubled itself much more slowly than the number of people who were to subsist upon it; and when their subsistence and all attendant expenses were subtracted, the process became much slower. Yet it was a favourable time and a favourable set of circumstances for capital to grow in. The property was secure, being under the protection of law well administered, and under the management of an united body of directors. The expenses were small, the position of the different stations being advantageous, and the required apparatus very simple. Production was at the same time easy; for the herrings came regularly, and the seasons had thus far been favourable. Here, then, capital might grow, if ever or anywhere; and it did grow; but the demands upon it grew still faster; and therefore Angus and Ella guarded the capital of their employers as if it had been their own, while they added to their private store as fast as was consistent with a due enjoyment of the fruits of their labour. Though they had nine children, they were at present in more favourable circumstances for saving than some of their neighbours who had few or none. Dan and his Noreen, for instance, saved nothing; how should they, when their hut scarcely protected them from the rain and snow, or their clothing from the chilling winds,—when there was not even the slightest preparation made for the tender little one that was soon to come into their charge? There can be no saving expected from those whose commonest wants are not supplied. The Murdochs were in nearly as poor a condition; and since they had never managed to avoid sinking, even in their best days, it was scarcely likely that they should now. Fergus toiled and toiled, and just continued to keep his place in the little society, but he could do no more. The consumption of his family just equalled the supply afforded by his labour, so that he could not, with all his efforts, set apart anything to begin saving upon. His nest-egg (whenever he thought he had one) had always disappeared before the day was out. There was nothing for it, but hoping that good seasons and full employment would last till his boys' labour should more than equal their consumption, and should not only release him from the charge of their maintenance, but assist in the support of the little ones, who must be nearly helpless for years to come.

If this society had been constituted like that of Rome, of which we have spoken, there would have been little or no saving, and therefore no provision for an increase in the number of its members. Where society is composed of a few very rich people and a multitude very poor, the least saving of all is made. The rich only *can* save in such a case, and they do not perceive a sufficient motive for doing so. They reckon on being always rich, and do not see why they should not enjoy their wealth to the utmost, year by year. Where society is composed of a few moderately rich and many sufficiently supplied with necessaries, there is a much better chance of an accumulation of capital, since the majority of the people have then a hope of raising their children to the rank of the moderately rich. They are free from the recklessness of the miserably poor, and from the thoughtless extravagance of the possessors of overgrown wealth. To this middling class belonged Angus, the widow Cuthbert, Ronald and the Duffs; and they therefore made the largest savings in proportion to their earnings. Mr. Mackenzie spent all his income, having no children, and feeling himself provided for for life. The naval superintendent, captain Forbes, a spirited young officer, was so far from attempting to save, that he flung his money about during his flying visits to the stations till he had none left, and barely escaped debt. But Duff, who was not placed beyond the danger of bad seasons, widow Cuthbert, and Angus, who had children dependent on them, and Ronald, who regarded the families of Ella and Fergus with strong affection, had motives to save, and did their full share towards making the capital of the society grow.

One day the next spring, Ronald appeared before his sister's door.

"Welcome, brother!" exclaimed Ella. "Is it a leisure day with you? And are you come to spend it with us?"

"It is a leisure day, and the last I shall have for long; and I am come to tell you why, and to consult with Angus about a little business of his. This is the reason that I came myself instead of sending Kenneth."

"I began to think you never meant to come, you have been so considerate in sparing Kenneth. But sit ye down,—aye, outside the door if you like, for it is a true spring day,—and Angus will be up from the boat presently."

Angus was soon seen hastening to meet Ronald, who then told his news. Captain Forbes had arrived at the Islay station in high spirits. A new market for their produce was unexpectedly opened in the

West Indies.[1] It was his belief that all the fish they could possibly prepare during the season would be insufficient to meet the sudden demand; and he came to see how many boats could be mustered, and how many labourers could be withdrawn from other employments to aid in the fishery.

"Now is Fergus's time," said Ella, "for getting his two boys hired at the station. They are young, to be sure; but as so many labourers are wanted, their services will be received, I dare say."

"Now is Rob's time for clearing off his debt to Fergus," observed Angus; "for I suppose, Ronald, wages will rise at the cooperage. More barrels will be wanted than you can easily prepare."

"No doubt," replied Ronald. "Now is your time, Angus, for building the platform you were talking of last year; and I came to offer what help I can. I will spare Kenneth for a week now to work with you; and I give you notice that you must take him now or not at all. And if there should be any difficulty about the little capital wanted for the work, I have a few pounds which are much at your service."

Angus thankfully accepted the offer of his boy's help, but had no occasion to borrow money. He should lose no time, he said, in erecting his platform, if the tidings Ronald brought should prove correct. Much time and labour in lading and unlading his vessel might be economized by the employment of a crane; and he thought he could not invest his savings better than in making such a provision at the commencement of a busier season than had ever been known in Garveloch.

Ella's apprehension was that the demand would be only temporary. On this head Ronald could give her no satisfaction, as he did not know enough of the circumstances to judge: but he thought that all who were called upon to use only their labour, or a small capital which yields a quick return, might rejoice in this sudden prosperity without any fear of consequences; and even Angus's investment of fixed capital would be perfectly safe. If it was doubtful the year before whether the erection of a platform and crane would not be worth while, it could scarcely fail to answer now, when there was to be a large addition to the profits of an ordinary season, even if that addition should be only temporary. Angus pro-

---

1   England maintained colonies in the West Indies, in which plantations were worked by bondslaves and natives who were "owned" by the white masters.

posed going to the spot to take measurements, and make an estimate of the expense.

"If you will wait till noon is past," said Ella, "I can go with you. I must be taught your plan, Angus, that I may answer for you when you are absent."

Another object in this delay was to set her brother at liberty to go where she knew his heart was all this time. While she was finishing her household business, uncle Ronald went down with some of the little ones to launch a tiny boat,—a present from Kenneth,—in one of the pools on the beach. Their mother heard their shouts of glee, and thought within herself that there were no festival days like those when her brother or her boy came from the station.

In a few minutes the children were playing without their uncle's assistance. He had gone to the widow Cuthbert's. Katie frankly held out her hand as he entered, and bade him welcome to Garveloch. She was just spreading the table for dinner, and invited him to sit down with herself and the children: but when he declined, she made no ceremony, but called the little ones from their play; and the meal went forward as if no guest had been there, except that Katie conversed freely with her friend Ronald.

"Hugh is much grown," observed Ronald. "I did not know him at first when he came to see me land."

"I knew you though," cried Hugh, "and I went to see whether you brought me a tub like the one you gave Bessie. I want a tub for my fish when I catch any."

"I will make you a tub bigger than Bessie's, and Kenneth shall bring it."

"I wish you would bring it," cried Hugh. "You promised me a boat the last time you came, a long, long while ago, and you never sent it."

"Yes, indeed I did, Hugh, and I thought Kenneth had given it to you."

Katie explained that it had been delivered safe, but had strangely disappeared before Hugh had seen it; and that as he never asked about it, she had not vexed him with explaining what had happened.

"Why did not you ask me for another?" said Ronald. "I do wish you would be free with me as an old friend."

"Indeed I always am," replied Katie. "I would ask a favour of you as easily as of Angus or Fergus."

After a moment's pause, Ronald told his tidings of the prospect of a busy season, and offered to purchase hemp for the widow and send it by Kenneth, before the price should rise, if she had not already a sufficient stock for her net-making for the year. Katie thankfully accepted his services, and looked so cheerfully round upon her children, when she heard of the approaching prosperity, that Ronald was glad he had taken courage to come and tell her.

When the meal was over, Katie took up her employment and seemed far from wishing that Ronald should go; but she kept little Hugh beside her to show Ronald how he was learning to help his mother in her work.

By the time several subjects of mutual interest had been talked over, Ronald recollected that the hour was long past when he ought to have met Angus on the beach, and he rose to go, offering to look in again in the evening before his departure; to which Katie made no objection.

Dinner was over at Angus's house, but Ella, who guessed where her brother was, would not have him called.—She suspected the truth,—that he came to observe whether there was any chance of his winning Katie at last, and to consult his sister, in case of being unable to discover for himself how Katie felt towards him. He was rather disheartened by the interview. She was so frank and friendly in her manner that he could not believe she felt any of the restraint he laboured under—anything more than the regard which she testified to his sister and brother. Ella could not contradict him. She was far from thinking the case a hopeless one; but she believed that time and patience were still and would long be necessary. She assured her brother that precipitation would probably ruin all; and that his best chance was in quietly waiting till he should have further opportunities of winning upon her. This determined Ronald not to speak at present, as, in his impatience of suspense, he had nearly resolved to do.

When the little party went down to the place where Angus proposed to erect his new building, several loungers gathered round to watch what was going to be done. Ronald was looked upon as so awfully learned a man, especially when using his rule and frowning over his calculations, that strangers,—such strangers as were in Garveloch,—did not venture to speak to him. They made their inquiries of the children in preference.

First came Noreen lagging along the shore in the gray cloak which she was supposed never to put off, as she had never been seen without it, winter or summer. Wrapt in it, and hanging over her arm, head downwards, was her baby, feebly crying, as usual, and as usual disregarded; for nothing short of a shrill scream seemed to be thought by Noreen worthy of attention. Her cap was nearly the same colour as her cloak, and her hair did not tend to ornament her further than by helping to conceal a black eye.

"Annie, darling, and how busy you all seem! And you nursing the babby as if you'd had one in your arms all your days, my darling."

"I dare not hold him as you hold your's," said Annie. "Look! The little thing's face is as black—O look!"

"As black as your eye," cried Bessie.

"Is it my eye, darling? O, it's a trifle that Dan gave me,—the villain,—when the spirits were in him."

"What! Did Dan strike you?" cried Annie, who was old enough to know that husbands and wives should not fall out like children.

"Strike me, darling! Yes, and the babby too. O, you should have heard the babby bawl as loud as me."

"Is not Dan very sorry?" asked Annie, coaxing the unfortunate infant.

"Is it sorry the ruffian would be? Not he; and why should he? 'Twas the spirits that made him a villain for the time; but he is the mildest husband of a noon-time that ever was seen. So, darling, don't you go and dream he isn't a good enough man for me. Heaven's blessing on him!—He never bothers me as your father would, Annie. We're just content, without all the measuring and building, and salting and packing, that you have to do at the father's bidding, my darling. What's all this trouble about now?"

Annie was too anxious to defend her father to answer the question immediately; so Noreen turned round to the little ones who were jumping from the ledges of rock.

"And what's all this trouble about, jewels?"

"The Captain is coming! the captain is coming!" cried they.

"Is it the captain going to have a new house on Garveloch?" cried Noreen. "O Dan, up to the gentleman as soon as he comes, and get the money others got before you last time; and when ye get it, don't be making a beast of yourself or a martyr of the babby, but remember the rent, jewel."

Dan found it much easier to remember the rent than to pay it, and had rather give his wife a black eye in private than be lectured by her in public; and he therefore looked sulky and bade her run after the captain if she chose, for that he would not bother himself for any reason in life.—Ella, who had overheard all, explained that there was no reason, as far as the captain was concerned; but that if Dan would bother himself to go out fishing, the rent would be no longer a trouble.

With all their recklessness and indolence, these people had pride;

and when they heard that everybody was likely to prosper this summer, Noreen began to talk of holding up her head, as she had a right to do, equal to any of them that little thought what her relations were at Rathmullin.

Dan esteemed it mighty provoking that the bread was taken from within his reach by them that were born to nothing but what they got with their dirty hands. If he had had a word with the captain as soon as others, he might have coaxed him into letting him have a boat; but it was always the way,—while he was content at home and just thinking of nothing at all, some vagabond or another stept into his shoes.

Ronald refrained from calling Dan to account for his term of abuse, knowing it to be in such frequent use in Ireland as to have lost much of its offensiveness. He assured Dan that the captain had work for everybody just now, and urged his making application to be hired without delay.

Murdoch stared with astonishment when he found that Angus was actually going to take down his curing-shed and remove it to the place where the stage was to be erected. It seemed to him as well as to Dan vastly too much trouble and expense; but Angus had taken into account the damage the fish sustain by being much exposed and shifted about previous to curing; and he believed that the expedition and security with which the produce would be hauled up, prepared, and shipped again, would soon repay him for what he was about to do.

The business of months seemed to be transacted in Garveloch this afternoon, on the strength of the tidings which Ronald brought. All doubtful matters (except the one which most nearly concerned Ronald) were brought to a decision. Angus decided, as we have seen, on making a large venture of fixed capital. Farmer Duff decided on hiring some more labourers while there was any chance of his getting them. Fergus decided on offering the labour of his two eldest boys at the station, believing that there would be work for all, however young. More than a few parties decided that their courtship should end in immediate marriage, and never doubted the perfect propriety of making use of a season of prosperity for the purpose. Dan decided on putting his hand to the oar at last. All who wished to hire labour decided on looking abroad for labourers, and betimes, if they wished to make good terms. All who had labour to let began to consider how high they might venture to fix its price.

This was no deceitful promise of prosperity,—to those at least who did not expect too much from it. The sanguine and the ignorant, who are ever ready to take an ell[1] where an inch is given, supposed that their island was enriched for ever. They heard of wages rising higher and higher, and never suspected they might fall. They saw that the only thing at present wanted was a greater number of labourers, and imagined that when their tribes of children were grown up, all would be right,—wages as high, food as plentiful as now, and as great an increase of employment as there would be of labour. It was well that all did not keep up their expectations to this pitch,—that some were aware how precarious was the present prosperity. A single bad season, the opening of a few more fishing stations, a change in the diet of the West India slaves,—any one of these, or many other circumstances, might reduce the Garveloch fishery to what it had been; while the numbers of those who depended upon it for subsistence were increasing with a greater and a greater rapidity.

The least sanguine, however, could not resist the feeling of exhilaration excited by what passed before their eyes: nor was there any reason that they should. Prudence and foresight do not interfere with the rational enjoyment of blessings; they rather add to it by imparting a feeling of security. The youngest and giddiest could not relish more than Angus and his wife the freedom from care they now enjoyed, the sight of plenty around them, and the knowledge that none need be idle, none need be poor; and if these, the young and the giddy, bestowed little thought on the probable issue of their present state, and escaped the anxiety with which they ought to have regarded the future, neither did they share the satisfaction of making provision for a season of storms.

The captain alighted in Garveloch, now and then, in his flight round the station. He was always in a prodigious bustle, and he made every body he met as fidgety as himself about the impossibility of getting labourers enough for the work to be done. Wherever he went, it was suggested to him that people might be hired from some other place, from which other place he had just heard that there was also a deficiency of labour.

Some people thought they might be satisfied with having as large a trade as their numbers could manage; but the captain was not satisfied without taking all that offered. Men and their families were brought from a distance, all the boys that could handle an oar or help

1   An ell is a unit of measure equal to 45 inches or 114 cm, as in the saying, "Give an inch and they'll take a mile."

to draw a net received wages; all the girls assisted their mothers to cure; so that, at this time, the largest families were the richest. These circumstances acted as an encouragement, and the captain's sanguine expectation that the demand would continue operated as a direct bounty on population; and, in consequence, numbers increased in Garveloch as rapidly as in any new colony of a fertile country.

The seasons which are favourable to the fishery,—in respect of weather,—are favourable to the harvest also. Farmer Duff reaped abundant crops the next two seasons, which unusual abundance just served to feed his customers. What would have been done in case of an average or an inferior crop having been yielded, few troubled themselves to determine. They had enough, and that was all they cared for.

Kenneth could not often be spared during these two seasons; but he came to attend the christening of a little brother and of two cousins. The only troubles he had to relate were of the difficulty of supplying the orders for barrels, and of the passion the captain was in when fish were spoiled for sale by being packed in old casks. The magistrate had the least to do of anybody. Hard times are the days of crime. There were still occasional quarrels; complaints of oppression on one side and sauciness on the other, and of a few acts of malice still perpetrated by people as stupid and helpless as Rob; but the crimes to which men are stimulated by want were not at present heard of. Were they over for ever?

Chapter VI: A Dreary Prospect

A time of leisure, as grievous to the most reckless and indolent as to the superior members of the society, came round ere long. First appeared hardship in the shape of an average crop; for the people having increased their consumption up to the amount of a remarkably abundant harvest, were of course stinted when the soil yielded only the usual return. No very disastrous consequences followed at first. There was much complaint and a little dismay when it was found that supplies must not be looked for from the neighbouring districts, since there also the season had been only moderately favourable, and there were mouths enough to feed in each place to leave no supplies over for Garveloch. The Garveloch people therefore were obliged to eat some of their fish instead of selling it, and to pay a very high price for their barley and oatmeal. Those who were able to give this price were willing to do it, seeing that the rise of price was a necessary consequence of the comparative scarcity;

that farmer Duff must pay himself for the outlay on his land, whether its produce were ample or scanty; and that its dearness alone could make the supply last till the next harvest came round. Those who were too poor to buy abused the farmer, saying that his crop was not scantier than it had been in many former years when he had sold it much cheaper, and that he was making use of a dispensation of Providence to fill his own pocket. They were slow to perceive that it was themselves and not the farmer who had made the change; that they had caused the increase of demand and the consequent rise of price.

It would have been well if nothing worse than the occurrence of an average season had happened. The number of people brought by a sudden demand for labour might have lessened. Some might have departed elsewhere, and others have devised plans for a new introduction or better economy of food; and after a short period of hardship, the demand for food might have gradually accommodated itself to the supply; for their society was not like the population of an overgrown district, where there may be mistakes in ascribing effects to causes, and where the blame of hardship may be laid in the wrong place. The people of Garveloch might survey their little district at a glance, and calculate the supply of provision grown, and count the numbers to be fed by it, and by this means discern, in ordinary circumstances, how they might best manage to proportion their resources of labour and food. But if any had endeavoured to do this, their expectations would have been baffled by the event, unless they had taken into the account the probability of bad seasons—a probability which the truly wise will never overlook.

A few seasons after the period of prosperity of which we have spoken, the dawn of a June morning broke as gloomily as if it had been November. Scudding clouds, from which came gushes of hail, swept over the sky and brushed the tallest points of rock as they passed. The wind came in gusts as chill as the wintry blasts, and before it the vexed ocean swelled and heaved, while its tumbling mass of waters seemed to forbid man to approach, much more to trust the frail workmanship of his hands to its overwhelming power. The night-light still glimmered from some of the dwellings in Garveloch, the islands of the Sound were not yet visible from the heights, and the peaks of Lorn were but beginning to show themselves against the eastern sky, when Angus came out stealthily from his dwelling, softly closed the door, drew his plaid about him, and paced down to the beach. He was proceeding to get out his boat, when his son Kenneth approached.

"Father," said he, "you are not going to trust yourself at sea to-day?"

"Help must be had, Kenneth. I must cross at the risk of my own life, or more will be lost. I have here the last of my savings; and since money is worth no more than pebbles in Garveloch, I must carry it where it may buy us food."

"And my mother—"

"Your mother is in the inner room, where she has been up with Jamie all night. I heard him very loud just now. His fever runs high, so that she will not miss me perhaps for hours. She neither saw nor heard me come out.—Now, Kenneth, say nothing about going instead of me. You know that my experience of the sea is greater than yours, and the best skill is little enough for such a voyage as mine is like to be."

"But my mother must soon know," urged Kenneth.

"Surely. Tell her that I hope to be back tomorrow night, with that which may ease her nursing. Farewell, my boy."

Kenneth was a brave, high-spirited youth. His heart was full when he saw his father put off among the stormy breakers, and he therefore said nothing. He helped to guide the boat to the last moment, wading as deep and struggling with the waves as long as he possibly could, till his father made a commanding sign that he should return. There was no use in speaking amidst the thunder of the waters. Kenneth wrung out his plaid, and climbing the rock, sat down, unheeding the wind, to watch his father's boat, scarcely visible in the grey light, as it won its weary way among the billows. Bitter thoughts rose fast within him;—his father in peril at sea; his mother worn with care and watching; his beloved little Jamie, the youngest of the large family, and their darling, sinking under the fever; all the others changing from what they had been, some in health, some in spirits, some in temper, and he unable to do anything to help them. Dismissed with others from the station because his labour was not now worth the food he consumed, he had come home to be, as he thought, a burden, but as his parents declared, a comfort, to his family amidst their cares, and daily looked round, and ever in vain, for some means of assisting them. As he now thought of the fruitlessness of all his efforts, tears rose and blinded him so that he could no longer discern any object at sea. As fast as he dashed them away they rose again, till he no longer resisted them, but let them flow as they had never flowed since childhood.

As he sat with his face hid in his plaid, he was roused by the pressure of his mother's hand upon his shoulder. She had spoken from a distance, but the roaring of wind and waters and the screaming of sea-fowl were more powerful than her voice, and her appearance took Kenneth by surprise—a surprise at which she smiled.

"Mother!" he cried, as he started up, and a burning blush overspread his face; "if I were a good son, it would be my part to smile when I found you with sinking spirits."

Ella smiled again as she answered—

"And when my spirits sink, I will look to you for cheer. Meantime, never fancy that tears are unworthy a brave man, or always a sorrowful sight to a mother. It is God's will, Kenneth, that there is cause for tears; and since there is cause, it is no pain to me to see them fall. If God calls you and me hither to look out upon a second year's storms, he knows that it is as natural for the heart as for the cloud to drop its rain; and never think, my boy, that I shall be a harder judge than he."

"But what brought ye out, mother, so early, into the cold?"

"I came to seek the cooling wind. Jamie fell asleep, and Annie came to take her turn beside him; and finding Angus gone, and my head hot and weary, I thought I should find more rest on the rock than in my bed. I see the boat, Kenneth. I know your father's purpose, and I guess you were praying just now for his safe return."

"And, O mother! I had some distrustful thoughts in the midst of my prayer. If he should not return, and even while he is gone, I can do nothing. Here I am, eating my daily portion, which I never helped to earn; being a burden when I thought—proud as I was— that I should be your main joy and help. O mother! this humbles one sadly. I never thought to be so humbled."

"Who that is humbled ever sees the stroke before it comes, Kenneth? Look round, and mark. Where many a smoke rose, only a short year since, from those cottages below, the fires are quenched, and with them is quenched the pride of those who revelled in plenty. Now, many are gone, and have left but four bare walls for us to remember them by. Some are gone to lie cold under yonder gray stones, and some few have found their way back over the sea. Those that remain have lost their pride: it was blown away with the cold ashes of their last fire; and it will not come back while they sit hungry and shivering. Which of these thought any more than you that they should be so humbled? When I gloried in my Jamie, as the brightest and handsomest of my children, I did not expect that he would be the first I should lay in the grave."

"Must he die, mother?"

"I take such to be God's will, Kenneth; but I once had a lesson, as you know, against reading his pleasure too readily. They that I thought lost came to dry land, and another lay under the water when I thought him safe on the hard rock. Since that day, I have ever waited for the issue; and so I will now. We will hope that Jamie may live, and we will be ready to part with any who were but just now in life and strength."

"It is but little we know, indeed," replied Kenneth. "It seems but yesterday that yon sea was almost as busy as a thronged city, with a hundred vessels following the shoals, and then crowding homewards with a full cargo; and now this year and last, not a boat has gone out, not a gleam of sun, not a blink of moonlight has been upon the sea; and as to the land, it is more changed still. Where the barley-fields were as green as a rich pasture three years ago, there are only a few straggling blades, just enough to tempt a man with thoughts of what a harvest is. This is a change we little feared to see."

"And yet," said Ella, "many did foresee, and all might have foreseen. When was there ever a time that the seasons did not change? Here we have been too slow to learn God's will. We knew that the same storms that took away our occupation must cut off our harvest; we knew that such stormy seasons come from time to time; and yet we acted as if we were promised plenty for ever. Our children look up to us for food, because we have given them no warning that it should cease; and they are right. But if we look up to God in the same manner we are wrong; for the warning was given long ago."

"I have heard uncle Ronald speak of it," replied Kenneth. "He has often feared that scarcity would come; but he told me that father, and widow Cuthbert, and the Duffs, would never be taken by surprise."

"If it had not been for our savings," replied Ella, "we should have had worse things to undergo than may be in store for us. Instead of trembling for Jamie, I might have been mourning the half of my children. Instead of grieving to see you wasting, Kenneth—how thin ye are grown!—I might have been—" She stopped.

"If I am thin, mother," Kenneth replied, "it is with care; and my care is that I can do nothing for bread for myself and you."

"I will take you at your word," replied his mother, with a smile. "We will try whether you will grow stouter for your conscience being at rest. But, mind, it shall be but a moderate trial, and I will share it with you."

Kenneth looked eagerly to his mother for an explanation of what was in her mind. Ella told him that there was positively no more grain to be bought before harvest. Farmer Duff had very wisely kept back enough for seed-corn, in case of the crop failing utterly, and had very reasonably laid up a sufficient store for his own household; and none was now left over. Ella's remaining store was not sufficient to afford even a stinted allowance to the whole family for the three months still to come; and she now, therefore, proposed that neither she nor her son should touch barley or oatmeal, but give up their share to the younger and tenderer members of the family.

Kenneth was grateful to his mother for her confidence. She had hitherto concealed the fact of the supply being nearly exhausted, in the hope that Kenneth, like the rest, would eat and think little of the future; but she now saw that he would be made happier by being allowed to share her sacrifices, and she therefore called upon him to do so.

Kenneth was not yet satisfied. It was not enough to be permitted to save food; he must find out how to obtain it.

"Not enough!" exclaimed his mother, mournfully. "My boy, ye little know what it is, and ye never can till the trial is made. Ye little know what it is to lie down at night cold and aching, and to toss about unable to sleep, when sleep seems the one thing that would give ye ease, since ye cannot have food. Ye little think what sleep is when it comes,—how horrible fancies are ever rising up to steal away the sweetness of rest—how all that ye see and all that ye touch turns to food, and turns back again before ye can get it to your mouth; or, worse, still, to fancy ye are driven by some evil power to strangle and devour whatever is most precious to you. Ye little think what it is to wake with a parched mouth and hands clenched, so that they are like an infant's all the day after, and the limbs trembling and the sight dim, as if fifty years had come over ye in a night. Ye little know, Kenneth, what it will be to loathe the food you and I shall have, and to see the thoughtless little ones crumbling the bannocks and eating them as if they were to be had as easily as the hailstones that have beat down the crops. Wait a while, my boy, before you say all this is not enough."

"You know too well, mother, what it is. Can it be that you have been fasting alone already?"

"I learned all this," said Ella, evading the question, "when I was nearly as young as you. There was a scarcity then, and we had a sore struggle. My father was never well after that season. There was no need, thank God, to stint the lads as we stinted ourselves; and, as for me, the only harm," she continued, smiling, "was, that your father found me less comely when he came back than I had been when he went away. There is also this good,—that there is one among us who has gone through evil times, and knows how to abide them."

"Teach me, mother. How shall I get such food as we may live on?"

"There will be no positive want of food yet, my boy, though it will be such as will not nourish us like that we have been used to. We must try shell-fish, without bannocks or potatoes; merely shell-fish, day after day; and the strongest soon grow weak on such diet."

"I would rather give up my share, sometimes," said Kenneth, "than gather them at the cost of what I see. I have been glad you were at home when the tide went down, and I would not let the little ones come and help, lest they should learn to fight like the hungry people on the shore. Dan, that ever kept his eyes half-shut at noon, now watches the first falling of the water, and bullies every one, if it be Noreen herself, that sees a shell before he snatches it."

"Their potatoes have not come up," observed Ella, "and they begin to be pinched the very first, because they had nothing to give for meal."

"And then," continued Kenneth, "the Murdochs have got the ill-will of all the neighbours, by their stripping every child they meet of whatever he may be carrying home. The very babies are learning to curse Meg Murdoch."

"And so you took their part," said Ella, smiling, "and let them strip you in turn. You are right not to let your little brothers go down with you to learn theft and covetousness; but you must not go on giving away your own share, now that you will have no bread at home."

"Then there are the fowl," said Kenneth. "They are not food for the delicate, to be sure, at this season; but we must try whether they will not nourish us till better days come. The worst of it is that very few are left, and those are the oldest and toughest."

"The neighbours that are poorer than we have been everywhere before us," said Ella. "But they are welcome. Since they trusted to chance, the first chances are their due. My eyes are dim with watching yon boat, and I can see nothing: is it still there, or has the mist come over it?"

Ella had scarcely withdrawn her gaze for a moment from her husband's struggle with the winds and waves. Kenneth, who had not thus strained his sight, could just discern the speck rising and falling on the dreary waste of waters.

"I see her still winning her way, mother; but you will scarce make her out again."

"I will not try now, but go home."

"And to bed," said Kenneth. "You are weary and half-frozen,

standing on this point as if ye came to meet the storm. Promise me you will rest, mother!"

"Perhaps I will if Jamie is still asleep. And do you hasten down, Kenneth, and gather whatever the tide may have thrown up. Now, don't part with all you get for your own share. I have called upon you for self-denial; and part of that self-denial must be not to give all the help you have been accustomed to yield."

"That is the worst part of it," said Kenneth; "but I remember, mother, that my first duty lies at home. O, if there were no hardship, how much less greedy and quarrelsome should we be! It is not in men's nature to quarrel for shell-fish every time the tide goes down."

"Remember," said Ella, "that better things also arise out of hardship. Do none learn patience? Do none practise self-denial?"

"But we have not known extreme hardship, mother."

"True. May the day never come when I shall see my children looking with jealousy upon one another! The jealousy of the starving is a fearful sight."

Kenneth's first trial of his new resolution awaited him when he went down to the shore to gather shell-fish. His appearance was usually a signal for the children, who were driven away by some one of the tyrants of the neighbourhood, to come down and put themselves under his protection. They had learned to reckon on his share being divided among them; for, while there was food at home, he could not find in his heart to refuse the little half-starved creatures their piteous requests. One found that some of her pickings were mere empty shells; another pleaded that she had no breakfast on the mornings when it was her turn to look for fish; and another declared that his father would beat him if he did not carry home his bonnetful. One or all of these pleas usually emptied Kenneth's store. One set of claimants had never yet been refused,—his cousins. Fergus's two eldest boys, who had earned good wages, and hoped to earn them again when the fishery should be resumed, were thrown back on their own resources in the interval. It was melancholy to see them wandering about the island in search of anything that might be rendered eatable, and at times reduced to beg of their cousin Kenneth as many shell-fish as he could spare. Kenneth felt that nothing but absolute famine could drive him to deny them; and he was therefore glad to perceive that they were not on the shore this morning. He gave notice to the little ones, who now gathered about him, that he could henceforth only help them by defending their right to whatever they could pick up. He must share equally with them from this day, and he hoped they would not ask that which he could no longer give. And now began the scenes which he was henceforth daily to witness among the children, and in time, upon a larger scale, among the parents. All the petty arts, all the violence, all the recklessness, to which the needy are tempted, began to show themselves first among those whose habits of self-control were weakest; and afforded a specimen of what might be looked for when the parents should be driven by want beyond the restraint of principles and habits which had been powerful in the absence of overwhelming temptation.

One of the little boys uplifted a vehement cry. "Willie has snatched my bonnet! O, my bonnet, my bonnet! It was fuller to-day than it has ever been yet."

"That is the very reason," cried Willie, a stout lad, who felt that he could carry everything among the little ones by strength of arm. "You never had enough before to make it worth while taking them. Now I have got them, I will keep them."

Kenneth, who was the representative of justice, struggled with Willie, and got back the property; but the lad vowed vengeance for his drubbing, especially against the complainant, who henceforth had no peace. All parties being left discontented, it was plainly a great evil that there had been temptation to recur to what Willie called the right of the strongest.

One of the little girls was found hidden behind a rock, eating all that had been collected for the family at home. Many cried "Shame!" and vowed she should never again be trusted within reach of more than her own share; to which she answered, that she should eat when she was hungry, and that those who had enough might supply her brothers and sister. This child would have had a rate levied upon all the more provident, for the relief of her fellow-paupers.

Two lads having quarrelled about the share due to one, the most hungry threw the whole back into the sea, by way of revenge as he declared. One would have thought he had heard Mr. Mackenzie speak of the possible, though extreme, case of men burning stacks because there was not enough corn.

Even this reckless boy was less provoking than one party, pre-eminent in poverty and dirt, who could not be persuaded to give over their sport, happen what might. They called together whatever animals could eat shell-fish, and put this food down the mouths of dogs and ponys,—both of which eat fish in the islands.

"How can you," said Kenneth, "bring more eaters down to the shore when we have too many already?"

"We must have our play," answered they. "Ours is the age for play, as we have heard our father say; and we are so cold and hungry almost all day, that it is very hard if we may not amuse ourselves when we can."

There was no use in pointing out to them that they were doing all they could to increase their own hunger; they only answered that they would have their sport as long as they could get it, and immediately whistled for more dogs.

To judge by their acts, these children did not perceive that, though they could not determine the quantity of fish which should be within reach, it was their fault that the number of eaters was needlessly increased. The half-starved multitudes of an over-peopled kingdom might take a lesson from their folly.

"Can this be the place," thought Kenneth, "can these be the children, where and among whom there was so much cheerfulness but a few seasons ago? How happy we all used to be picking up our fish! And now, some still laugh louder than ever; but the mirth of the destitute is more painful to witness than the grave looks of those who have something left. O, for peace and plenty once more!"

Chapter VII: The Discipline of the Teachable

As Ella slowly took her way homewards, she caught a glimpse of two men coming up the winding path she was descending. Forgetting the impossibility that Angus should be already returned, and seeing that one was Fergus, she supposed that her husband and brother were coming to meet her. On her turning a point, they were in full view. It was Ronald instead of Angus. Terror seized the anxious wife, who was weakened by watching and care.

"O Angus, Angus!" she cried, in tones which made the rocks ring again. "O, he is lost, and ye are come to tell me!"

Before her brothers could reach her, she had sunk down, unable to keep her hold of the rock, while the earth seemed to swim round and quake beneath her. She was lost in a fainting-fit before a word of comfort could reach her ear.

"This must be fasting as well as care," said Ronald, as he chafed her hands, while Fergus sprinkled water over her face. "Never before was Ella seen to sink, much less upon a false alarm. It must be sore suffering that could bring her to this."

Fergus's tears were falling fast while he replied,—

"'Tis the parent's heart that suffers, Ronald. 'Tis for her little Jamie that she has watched and struggled till she faints, spirit and body together."

"She is coming round," said Ronald. "There is colour in her lips.

Now see if her spirit does not rally as soon as her limbs, or sooner. She will be more surprised at herself than we are."

"Hush! she opened her eyes just now. Raise her a little more."

"Why, Ella," said Ronald, smiling, as he leaned over her, "ye never gave me such a greeting before. Why are ye so sorry to see me to-day?"

"Is nothing the matter?" asked Ella steadily. "I dreamed there was;—something about Angus."

"It was only a dream, as far as I know. I have but just landed, and I came to you for news of Angus and all of you."

By this time Ella had started up, and refusing further assistance, supported herself by leaning against the rock.

"I thought Fergus looked sad, I thought he looked wretched," she continued, gazing wistfully into her younger brother's face.

"May be ye're right, Ella; but it was not for you. A man has enough to make him look grave in times like these. But I did not mean to frighten you."

"Times like these make us all selfish," said Ella, "and that is the worst of them. There was a time, Fergus, when I should have been quicker-sighted to your sorrow than my own.—But come with me to shelter before yon cloud bursts. I have been too long from my sick child already. Come with me both of ye, and take the poor welcome I can give. O, it is a comfort, Ronald, to see ye here!"

Her step was little less firm, as her brothers observed, than their own. At her own door she charged them to make no one uneasy by speaking of her fainting-fit. It was a strange fancy, she said, which would not come over her again.

"Mother, how white you look!" exclaimed Annie, as they entered.

"I am cold, my lass. The wind is piercing on the heights; so put some more peat to the fire, and see how you can make your uncles comfortable while I go to Jamie."

Jamie was still in his uneasy sleep. He lay on his back, his mouth open and parched, as if not a drop of liquid had ever touched his tongue, his breathing irregular, his bony fingers sometimes twitching, sometimes drooped with an appearance of utter helplessness. While his mother passed her hand over his temples, and watched his pulse and his countenance, she did not perceive that any one had followed her into the chamber. Presently she heard stifled sobs, and saw that Fergus was kneeling at the foot of the child's crib, hiding his face in his plaid.

"God help you! God comfort you!" she heard him say.

"You think he will die, Fergus; and you tremble for your own two sick children. But hope—at least till you see them as ill as Jamie. I have hoped till now."

Fergus's grief became more violent. His two infants had died in the night. The fever had made quicker work where its victims were already weakened by want. Fergus came to bid his brothers to the funeral.

Ella led him out of the chamber, and placed herself by him, but so that she could see all that passed by her child's bedside. She was more than ever thankful that Ronald had come, when he succeeded in gaining Fergus's attention to what he had to say on the present state of affairs.

He could give little comfort about the prospect of an early supply of grain from the neighbouring islands, as there was a nearly equal degree of distress throughout. The season that was unfavourable to one, was so to all; and the same causes which stopped the fishery laid waste the land. But though immediate relief was not to be looked for, it was hoped that help was on the way. Memorials to government had been sent from the different stations, and Captain Forbes was now making a circuit of the islands in order to estimate the degrees of distress, and to judge how best to apply the funds the Company proposed to set apart for the relief of the inhabitants. He would soon be in Garveloch, and presently after it was possible a vessel might arrive with pease [green peas], potatoes, or grain. Ronald had no sooner heard of this prospect of relief than he made his way over the stormy sea to cheer his sister and brother with the news. There was doubtless another, Ella observed, whom he would wish to tell, though she was thankful to say that widow Cuthbert suffered less from the pressure of the times than any family in Garveloch, unless it was the Duffs.

Ronald took no notice of this at present; he reserved what he had to say about Katie till Fergus should be gone; and proceeded to explain that he had endeavoured in vain to make a purchase of meal that he might bring with him. There was none to be had for love or money. But as those who could pay best were served first, he had received a promise that he should purchase a portion of the first cargo that passed the station. He desired that it might be equally divided between the families of his sister, his brother, and the widow Cuthbert, and that some one should be in the watch to secure the package addressed to Fergus, as soon as the sloop should approach. Before he even thanked his brother, Fergus anxiously inquired when the supply would come? There was no knowing. It might be a fortnight; it might be two months. He did feel and express himself grateful, however, and said something, to which Ronald would not listen, about repaying, in happier days, that part of the debt which could be repaid, and then rose to go and tell his wife that food was or would be on the way. Ronald called him back as he was going out at the door, to entreat that he would never revive the subject of payment.

"I have only myself to work and care for," he said, "and whatever is left over is the natural portion of my kindred. You would inherit it at my death, you know, Fergus; and it is only putting it into your hands when you really want it, instead of waiting till it might be less acceptable to you and yours."

Upon this ensued, as soon as Ronald and his sister were quite alone, a conversation relating to the widow Cuthbert. It was long and earnest, and interrupted only by the attentions necessary to the little patient. The child, on waking, knew his uncle Ronald, and submitted to be soothed and quieted by him while Ella sat spinning beside the crib.

They were thus engaged in the afternoon when Katie entered. She brought a nourishing mess for little Jamie, as she had done more than once before since his illness began. She was surprised to see Ronald, for visitors were rare in such a season of storms. She declared herself vexed at having entered without warning, when she saw him preparing for immediate departure; but he said he must be at the station before night, and had remained too long already; and as his sister did not press his stay, Katie said no more about it, but took his offered hand, and cheerfully confirmed what Ella had told him of the health and comfort of her family. There was no need to ask after her own, for she looked, perhaps from the force of contrast with every body else, more fresh in health and easy in spirits than in many former days when less care prevailed.

"Go, my dears," said Ella to the children in the outer room, "and help your uncle with his boat, and then ye can watch him away round the point; and mind ye mark whether any other vessel is in sight. And yet Angus said he should not be back this day."

"And now," said Katie, when she had done watching how her friend coaxed little Jamie into swallowing the food she brought, "you must let me have my own way entirely, Ella; for you know me for a willful woman."

"Let me hear your will before I promise, Katie."

"My will is to change house and family with you to-night. You must put my children to bed for me, and eat my supper, which you will find in the cupboard, and then lie down in my bed, and sleep till the sun is high. You can trust me to nurse Jamie, I know, from what you said when my Hugh struggled through the measles; and you may quite depend on it, Kenneth says, that your husband will not return to-night."

Ella had no foolish scruples about accepting this neighbourly offer. She had watched many nights, and was so nearly exhausted, that this was a very seasonable help, she thought, to the better performance of her duties the next day. She had been ever ready to give similar assistance to her neighbours in like cases; and knowing the pleasure of doing friendly acts, she would not refuse it to Kate. She therefore agreed at once, adding,—

"I am sure you would not offer this if you had any fear of your children taking the fever from me or you."

"Certainly not, Ella. You know nobody was more careful than I when the small-pox was in the island; and I offended several neighbours by not letting my children so much as speak with theirs; but this kind of fever is not given and taken, as I have good reason to be sure."

In a little while, seeing that Ella was moving about as if to prepare for her comfort during the evening and night, she called her to come and sit down, and not trouble herself with any more cares this day.

"That which will do for you," she said, "will do for me; and if I want anything, there will be Annie to tell me where to find it."

"I'm willing enough to sit down with ye," said Ella, when she had fed the fire, and resumed her spinning, "because—"

"Because you cannot stand; is not that it, Ella? You still look as white as if you had seen a ghost. So you took Ronald for a ghost this morning?"

"Fergus should not have told you that silly story. No; I am willing to be alone with you, because I have much to say about Ronald. You need never more look as you do now, Katie. I am going to lay a different plea before you this day; and if ye will grant it, it will be my last."

Katie bent over her work, and made no reply; so Ella proceeded.

"You know as well as I how long Ronald has loved you, and how sore a struggle your marriage was to him, and that there have been times since when he has hoped; but you have never known, as I have, how tossed in mind he has been for more than three years past. He has come and gone, and come again, Katie, watching your feelings, and waiting for what he thought your pleasure, till he often lost all power of judging what he should do, and how he should speak to you."

"I am sure," said Katie, "it was as far from my wish as from my knowledge that his mind should be so tossed. I never willingly left any one in uncertainty, and I have far too much respect for Ronald, far too much—"

"Neither he nor I ever had such a thought, Katie, as that ye would trifle with him or any man. If he had, ye would soon have seen an end of his love. The uncertainty was no fault of yours, and it was only from particular causes that it lasted so long. He has said many a time that if you had been a young girl, he would have spoken out and known your mind at once; but your husband was his friend, and there was no measuring what your feelings might be now, and he feared above all things wounding them; and so he lingered and lingered and never spoke, till circumstances have decided the matter he could not decide for himself. He wishes you to know, Katie, that you may lay aside all fear of him. He gives you his word of honour he will never sue you; and if, as he suspects, he has occasioned you uneasiness, he entreats your pardon, and hopes you will dismiss it all from your mind."

"Is this the plea you spoke of?" asked Katie.

"No; the plea I spoke of may be, perhaps, more easily granted. Let me entreat for him that you will regard him freely as an old friend, as a brother. He will think no more of marriage; and I know nothing would make him so happy as being able to watch over and help us all equally. Your children love, him, Katie; and if you will only do as I do, give him a welcome when he comes and a blessing when he departs, and ask him for aid, and take what he offers, and let him keep watch upon your children for their good, there may be an end of all difficulty, and my brother may be happier than he has been for many a year. It will ever be painful to be like strangers or common acquaintance, and you have his word of honour,—and whose word is so sure?—that he will not seek to be more than friend; the only way for his peace and your ease is to be really friends,—as if ye were both the children of the same parents. Let Ronald be your friend as he is mine."

"I am not aware," said Katie, "of either act or word which need make me scruple to give and take friendship in the way you wish. But, Ella, you must answer me one question plainly; is it anything in myself which made Ronald change his views? I should not have asked this if you had not said that he gave up marriage altogether; but since I know that his thoughts are not turning upon any one else, I should like to be told whether he has less esteem for me than before I married?"

"If he had, would he seek your friendship as he does? If he esteemed or thought he ever should esteem you less, he would just keep away from Garveloch, and tell nobody why, unless perhaps myself. No; he feels as he ever did; and lest you should doubt me, I will tell you all I know of his conscience and his judgment on this matter. It is the state of society in the islands, Katie, that makes him and other thoughtful men give up the intention of marrying."

"And some that are not thoughtful too, Ella. I could tell you of more than one that would fain have had me when there was prospect that my boys would be a little fortune to me,—I mean when labour was scarce,—that have now slunk away, and will never hold out a hand to me again, I dare say, till my family promise to be a profit instead of a burden."

"You do not take Ronald to be one of these!" cried Ella indignantly. "You cannot think that he is one to come forward and go back as your fortune waxes and wanes, whether that fortune be your children or your savings! It is not for himself only, but for you and your children, and for us and for society, that he thinks and acts as he does."

Katie did not doubt it.—Ronald was far from selfish.

"If all was bright with us again in a single month," said Ella, "he would keep in the same mind; for he sees that prosperity can never last long among us, while we make no provision against the changes that must ever befall, while seasons are sometimes stormy and our commerce liable to variations. We have made an abundant season and a brisk demand into curses, by acting as if they were always to last; and now we want many such as he to soften our miseries, which he could not do if he were burdened like us."

"But it is hard," observed Katie, "that he must deny himself because his neighbours are imprudent."

"Yet his lot is best, Katie. It is sweet to him to help us in our need; and he is spared the sorrow of seeing his little ones pine for that which he cannot give. Yet he cannot but feel that he bears more than his share in giving up marriage altogether. If there were no O'Rorys to marry at eighteen, and if most others had the prudence to wait some years longer than they do, all who wish might marry and deserve no blame."

"But who thinks of praise or blame about the act of marrying?" said Katie. "I own that they ought. When one looks round and sees how sin and sorrow grow where hunger prevails, one cannot think any man guiltless who overlooks the chance of his increasing the poverty of society. But how few consider this! Those who think themselves conscientious, go no farther than to consider whether they are marrying the right person. They spend no thought on the time and the manner, or on their duty to society."

"It is so even here," said Ella, "where we can trace the causes of distress: and in great cities, where it is easy to lay the blame in the wrong place, and where the people become the more reckless the poorer they grow, the evil is much greater. There children are born whose youthful parents have neither roofs to shelter, nor clothes to cover them; and the more widely poverty spreads through the multitude of labourers, the faster is that multitude doubled. You have seen enough of cities, Katie, to know that this is true."

"Yes; and all this is done in the name of Providence. I always expected next to hear Providence blamed for not giving food enough for all this multitude."

"Such blame would have been as reasonable as the excuse," said Ella. "But how slow we are to learn the will of Providence in this case, when it is the very same that we understand in other cases! Providence gave us strength of limbs and of passions: yet these we restrain for the sake of living in society. If a man used his hands to pull down his neighbour's house, or his passion of anger to disturb the society in which he lives, we should think it no excuse that Providence had given him his natural powers, or made him enjoy their exercise. How is it more excusable for a man to bring children into the world, when there are so many to be fed that every one that is born must help to starve one already living?"

"Since Providence has not made food increase as men increase," said Katie, "it is plain that Providence wills restraint here as in the case of other passions."

"And awful are the tokens of its pleasure, Katie. The tears of mothers over their dead children, that shrunk under poverty like blossoms withering before the frosts, the fading of the weak, the wasting of the strong, thefts in the streets, sickness in the houses, funerals by the wayside—these are the tokens that unlimited increase is not God's will."

"These tell us where we are wrong, Ella. How shall we learn how we may be right?"

"By doing as you have done through life, Katie; by using our judgment, and such power as we have. We have not the power of increasing food as fast as our numbers may increase; but we have the power of limiting our numbers to agree with the supply of food. This is the gentle check which is put into our own hands; and if we will not use it, we must not repine if harsher checks follow. If the passionate man will not restrain his anger, he must expect punishment at the hands of him whom he has injured; and if he imprudently indulges his love, he must not complain when poverty, disease, and death lay waste his family."

"Do not you think, Ella, that there are more parties to a marriage than is commonly supposed?"

"There is a party," replied Ella, smiling, "that if it could be present, would often forbid the banns; and it is this party that Ronald has now consulted."

"You mean society."

"Yes. In savage life, marriage may be a contract between a man and woman only, for their mutual pleasure; but if they lay claim to the protection and advantages of society, they are responsible to society. They have no right to provide for a diminution of its resources; and therefore, when they marry, they form a tacit contract with society to bring no members into it who shall not be provided for, by their own labour or that of their parents. No man is a good citizen who runs the risk of throwing the maintenance of his children on others."

"Ah, Ella! did you consider this before your ten children were born?"[1]

"Indeed, Katie, there seemed no doubt to my husband and me that our children would be well provided for. There were then few labourers in Garveloch, and a prospect of abundant provision; and even now we are not in poverty. We have money, clothes, and furniture; and that we have not food enough is owing to those who, having saved nothing, are now far more distressed than we are. Let us hope that all will take warning. My husband and I shall be careful to teach those of our children who are spared to us how much easier it is to prevent want than to endure it."

"You and I will do what we can, Ella, to make our children prudent in marriage; and if all our neighbours would do the same, we might look forward cheerfully. But so few take warning! And it is so discouraging to the prudent to find themselves left almost alone!"

"Nay, Katie; it is not as if all must work together to do any good. Every prudent man, like Ronald, not only prevents a large increase of mischief, but, by increasing capital, does a positive good. Every such act of restraint tells; every such wise resolution stops one drain on the resources of society. Surely this knowledge affords grounds for

---

1   The text states earlier, several times, that Ella has nine children, not ten.

a conscientious man to act upon, without doubt and discouragement."

"How differently is honour imputed in different times!" said Katie, smiling. "The times have been when they who had brought the most children into the world were thought the greatest benefactors of society; and now we are honouring those most who have none. Yet both may have been right in their time."

"A change of place serves the same purpose as change of time," replied Ella. "If Ronald were in a new colony, where labour was more in request than anything else, he would be honoured for having ten children, and doubly honoured for having twenty. And reasonably too; for, in such a case, children would be a gift, and not a burden to society."

"It is a pity, Ella, that all should not go there who are too poor to marry properly, and have no relish for the honour of a single life. Dan and his wife would be a treasure to a new colony."

"If they and their children would work, Katie; not otherwise. But the poor little things would have a better chance of life there. If Noreen stays here, she may be too like many a Highland mother;— she may tell of her twenty children, and leave but one or two behind her."

"My heart aches for those poor infants," said Katie. "One would almost as soon hear that they were put out of the way at their birth, as see them dwindle away and drop into their little graves one after another, before they are four years old. I have often heard that neither the very rich nor the very poor leave such large families behind them as the middling classes; and if the reason is known, it seems to me very like murder not to prevent it."

"The reasons are well known, Katie. Those who live in luxury and dissipation have fewer children born to them than any class; but those that are born are guarded from the wants and diseases which cut off the families of the very poor. The middling classes are more prudent than the lowest, and have therefore fewer children than they, though more than the luxurious; and they rear a much larger proportion than either."

"One might look far, Ella, among the lords and ladies in London, or among the poor Paisley weavers,[1] before one would find such a healthy, hearty tribe—"

---

1   Paisley is a city in Scotland, west of Glasgow, known for a weaving pattern featuring a curved design.

"As yours," Katie would have said; but seeing Ella look upon her little Jamie with a deep sigh, she stopped short, but presently went on—

"It seems to me that a lady of fashion, who gives up her natural rest for feasting and playing cards all night long in a hot room, and lets herself be driven about in a close carriage instead of taking the air on her own limbs, can have no more wish to rear a large healthy family than Noreen, who lets her babe dangle as if she meant to break its back, and gives the poor thing nothing but potatoes, when it ought to be nourished with the best of milk and wholesome bread. Both are little better than the mothers in China. O Ella! did your husband ever tell you of the children in China?"

"Yes, but I scarcely believed even his word for it. Who told you?"

"I have read it in more books than one; and I know that the same thing is done in India; so I am afraid it is all too true. In India it is a very common thing for female children to be destroyed as soon as born."[1]

"The temptation is strong, Katie, where the people are so poor that many hundred thousand at a time die of famine. But child murder is yet more common in China, where no punishment follows, and nothing can exceed the distress for food. In great cities, newborn babes are nightly laid in the streets to perish, and many more are thrown into the river, and carried away before their parents' eyes."

"It is even said, Ella that there are persons whose regular business it is to drown infants like puppies."

"O horrible! And how far must people be corrupted before they would bear children to meet such a fate!"

"There is nothing so corrupting as poverty, Ella; and there is no poverty like that of the Chinese."

"And yet China is called the richest country in the world."

"And so it may be. It may produce more food in proportion to its bounds—it may contain more wealth of every sort than any country in the world, and may at the same time contain more paupers. We call

---

1   Katie refers to the practice of female infanticide, traditionally committed in cultures wherein females were less valued than males. In particular, boy children were valued as better providers for their aging parents than girls. Although less a problem in England than in eastern societies, the proliferation of abandoned children in Britain led to the establishment of "baby-farms," orphanages, and foundling hospitals as alternatives to abandonment or infanticide.

newly-settled countries poor countries because they contain comparatively little capital; but the happiness of the people does not depend on the total amount of wealth, but on its proportion to those who are to enjoy it. What country was ever poorer than Garveloch twenty years ago? Yet nobody was in want. What country is so rich as China at this day? Yet there multitudes eat putrid dogs and cats, and live in boats for want of a house, and follow the English ships, to pick up and devour the most disgusting garbage that they throw overboard."

"Suppose such should be the lot of our native kingdom," said Ella, shuddering. "Such is the natural course of things when a nation multiplies its numbers without a corresponding increase of food. May it be given to all to see this before we reach the pass of the Chinese!—and even if we never reach it—if, as is more likely, the evil is palliated by the caution of the prudent, by the emigration of the enterprising, and by other means which may yet remain, may we learn to use them before we are driven to it by famine and disease!"

"It is fearful enough, Ella, to witness what is daily before our eyes. God forbid that the whole kingdom should be in the state that Garveloch is in now!"

"In very many towns, Katie, there is always distress as great as our neighbours' now; and so there will be till they that hold the power in their own hands—not the king, not the parliament, not the rich only, but the body of the people, understand those natural laws by which and under which they subsist."

Many would be of Ella's opinion, if they could, like her, see the operation of the principle of increase within narrow bounds; for nothing can be plainer, nothing more indisputable when fully understood. In large societies, the mind of the observer is perplexed by the movements around him. The comings and goings, the births, deaths, and accidents, defy his calculations; and there are always persons at hand who help to delude him by talking in a strain which would have suited the olden time, but which is very inappropriate to the present state of things. In every city, however crowded with a half-starved population, there are many more who do their utmost to encourage population than can give a sound reason for their doing so; and while their advice is ringing in the ears, and their example is before the eyes, and there is no lack of inaccurate explanations why our workhouses are overflowing, our hospitals thronged, and our funeral bells for ever tolling, it is difficult to ascertain the real state of the case. But when the observation is exercised within a narrow range, the truth becomes immediately apparent,—it becomes evident that since capital increases in a slower ratio than population, there will be sooner or later a deficiency of food, unless the more vigorous principle of increase be controlled. If the welfare of a nation depended on the hare not reaching the goal before the tortoise, there might be some who would insist till the last moment that they moved at an equal pace, and ought, therefore, to be let alone; but there would be some who, trusting to their own eyes, would take precautionary measures: they might let the hare run till she overtook the tortoise, but then they would put on a clog. If any complain that this is not a fair race, the answer is that the hare and the tortoise were not made to vie with each other in speed; and if we set them to do it, we must manage the competition with a view to the consequences.

Ella and Katie, sensible and unprejudiced, and rendered quick-sighted by anxiety for their children, were peculiarly qualified for seeing the truth when fairly placed before them. Their interest in Ronald, as well as in their own offspring, gave them a view of both sides of the question; and there remained not a doubt, after calculating numbers and resources, that there must be some check to the increase of the people, and that the prudential check is infinitely preferable to those of vice and misery.

Of the griefs attending the latter, Ella could form some idea—though her feelings were not embittered by self-reproach—when she looked in the face of her sick child, who was now resting his aching head on her bosom. She could not leave him, though it was growing late, till he closed his heavy eyes, and let her lay him on his pillow. Then Annie came to bear the widow company for an hour or two; and Ella went to pass the night in her friend's dwelling.

"We shall never have any reserves in our confidence henceforth, Ella," said Katie, smiling. "There has been but one subject on which I was not always glad to hear you speak; and now that one is settled for ever."

Ella was glad that Katie had thus spoken, for she had not been perfectly sure of her friend's state of feeling. She now gazed affectionately on that youthful face, touched but not withered by early sorrow, and kissed the forehead of the friend she loved like a younger sister, and whom she could not have regarded as such more tenderly if they had been made sisters by marriage.

Chapter VIII: The Discipline of the Unteachable

Angus was restored safe to his home; but his return was melancholy enough. He was blown over the Sound by a storm, and landed at the moment that the funeral train who bore the bodies of Fergus's two children were winding up the rocks to the burial-place. The anxious father was naturally possessed with the idea that this was the funeral of the child he had left so ill; and he was confirmed in the supposition by seeing none of his family on the beach to await his arrival. Kenneth and his brothers were among the mourners, and Angus therefore found his wife and the girls alone when, with a throbbing heart, he entered his own dwelling. Ella met him with a calm but sad countenance, which, together with the silent awe with which the children looked up to him, answered but too plainly the question he would have asked. Little Jamie had died a few hours before in his mother's arms. The last words he spoke had been to call for his father.

"O, why was I not here?" exclaimed the mourning parent, laying his cheek to that of his boy, as if the cold body could be conscious of the caress. "It must have been an evil spirit that decoyed me away."

"Alas, then, your voyage has been in vain!" said Ella. "You have brought no bread."

Angus shook his head mournfully, and cast down the pouch of useless money that came back as full as it went out. The scarcity extended throughout the neighbourhood, and no food was to be bought at any price. Ella saw her husband's look of despondency, and rallied. She reminded him that they had a stock of meal, though a scanty one, and she held out the hope, suggested by Ronald's information, that a sloop would soon arrive with food enough to afford a temporary supply to all the inhabitants.

It had been agreed between Fergus and his sister that a constant watch for this vessel should be kept from daybreak till dark by the elder children of the family. Annie was now at the post in the absence of Kenneth, and Ella tempted her husband out with her, to pronounce whether the look-out was well chosen. She saw that his grief was too new to allow him to receive the condolence of neighbours who might step in on their return from the funeral. She was glad she had done so when she saw Annie putting back the hair which the stormy wind blew over her face, and evidently straining her sight to discern some object at sea. Angus had his glass [telescope] with him, and in the intervals of the driving mists, he plainly perceived a sloop coming up from the south.

"Away with you, with me for your helper!" cried Ella. "We will be at sea before any one knows what is coming; and then we shall escape contention and the sight of contention. And you, Annie, tell none but your uncle and Kenneth where we are gone. If it should not be the right sloop, it would be cruel to raise false hopes."

"Besides, mother, the people would tear ye to pieces, or at least the boat—they are grown so savage."

"They would very likely fancy we were going to snatch their share, instead of to receive a regular purchase. Farewell, my lass," she continued, as they reached the boat; "Kenneth will soon be with you, and ye may give us a smile when we land, if yon be the vessel we take her for."

"But, O father, the squalls are so rough! I fear to let you go."

"Never fear, Annie. The Flora knows the greeting of a summer squall. She will win her way out hardly enough; but you will see her bounding back as if she was racing with the gale."

There were many loungers on the beach when Angus and Ella cleared out. Some were invalids, who could not be kept within their cheerless homes even by the chill and boisterous weather. Many were idlers; and all made sport of what they thought the useless toil of going to sea at such a time. Their jokes would have been painful and perhaps irritating to Angus if he had not had reason to hope that relief was on the way to himself and them.

"Did ye bring home such a cargo this morning that ye are tempted to try your luck again?" cried one.

"Make haste!" exclaimed another, "or ye'll scarcely find the shoal. It's a brave summer day for casting a net."

"Or for angling," observed a third. "Where are your lines, neighbour? Nothing like a smooth sea for ladies' fishing."

"Ye must treat us each with a supper when you come back, Angus," said a fourth, "unless indeed the fishes should make a supper of you."

"I trust there may be a supper for every one in Garveloch this night," observed Ella, as the final shout reached the rolling and pitching vessel; and these cheering words were the last she spoke, as all her husband's attention and her own was required to direct their rough and somewhat perilous course.

Never was such a commotion excited in Garveloch as upon the spread of the tidings that a vessel had arrived at the quay with a certain quantity of grain and an ample supply of pease. The eagle was startled from her nest by the uproar. The more shrill grew the blast, the louder rose the voices; the higher swelled the tide over the bar, the greater was the eagerness to cross it as the shortest way to the quay. The men sent their wives home for whatever little wealth they had to offer in exchange, in case the food was to be purchased and not given, while they themselves hastened to secure the point whence they might best bid or entreat. Here a poor invalid, putting forth his utmost power to keep up with his competitors, was jostled aside or thrown down by the passers by. There a band of children were beginning a noisy rejoicing for they scarcely knew what; some among them half-crying in the midst of their shouting from hunger and pain, which would not be forgotten. The only quiet people in the island were Angus's family, and their ill-thriving neighbours round the point.

When the Flora, dimly seen in the twilight, came bounding in as her master had foretold, no one awaited her on the beach but those who had watched the whole expedition, Fergus, Kenneth, and his sister. The expected supply of meal was safe, and Fergus lost no time in conveying it out of sight, and into a place of safety.

"I brought down the money, father," said Kenneth, producing the pouch, "that you might buy more at the quay, if you wish it, before it is all gone."

"No, my boy," said Angus. "We have enough for the present, and I will neither take what others want more than we, nor raise the price by increasing the demand."

The Murdochs and O'Rorys were the last to know what had happened, as little was heard of the tumult beyond the point. They were extremely and almost equally wretched, and were far from attempting to soften their distresses by sympathy and neighbourly offices. Those who are most heedless of adversity in prospect, do not usually bear it best when it comes; and so it proved in the instance of both these families. Murdoch, who, when he might have been prosperous, was too lazy to do more than trust he should get through well enough, now cast all the blame of his destitution on Dan's assurances that it would be the easiest thing in life to live, if he would only grow potatoes. Dan, who was content any way when causes of discontent were only in prospect, forgot there was such a thing as content when the natural consequences of his recklessness came upon him. It had been a terrible day when the absolute want of food had driven both to dig up their seed potatoes. Murdoch had foresight enough to be appalled at the prospect of the long destitution which this measure must cause. Dan laughed at him for supposing that anything better could be done in a season so wet that every root would rot in the ground instead of growing; but he did not the less grumble at "the powers" for giving him nothing better to eat than half-rotten roots, that afforded no more strength than his own puny infant had and was losing day by day. Noreen often looked rueful with two black eyes, and did not insist so vehemently as formerly on her Dan being "the beautifullest husband in nature;" and as for the child, its best friends could only hope it would follow Noreen's former dangling "babbies," and be laid in peace under the sod.

The first news these neighbours had of the arrival of the vessel from the station was from Kenneth, who good-naturedly remembered to run and give them the information in time to afford them a fair chance in the scramble. Murdoch seized his staff and was off in an instant.

"Stay, neighbour," cried Kenneth, who was not aware of the extent of Murdoch's poverty; "the buyers have the first chance you know. Better not go empty-handed."

Murdoch thought he was jeering, and shook his stick at him with a gesture of passion, which Kenneth could not resent when he saw how the old man's limbs shook, and how vain were his attempts at unusual speed.

Dan jumped up at the news, snatched his baby, and gave it a toss which was enough to shake its weak frame to pieces, seized upon Noreen for a kiss in answer to the shriek with which she received the child, snatched the pot in which the last batch of rotten potatoes was boiling, and threw out its contents into the puddle beside the door, and ran off, laughing at his wife's lamentations for the only bit of food she had had to put between her teeth this day. Kenneth now perceived that Dan could bestir himself upon occasion; and indeed the Irishman's glee was so obstreperous, that it might have been supposed his mirth was owing to his favourite "sperits," if it had not been known that he had been long without the means of procuring himself that indulgence.

Such a man's mirth is easily turned to rage. On reaching the sloop, which was fast emptying of its contents, Dan found that he stood a worse chance of a supply than anybody in Garveloch, except Murdoch, who still lagged behind. To come empty-handed and to come late was a double disqualification; and to be kept at a distance by force put Dan into a passion which was only equalled by his neighbour's, when he also arrived at the scene of action. It was the policy of the bystanders to turn their rage upon each other. As soon as an opening appeared among the group on the quay, through which the sloop might be approached, they pushed the old man forward, and held Dan back, urging that a hearty youth like him, and a stranger, would not surely force his way before an old man, who had been born and bred in the place; but Dan kicked, struggled, dealt his blows right and left, and at last sprang upon Murdoch, snatched off his bonnet, and buffeted him about the face with it.

"You graceless wretch!" exclaimed all who were at leisure to look on.

"Let him uncover gray hairs that helped to make them gray," said Murdoch, in a voice of forced calmness. "It was he that lured me to poverty, and now let him glory in it."

"It's owing to your gray hairs I did not beat you blind this minute," cried Dan. "I'd have you keep a civil tongue in your head, if you'd have your eyes stay there too."

"I would peril my eyes to say it again," cried the old man. "It was you that lured me to poverty with saying that Ireland was the brightest and merriest land under the sun, and the only country where a man may live and be content without trouble."

"By the holy poker, so it is, barring such reprobates as you are in it."

"You told me that I spent my labour for nothing, and worse than nothing, when I grew oats and barley. You told me that I might get three times as much food out of the ground, by growing potatoes instead. You—"

"All true, by the saints, villain as you are to doubt my word! There's three times the victuals in an Irishman's field, and three times the children in his cabin, and three times the people on the face of the blessed land, that there is where the folks are so mighty high that they must have bread."

"And three times the number die," said a voice near, "when a bad season comes."

"And what if they do?" cried Dan: "'tis a blessed land for all that, with a golden sun to live under, and a green turf to lie under."

"It's a vile country," cried Murdoch, emboldened by hope of support from the bystanders. "Your children are as hungry as cannibals, and as naked as savages. When the sun shines, you thank the powers and lie still in your laziness—"

"There's reason for that," interrupted Dan. "There are so many to do the work, we can't settle who is to begin; and so we're content to take no trouble; and this is the most your Rob and Meg have learned of me."

"And then when there comes a blank harvest, you fight over one another's graves."

"Sure the powers forgive the sin," creed Dan. "Craving stomachs drive to blows, and then the priest is merciful."

"More merciful than you are to one another when the fever comes, cruel savages as you are! If your own mother took the fever, you would turn her into a shed by the road side, and let her tend herself. You would go quietly smoking your pipe past the very place where your own father lay dying, and never speak a word or move a finger for him."

" 'Tis false as to not speaking a word. We pray for them in the fever day and night; and many's the mass I have vowed against I grow richer. The fever is a judgment of Heaven, and where is the good of catching it if we can help it? They that sent it will take care of them that have it, and what is our care to theirs?"

"Shame! Shame!" was the cry from all sides; and some who were on their way home with a pan full of meal or a basket full of pease, stopped to listen why.

"Shame! Shame!" cried Dan, mimicking the shouters. "You just don't know what you're talking about; for them that have the fever don't cry shame."

"Not in their hearts?"

"Never a bit;—and don't I know that had an uncle in the fever twice, and moved him for fear we should fall down in it too? Didn't he come crawling out the first time when we were bringing a coffin and supposing him dead, and did not he help the wail for himself before we saw him among us? And would he have wailed in a joke, if he had cried 'Shame!' in his heart and who such a judge as himself?"

"What happened the next time, Dan?"

"The next time 'twas his ghost in earnest that went to the burial; and a pretty burial it was. O, there's no place like old Ireland for care of the dead! We beat you there entirely, you unnatural ruffians, that never give so much as a howl to your nearest flesh and blood!"

The listeners thought it better and more natural to help the living than to honour the dead. It did not seem to occur to either party that it was possible to do both. The dispute now ran higher than ever, Murdoch laying the blame on Dan of having made all his resources depend on a favourable season, and Dan defending everything Irish, down to poverty, famines, and pestilential fevers; the first a perpetual, and each of the others a frequent evil. A fight was beginning, when order was restored by an authority which might not be resisted. Mr. Mackenzie was on board, having taken this opportunity of visiting several islands which were under his charge as a magistrate. Seeing the uproar on the quay likely to increase every moment, he stepped on shore, ordered two or three stout men to part the combatants, and gave poor old Murdoch into the care of Angus, who was standing by, desiring that his wants should be supplied, and that he should be sent home out of the reach of provocation from Dan. Angus looked kindly after the interests of his old master, now so humbled as not to resist his help; and then sent a neighbour with him to guard him from robbery on his way home. It might have been thought that Rob would have been the fittest person to undertake this natural duty; but Rob was nowhere to be seen. He had appeared one of the first on the quay, and had bought a supply of food with a little silver crucifix which he had contrived to steal from Noreen, and which she had kept, through all her distresses, as a sort of charm. Rob was now hidden in a snug corner, eating a portion of his provision, and drinking the whiskey for which he had exchanged the rest.

Mr. Mackenzie accepted Angus's invitation to spend the night under his roof. He agreed all the more readily from perceiving that he could gratify the feelings of the parents by taking part in the funeral of their child the next day; by carrying his head to the grave, as the expression is.

Mr. Mackenzie would know from Angus all that he could tell of Murdoch's history, and of what had happened to Dan since he settled in Garveloch. The present state of the island was a subject which always made Angus melancholy. The place was so changed, he said; there were many people that you would scarcely believe to be the same as before their distresses began.

"Such is always the case, Angus, where there are more people than can live without jostling. People act upon opposite maxims according to their circumstances. If there is abundance for every body, they are very ready to cry, 'The more the merrier;' if the provision is scanty, they mutter, 'The fewer the better cheer,' and each snatches what he can for himself."

Ella was at this moment distributing the evening meal. At these very words she placed before her son Kenneth a barley-cake,—the first he had tasted for some time,—with a smile which he well understood. He had known something of the sufferings his mother had described as the consequence of their mutual resolution not to touch the food on which they usually subsisted; but, till this evening, he had supposed the trial only begun, and felt almost ashamed to be released so soon. As he broke his bread, a blush overspread his whole face; and when he next looked up, he met Ella's eyes filled with tears. Mr. Mackenzie observed, but did not understand; and Angus himself would have found it difficult to explain, though Kenneth's altered looks caused a suspicion that he had exercised more than his share of self-denial.

"I have seen so much of the snatching you speak of, and of

defrauding too," said Angus, when all but himself and his guest had withdrawn, "as to make me think we are now little better off than in cities, compared with which I used to think our island a paradise. There has, I believe, been crime enough committed within the circuit of a mile from this place, to match with the alleys and cellars of a manufacturing city. The malice of the people in their speech, the envy in their countenances, the artifices in their management, the violence of their actions, are new in this place and these people. I hoped to have kept my children out of sight and hearing of these things for ever."

"Never nourish such a hope, friend," said Mr. Mackenzie, "unless you can keep want out of sight and hearing too. Virtue and vice depend not on place, but on circumstance. The rich do not steal in cities, any more than the starving respect property in a retired island like this. If we could increase our supply of necessaries and comforts in proportion to the wants and reasonable desires of all, there would be little vice; and if we did no more than rightly estimate and administer the resources we already possess, we might destroy for ever the worst evils of which society complains."

"Surely, Sir, it might be done, if society were but animated with one mind. It is in the power of few, I suppose, to increase the supply of necessaries and comforts perpetually and very extensively; and no power on earth can do it so as to keep pace with the constant demand for them."

"Certainly, if that demand be unchecked."

"I was going to say, Sir, that it is in the power of every one to help to equalize the demand. It seems to me, that whoever acts so as to aggravate want, becomes answerable for the evils caused by want, whether he injures his neighbour's capital, or neglects to improve his own, or increases a demand upon it which is already overwhelming."

"You will be told, friend, if you preach your doctrine to unwilling ears, that one set of vices would rage only the more fiercely for those which result from want being moderated."

"I know," replied Angus, "that some are of opinion that there is always a balance of vices in society; that, as some are extinguished, others arise. This seems to me a fancy that nobody can prove or show to be reasonable."

"I am quite of your opinion, Angus; and if I were not, I am sure I should find it difficult to assert that any set of vices could be more to be dreaded than those which arise from extreme poverty. I would not draw a comparison in favour of any acknowledged vice over any other; but I can conceive of no more dreadful degradation of character, no more abundant sources of misery, than arise out of the overpowering temptations of want. You have seen instances, I doubt not, among the lower, as I among the higher classes, of the regular process by which honourable feelings are blunted, kindly affections embittered, piety turned into blasphemy, and integrity into fraud and violence, as the pressure of poverty becomes more and more galling."

"I have seen so much of this, Sir, as to make me believe that very few, if any, pass through the trial of squalid and hopeless poverty with healthy minds. Moreover, I believe such poverty to be the hot-bed of *all* vices. I shall never be convinced, unless I see it, that any vice in existence will be aggravated by the comforts of life being extended to all, or that there is any which is not encouraged by the feelings of personal injury, of hatred towards their superiors, or recklessness concerning their companions and themselves, which are excited among the abject or ferocious poor."

"Evil seems to be an admonition of Providence to men to change that part of their conduct which brings on that evil," observed Mr. Mackenzie; "and happy are they who take the warning in time, or remember it for their future guidance. Extensive fires warn men not to build houses of wood; pestilence may teach cleanliness and ventilation; and having thus given their lesson, these evils become rare, or cease. What, therefore, may famine teach?"

"Care not to let eaters multiply beyond the ordinary supply of food. I hope we people of Garveloch shall take the warning. I am sure it is distinct enough."

"Yes, Angus. You ate up the unusual supply of two abundant seasons. An average one produced hardship. An unfavourable one has brought you to the brink of a famine. This is Providence's way of admonishing."

Chapter IX: Troubles Never Come Alone

The sufferings of the islanders were not yet over, as all foresaw who were accustomed to watch the succession of events. The natural consequence of a famine in former days was a plague; and it is still too well known in Scotland and Ireland that sickness follows scarcity. Garveloch went through the natural process. There never was such a winter known there as that which succeeded the scarcity. Rheumatism among the aged, consumption among the youthful, all the disorders of infancy among the children, laid waste the habitations of many who thought they had never known sorrow till now. Many a gray-haired matron, who used to sit plying her distaff[1] in the chimney-corner, and singing old songs to the little ones playing about her, had been shaken by the privations of the summer, and now lay groaning in the torments of the disease which was soon to take her hence, although, with due care, so vigorous a life might still have been preserved for a few years. Here, a father who was anxious to be up and doing for his children, on the sea or at the station, was in danger of coughing his life away if he faced the wintry air, and fretted in idleness within his smoky cottage. There, a mother who had hungered through many a day to feed her children, now found that she had broken down her strength in the effort, and that she must leave them to a care less tender than her own. In other cases, the parent and her little ones seemed hastening together to another world, and two or three of one family were buried in the same grave. The mortality among the children was dreadful. The widow Cuthbert could scarcely believe her own happiness when she saw all her little family daily seated at the board in rosy health and gay spirits, when not a neighbour had been exempt from loss. She would scarcely suffer her boys out of her sight; and if accidentally parted from them, trembled lest she should hear complaints or see traces of illness when she met them again. There had been sickness in Ella's family, but none died after little Jamie. Ronald kept watch over them all. Many were the kind presents, many the welcome indulgences he sent or carried to the sick members of his sister's and brother's family this year. Katie needed no such assistance. If she had, she would have freely accepted it; but frequent inquiries and much friendly intercourse served quite as well to show the regard these friends bore to each other.

The supplies of food were still so precarious as to make every body anxious except those who could purchase a store. Now and then a boat with provisions came from a distance, and the cod-fishing turned out tolerably productive to those who had health and strength to pursue the occupation. So much was wanted, however, for immediate consumption, that business nearly stood still at the station. Kenneth had been recalled thither when there seemed to be a prospect of employment for him; but he had now made the last barrel that would be wanted before next season, and began to be very melancholy. He sauntered along the pier, around which there was no

---

1   A distaff is an implement used for spinning wool and flax threads by hand.

busy traffic; he lounged about the cooperage, taking up first one tool and then another, and wondering when the hammer and the saw would be heard there again. Many a time did he count the weeks that must pass before he should be once more earning his maintenance, and reckon how large was the debt to his uncle which he was incurring by his present uselessness. Ronald could not succeed in making him cheerful for a day together, or in inducing him to employ himself; and he began to fear that either illness was creeping on the young man, or that his fine spirit was broken by the anxiety he had undergone and the miseries he had beheld. He would have sent him over to Ella, whose influence was all-powerful with her son; but Ella had cares enough at home just now. Having messages from Kenneth as frequently as usual, she was not more than usually anxious concerning him.

Angus's activity and cheerfulness never gave way. He ascribed their power to his wife's influence; while she found a never-failing support to her energies when he was present. She owned to Katie how easily she could give way to despondency when he was absent for days together, and how she felt strong enough to do and bear anything when his boat came in sight again. The fact was, they did owe each other all they believed they owed. There was a lofty spirit of trust in Ella, as animating to her husband as his experience in life and devotion to his home were supporting her. Katie looked with a generous sympathy on the enjoyment of a happiness of which she had been deprived, and wished no more for herself than that she might be as secure from trials with her children as she believed Angus and Ella to be. No sorrows could, as she told Ella, be inflicted by the children of such parents—by children so brought up as theirs. Ella never admitted this assurance without reservation; for she knew too much of human life to expect that any one of its blessings should be enjoyed for ever without alloy.

It was during the absence of her husband on one of his trading excursions that the children came crowding round the door, to ask Ella to come and listen to the new music some gentlemen in fine clothes were playing as they went up the pass. Katie was brought out by her little people at the same moment. The children climbed the height to get another view of the strangers, and their mothers followed. A recruiting party was ascending between the rocks at the same moment that more companies than one were leaving the burying-ground. The children clapped their hands and began to dance to the booming drum and shrill fife; but Ella immediately stopped them.

"Don't ye mark," she said, "there's Rob and Meg Murdoch coming down the hill? Would ye like to see anybody dancing in your sight when you have just laid your father's head in the ground?"

"I saw Rob drunk this very morn, mother, and he danced as if his father had been there looking on."

"If Rob behaves as if he had no feeling, that is no reason why you should seem to think he has none."

"Look at Meg!" cried another child. "She is laughing as if it was a bridal instead of a funeral."

Ella was shocked, though not much surprised, to see Meg run forward to meet the soldiers, as if they were old acquaintance, and linger behind with them when her party, including her stupid brother, had cracked their joke and passed on. It occurred to her that Meg's brother-in-law might be among the soldiers and she said so by way of excuse; but immediately called the children down from the height, unwilling that such an example of unfeeling levity should remain before their eyes. They were naturally somewhat unwilling to lose sight of the scarlet coats, having never beheld any before.

"Ye will see such often enough, now, my dears," said their mother, sighing. "These people know how to choose their time. The fife is ever merriest when the heart's music is hushed; and whenever people are at their wit's end with want and sorrow, the red-coats come and carry away such as are glad to drown thought and seek change instead of waiting for it."

"Yes, indeed," replied Katie: "a funeral at the top of the hill, and a recruiting party going to meet it, is natural enough; and so it would have been to see lads made to drink in the king's name when their stomachs were craving food. I wondered we had had no recruiting before; for the worse the times, the more are ready to leave home behind them, and go and serve the king."

The children understood nothing of all this but that they should see the soldiers again, which indeed was the point which most concerned them at their age. They listened long for the drum—they took turns as scouts to watch which way the soldiers went, and to give notice if they should approach. Now they were traced up to Duff's farm, heard to play before the door, and seen to be invited in. After a while, they proceeded with a few followers at their heels, by a roundabout way to the Murdochs' cove. Meg was their guide, walking in front, arm-in-arm with a soldier—a fashion of marching to which it was supposed she had been just drilled. The music being heard approaching behind the rocks, the children scampered off to meet it; and after a considerable time, during which shouts arose which made the mothers wish their boys at home again, the children appeared as the advanced guard of the procession, waving their bonnets, and pretending to march like the grand folks behind them. It was soon apparent that all present were not as happy as they. Meg indeed laughed so as to be heard above the music, and one or two raw lads looked full of pride and heroism, and took off their bonnets from time to time to look at the gay ribbons with which they were ornamented; but all the bustle and noise—nothing remarkable perhaps in an English city, but very astonishing in Garveloch—could not call off attention from a woman's rage, or drown the screams of a woman's scolding voice. The vixen was Noreen; and if ever a vixen had an excuse for her violence, it was she at this moment; for Dan, the husband for whom she had, as she declared, left the beautifullest home of the beautifullest country in the world—Dan, whom she had defended through thick and thin, for having "kilt" her and "murthered" her "babbies,"—Dan, who had said so often that a man needed nothing in life more than a cabin and a potato-ground, and an "iligant" wife, had enlisted, and was going to leave her and her last remaining child to starve. Had not he a cabin? she wanted to know; and had not he a potato-ground, as good as any at Rathmullin? and had not he called her his "iligant Noreen" before the fancy came across him to break her heart?

Since it did not please Dan to answer her questions, no one else was bound to do so. It was difficult to say whether he was drunk or not. He kissed his wife in return for her cuffs, and behaved like a madman; but such was his way when he was roused to mirth.

Shocked at the sight, Ella was about to withdraw, when Katie expressed her wonder whether this scene was to be acted in all the islands. She had connexions in more than one, and began to be anxious lest some of them should be tempted to go abroad. Ella therefore accosted the sergeant, a good-natured-looking man, and asked if his recruiting was likely to be prosperous among the islands? He found the people very loyal, he replied, and many fine young men ready to serve their king and country. He should visit every place in the district in turn, and had already made a pretty wide circuit. He had this morning come from Islay.

"You would scarce enlist many there," observed Ella. "A few months ago would have been your best time for Islay; now the fishery begins to open a prospect again."

"I beg your pardon, madam; we have been particularly successful in Islay." And he pulled out a list of names, displayed it hastily, and was about to put it up again when Katie snatched it, and after the first glance looked at her friend with such a gaze of anguish as at once told Ella the truth.

"Is Kenneth's name there?" she asked, in a low, hoarse voice.

"That young man," said the sergeant, who had been speaking to one of his people, and did not perceive Ella's emotion, "that young man to whose name you point—and a very fine youth he is, six feet and half an inch—belongs to this place. He is to come over this afternoon to take leave of his family, and proceeds with me in the morning."

Ella retreated hastily towards her own door; she turned round on reaching the threshold, and motioned to Katie not to follow her; but Katie would not be repulsed. With streaming eyes she attempted to make her way by gentle force. Ella recovered her power of speech.

"Leave me, Katie. I can speak to no one but Angus. O Angus! why are you away? O! how shall I tell the news when he comes back?"

When Katie had led her friend into the inner room, she left her to her grief, thinking that the best kindness was to keep watch that no one intruded. The widow felt as if her own heart was bursting when audible tokens once or twice reached her of the fearful conflict which rent the mother's heart. In the fervour of her love and compassion for Ella, she was full of indignation against him who had caused all this misery; and when this indignation had reached its highest pitch, the latch of the door was uplifted, and Kenneth stood before her. His pale countenance, with its expression of mournful determination, might have disarmed her anger at a moment of less excitement; but Katie would not bestow on him a second glance or a greeting.

"Where is my mother?" he inquired. "My father, I find, is absent."

"Seek her yourself," replied Katie, pointing to the chamber. "If you did not fear to wring her heart, you will scarce shrink from seeing her grief."

"She knows then!" said Kenneth. "I would fain have told her myself—"

"You need not covet the task," replied Katie, her features working convulsively. "You would have cast yourself into the sea before now if you had seen her take the tidings." And the widow gave vent to what was boiling in her mind.

Kenneth did not at first interrupt her; and when he attempted explanation, was not allowed to proceed. Katie had never before been so unreasonable as now on her friend's behalf.

"Make way!" said Kenneth, at length, in strong emotion. "My mother will hear me."

Ella at this moment threw open the door of the chamber, and stood, still trembling but erect, and spoke calmly.

"Katie!" she said, "I thought you had known Kenneth and me better. He has ever been dutiful: why then condemn him unheard? I have told you my confidence in him; and is it kind, then, to make a mockery of my trust?"

Katie's anger was now all turned against herself. She cast an imploring look at them both, and rushed out of the house before they could detain her.

"Bless you, mother, for trusting me!" cried Kenneth.

"But O, my boy, what a sore trial to my trust! What has possessed ye, Kenneth, that ye must leave us? When we have suffered together so long, and were beginning to hope together again, what could make ye plunge us into a new trouble?"

"It was hastily done, mother, but done for the best, and not from discontent with home, or a love of wandering. I could not see so clearly as you that times are about to mend. I could not endure to be a burden to uncle Ronald, and my heart was sick with hoping and hoping, and finding nothing to do after all. Then there are so many brothers growing up to fill my place; and my going will make room for one of them at the station. And then there was the bounty too. I thought I should have had pleasure, mother, in giving you the first purse of money I ever had; but nothing will give me any pleasure again if you think I have been wilfully wrong."

"Not wilfully wrong, Kenneth; I never thought you could be that—not even in the first moment when—"

She could not proceed. Her son continued:

"I would fain hear ye say more, mother. O, can ye tell me that you think me right?"

"Do not let it weigh with you, my son, whether I think you judged rightly or not. You felt dutifully and kindly, and you have as much right to judge of your duty as I. You shall never want my blessing nor your father's. It is to your wish to do your duty that we give our blessing; and it will therefore follow you over the world."

Kenneth had much to say on duty to one's country, and on the question who could best be spared to serve in her armies; in the pursuit of which argument he brought the proof round to himself. His mother, feeling that the deed could not be undone, encouraged his feelings of patriotism, sanctioned his desire to fulfil a public duty, and contented herself with the silence of dissent when she thought him mistaken.

"Mother," cried Kenneth, at length, bursting into tears, "you make a child of me by treating me like a man. I knew you would be patient, I knew you would be indulgent, but I scarcely hoped that even you could so soon, so very soon, give me the rights I have been so hasty to claim. If you had blamed me, if you had spoken with authority, I could have commanded myself better when it comes to the last."

"We are all weak," murmured Ella, melting also into tears. "God forbid we should judge one another! We are least of all fit to do so when our griefs are tossing so as to wreck our judgments. Authority, Kenneth! No; this is not the time for me to use it. If it were merely whether ye should cross to Islay to-day or to-morrow, I might have spoken unawares with authority; but when the question is, what your duty in life is to be, and when that question is already decided, all that a mother can do is to give her blessing."

The many dreary hours of this night were too few for what had to be said and done by the elder members of this mourning family. Soon after day break Angus returned; so that Kenneth had not the additional misery of departing in uncertainty whether he should be followed by his father's blessing. Angus had in his young days been sent abroad by a spirit of adventure; so that he was even better prepared than Ella to sympathise in Kenneth's feelings and convictions. He commanded himself when the event was first told him; accompanied his son to a considerable distance; and from the hour of his return spoke to none but Ella of the blank the wanderer's absence caused, or of the anxiety with which he watched for tidings of the war.

Chapter X: Conclusion

A recruiting party was, as Ella had foretold, a frequent sight in Garveloch as long as the distress lasted; and one of the present consequences to her and her husband of the favourable season which followed was, that the red-coats ceased to appear, and the hated sound of the drum and fife to make them start. As soon as the fishery was resumed, there was work enough for all who remained on the island, and therefore little encouragement to serve the king out of his own dominions. News of Kenneth came very rarely—about as often as rejoicings for a victory. Some of Angus's neighbours were wont to come and tell him of such events as if they were certain of bringing welcome news, provided he knew that his son was safe. Fergus's lads, especially, who regretted that they were too young to enlist at the same time with Kenneth, seemed disposed to take the first opportunity of doing so that might occur, and to have no doubt that the best service they could render to their island was to leave it.

"How can you suppose," said Angus to them one day, "that I can rejoice in the slaughter you tell me of? How can you imagine it can give me pleasure to look forward to our strong youths leaving our shores?"

"I thought, uncle," said one—"I am sure I heard somebody say you believed that we wanted thinning, and that war must therefore be a very good thing."

"I said so," said Captain Forbes, who stood within hearing. "You think, Angus, that there are too many people for the supply of food; and therefore the more that die, the better cheer there is for those who remain. Did you not tell Mr. Mackenzie so?"

"Better say at once, sir, that we ought to pray for a pestilence. Better send for our enemies to slaughter us as fast as they can, sparing only a proper number to enjoy what we leave behind."

"But I am sure you used to complain of our numbers, Angus, and ascribe our distress to them."

"But it does not follow, sir, that I would have them removed by violence. All I wish is, that society should be as happy as it can be made; and it would be somewhat strange to inflict the extremest misery with this view. I never had such a thought, I assure you, as of running into a greater evil to avoid a lesser."

"Many people, however, think occasional wars and plagues very good things to keep down the population."

"So I have heard, but I think very differently. The one circumstance which, above all others, cheers me respecting the state of society, is that population is, to a considerable extent, checked by better means than formerly. There are fewer lives lost by war, plagues, and the accidents of common life, while the increase of population is not in proportion to the removal of these dreadful checks."

"How do you account for this?"

"Marriage is less general, and takes place at a later age—at least among the middling classes, whose example will, I trust, be soon followed by their poorer neighbours. Whenever any one class gains a clear understanding of the reasons why a thing has been, and why it should no longer be, there is room for hope that other classes will in time enter into their views, and act accordingly. There is hope that governments will in time cease to make war and encourage population,—that is, to call people into existence for the purpose of cutting one another's throat. There is hope that the poor will in time be more eager to maintain than to multiply their families; and then, lads, there will be no more drumming and fifing in Garveloch, and no need to wander abroad in search of danger and death, in order to show patriotism."

"When will that be, uncle?"

"I am no prophet; but I will venture to prophesy that it will happen somewhere between the third and the thirty-thousandth generation from the present—that is, that it will take place, but not yet."

"You have said a great deal," observed the captain, "about the reasons why there should no longer be want; but you slipped quietly enough over the reason why there has ever been want."

"It was not my intention to do so," said Angus, smiling, "for it appears very clear to me. It was growing need which urged men towards all the improvements which have ever taken place. The appropriation and security of property, improvements in government, art, and sciences—in short, all the institutions of society took their beginning from the growing wants of men; and those growing wants were caused, of course, by increase of numbers. This is quite enough to satisfy us that the principle of increase is a good one; while, if we see that our institutions can now be preserved and improved under other and higher kinds of stimulus, it is time that we were controlling the principle within the bounds of reason and happiness."

"It is done for us when we do not look to it ourselves," the captain replied, sighing as he cast a glance around him. "How full is the burying-ground,—how empty are the houses compared with what they were but a few months ago! It reminds me of some of the places in the east, where we were ordered to march in the rear of the plague. They will soon be filled again, if the fishery does well. That is a comfort."

"And it reminds me that I have no time to lose," observed Angus. "Will you be my passenger to the station, captain?"

Nobody had time to lose this season in the island, but those who were willing to run the risk of future scarcity. Labour was in great request, and, of course, well paid. Angus found ample employment for his crane, and received very good interest for the capital laid out upon it. His younger sons worked it with as much zeal as Kenneth had shown in its construction; but their father, proud as he was of them, thought in his inmost heart that no other of his flourishing tribe equalled the eldest, or could make up for his loss; and the haunting dream of the night, the favourite vision of the day, was of Kenneth's return, to leave his native land no more. This was Angus's meditation while plying the oar, and this his theme in his own chimney corner. It was much to hear of Kenneth's honour and welfare, but while no hope of peace came with the tidings, they were not perfectly satisfying.

The only person to whom the improvement in the times brought any trouble was the widow Cuthbert. Her former lovers—not Ronald, but those who had broken off acquaintance with her when her young family seemed a dead weight in the scale against her own charms—now returned, and were more earnest than ever in their suit. Katie had discretion enough to be aware that the only respect in which she had become a more desirable match than before was in the growth of her boys, whose labour might soon be a little fortune to her, if she chose so to employ it. She was therefore far from being flattered at becoming so much in request, and honoured and valued the disinterested friendship of Ronald more than ever.

The present time, even with the drawback of Kenneth's absence, was the happiest period of Ronald's life. He made his little home at the station sociable and comfortable, by gathering his nephews and nieces about him; and his visits to Garveloch became more frequent and more welcome continually when his prosperous business allowed him leisure for the trip. Fergus, weighed down with care, had grown old before his time; and to Ronald's assistance it was owing that his family preserved their respectability till the lads were able to take on themselves a part of the charge which had been too heavy for their father.

Ella was the last of the family to show the marks of change. Her mind and heart were as remarkable for their freshness in age as they had been for their dignity in youth. Inured to early exertion and hardship, she was equal to all calls upon her energies of body and spirit. She was still seen, as occasion required, among the rocks, or on the sea, or administering her affairs at home. She was never known to plead infirmity, or to need forbearance, or to disappoint expectation. She had all she wanted in her husband's devotion to her and to his home, and she distributed benefits untold from the rich treasury of her warm affections. She had, from childhood, filled a station of authority, and had never abused her power, but made it the means of living for others. Her power increased with every year of her life, and with it grew her scrupulous watchfulness over its exercise, till the same open heart, penetrating eye, and ready hand, which had once made her the sufficient dependence of her orphan brothers, gave her an extensive influence over the weal and woe of Garveloch.

Summary of Principles illustrated in this volume

The increase of population is necessarily limited by the means of subsistence.

Since successive portions of capital yield a less and less return, and the human species produce at a constantly accelerated rate, there is a perpetual tendency in population to press upon the means of subsistence.

The ultimate checks by which population is kept down to the level of the means of subsistence are vice and misery.

Since the ends of life are virtue and happiness, these checks ought to be superseded by the milder methods which exist within man's reach.

These evils may be delayed by promoting the increase of capital, and superseded by restraining the increase of population.

Towards the one object, a part of society may do a little: towards the other, all may do much.

By rendering property secure, expenditure frugal, and production easy, society may promote the growth of capital.

By bringing no more children into the world than there is a subsistence provided for, society may preserve itself from the miseries of want. In other words, the timely use of the mild preventive check may avert the horrors of any positive check.

The preventive check becomes more, and the positive checks less powerful, as society advances.

The positive checks, having performed their office in stimulating the human faculties and originating social institutions, must be wholly superseded by the preventive check before society can attain its ultimate aim—the greatest happiness of the greatest number.

A Manchester Strike

[The advent of machinery offers the most potent symbol of the Industrial Revolution, representing cultural progress while depriving skilled trades- and crafts-people of their livelihoods, challenging ruling-class complacency and, for the rising middle-classes, generating unprecedented wealth. The "machinery question" initiated new avenues for social inquiry by raising issues effecting every level of society that demanded solutions appropriate to the early modern era. The efficiency of machine labor in terms of production time and consistency of finished product proved highly seductive to manufacturers aiming to realize the most profit for the least investment. As cottage industries were replaced by factories, machines, and "hands," many thousands of workers in traditional occupations found themselves redundant in this new economy that defined the human worker as just another cog in the technological wheel. Disenfranchised and dehumanized, some displaced workers responded by smashing the machinery as it was *en route* to the factories; but in their attempts to stem the tide of progress, the efforts of the Luddites ("framebreakers") and similar activists proved futile.

As industry grew and factory labor became the norm, protests focused more directly on worker-management relations, culminating in the trade union movement so threatening in its capacity to foster a mass uprising. Initially, every factory was seen as a "potential centre of political rebellion. The mill appeared as [a] symbol of social energies…[that] embodied a double threat to the settled order" (E.P. Thompson 207). The first threat was economic, represented by the rising middle classes made rich by industry. The second threat was sociopolitical, represented by the masses of discontented working poor. Uneasy social relations continued to surface with the conspicuous prosperity of the *nouveax riches*, with the concentration of the masses in urban centers, and with the dramatic disparity in quality of lifestyle between the two. Maxine Berg notes that "the terms of debate on the machinery issue were set by political economy" (18), and Harriet Martineau, who early asserted herself as a primary participant in that debate (for example, "The Rioters" in 1827 and "The Turn-out" in 1829), revisited these issues periodically throughout her career.

Several *Illustrations* tales feature industrial themes, including "Life in the Wilds" and "The Hill and the Valley." But Martineau's fullest treatment is "A Manchester Strike," which provides a compelling depiction of suffering among the industrial working poor. Martineau's tale anticipates subsequent industrial novels in its sympathetic portrayal of workers blinded, maimed, and crippled by industrial exploitation, spiritually broken by unremitting hopelessness, and driven to alcoholism through desperate poverty. The example provided by the industrial city of Manchester illustrates Martineau's observation that Britain's industrial poor fare little better than slaves on American plantations. After witnessing slavery in America, Martineau wrote: "We have a population in our manufacturing towns almost as oppressed, and in our secluded rural districts almost as ignorant, as your negroes. These must be redeemed" (letter to Abby Kelley, June 20, 1838).[1] But as industry grew, so too did the oppression of the working class accelerate. In 1850, she wrote sympathetically of the deplorable "state of operatives...men wild with hunger" and of the abuse of apprentices who are treated as "the most barbarous and depraved of slaveholders treats his slaves" (*History* 3:167-88).[2] Despite a remarkably vital reform movement, on both grass-roots and bureaucratic levels, conceptual understanding of industrialization's cultural impact remained elusive, obscured by the sheer size and magnitude of a social force destined to change society throughout the world permanently and irrevocably.

Among the topics explored in this tale are workers' health broken by excessive heat and polluted air in factories; child labor; the hand-to-mouth existence constantly threatened by under- or unemployment; attitudes toward worker's rights; and the threat posed by workers' organizing. "A Manchester Strike" also dramatizes the intersections between Malthusian population theory and the wages fund doctrine, particularly the problems arising when all working family members are employed in the same trade and that trade is in economic decline. In her concluding *Summary* of "A Manchester Strike," Martineau argues that the proportion of the wages fund received by workers depends on the number among whom it is divided. The rate of wages thus depends less on manufacturers' wealth than on the proportion between capital and population. In Manchester, as in Garveloch, population growth determines how many jobs are available and how the subsistence fund is distributed.

---

1   Deborah Logan, ed., *Writings on Slavery and the American Civil War by Harriet Martineau* (DeKalb, IL: Northern Illinois UP, 2002), 42-43.

2   The analogy was a popular one: writing of its opposition to the "Factory Regulation Bill," the *British Labourer's Protector and Factory Child's Friend* (1832-33) deplores Parliament's attempt to "humanize in some measure a system of labour...[which is] the most barbarous, known in any age of the world" (149). The article anticipates a time "when there will no longer be a denial by the legislature of that JUSTICE and LIBERTY, which the *factory child* and the *negro slave* are equally ENTITLED TO."

Martineau's working class hero, William Allen, is gentle, long-suffering, and intelligent. Although weighed down by his wife's defeated listlessness and daughter Martha's physical maladies, Allen does not succumb to drink, as do many of his neighbors; rather, he maintains his strength of character and his respected standing in the community. Chosen to represent his co-workers and to air their grievances to management, Allen is a reluctant hero destined to become the communal scapegoat, a pawn to be manipulated between the factory owners, the workers, the union agitators, and the strike breakers. Because manufacturers refuse to hire a disgraced worker and settlement laws prohibited movement away from one's native parish to seek work elsewhere, Allen is forced to become a humble street-sweeper, making provision for his family even more difficult than when he was a factory worker. This working-class hero fades into obscurity and ignominy as a result of simply asserting his principles and articulating his views on human justice. Allen's defeat warns against working-class combining (an early form of trade unionism), a grim reminder of the futility marking the lives of the working poor at this time.]

Notice. The author hopes that as she has no acquaintance with any one firm, master, or workman in Manchester, she will be spared the imputation of personality. Her personages are all abstractions.

Chapter I: The Week's End

One fine Saturday evening in May, 18—, several hundred work-people, men, girls, and boys, poured out from the gates of a factory which stood on the banks of the Medlock, near Manchester. The children dispersed in troops, some to play, but the greater number to reach home with all speed, as if they were afraid of the sunshine that checquered the street and reddened the gables and chimnies.

The men seemed in no such haste; they lingered about the factory, one large group standing before the gates, and smaller knots occupying the street for some distance, while a few proceeded slowly on their way home, chatting with one or another party as they went. One only appeared to have nothing to say to his companions, and to wish to get away quietly, if they would have let him. He was one of the most respectable looking among them, decent in his dress, and intelligent though somewhat melancholy in countenance. He was making his way without speaking to anybody, when first one and then another caught him by the button and detained him in consultation. All seemed anxious to know what Allen had to relate or to advise; and Allen had some difficulty in getting leave to go home, much as he knew he was wanted there. When he had at length escaped, he walked so rapidly as presently to overtake his little daughter, Martha, who had left the factory somewhat earlier. He saw her before him for some distance, and observed how she limped and, how feebly she made her way along the street (if such it might be called,) which led to their abode. It was far from easy walking to the strongest. There were heaps of rubbish, pools of muddy water, stones and brickbats[1] lying about, and cabbage-leaves on which the unwary might slip, and bones over which pigs were grunting and curs snarling and fighting. Little Martha, a delicate child of eight years old, tried to avoid all these obstacles; but she nearly slipped down several times, and started when the dogs came near her, and shivered every time the mild spring breeze blew in her face.

"Martha, how lame you are to-day!" said Allen, taking her round the waist to help her onward.

"O father, my knees have been aching so all day, I thought I should have dropped every moment."

"And one would think it was Christmas by your looks, child, instead of a bright May day."

"It is very chill after the factory," said the little girl, her teeth still chattering. "Sure the weather must have changed, father."

No; the wind was south, and the sky cloudless. It was only that the thermometer had stood at 75° within the factory.

"I suppose your wages are lowered as well as mine," said Allen; "how much do you bring home this week?"

"Only three shillings, father; and some say it will be less before long. I am afraid mother—"

The weak-spirited child could not say what it was that she feared, being choked by her tears.

"Come, Martha, cheer up," said her father. "Mother knows that you get sometimes more and sometimes less; and, after all, you earn as much as a piecer as some do at the hand-loom. There is Field, our neighbour; he and his wife together do not earn more than seven shillings a week, you know, and think how much older and stronger they are than you! We must make you stronger, Martha. I will go with you to Mr. Dawson, and he will find out what is the matter with your knees."

---

1 Brickbats are broken bricks used as missiles or weapons.

By this time they had reached the foot of the stairs which led up to their two rooms in the third story of a large dwelling which was occupied by many poor families. Barefooted children were scampering up and down these stairs at play; girls nursing babies sat at various elevations, and seemed in danger of being kicked down as often as a drunken man or an angry woman should want to pass; a thing which frequently happened. Little Martha looked up the steep stairs and sighed. Her father lifted and carried her. The noises would have stunned a stranger, and they seemed louder than usual to accustomed ears. Martha's little dog came barking and jumping up as soon as he saw her, and this set several babies crying; the shrill piping of a bulfinch was heard in the din, and over all, the voice of a scolding woman.

"That is Sally Field's voice if it is anybody's," said Allen. "It is enough to make one shift one's quarters to have that woman within hearing."

"She is in our rooms, father. I am sure the noise is there; and see, her door is open and her room empty."

"She need not fear leaving her door open," observed a neighbour in passing. "There is nothing there that anybody would wish to carry away."

Allen did not answer, but made haste to restore peace in his own dwelling, knowing that his wife was far from being a match for Sally Field. As he flung open the door, the weaker party seemed to resign the contest to him; his wife sank into a chair, trembling all over. Her four or five little ones had hidden themselves where they could, some under the table, some behind the bed, having all been slapped or pushed or buffeted by Sally for staring at her with their thumbs in their mouths. She was not aware that Sally Field in a passion was a sight to make any one stare.

Allen carried Martha to a seat in preparation for turning out Sally Field and locking the door upon her, which he meant to do by main force if gentler means should fail. Her surprise at seeing him, however, and perhaps some degree of awe of his determined countenance, made her pause for a moment.

"What is all this, wife?" inquired Allen.

"I am sure I don't know. Sally has been rating me and the children this hour past, and heaven knows what for."

Sally proceeded upon this to declare a long list of offences of which Allen's family had been guilty towards her, and Allen suffered her to go on till she had exhausted her breath. When at length she lost her voice—a catastrophe which happens sooner or later to all scolds,—he took up the word.

"I'll tell you what, Sally," said he; "I am very sorry for you, and very much ashamed of you, and I should be more angry on my wife's account than you ever saw me if I did not know you well, and understand what is at the bottom of all this. Remember, Sally, I have known you and your husband since you were this high, as well as if you had been children of my own. Don't put me in mind how young you are. Don't make me treat you like a child when you have taken upon you so early to be a woman. Don't make me call your husband to take care of you as if you could not take care of yourself."

"Call him! call him and welcome, if you can find him," cried Sally. "Show me where he is, and I'll find a better use for my tongue than in scolding your mean-spirited wife there that looks as if she were going to die whenever one speaks. Go, pray, call my husband."

"Aye, aye; that's the grievance, I see," said Allen. "We all have our grievances, Sally, and it is great folly to make them worse of our own accord. Do you expect to tempt your husband to stay at home with you by scolding as you were doing just now?"

"Do you leave your wife for the twenty-four hours together?" cried Sally. "Do you make yourself drunk with your last shilling?—and yet any man had rather see his wife in a passion now and then than have her such a poor, puny, crying creature as your wife is."

"Hush, hush, mistress!" interrupted Allen. "I will lock the door upon you this moment, and would have done it before but that you would raise a mob in the street if I turned you out. Sally, you know you have not a friend in the world if you quarrel with us, and what will you do with your sore heart then?"

The poor creature's passion now dissolved in tears. She threw herself on the bed and sobbed bitterly. She was left to herself for some time. Allen produced his week's wages, and settled with his wife how they should be disposed of, and persuaded her to go out herself and make the necessary purchases, saying that he would search for Field and try to get him home. Allen's wife sighed.

"You are not afraid to trust me in an alehouse?" said he smiling.

"Bless your heart, no; that I never was nor ever shall be: but I was thinking of what you said, that we all have our grievances. Here is three shillings less wages this week."

"Yes, and another sixpence off Martha's too: but don't fret, wife; we must do as others do, and be glad if nothing worse happens. See to poor Martha's knees before you go out; she is more lame than ever to-day.—And now, Sally, if you will promise me to go to your own room, and stay there till I bring your husband back, and if you will give me your word to keep the peace with him whatever he may have been doing, I will go and search him out, and see what I can do to make him behave better to you."

Sally promised to keep the peace, but begged to stay and take care of the children till their mother should return. Seeing however that Martha looked up beseechingly in her father's face, and that the little ones clung to their mother's apron, she cursed herself for having deserved that they should be afraid of her, and ran down to bolt herself into her own room and recover her composure as she might.

As there was no fire, and as Martha was very discreet for her years, the parents promised the children to lock them up, that no scold might come and terrify them while they had to take care of themselves. Martha was advised to sit still, and her bulfinch was taken down from the window and placed beside her to be fed and watered; the other little things promised to be good, and their father and mother went, the one to the Spread-Eagle and the other to the market.

It required no great sagacity to prophesy that Field would be found at the Spread-Eagle. He varied his excursions a little, according to times and seasons: but those who knew his ways could easily guess at which of his haunts he might be expected when missing from home. When he stole out before getting to his loom in the morning, or after leaving it late at night, he generally stepped only to the dram-shop, for a glass of gin to warm him for his work, or to settle him to his sleep, as his pretence was; but when he had finished his piece and got his pay, he felt himself at liberty to go to the Spread-Eagle and have a carouse, from which he returned in the dark, sometimes reeling on his own legs, sometimes carried on other men's shoulders. This habit of drinking had grown upon him with frightful rapidity. He had, a year before, been described by his employers as a steady, well-behaved lad. He had fallen in love with Sally and married her in a hurry, found her temper disagreeable and his home uncomfortable, tried in vain to keep her in order, and then, giving up all hope, took to drinking, and would not tolerate a word of remonstrance from any one but his old friend Allen.

There were more customers this evening at the Spread-Eagle than was usual even on Saturdays. Allen was warmly welcomed as he entered, for it was supposed he came to keep company with his companions from the same factory. Almost all present were spinners and power-loom weavers under the firm of Mortimer and Rowe; and the occasion of their assembling in greater numbers than usual, was the reduction of wages which had that day taken place. Room was made for Allen as soon as he appeared, a pipe and pot of porter[1] called for, and he was welcomed to their consultation. But Allen looked round instead of taking his seat, and inquired for Field. The landlord pointed to a corner where Field lay in a drunken sleep under a bench.

"Let him lie," said one. "He is too far gone to be roused."

"What concern is it of yours?" cried another. "Come and listen to what Clack was saying."

"You shirked us in the street," said a third: "now we have caught you, we shall not let you go."

The landlord being really of opinion that Field had better lie where he was for an hour or two, Allen sat down to hear what was going on.

Clack turned to him to know what their masters deserved for lowering their wages.

"That depends upon circumstances," replied Allen. "Be they much to blame or little, something must be done to prevent a further reduction, or many of us will be ruined."

"Shake hands, my fine fellow!" cried Clack. "That was just what we had agreed. It is time such tyranny was put down, and we can put it down, and we will."

"Gently, gently," said Allen. "How do you think of putting it down?"

"Why should not we root out the one who is the most of a tyrant, and then the others may take warning before it is too late? We have nothing to do but to agree."

"No easy matter sometimes, friend."

"Stuff! we have agreed before upon a less occasion, and when there was danger in it. Had not we our combinations, when combination was against the law? and shall not we have them again now that the law lets us alone? Shall we be bold in the day of danger and shrink when that day is over?"

"Well, well, neighbour: I said nothing about being afraid. What would you have us agree to do?"

"To root out Messrs. Mortimer and Rowe. Every man in our union must be sworn not to enter their gates; and if this does not frighten the masters and make them more reasonable, I don't know what will."

"And if, instead of being frightened, the masters unite to refuse

---

1 Porter is dark malt ale.

us work till we give up our stand against Mortimer and Rowe, what are we to do then?"

"To measure our strength against theirs, to be sure. You know they can't do without us."

"Nor we without them; and where both parties are so necessary to each other, it is a pity they should fall out."

"A pity! To be sure it is a pity; but if the masters drive us to it, the blame rests with them."

"I hope," said a timid-looking man, Hare by name, who had a habit of twirling his hat when silent, and of scratching his head when he spoke, "I hope, neighbour, you will think what you are about before you mention a strike. I've seen enough of strikes. I had rather see my children on the parish than strike."[1]

Clack looked disdainfully at him, and said it was well that some dove-like folks had not to manage a fight against the eagle. For his part, he thought any man ought to be proud of the honor of making a stand against any oppression; and that he had rather, for his own share, have the thanks of the Union Committee than wear Wellington's star.[2] Would not his friend Allen say the same?

No. Allen agreed with Hare so far as thinking that there could be few worse evils than a strike; but at the same time it was an evil which might become necessary in certain cases. When convinced that it was necessary in defence of the rights of the working-man, he would join in it heart and hand; but never out of spite or revenge,—never to root out any master breathing.—So many agreed in this opinion, that Clack grew more eager than ever in defending himself and blaming the masters in question.

"Dare any one say," he cried, "that the Dey [governor] of Algiers himself is a greater tyrant than Mortimer would be if he dared? Does not he look as if he would trample us under foot if he could? Does not he smile with contempt at whatever is said by a working-man? Does not he spurn every complaint, and laugh at every threat? and if he takes it into his lofty head to do a kindness, does not he make it bitter with his pride?"

---

1 "On the parish" or "on the dole" means being supported by public charity.
2 Arthur Wellesley, first Duke of Wellington (1769-1852), member of Irish Parliament, British general, statesman, secretary of state, and prime minister (1828-30). Wellington served in India and is best known for his 1815 victory over Napoleon at Waterloo that ended the Peninsular Wars.

"All true, Clack, as everybody knows that works for Mortimer; but—"

"And as for Rowe," interrupted the talker, "he is worse if possible, in his way."

"I don't know," said Hare, doubtfully. "Mr. Rowe came once and talked very kindly with me."

"Aye, when he had some purpose to answer. We are all, except you, Hare, wise enough to know what Rowe's pretty speeches mean. You should follow him to the next masters' meeting, man, and hear how he alters his tone with his company. The mean-spirited, shuffling knave!"

"Well, well, Clack; granting that Mortimer is tyrannical and Rowe not to be trusted,—that does not alter the case about rooting them out. To make the attempt is to acknowledge at the outset that the object of our union is a bad one: it will fill the minds of the operatives[1] with foul passions and provoke a war between masters and men which will end in the destruction of both. Whenever we do strike, let it be in defence of our own rights, and not out of enmity to individuals among our employers."

Clack muttered something about there being shufflers among the men as well as the masters; to which Allen replied that the way to make shufflers was to use intimidation. The more wisdom and moderation there was in proceedings of any body of men, the better chance there was of unanimity and determination. He repeated that, as long as the Union of which he was a member kept in view the interests of the body of operatives, he would be found ready to do and to sacrifice his share; but as soon as it should set to work on other objects, he should withdraw at all risks.

Before he had done speaking, the attention of his companions was called off by an unexpected addition to their company. Music had been heard gradually approaching for some minutes, and now the musician stood darkening the door and almost deafening the people within with the extraordinary variety of sounds he produced. An enormous drum was strapped across his body; a Pan's pipe employed his mouth, and his hat, with a pointed crown and a broad brim, was garnished with bells. A little girl, fantastically dressed, performed on the triangle, and danced, and collected halfpence from the bystanders. While the musician played a jig, jerking his head incessantly from side to side, nobody thought of looking particularly at him: but when he turned to the company within doors and set his little companion to sing to his playing

---

1 Operatives refers to industrial factory workers.

"Should auld acquaintance be forgot,"

several of the debaters began to fancy that they knew the face and figure of the musician. "It is—yes, it certainly is Bray!" said one to another; and many a hand was held out to him.

"I thought you were not likely to forget old acquaintance, even if they come in a new dress," said Bray, laughing heartily, and proceeding to deposit his decorations with one or another of his former companions. He put his hat on Allen's head, slipped the strap of his drum over Clack's shoulders, and gave the triangle to Hare.

"Come," said he, "let us have a concert. It is my turn to see spinners turn strollers. Come, Allen, shake your head, man, and let us hear what comes out of it."

"How we have wondered," exclaimed Allen, "what had become of you and yours! Is that poor little Hannah that used to be so delicate?"

"The same that your good wife nursed through the measles. She would hardly know her now."

Allen shook his head.

"Ah, I see what you mean," said Bray. "You had rather see her covered with white cotton flakes than with yellow ribands [ribbons]; but remember it is no fault of mine that she is not still a piecer in yonder factory; and I don't know that I need call it my misfortune any more than my fault. Look how strong and plump she is! so much for living in the open air, instead of being mewed up in a place like an oven. Now, don't take off the hat on purpose to shake your head. What can a man do—" and looking round, he appealed to the company, "what can a proscribed [exiled, outcast] man do but get his living, so as not to have to ask for work?"

A loud clapping and shuffling of feet was the answer to his question. The noise half roused the drunken man in the corner, who rolled himself over to the terror of little Hannah, who had got as far as she could out of the way of the smokers, among whom her father had been so well received. Allen rose to go, having some hope that Field might be safely set on his legs again by this time. He asked Bray whether he meant to stay in the neighbourhood, and where he would lodge.

"You must stay," cried one, "and play a tune before your old masters' gate."

"You must stay," said another, "and see how we manage a strike now-a-days."

"A strike! Are you going to try your strength again? You will make me wish I was one of you still; but I can head the march. Stay? Yes, I'll stay and lead you on to victory. Hurra! I'll go recruiting with my drum. I'll manage to meet Mortimer, when I have a procession a mile long at my heels!"

"You lay by your drum on Sundays, I suppose?" said Allen.

"Yes, yes. We keep within and take our rest on Sundays. It is as great a treat to us to sit within doors all day once a week, as it is to some other folks to get into the green meadows. If the landlord can give us lodging, you will find us here in the morning, Allen."

"Let Hannah go home with me, Bray. I know my wife will be glad to see her and to hear her story, and this is no place for a child. If I can rouse yon sleeper, I will go now, and send my wife with a cloak or something to hide the child's frippery,[1] and then she will spend tomorrow in a fitter place than a public-house [pub]."

Bray sat gravely looking at his child for a few moments, and then started up, saying that he would undertake to rouse the sleeper. Blowing the Pan's pipe close by his ear made him start, and a rub-a-dub on the drum woke him up effectually: so that he was able, cross and miserable, to crawl homewards with the help of Allen's arm, and to be put to bed by his wife with the indistinct dread in his mind of a terrible lecture as soon as he should be in a condition to listen to it.

Chapter II: Child's Gossip

Much business was transacted at the Spread-Eagle on the Sunday by the committee of the Union. It was the general opinion that a great struggle between masters and men was on the eve of taking place, and measures were adopted for finding out what was the disposition of the operative spinners respecting a general strike, if an equalization of wages was not to be obtained by other means. It had been agreed on the Saturday night that twenty-five members of the Union should employ the Sunday in obtaining the names of as many as were willing to turn out, or to subscribe for the assistance of those who should turn out, in case of opposition from the masters. These twenty-five men were to bring in their reports on Sunday night; after which, if the affair should look promising, a petition was to be addressed to the masters, for a public meeting, at which an equalization of wages was to be agreed on.

Clack was somewhat at a loss how to apportion his own business,

---

1   As a street performer, Hannah wears an elaborate or gaudy dress, which is out of place in her old neighborhood.

and that of other people, on this occasion. Having a very high opinion of his own powers of persuasion, and being confident of his knowledge of law, he wanted to be everywhere at once, and to guide all the movements of the people he employed. As this was impossible, however, he thought it best to remain in some known place of appeal where parties might come to him for direction and information. He therefore sat at the Spread-Eagle all day big with importance, and dissatisfied only because his underlings could not be about their business abroad, and listening to him at the same time.

The Allens knew nothing of what was going forward. Mrs. Allen was so full of interest and curiosity about little Hannah Bray, that she had no thoughts to bestow on public affairs, as the transactions of the Union were commonly called. Her husband had gone early into the country with Bray this day dressed like other people, to visit some relations of the latter, who did not know what had become of him after he had been refused employment in Manchester, and obliged to betake himself to some new mode of obtaining a livelihood.[1]

Little Hannah slept till the sun was high on the Sunday morning, and might have slept longer if Mrs. Allen had not feared she would not get breakfast over in time for church. Hannah jumped up with the excuse that the place was so quiet, there was nothing to wake her.

"Indeed!" said Mrs. Allen. "We think the children and the neighbours make a great deal of noise; but I suppose you sleep in public-houses for the most part."

Hannah observed that people call so loud for what they want in public-houses, and they care so little for hours, that there is no knowing when you may sleep quietly.

"Have you no other frock than that, my dear?" asked Mrs. Allen. "I suppose you go to church on Sundays, and you cannot possibly go in all those gay ribands."

"O no," said Hannah. "I have a dark frock for Sundays, and a straw bonnet; but they are in father's pack, and I suppose that is at the Spread-Eagle."

"And he is gone into the country for the day. Well, you must change with Martha when church time comes. Poor Martha has but

---

1 Once an operative was known as an agitator, he/she was blacklisted by all area factories and so unable to work. After becoming a proscribed or outcast operative, Bray, with his daughter Hannah, becomes a homeless street performer—an ominous example to set before William Allen at this particular time.

one tidy frock; but she is too lame to go out to-day, even as far as the apothecary's; and I am sure she will lend you her frock and tippet[1] to go to church in."

Martha was willing to lend but had rather put on her factory dress than Hannah's red frock with yellow trimmings. Hannah hinted that she should like to stay within with Martha all day; and the indulgent mother, seeing Martha's pleasure at the prospect of a companion and nurse of her own age, left the little girls to amuse themselves, while she took the younger children to church with her as usual.

"Father says he heard you sing last night," said Martha when they were left alone. "Will you sing to me?"

"I am so tired of singing!" pleaded Hannah. "I don't know many songs, and I sing them so very often! Won't that bird do as well? Let me get down the cage, may I?"

"Yes do, and we will give him some water, poor fellow! He is my bird and I feed him every day. Somebody that could not afford to keep him sold him to father, and father gave him to me. Had you ever a bird?"

"No, but I had a monkey once. When we went away, father got a monkey, and I used to lead him about with a string; but I was glad when we had done with him, he was so mischievous. Look here how he tore my arm one day, when somebody had put him in a passion with giving him empty nutshells."

"What a terrible place!" said Martha. "Was it long in getting well?"

"No; father got an apothecary to tie it up, and it soon got well."

"My father is going to show my knees to Mr. Dawson, the apothecary. Do look how they are swelled; and they ache so, you can't think."

"O, but I can think, for mine used to ache terribly when I walked and stood before the wheels all day."

"But yours were never so bad as mine, or I am sure you could not dance about as you do."

"Not so bad, to be sure, and my arms were never so shrunk away as yours. Look, my arm is twice as big as yours."

"I wonder what's the reason," sighed Martha. "Mother says I get thinner and thinner."

"You should have meat for dinner every day as I have," said Hannah, "and then you would grow fat like me. Father gets such good

---

1   A tippet is a scarf of wool or fur worn around the neck.

dinners for us to what we used to have. He says 'tis that, and being in the air so much that prevents my being sickly, as I used to be. I don't think I could do the work that I used to do with all that noise, and the smell of oil and the heat."

"And I am sure I could not sing and dance as you do."

"No, how should you dance when you are so lame?"

"And I don't think I can sing at all."

"Come, try, and I will sing with you. Try 'God save the king.'"

"It is Sunday," said Martha gravely.

"Well, I thought people might sing 'God save the king' on Sundays. I have heard father play it on the drum, just before the Old Hundred. You know the Old Hundred."[1]

Martha had heard this hymn-tune at church, and she tried to sing it; but Hannah burst out a laughing.

"Lord! Martha, your voice is like a little twittering bird's. Can't you open your mouth and sing this way?"

"No, I can't," said Martha, quite out of breath; "and besides, Hannah, you should not say 'Lord!' Father and mother never let us say those sort of words."

"Nor my father either. He is more angry with me for that, than for anything; but it slips out somehow, and you would not wonder if you knew how often I hear people say that, and many worse things."

"Worse things?" said Martha, looking curious.

"Yes; much worse things; but I am not going to tell you what they are, because father made me promise not to tell you about any of the bad people that I have heard swear and seen tipsy. Was your father ever tipsy?"

"Not that I know of; but our neighbour Field is often tipsy. I am afraid every day that he will topple down stairs."

"My father was tipsy once," said Hannah, "and he beat me so, you can't think."

"When? Lately?"

"No, just after we began to stroll. Though it is so long ago, I remember it very well, for I was never so frightened in my life. I did not know where to go to get away from him; and the people pushed him about and laughed at me the more the more I cried. I asked him afterwards not to get tipsy any more, and he said he never would, and he never has. It was only because we had got more money that

---

1 "Old Hundred" refers to an old Protestant hymn.

day than we ever got in a day before: but it soon went away, for when father woke the next morning, his pocket was quite empty."

"And did you soon get some more money?"

"O yes; we get some every day except Sundays. I carry the hat round every time we stop to play, and I always get some halfpence and sometimes a silver sixpence."

"Ah! then, you get a great deal more than I do, Hannah. I brought home only three shillings this week."

"I take much more than that, to be sure; but then it is my father's earning more than mine. His great drum sounds farther and brings more people to listen than my triangle."

"Is your triangle here? I wish you would teach me to play," said Martha. "Now do. If you will, I will ask mother to show us the pictures in grandfather's bible when she comes home."

Hannah had been very fond of these pictures when she was recovering from the measles; and this bribe and her good nature together overcame her disgust at the instrument she had to play every day and almost all day long. She indulged herself with a prodigious yawn, and then began her lesson. When Mrs. Allen came back, she found the bulfinch piping at his loudest pitch to the accompaniment of the triangle, Hannah screaming her instructions to her new pupil, and poor paleface little Martha flushed with flattery and with the grand idea of earning a great many silver sixpences every day if her father would let her make music in the streets instead of going to the factory.

Chapter III: No Union of Masters

The achievements of the twenty-five who canvassed for support during Sunday were such as to put Clack into high spirits. The list of names with signatures or marks annexed, amounted to several thousands; and if the orator had been allowed to have his own way, he would have proclaimed war against the masters at once, and the turn-out would have begun on the Monday morning: but there were a few soberer folks than himself engaged in the consultation; and these smiled at this brag of the many thousand pounds that would pour in from Leeds, Coventry, Liverpool, Glasgow, and other places, and insisted upon offering the masters the option of a peaceable agreement before any measures of opposition were taken.

Clack retorted that these men were afraid of their wives, and declared that they might wait long for a strike if it was necessary to refrain till the women voted for it, since there was never a woman yet who did not hate a turn-out as she would the plague.

This observation called forth some joke at his expense, for Clack was known to be engaged to be married, and it was thought he spoke from awkward experience. In the eagerness of defence he went a step too far. He asked if it was likely, knowing the disposition of the women on this subject, that he should consult any breathing as to the part he should take, or provoke opposition from any female tongue, or care for it if he should happen to meet with it. These words were, as he might have expected, carried to the ears which should never have heard them, and prevented his next meeting with his betrothed from being the pleasantest in the world. While a storm was brewing at a distance in consequence of his indiscreet boast, Clack made himself very merry with those who were less bold than himself.

"Where is Hare to-day? Henpecked, I warrant. Did not he promise faithfully to be one of the twenty-five?"

"Yes, and he is no where to be found," said a neighbour.

"But I wonder, Clack, you troubled yourself to take a promise from such a shilly-shally fellow as Hare. His being married has nothing to do with it: he was never in the same mind for an hour together from his youth up."

"How did he get married then?"

"O there was another and a steadier mind concerned in that matter, you know: not that I mean any harm against his wife: she is as mild as she is sensible. I only mean that her judgment strengthens his when they have to act together."

"Then I suppose she does not like the idea of a strike any better than the other women, and persuades him not to come?"

"More likely she knows nothing of it. If there is one thing rather than another that Hare is afraid of, it is combination.[1] That imprisonment of his father under the old combination laws made him a coward for life; and there is no use in telling him that the law leaves us to manage our own business now as long as we keep the peace."

"He does, indeed, make a pitiful figure between his dread of belonging to the Union and his horror of being left out. But why

---

1 Combination Laws (1780, 1799) made workers' organizing (combining) against factory owners for any purpose (safer working conditions, adequate wages) illegal. Even on suspicion of organizing, workers were tried and imprisoned or transported and, sometimes, executed. The Laws were repealed in 1824 but reinstated in 1825 to prohibit strikes.

do we waste our breath upon him? Who has seen Allen to-day, and why does he not come? We shall count his modesty for backwardness if he does not take care."

"Don't be in a hurry to blame a better man than yourself," said a neighbour. "Allen has been in the country all day."

There was no offence in such a comparison; for Allen was generally looked up to as the first man in that branch of the Union, though he was so little aware of his own merits that he did not come forward so much as he should have done, except on urgent occasions; and then he never failed to do all that was expected of him.

When the petition to the masters to hold a public meeting was prepared, and when Clack had appointed himself and two others to carry it round the next day, the Committee terminated their present sitting.

The first man to which the deputies addressed their petition was that of Mortimer and Rowe.

"Are the partners at home?" they inquired.

"I don't know whether Mr. Mortimer is here yet, but there is Mr. Rowe. Sir! Mr. Rowe!" called the clerk, as he saw the junior partner making his escape, "these men wish to speak with you, sir, if you please."

Mr. Rowe, perceiving that he had been seen, came forward to be spoken with.

"A public meeting,—equalization of wages,—aye, very fair: hum! very well, my good fellows. Well: what do you want me to do?"

"To give your voice in favour of this public meeting."

"Why, you know you have a good friend in me. You surely cannot anticipate any difficulty with me. I am a friend of peace, you know. No man more so."

"Aye, sir: but there is more than one sort of peace. The masters have called it peace when they had all their own way, and their men were cowed by the law and dared not openly resist. The men call it peace when the two parties have confidence in each other, and make a cordial agreement, and keep to it. This is what we want at the present time."

So said Gibson, whose turn it was to be spokesman; but Clack could not help putting in his word.

"And if either party refuses peace, you know, sir, the next thing is war."

"O, no war!" said Mr. Rowe. "A cordial agreement, as you say, is the right thing. So, for this purpose you wish for a public meeting. Well; I shall be happy to attend a public meeting, if—"

"We are happy to find you so agreeable, sir. Will you just sign for self and partner, if you please."

"Sign! I see no signatures."

"Because you happen to be the first person we have applied to, sir; that is all. We hope for signatures plenty before the day is over. Will you please to sign, as you approve of the meeting?"

Mr. Rowe suddenly recollected that he must consult his partner who sat in a back room. The men had not to wait long. The junior partner, indeed, did not appear again, but Mr. Mortimer issued forth, looking not a whit less haughty than usual. He begged the deputies would make the best of their way off his premises, as he had nothing to say to them.

What were his sentiments respecting the meeting, if they might inquire?

His sentiments were, that the masters had been far too tolerant already of the complaints of the men; and that it was time the lower orders were taught their proper place. He had neither leisure nor inclination to argue with any of them, either there or elsewhere; so the sooner they took themselves off the better.

"You may live to change your sentiments, sir," observed Gibson.

"Beware of threats!" said Mr. Mortimer. "There is law yet for the punishment of threats, remember."

"I have neither forgotten the law, Mr. Mortimer, nor used threats. I said, and I say again, you may live to change your sentiments; and, for your own sake, it is to be hoped you will. Good morning, sir."

"He is too busy even to wish us good morning," observed Clack. "How coolly he looked over the letter he took from his clerk, as if we were not worth attending to for a moment!"

"Haughty as he is," said Gibson, "I would sooner bear with his pride than Rowe's behaviour or Elliott's."

"They are young men, Gibson, and Mortimer is old, and we would sooner bear with an old man's mistakes than a young man's, be they what they may! Where next? To Elliott's?"

"Yes, we are sure of being ill-treated there; so the sooner it is over the better."

As they approached Mr. Elliott's house, they perceived that gentleman mounted on his favourite hunter, and in the act of leaving his own door. He was too much occupied with his own affairs to see them coming, for the most important part of his morning's business was setting off for his ride; and he had eyes for little else while he was admiring the polish of his boots, adjusting his collar, settling the skirts of his coat, and patting his horse's neck. Clack was not the man for ceremony; he came straight up before the horse, and laid his hand on the handsome new rein, saying, "By your leave, sir—"

"Hands off," cried Elliott, giving him a cut across the knuckles with his riding whip. "How dare you stop me? How dare you handle my rein with your greasy fingers?"

"How would you get such a rein, I wonder, sir, if we did not grease our fingers in your service?" said Clack, indignantly.

"I'm in a hurry," said Elliott; "you can speak to the people within, if you want any thing."

"We will not detain you, sir," said Taylor, who was now spokesman, "but nobody but yourself can answer our question." And he told the story in a few words, and put the petition into the gentleman's hands.

Elliott glanced his eye over it as well as the restlessness of his horse would permit, and then struck it contemptuously with his riding-whip into the mud, swore that that was the proper place for such a piece of insolence, rode up against the men, and pranced down the street without bestowing another look or word upon them.

"Pride comes before a fall; let the gentleman take care of himself," said Gibson, quietly picking up the petition and wiping off the mud with his handkerchief.

Clack talked about using his greasy fingers to cram the soiled petition down the gentleman's throat, and seemed disposed to harangue the laughing bystanders; but his more prudent companions took him by the arm and led him away. Mr. Elliott's clerk, who had seen the whole proceeding from an upper window, and was ashamed of his master's conduct, came after them, out of breath, to ask them in while he copied the petition, which was not, as he observed, fit to show to any other gentleman. Gibson thanked him for his civility, but observed that the soiled paper would tell part of their story better than they could tell it themselves. The clerk, therefore, slowly returned, saying to himself that it is a pity when young men, coming to a large fortune obtained in trade, forget by whose means their wealth was acquired, and by what tenure it is held.

After visiting several manufacturers, some of whom were more and others less favourable to their claims than they expected, the deputies requested an interview with Mr. Wentworth. Mr. Wentworth had been rich as a young man, had failed through unavoidable misfortunes, and had worked his way up again to a competence, after having paid every shilling he owed. He was now an elderly man, homely in his person, somewhat slovenly in his dress, not much given to talk, and, when he did speak, causing some surprise and weariness to strangers by the drawling twang of his speech. Those who knew him well, however, had rather hear his voice than any music; and such of his men as belonged to the Union agreed that ten words from him were worth a speech of an hour long from Clack. There was, to be sure, no need for so many words from him as from other people, for he practised a great variety of inarticulate sounds, the meaning of which was well understood by those accustomed to converse with him, and deserved all the purposes of a reply.

Mr. Wentworth was sitting at his desk when the deputies were introduced. As they uncovered their heads and made their bow, some murmurings and clutterings reached them which they understood as a welcome. He looked steadily at them from under his shaggy eyebrows while they explained their business, and then took the petition to look over.

"You can hardly have any paper-makers in your Union," said he, chuckling as he unfolded the sheet; "or are you saving your pence against a strike, that you can't afford paper as fair as your writing?"

"Aye, aye; wait a while and you will see him grow wiser," was his observation on hearing the story of Elliott's insolence. "We were all boys before we were men.—Hum:—equalization.—Who will avouch that this equalization is all that you want?"

"I, sir," said the ever-ready Clack—"I drew it up, and so I ought to know."

Gibson observed, that though no further object was expressly contemplated by the Union, he would not answer for their not increasing their demands as they proceeded. If there was any attempt to equalize the wages by reducing all to the lowest now given, the Union would demand an advance.

"Who gives the lowest?" inquired Mr. Wentworth.

"Except some upstarts whom we can easily manage, Mortimer and Rowe give the lowest, and you, sir, the next lowest, and Elliott the highest."

"Who was lamenting lately that the combination laws were repealed, so that the masters cannot be prosecuted for oppression? Who proposed to burn them in effigy, tied to one another's necks?"

The deputies looked at one another, and then answered that all this was only private talk of one of their meetings; it was never meant for earnest.

"Well, I only let you know that you may look about your Committee-room and find where the little bird builds that carries the matter; and if you can't find her, take care that she has nothing to carry that you would be ashamed to own. Did you learn from her that the masters combine against you?"

"We learn it from our own eyes, and ears, and senses," said Clack. "Have not masters oppressed their men from the beginning of the world?"

"Indeed I don't know," said Mr. Wentworth. "If Adam had a gardener under him in Paradise, they might have tried to turn one another out, but I never heard of it."

"Stuff and nonsense, sir, begging your pardon. Don't we know that masters always have lorded it over the poor? They were born with a silver spoon in their mouths, and —"

"I wonder where mine is," observed Mr. Wentworth; "I will look in my mother's plate chest for it."

The orator went on,—

"They openly treat us like slaves as long as they can, and when we will bear it no longer, they plot in secret against us. They steal to one another's houses when they think we are asleep; they bolt their doors and fill their glasses to their own prosperity, and every bumper that goes down their throats is paid for with the poor man's crust."

"They must have made the little bird tipsy, Clack, before she carried you such a strange story as that."

"Don't tell me, sir, that it is not true! Don't tell me!"

"I am not telling you anything; for the plain reason, that I have nothing to tell. I only want to ask you one or two things, as you seem to know so much more than we do. Pray what have the masters combined for just now?"

"To lower our wages, to be sure."

"And yet Mortimer pays one rate, and I another, and Elliott another. Why don't I ask as much labour for my money as Mortimer?"

"You dare not," cried Clack.

"You know it's not fair," said Taylor.

"You are not the man to grind the poor," said Gibson.

"You have not hit it, any of you. You all seem to think it is a matter of pure choice with us, what wages we give."

"To be sure," said Clack, "and that is the reason we want parliament to settle the matter at once and for ever."

"Parliament has no more choice in the matter than we masters," drily observed Mr. Wentworth. "If ever Parliament passes a bill to regulate wages, we must have a rider put to it to decree how much rain must fall before harvest."

Clack muttered something about not standing any longer to be trifled with; but his companions thought it possible that Mr. Wentworth might have something to say that was worth hearing, and persuaded the orator to be quiet. Gibson inquired,—

"Where then does the choice rest, sir, if neither with the government nor the masters?"

"Such power as there is rests with those who take, not with those who give wages. Not such power as tips our friend's tongue there," nodding at Clack, "not such power as you gain by the most successful strike, not such power as combination gives you, be it peaceable or threatening; but a much more lasting power which cannot be taken from you. The power of the masters is considerable, for they hold the administration of capital; but it is not on this that the rate of wages depends. It depends on the administration of labour; and this much greater power is in your hands."

The deputies thought that they who pay wages must always have power over those who receive.

"That is as much as saying that wages are a gift. I thought you had supposed them your right."

All were eager to urge the rights of industry.

"Aye, all very true; no right can be clearer when we see what wages are. Come, Clack, tell us, (for who knows if you don't?) tell us what wages Adam gave his under gardeners. You can't say? Why, I thought you knew all that the masters did at the beginning of the world. Well, when Adam was some hundred years old, (you may trust me, for I am descended from him in a straight line,) he said to Eve, 'Stay you here and spin with the women, while I go yonder and set my men to delve; and don't expect us back in a hurry, for tillage is tough work here to what it was in Eden, and we must gather our crops before we can bring them to market. Come, my good fellows, work hard and you shall have your shares.' 'And pray, sir,' said the men, 'what are we to live upon while our fruit and vegetables are growing?' 'Why,' says Adam, 'instead of my sharing the fruit with you when it is grown, suppose you take your portion in advance. It may be a convenience to you, and it is all the same thing to me.' So the men looked at the ground, and calculated how much digging and other work there would be, and then named their demand; not in silver money with king George's head upon it, but food and clothing, and tools."

"Then at harvest time," observed Gibson, "the whole produce belonged to Adam?"

"Of course. The commodity was made up, like all commodities, of capital and labour: Adam's capital and the men's labour."

"And of a deal besides," cried Clack. "If it was grain, there was the root, and the stalk, and the ear; and if it was fruit, there was the rind, and the pulp, and the juice."

"Begging your pardon, friend, there was nothing but capital and labour. Without labour, and the soil and the tools which made the capital, there would have been neither grain nor fruit; and if grain and fruit grew wild, they could be no commodity without labour, any more than the diamond in the mine, and the pearl in the sea, are a commodity before the one is dug, and the other fished up. Well, Adam and his men expected to get as much by their crop as would pay for their subsistence and their toil; and this much the men asked, and Adam was willing to give, and a fair surplus remained over for himself. So they made their bargain, and he bought their share of the commodity, and had to himself all the flax and other things that his produce exchanged for in the market. And so that season passed off, and all were contented."

"And what happened next season, sir?"

"Next season, twice the number of men came to ask work in the same plot of ground. Adam told them that he had very little more wages to pay away than he had the year before, so that if they all wanted to work under him they must be content with little more than half what each had formerly earned. They agreed, and submitted to be rather pinched; but they hoped it would be only for a time, as it was a very fine harvest indeed, so much labour having been spent upon it, and there being a fine profit into Adam's pocket."

"Did they wear pockets then, sir?"

"No doubt; for the women were improving their tailoring, as much as the men their gardening, and expecting, like them, to increase their gains in consequence; and so they would have done, but that four times the number of labourers appeared next year, so that, notwithstanding the increase of capital, each had not so much as one-third the original wages; and the men grew very cross, and their wives very melancholy. But how could Adam help it?"

"Why did not the men carry their labour elsewhere?" asked Clack contemptuously.

"Why do you go on spinning for Mortimer and Rowe, when Elliott pays higher wages?"

"Because nobody is taking on new hands. I can't get work."

"Well, nobody was taking on new hands in Adam's neighbourhood; all the capital was already employed."

"But I don't mean to go on so," said Clack. "I shall strike with all the rest of Mortimer's men, if we don't get better paid."

"Aye, it is as I thought, Clack. Adam's head labourer was your grandfather, for he said just the same thing you are saying; and what is more, he did it. They all turned out, every man of them, and let the field take care of itself."

"And what happened?"

"Only half a harvest came up; so that, of course, wages were lower than ever next year. The worst folly of all was that they went on to blame Adam, though he showed them that the harvest would not even pay its own expenses; much less leave anything to divide between him and them. 'You talk to me,' says he, 'as if I could get capital down from the clouds as fast as I please: whereas you might have seen from the beginning, that I have a certain quantity and no more. If you choose to bring a thousand labourers to live upon the capital which was once divided among a hundred, it is your fault and not mine that you are badly off.'"

"If the thousand men agreed to live for so little, it was their own affair, to be sure."

"And if they did not agree, their bidding against each other could not shift the blame upon Adam. If there was such competition among the men as to enable him to obtain more labour for the same wages, he was not to blame, was he, for employing three men for what he had at first paid to one?"

"Nor were the men to blame, sir, for bargaining for such wages as were to be had."

"Certainly. Where then was the evil?"

"Clearly in there being too many hands for the work to be done," replied Gibson. "But who could help that, sir?"

"Nobody could relieve the immediate pressure, Gibson, unless some had the means of taking themselves off, or of applying their labour to some employment which was less overstocked; but all had it in their power to prevent the evil returning. By foresight and care, labour may be proportioned to capital as accurately as my machinery to the power of my steam-engine."

"What has all this to do with our petition?" asked the orator, who was impatient of remaining so long in the background.

"A great deal," replied Gibson. "Mr. Wentworth means to point out how much rests with the masters, and how much with the men, and to warn us against a strike. But, sir, about equalization of wages: you think that fair enough, I suppose. In the very same market, and under the very same circumstances, labour ought to be paid at the same rate, surely?"

"One circumstance, you know, is the extent of the master's capital, which is seldom the same in any two cases, and on which his power of waiting for his returns depends. But I agree with you that a man cannot safely lower his rate of wages much and permanently below that of his competitors, and that an equalization of wages is desirable for all parties; so I will sign my agreement to your wish for a public meeting. Coming, Charles, coming."

Gibson had observed Mr. Wentworth's old gray pony in the yard for some time, and he now saw that Charles looked tired of leading it backwards and forwards while the animal turned its head one way and another, as if looking for its usually punctual master. While helping the gentleman on with the heavy great-coat, which he wore winter and summer, the deputy apologized for having kept the rider and his steed so long asunder.

"Never mind," drawled Mr. Wentworth. "Dobbin and I have two rounds, a long, and a short; and I dare say he has made up his mind already which it will be to-day. If I have helped you to a short cut to your business, you will not think your time wasted any more than I." Then as he buttoned the last button, and pulled his hat over his brows, "That's well: all tight. Hey ho, Dobbin! Good day to ye all."

The shaggy pony pricked up his ears, quickened his pace, and well nigh nodded to his master at the sound of his voice. When Mr. Wentworth scrambled up into the saddle and left the yard at a funeral pace, the deputies looked with much more respect on him and his equipage, than on the brilliant spectacle they had met at Elliott's door.

Chapter IV: Union of Men

As soon as it was ascertained that, though many of the masters declined committing themselves by signing their names, most or all of them would attend the desired meeting, Clack took upon himself to issue a placard, whose large red and black letters attracted the eyes of all who could read. It made known the intention of the masters to meet at the York Hotel, on the Wednesday afternoon, and of the Committee of the men to hold a previous meeting at the Spread-Eagle, in the morning, in order to prepare resolutions to be laid before the masters. The Committee was to be escorted to and fro by a circuitous route by a procession; and the place appointed where those were to meet who wished to make apart of the show, was St. George's Fields. The placard began and ended by an appeal to the people to guard their rights against oppression. Many were surprised at the anxiety of the leading men among the spinners to disown this placard. It seemed to the crowd very spirited and eloquent, and they began to look out their decorations for the procession.

Bray was one of the first on the spot, piping, drumming, and shaking his bells at the appearance of every new group. Other musicians joined the train, flags were displayed, the women gathered to look on, the children cheered and brought green boughs, and all had the appearance of rejoicing, though it would have been difficult for any one to say what there was to rejoice about. Many had no clear idea of what was doing or going to be done: some had no idea at all, and those who knew best thought it a pity that such a display should have been made as might bear the appearance of being intended to intimidate the masters. The Committee were so generally of this opinion, that they did not attend, but went quietly, one by one, to the Spread-Eagle; so that, in fact, the procession was formed to escort Clack, and nobody else. This was all the more glorious for him, he thought; and he walked proudly just behind the chief musician, Bray, now shaking hands from side to side, now bowing with his hand on his heart, now bidding all halt and giving the signal for groans or cheers. There were three groans at Mortimer and Rowe's, and three cheers at Elliott's, which were received with infinite disdain by that gentleman as he sat at his breakfast table, balancing his egg-spoon and glancing at the newspaper. The procession next overtook Mr. Wentworth in Chancery Lane, pacing to business on his gray pony. All eyes were turned to Clack for a signal whether to groan or cheer. There was, in the meanwhile, a faint beginning of each, at which the pony looked more astonished than his master, who only chuckled and murmured in his usual manner as he looked upon the assemblage with a quiet smile.

"What do you expect to get by this fine show?" said he to a youth near him.

"Cheap bread! Hurrah!" cried the lad waving his bludgeon, and wishing there was a loaf on the top of it.

"And you, and you, and you?" said Mr. Wentworth to one and another as they passed.

"No potato peelings! Reform and good wages! Liberty and cheap bread!" cried they, according to their various notions. The children's only idea was (and it was the wisest) that it was a holiday, with a procession and a band of music.

When Clack had got a little a-head of the slow-moving pony and its rider, he decided to halt and hold a short parley. Advancing with a bow, he said,

"You call yourself the poor man's friend, I believe, sir?"

"No man's enemy, I hope," replied Mr. Wentworth.

"Then allow us the honour of giving you three cheers on your pledge to support our interests this evening. Hats off!"

"Better wait awhile," said Mr. Wentworth. "Cheers will keep, and I dislike unnecessary pledges."

Clack looked suspicious, and nods and winks went round.

"We might differ, you know, as to what your interests are, and then I might seem to break my word when I did not mean it."

"Let him go free," said a bystander. "He knows the consequences if he opposes us."

"That is rather a strange way of letting me go free," observed the gentleman, smiling. "However, friend, threats are empty air to a man who knows his own mind; and my mind is made up to consider the interests of all, come groans, come cheers."

"It is not everybody, sir, who would speak so independently,—to our faces too."

"True, friend. All the masters and all the men have not my years, and have not learned to look steadily in honest faces; and that is why I am sorry to see this parade, which looks too much like intimidation. Come now, be persuaded. I will give you house-room for your flags, and my old friend Bray there shall not lose his job; he shall make it a holiday to the children in my factory."

It was too much to ask of Clack. He could not give up his procession, and so made haste to march on. As Mr. Wentworth turned in at his factory gate in Ancoats Street, every man in the long train bowed respectfully. In his case, the regard of his neighbours was not measured by the rate of wages he paid.

The procession, having deposited Clack at the Spread-Eagle, was by no means so ready to depart as to arrive. They insisted that it should be an open meeting, and that they should have a voice in the demands to be offered to the masters. They rushed through the house to the skittle-ground[1] behind, caused a table with paper and ink to be placed in an arbour, and, setting the Committee entirely aside on the plea that this was a special occasion, began to call aloud for Allen to take the chair. Allen was nowhere to be found on the premises, for the good reason that he was at his work, and knew little of what was going on. Being sent for, he presently appeared and asked what he was wanted for.

---

1   Skittles is a British version of the game of bowling, a traditional pub
    game played with nine pins and a wooden ball on a special lane or alley.

"To take the chair."

But Allen was too modest to accept the honour at a word; he drew back, and urged his being totally unused to come forward at public meetings, and named several who understood the management of that kind of business better than himself. Those that he named were all single men; for he bore in mind,—and this certainly added to his reluctance,—that the sin of taking a prominent part in a combination of workmen, is apt to be remembered against the sinner when the days of trouble are over; and he felt that a family man was not the one who ought to be made to incur the risk. When further pressed, he did not scruple to declare this to be one of his objections; but the people were in the humour to overcome objections, and they promised faithfully that he and his family should not be injured; that if discharged from the factory, they should be maintained by the Union; and that as no one knew so much of their affairs as Allen, as he could express himself with moderation in speech, and with ease on paper, he was the man to be at the head of their affairs, and that it was his bounden duty to accept the office.

Allen could not deny this, and did not, therefore, dally with his duty; but it cost him a bitter pang. While Clack listened and looked on with a feeling of jealousy, and thought it a moment of triumph such as he would fain have enjoyed himself, he little knew how little Allen was to be envied. He could not guess what feelings rushed on Allen's mind at the moment that he took the decisive step into the arbour and seated himself at the table, and received the pen into his hand. Thoughts of the dismay of his timid wife, of the hardships to which he might expose his children, of the difficulties of his office, and the ill-will which its discharge must sometimes bring upon him,—thoughts of the quarrels in which he must mediate, and of the distress which, in case of a turn-out, he must witness, without much power to relieve,—might have overcome a man of firmer nerve than Allen; but though they distressed, they did not conquer him, convinced as he was that he ought not to evade the choice of the people. His fellow-labourers allowed him a few minutes to collect his thoughts before addressing them, and while he was seemingly arranging the papers before him, they packed themselves and one another closely, in order to leave room for new comers, without creating a noise and bustle. Those who stood nearest the arbour hung the flags so as to make a sort of canopy over it, and a few of the most efficient of the standing Committee took their places on each side of Allen.—His address was in natural accordance with the feelings which had just passed through his mind:—

"Combinations are necessary, my fellow-labourers, when one set of men is opposed to another, as we are to our masters. The law could not prevent combinations, even when severe punishments visited those who were engaged in them; which was a clear proof that men must combine, that the law was of no use, and ought therefore to be done away. Let me congratulate you that these severe laws are done away; that a man cannot now be shut up in prison for many months together for agreeing with his companions to withhold their labour in order to increase its price. Let me congratulate you that when a man cannot be caught in the trap of the combination laws, he can no longer be punished under a law against conspiracy, which was made long before such a thing as combinations of workmen were thought of. We can now meet in the face of day, and conduct our bargains with our masters either by agreement or opposition, without any one having a right to interfere, as long as we keep the peace. Evils there are, indeed, still; and such a thing is still heard of as persecution in consequence of a combination; but such evils as are inflicted by the crushing hand of power light on a few, and the devotion of those few secures the exemption of the rest. It is certainly an evil to a peaceably disposed man to see himself regarded with a fierce eye by those to whom he no longer dares touch his hat lest he should be accused of suing for mercy. It is certainly an evil to a man of independent mind to be placed under the feet of any former enemy, to receive his weekly subsistence from the hands of his equals, and to fancy that the whisper is going round—'This is he who lives upon our gathered pence.'—Such evils await, as you know, him who comes forward to lead a combination; but they belong to the state of affairs; and since they can neither be helped, nor be allowed to weigh against the advantages of union, they should be, not only patiently, but silently borne. Well is it for the victim if he can say to himself that now is the time for him to practise the heroism which in grander scenes has often made his bosom throb. He may even esteem himself honoured in his lot being somewhat of the same cast,—though his own consciousness alone may perceive the resemblance,—something of the same cast, I say, with that of venerated statesmen who have returned to the plough to be forgotten in their own age, and remembered in another,—with that of generals who have held out the decrepit hand with a petition to the gay passers by to give a halfpenny to the deliverer of their country.— Nay, no cheers yet! Your cheers only recall me with shame to that which I was going to say when my personal feelings led me away,— led me to compare that which is universally allowed to be moving because it is noble, with that which, if moving at all, is so only because it is piteous. As I was saying, combinations are ordered by laws more powerful than those which, till lately, forbade them; and this shows the wisdom of the repeal of the latter. If it had been wished to prevent our meeting for caprice or sport, laws might have availed. If their object had been to hinder the idle from meeting to dissipate their tediousness, or the gamesome from pursuing that on which no more valuable thing was staked than their present pleasure, these laws might have been successfully, though somewhat tyrannically, enforced. But such are not they who form combinations: but rather such as have their frames bowed with over-toil, and their brows knit with care, such as meet because the lives and health of their families, their personal respectability, and the bare honesty of not stealing a loaf from another man's counter, are the tremendous stake which they feel to be put to hazard. Sound and wise laws can restrain the fiercest passions of the few, because, being sound and wise, they are supported by the many; and it is therefore clear that when laws give way like cobwebs before the impulse of a body of men too united to be brought together by caprice, those laws are neither wise nor sound. Such were the combination laws, and therefore were they repealed. Never again will it be attempted to set up the prohibition of parliament against the commands of nature,—a threat of imprisonment against the cravings of hunger. Security of person and property being provided for, (as, indeed, they were already by former laws,) we are left free to make the best agreement we can for the sale of our labour, and to arrange our terms by whatever peaceable methods we choose.

"Combination on our part is necessary from power being lodged unequally in the hands of individuals, and it is necessary for labourers to be balanced against the influence and wealth of capitalists. A master can do as he pleases with his hundred or five hundred workmen, unless they are combined. One word of his mouth, one stroke of his pen, can send them home on the Saturday night with a blank prospect of destitution before them; while these hundred or five hundred men must make their many wills into one before his can even be threatened with opposition. One may tremble, another may mourn, a third may utter deep down in his heart the curses he dares not proclaim; but all this is of no avail. The only way is to bring opposition to bear upon the interests of the master; and this can only be done by union. The best of the masters say, and probably with truth, that their interests demand the reductions under which we groan. Be it so: we have interests too, and we must bring them up as an opposing force, and see which are the strongest. This may be,—allow me to say, must be—done without ill-will in any party towards any other party. There may be some method yet unknown by which the interests of all may be reconciled; if so, by union we must discover it. But if, indeed, interests must continue to be opposed, if bread must be fought for, and the discord of men must for ever be contrasted with the harmony of nature, let the battle be as fair as circumstances will allow. Let the host of pigmies try if they cannot win a chance against the regiment of giants by organizing their numbers, and knitting them into a phalanx.[1] The odds against them are fearful, it is true; but more desperate battles have been sustained and won. I have not indeed, as the friend at my elbow reminds me, represented our case so favourably as I might have done. Many here think that the power is in our own hands; some that the chances are equal, and the less sanguine, that the chance fair.—I have spoken of the general necessity of union, and not with any intention of taking for granted that we are on the eve of an express struggle. This depends on circumstances yet to be disclosed. Some change, and that a speedy one, there ought to be in the condition of the working classes: they cannot go on long labouring their lives away for a less recompense than good habitations, clothing, and food. These form the very least sum of the just rewards of industry; whereas a multitude are pinched with the frosts of winter, live amidst the stench of unwholesome dwellings in summer, have nearly forgotten the taste of animal food, and even sigh for bread as for a luxury. The question to be debated, and to be put to the trial if necessary,—and I wish every master in Manchester was here to take down my words for his further consideration, is whether a social being has not a right to comfortable subsistence in return for his full and efficient labour."—Allen's pause was interrupted by a voice from behind the crowd, declaring,—

"No doubt, no doubt, my good fellows: a clear right, and I wish with all my heart you may win your right."

It was Rowe, who had entered as if for the purpose of convincing

---

1   Pigmies, also pygmies, a tribe in central Africa of small stature, compared with Europeans. A phalanx is a body of troops, organized in opposition, presenting a united front. Allen draws an analogy between the disempowered workers (pygmies) and the middle-class manufacturers (giants), urging that, despite the odds, presenting a united front (phalanx) through union organizing was essential to facilitating social and economic change for the workers.

the men that he was on their side. An opening was made from the table to the outskirts of the crowd; but Rowe slunk back in opposition to all attempts to push him forward. The fact was, he saw another person present whom he little expected to meet, and before whom he was sorry to have committed himself. Mr. Wentworth advanced through the opening, with his memorandum book in his hand:—

"I am willing to put down your question, Allen, for further discussion, provided you add a clause to it:—'Whether a member of society has not a right to a comfortable subsistence in return for full and efficient labour, *provided he does not, by his own act, put that subsistence beyond his reach?*'"

Allen smiled, and all within hearing stared at Mr. Wentworth's simplicity in adding this clause which nobody could dispute.

"We have certainly nothing to object to your addition, sir," said Allen. "Only I cannot think it necessary."

"Let it stand, however, for my satisfaction; and now go on with what you have to say."

A seat was offered to Mr. Wentworth, and proclamation was made of one for Mr. Rowe, who, however, had disappeared. Allen proceeded:—

"I have only a few words to add respecting the terms on which I will consent to resume my present office on any future occasion, or to accept of any power you may wish to put into my hands. I must be supported by you in all measures taken to preserve our own peace and that of the masters; and to this end, there must be the utmost strictness in the full performance of all contracts. Whether the present dispute be amicably settled this very evening, or whether it be protracted, or a partial or a general strike should take place,—none of these things can set aside a contract previously entered into. Integrity must be our rule as much as liberty is our warrant and justice our end. The first man who deserts the work he has pledged himself to perform, puts the weapon of the law into the hands of our opponents; the first who is legally convicted of a breach of contract, brands our cause with indelible disgrace. We want no truants here, and we will own none but honest labourers to be of our company; and unless I am aided in preserving the reputation of our cause, I declare,—whatever may be thought of the importance of the threat,—that from that moment I withdraw my countenance and my help. If at the period of any strike, any part of my contract with my employers is undischarged, I shall hold it to be my duty to work for them during the stated number of hours, even if I should repair from their factory to preside over a meeting like the present; and the same is expected of every man who enrolls himself in our bands. Honour towards our masters is as necessary as fidelity to each other."

The meeting having signified an unanimous assent to what Allen had said, he proceeded to draw up a statement of wages to be presented to the masters. A great number of men pushed and jostled one another in order to get near the table and state their grievances; for some under every firm supposed their wages to be the lowest wages, and Elliott the highest.—Mortimer and Rowe were therefore to be requested to answer this evening, yes or no, whether they would give Elliott's rate of wages. Allen, Clack, and Gibson were deputed to wait on the masters with the written demand.

The meeting broke up for a while, and the quietest and most industrious of the men went home, while the rest prepared to parade again through the streets.

Allen withdrew one of the last, as he wished to see the place quiet before he left his post. As he turned from the door of the public-house, his hands in his pockets and his eyes bent on the ground in deep thought, he was startled by someone taking his arm. It was his wife, who had been watching and lingering in the neighbourhood till she was tired and frightened.

"Why, Mary," said her husband, smiling, "you will make me lose my good name. This is the way wives haunt the public-house when their husbands are given to drink."

Mary could trust her husband for soberness if ever woman could; but she feared his being drawn in to join against the masters, and bring ruin on his family.

Allen answered that he was not the man to be *drawn in* to do what his wife knew he disliked as much as she could do; but he might of his own free choice determine to do what she feared; and, in that case, he trusted the discharge of his public duty would not be embittered by domestic opposition and discontent. His prospect was not a very cheering one, however, in this respect. When fairly seated in his own home, his wife seemed prodigiously inclined to lock the door and pocket the key; and she cried so piteously at the bare idea of a strike and its distresses, that Allen longed to go to sleep, and forget all that had been done, and all that was in prospect.

Chapter V: No Progress Made

The masters' meeting was a tedious affair to all parties. The chairman and the three deputies held such long disputes, as to whether wages were really much lower than formerly, that the people who waited in anxious expectation at the Spread-Eagle, began to wonder whether the deputies had lain down to take a nap, or found their business a different kind of affair from what they had expected. If they had known what point was in dispute, they would have wondered what room there was for argument, as any man among them could have told what he was paid two years before, and what now. They all knew that they were now paid by Mortimer and Rowe, only three and fourpence per one thousand hanks,[1] while some time before, they had upwards of four shillings. How, they would have asked, could there be any doubt as to whether wages were lowered?

Clack was profuse in his expressions of astonishment at the stupidity of those who made a question of so plain a matter; but his wonder did no more toward settling the point than the shuffling of the chairman, who did not understand the true state of the case, and could therefore render no service in throwing light upon it.

If it had not been for Mr. Wentworth, and one or two more who held his view, nothing at all would have been done.

"Nobody doubts," observed Wentworth, "that you now take so many shillings less than you took five years ago; but that matters nothing to you or to us."

The chairman and Clack stared in about an equal degree.

"My dear sir, that is the very point," said the one.

"I always thought you had had a heart to feel for the poor," cried the other.

"I beg your pardon," said the gentleman quietly, "it is not, sir, the point in dispute, and I trust, Clack, my observation does not carry any great cruelty in it. If a penny a week would enable a man to buy all necessaries for himself and his family, and if a pound would do no more, would it signify to any man whether his wages were a penny or a pound?"

"Certainly not; but who ever heard of such wonderful pennies?"

"I have heard of shillings which you might think nearly as wonderful as such pennies: shillings which would buy more than twice as much at one time as at another."

"To be sure," said Clack, laughing contemptuously, "every child knows that the price of bread and other things rises and falls."

"Very well. Your concern is about how much of bread and other things you get in return for your labour, and not how many shillings.

---

1 A hank is a length of thread, typically 840 yards of cotton or 300 yards of linen.

Shillings are of no value to you but for what they buy. If half the money in the kingdom were to be carried off by fairies this night, so that you could have only half your present nominal wages, you would be no worse off than at present. The same quantity of food and clothing would be in the market, and you would get as much for sixpence as you now get for a shilling. This is why I said the nominal amount of your wages mattered little. I said nothing about the real amount."

"But you do not deny, sir," said Allen, "that our real wages are less than they were?"

"I am afraid it is as true as that our profits are less. There is less surplus remaining over our manufacture for us to divide. If this division were made in kind, instead of your being paid in money in advance, you would see the real state of the case,—that we cannot afford higher wages."

"In kind! Lord, sir," cried Clack, "what should we do with a bundle of yarns on Saturday night? what baker or grocer would take them?"

"None I dare say; and therefore, for the convenience of the parties, payment for labour is made in money; but it is not the less true that your wages consist of the proportion you receive of the return brought by the article you manufacture. You know how the value of this return varies; how, when an article is scarce, it brings in a large return, and how, when it is plentiful, our customers give less for it; and you must therefore see how your wages vary independently of our will."

"But whose doing is it, sir, that the return varies so much?"

"It is partly your doing; I mean that of those who bring labour to market. We masters have nothing to do with the quantity of labour brought to sale any further than to purchase it. If you bring so much as to reduce its price too far, whose fault is that?"

"To be sure we cannot expect you to pay high, when you can purchase labour cheap," said Allen, "any more than we would give sixpence for a loaf, if we could get as good a one for fivepence."

"If," observed one of the masters, "you brought only half the present quantity of labour to us, we must, whether we liked it or no, pay double for it. If you choose to bring up large families who will in turn rear large families to the same occupation, it is a necessary consequence that wages will fall to the very lowest point."

"What do you call the lowest point?"

"That at which the labourer can barely subsist. If he cannot subsist, he cannot labour, of course. If he can do more than merely subsist, his wages are not at the lowest point."

"Ours are so now," said Gibson, despondingly.

"Not exactly so," replied the manufacturer. "Don't fancy that I wish them lower, or would not make them higher if I could; but I cannot allow that they are at the lowest. Do you know no Irish hand-loom weavers who make only four shillings a week?"

"Poor creatures! yes; but how do they live? Crowded together on straw, with mere rags to cover them, and only half as much food as they could eat. It is dreadful!"

"It is; and God forbid we should see many more sinking down into such a state! I only mentioned their case to show you that your wages may still fall, if the labourers' proportion of the returns to capital is still further divided among a number. Upon the proportion of your labour to our capital depends the rise and fall of wages through the whole scale of payment."

"What would you call the highest rate?" inquired Allen.

"The greatest possible proportion of the return that the capitalist can spare, so as to leave it worth his while to manufacture; and this highest rate is, of course, paid only when labour is difficult to be had."

"We cannot wait till that time," said Clack. "If we waited till a war or a fever carried off part of our numbers, it would do little good; for there are plenty of young ones growing up. We must bestir ourselves and see if a strike will not do as well. The plague would no doubt be more acceptable to gentlemen, as long as it did not stop their manufacture, like a strike; but the poor must raise themselves by such means as are in their own hands, and not wait for judgment of Providence."

"I quite agree with you," said Mr. Wentworth. "Providence would have men guide themselves by its usual course, and not by uncommon accidents. But I doubt whether a strike is one of the means which will gain your point. It will leave your case worse than in the beginning, depend upon it. A strike works the wrong way for your interest. It does not decrease your numbers, and it does decrease the capital which is to maintain you."

Clack would hear nothing against a strike. Let the masters all give the same wages as Elliott, or prepare for a strike. Rather to silence the orator than with hope of much benefit from the observation, Gibson said that a pernicious multiplication of hands took place from the big piecers being allowed to spin. The masters for the most part like that they should, because they soon got to employ them to spin at less wages; and too many of the men liked it, also, because it saved them trouble: and some would even sit down to read, while their piecers were looking after the wheels; but it seemed to him very hard that good spinners should be sometimes out of work, while piecers were practising their business.

The masters thought that any regulation of the kind Gibson wished for, would only have a slight effect for a short time; it could not permanently keep down the spinning population to the number required to ensure sufficient wages.

Clack would not be diverted any longer from the plain question, would Messrs. Mortimer and Rowe raise their wages to Elliott's rate? Rowe took a long pinch of snuff to avoid answering. Mortimer sat bolt upright with his arms folded, and replied, "Certainly not." Others of the masters tried to mediate, proposing that Elliott and Mortimer should meet half-way, that is, at Mr. Wentworth's rate: but this proposal was rejected by all parties. Elliott said he left these things to the people under him; but he believed his clerk was popular with the operatives and wished for no change any more than himself; so that he should not reduce. Mortimer would not be dictated to by a mob; and the representatives of this 'mob' declared their intention of calling Wentworth to account, when they had done with Mortimer, and that his rate must not therefore be proposed for adoption. And thus the matter was no nearer being settled than before.

"Pray is it true," inquired Mortimer, "that you have talked of rooting me out?"

"Such a thing has been mentioned in private, sir," replied Allen, "but immediately scouted. It was never proposed at any public meeting, and will not be mentioned again I dare say."

"So! you have more prudence than I gave you credit for. I almost wish you had made the trial, that you might end by learning your own place. You would soon have known what comes of dictating to us."

This was a signal for Clack to renew his oratory. The peace makers on both sides found it was time to separate, as there seemed no chance of coming to any agreement. The three men made their vow and withdrew,—Allen with a heavy heart, leaving the masters to agree that the affair must be gone through with firmness and temper; that is, some were for firmness, and some for temper. Mortimer was annoyed at being exposed to an annoyance from people so much beneath him; and Wentworth and others thought that the shortest way to a good issue was to regard the claims of the people with respect, their mistakes with gentleness, and their distresses with compassion.

Before Allen could speak a word in reply to the inquiries of his eager companions, Clack began in a strain of indignation to pronounce him a trimmer,[1] for having answered Mortimer as he did about the proposal to root him out. The men being disposed at the moment to listen to everything that regarded the punishment of Mortimer, were hard upon Allen, though not so abusive as Clack. Allen kept his temper, stood the brunt of that to which his rectitude of principle exposed him, stayed till the business of the evening was finished, and then pondered, on his way home, the hard chance by which he was exposed to the displeasure of the masters, the unreasonableness of his comrades, and the timid complaints of his wife. Allen was not made for ambition.

Before the operatives separated, it was agreed that all employed at a lower rate of wages than Elliott's should turn out the next morning, except the children, whose maintenance would cost so much that it was desirable they should earn as long as allowed to do so. Meetings were to be held from day to day, first to appoint a fresh committee, and afterwards to take measures for securing assistance from fellow-labourers at a distance.

Bray, who had taken care that the meeting should not want for harmony of one kind at least during its sitting, betook himself at its close to the York Hotel, just when the masters were dispersing, and with some degree of impudence stated his desire to be impartial, and his readiness to drum the gentlemen home, if they would please to marshal themselves, as he had played in front of the men in the morning. Elliott called for a waiter to turn the fellow away, and Wentworth observed that he feared his travels had not improved the quality of his wit.

Chapter VI: Night and Morning

"How is Martha?" was Allen's first inquiry on meeting his wife at the head of the stairs. Martha had been asleep when he had returned in the middle of the day; for it was now her turn for night-work at the factory, and what rest she had must be taken in the day. Her mother said that her lameness was much the same; that she had seen Mr. Dawson, the apothecary, who pronounced that rest was what her weak limbs most required; and that as perfect rest was out of the question, her mother must bandage the joint while the child was at her work, and keep her laid on her bed at home. Here was the dif-

---

1 A trimmer is one who has no firm position on issues but adapts according to the situation or reigning mood of others.

ficulty, her mother said, especially while Hannah was with her, for they were both fond of play when poor Martha was not too tired to stir. She was now gone to her work for the night.

The little girl repaired to the factory, sighing at the thought of the long hours that must pass before she could sit down or breathe the fresh air again. She had been as willing a child at her work as could be till lately: but since she had grown sickly, a sense of hardship had come over her, and she was seldom happy. She was very industrious and disposed to be silent at her occupation; so that she was liked by her employers, and had nothing more to complain of than the necessary fatigue and disagreeableness of the work. She would not have minded it for a few hours of the day; but to be shut up all day, or else all night, without any time to nurse the baby or play with her companions, was too much for a little girl of eight years old. She had never been so sensible of this as since her renewed acquaintance with Hannah.

This night, when the dust from the cotton made her cough, when the smell and the heat brought on sickness and faintness, and the incessant whizzing and whirling of the wheels gave her the feeling of being in a dream, she remembered that a part of Hannah's business was to walk on broad roads or through green fields by her father's side, listening to the stories he amused her with, and to sit on a stile or under a tree to practice a new tune, or get a better dinner than poor Martha often saw. She forgot that Hannah was sometimes wet through, or scorched by the sun, as her complexion, brown as a gipsy's, showed; and that Hannah had no home and no mother, and very hard and unpleasant work to do at fairs, and on particular occasions. About midnight, when Martha remembered that all at home were probably sound asleep, she could not resist the temptation of resting her aching limbs, and sat down, trusting to make up afterwards for lost time and taking care to be on her feet when the overlooker passed, or when any one else was likely to watch her. It is a dangerous thing, however, to take rest with the intention of rousing oneself from time to time; and so Martha found. She fairly fell asleep after a time, and dreamed that she was attending very diligently to her work; and so many things besides passed through her mind during the two minutes that she slept, that when the overlooker laid his hand upon her shoulder, she started and was afraid she was going to be scolded for a long fit of idleness. But she was not harshly spoken to.

"Come, come, child; how long have you been asleep?"

"I don't know. I thought I was awake all the time." And Martha began to cry.

"Well, don't cry. I was past just now, and you were busy enough; but don't sit down; better not, for fear you should drop asleep again."

Martha thought she had escaped very well; and winking and rubbing her eyes, she began to limp forward and use her trembling hands. The overlooker watched her for a few moments, and told her she was so industrious in general that he should be sorry to be hard upon her; but she knew that if she was seen flagging over her work, the idle ones would make it an excuse to do so too. Martha curtsied, and put new vigour into her work at this praise. Before he went on in his rounds, the overlooker pointed to the window and told her morning was come.

It was a strange scene that the dawn shone upon. As the grey light from the east mingled with the flickering, yellow glare of the lamps, it gave a mottled dirty appearance to everything; to the pale-faced children, to the unshaved overlooker, to the loaded atmosphere, and even to the produce of the wheels.

When a bright sunbeam shone in through the window, thickened with the condensed breath of the work-people, and showed the oily steam rising through the heated room, the lamps were extinguished, to the great relief of those who found the place growing too like an oven to be much longer tolerable. The sunbeams rested now on the ceiling and Martha knew that they must travel down to the floor and be turned full on her frame and some way past it, before she could be released; but still it was a comfort that morning was come.

She observed that the overlooker frequently went out and came back again, and that there was a great deal of consultation among her betters as the hours drew on. A breath of fresh air came in now and then from below, and news went round that the gates were already open, two hours earlier than usual. Presently the tramp of heavy feet was heard, like that of the weavers and spinners coming to her daily work. Martha looked up eagerly to the clock, supposing that the time had passed quicker than she had been aware of; but it was only four o'clock. What could bring the people to their work so early? They could scarcely have mistaken the hour from the brightness of the morning, for it had now clouded over, and was raining a soaking shower. More news went round. Those who had arrived had barely escaped being waylaid and punished for coming to work after a strike had been proclaimed. They had been pursued to the gates and very nearly caught, and must now stay where they were till nightfall, as they could not safely appear in broad daylight, going to and returning from their dinners. Many wondered that they had ventured at all, and all prophecied that they must give up to the will of the Union if they wished to be safe. The overlooker, finding much excitement prevailing on the circulation of the news, commanded silence, observing that it was no concern of any of the children present. There was no strike of the children, and they would be permitted to go and come without hinderance. Martha determined to get away the first moment she could, and to meet her father, if possible, that he might not encounter any troublesome people for her sake.

Allen was watching the moment of release as anxiously for his little daughter as she could have done for herself, and he was to the full as weary as she. On the previous evening he had carried home paper and pens, preferring to write the necessary letters at his own dwelling to spending the night at the Spread-Eagle. He got his wife to clear and wipe down the deal table, when she had put all the children to bed; and then he sat down to compose a pattern letter, stating the circumstances which had led to a strike, and urging an appeal to their fellow-workmen in distant places for aid in the struggle which might be deemed a peculiarly important one. Having tolerably well satisfied himself that the letter was the proper thing, he read it to his admiring wife, who by turns smiled because she was proud of her husband, and sighed to think how perilous an office he had undertaken. She then went to bed and was soothed to sleep by the scratching of his nicely-mended pen. From this time all was silence in the apartment, except the occasional crackle when Allen folded his paper, or the cautious taking up and laying down of the snuffers when the long candle-wick craved snuffing, or the passing squalls of the baby, who, however, allowed himself to be so quickly hushed as not materially to disturb the scribe.

When nearly twenty copies of his letter had been written, each varying a little from the original, according to the differing circumstances of those to whom it was addressed, Allen was so weary that he could write no longer without some refreshment. He put out his light, and opened the window for a minute to breathe the fresh air. The pattering of the rain wakened his wife, who roused herself to fret over the weather and wonder how Martha was to get home. Her husband told her he meant to go for the child, and would carry a shawl to wrap her in. If Mary had known what lions were in her husband's path, she would not have let him go.

There was but one man visible when Allen went forth, and he was walking rapidly at some distance. It was Hare,—who, having never been well disposed towards a turn-out, and being supported in his dislike of it by his wife, hoped to avoid mischief and continue his earnings by going to the factory before people should be looking for him, and doing his work as usual, without talking about wages to anybody. Such devices did not suit the purposes of the Union, and were guarded against, as in all similar cases. Hare thought it just possible that he might meet with opposition, and looked as far before him as his eyes could reach; but he did not suspect an ambush on either hand. When he continued in the same direction, however, so as to render it certain that he was making for the factory, six men issued, one by one, from opposite alleys, and formed a line across the street. Hare's name was shouted to some one still concealed, coupled with a question whether he was under contract.

Having received their answer, they coolly told their trembling fellow-workman that as he had not the pretence of any contract, and was nevertheless going to work at an unfair price, he must be ducked. They had a rope ready, and would deliver him up to be dragged through the river.

Hare turned from one to another with as large a variety of excuses as he could invent at the moment. Among the rest, he vowed that he came to watch who would be wicked enough to go to work at this same factory after having sworn to strike. He was laughed at, let off with a roll in the kennel and with being hunted part of the way home, whither he ran to seek refuge with his wife in panting terror, and presenting a woeful spectacle of disgrace. He perhaps owed it to his known cowardice that he fared no worse; as his companions were well assured he was sufficiently daunted not to attempt to cheat them a second time.

Allen proceeded at his best pace while this judgment was being inflicted on Hare, never supposing that he could be suspected of taking work unfairly: but like all eminent men, he had his enemies, and these chose to take for granted that he could not be going to the factory with any honest design. He was seized, girded with the dreadful rope, and hauled towards the river, though he produced the shawl, demanded time to call witnesses, and used all the eloquence he could command. His last resource was to explain that the supplies from a distance must be delayed if any harm happened to him. This occasioned a short pause, during which the night-children came forth from the factory. One of the ambush, who had some sense of justice, and wished to find out the truth about Allen, ran up to Martha, as soon as she appeared, and before she could know what had happened, and asked her whether her father was not late in coming to work this morning?

"He is not coming to work at all," said the child; "but he said he would come for me. Perhaps the rain made him stay at home."

This testimony released Allen, and disappointed some of the lads who stood round of a frolic, which they had desired to fill up the time till they could proceed to a frolic of a different kind. They looked up at the clouds, and hoped the rain would not make the parson cheat them. They were going to be married. Several had begun to think of this some time before (as lads and lasses that work together in factories are wont to do); and this seemed the very time, when they had a holiday they did not know what to do with, and were sure, they believed, of ten shillings a week as long as the turn-out should last. So, amid the warning looks of elderly friends, and the remonstrances of parents who justly thought this the worst possible time to take new burdens upon them, several thoughtless young couples went laughing through the rain to the altar, and snapped their fingers at the clergyman behind his back because his careful enquiries brought to light no cause why the solemnization of matrimony should not proceed.

Chapter VII: A Committee

This was an eventful day. The masters published a placard, (not, however, signed by all,) threatening to turn off every man in their employ who should continue, after a certain day, to belong to the Union. The effect was exactly what the wisest of them expected; the turn-out became general; and the workmen, being exasperated, put new vigour into all their proceedings. Their Committee was enlarged and instructed to sit daily. Delegates were dispatched on tours to distant places, with authority to tell the tale, and collect supplies; and the people at home consented to receive, for their weekly maintenance, no more than half what the young bridegrooms had settled as the probable allowance. Five shillings a week was to be allowed as long as the children remained at work; and in case of their employment failing, the sum was to be increased in proportion to the capability of the fund. Weekly meetings were ordered to be held in St. George's Fields, at which any one should be welcome to attend; and it was agreed that it would be worth while going to some expense to have the proceedings of the body made public through the newspapers.

Allen was strongly in favour of having only three members of the Committee sit daily for the dispatch of common business; viz., the treasurer, secretary, and one of the other members, in rotation, for the sake of a casting vote. He knew enough of such Committees to believe that ill-natured tittle-tattle was particularly apt to find its way into them, and that quarrels between masters and men were often kept up by these means long after they would naturally have died out; and that a weekly sitting, at which the three members should be accountable for all they had done, would be sufficient for the interests of the association. The proposal gave offence, however; some supposing that he wanted to keep the power in few hands, others being unwilling to enjoy the pomp and privilege of their office no oftener than once or twice a week, and some honestly thinking that the voices of all were wanted for the decision of questions daily arising. Allen would have cared little for his motion being rejected; but, in spite of all the allowance he strove to make, it vexed him to the heart to hear evil motives assigned for every proposition which did not please the people. He often said to himself that it must be a very different thing to sit in a committee of gentlemen where opinions are treated as opinions, (*i.e.*, as having no moral qualities, and to be accepted or rejected according to their expediency,) and in a committee of persons who expose their deficiencies of education by calling all unkind or foolish who differ from themselves. Such remarks appeared to Allen to proceed from the same spirit which tortured martyrs in former days, and proscribed the leaders of a combination in the present.

Any one committee-meeting afforded a pretty fair specimen of all. Sometimes there were more letters than at others, sometimes larger, sometimes smaller remittances than had been expected, and occasionally none at all. Sometimes there was a dearth of gossip about the sayings and doings of the masters, and then again an abundance of news of spiteful devices and willful misrepresentations and scornful sayings, for which there should be a sure retribution. But the same features distinguished all; and one sketch will therefore describe the whole.

A little before ten, the committee-men might be seen tending towards St. George's road. They could win their way but slowly, for they were continually waylaid by one or another who had some very important suggestion to make, or question to answer; or a piece of news to tell which would sound well in committee. Allen was the most sore beset.

"Lord! Allen, what work yours must be with such a many letters to write! Why, it must cost a mint of money to pay postage."

"All for the cause, you know. Let me go, will you? I am rather late."

"Not a clock has struck yet, man, and I want to know whether it's true about the large order that's gone to Glasgow because Elliott can't execute it?"

"All true, perfectly true. Good bye."

"Well, but have you seen Elliott since? Lord! I should love to see him look chap-fallen when he finds the power is with us."

"'Tis for us to look chap-fallen, I think," said Allen, trying to disengage his button; "where's the power if more such orders go the same way?"

"Stop, Allen, one more thing more. Do you know, several of us are of a mind that it is a disgrace to the Union that Wooler, with his large family, has no more on a pay-day than Briggs."

"Briggs has a sick wife, and his children are too young to work."

"Wooler must have more, however, and that you'll find to your cost, if you don't take care. Pretty encouragement to turn out, indeed, if such a man as he is to be sacrificed to worse men than himself!"

"Let him carry his complaint to the proper place, if he is discontented. The committee ordered his allowance, and it is they must alter it, not I."

Allen now thought he had made his escape; but his gossip called after him that he had something to tell him on which the whole fate of the strike depended. Allen was all ear in a moment. It was said, and on very good authority, that the masters would never employ a Manchester man again. They had sent to Glasgow and to Belfast, and all over England, and if they could not get workmen enough by these means, they would bring them in troops from abroad.

"Who told you this?" said Allen, laughing.

"That's between him and me," replied the gossip mysteriously, "but you may rely upon it, it is true."

"Aye, we have been told so twice a day since we turned out," said Allen; "but that is no reason why we should believe it. You might as well tell me they mean to take their mills on their backs and march over the sea to America."

"You may laugh, sir, but I'm far from as sure as you that we are not going to ruin."

"I am sure of no such thing," replied Allen. "I wish I were; but if we are ruined, it will not be by French people spinning in Chorlton Row."[1]

---

1   Chorlton Row is a township in Manchester, a slum area that grew up
    around the Chorlton Mills known as "Little Ireland." Now called
    Chorlton-on-Medlock, it is part of Manchester University Campus.

A knot of smokers, each with as much to say, stood or lolled about the door of the Spread-Eagle. Allen looked at the window of the committee-room, and wished he could have got in that way; but there was no escape from the file of questioners. Several of his companions were ready to tell him that he was late, when he at length took his seat at the end of the table, and began to arrange his papers.

"I know it; but I left home half an hour since. I have been stopped by the way."

"And so you always will be. You're so soft, man, you're not fit for office if you can't say 'no.'"

Dooley, the representative of the Irish hand-loom weavers, here took up Allen's defence, urging that it would be too hard if the people out of office might not make their remarks to those who were in; and that a secretary must be as stony-hearted as the last speaker to refuse them a hearing.

"Come, come; to business," cried Allen, to stop the dispute. "But first shut the door, Brown, and make every one knock that wants to come in. If they won't obey at once, slip the bolt. We must preserve the dignity and quiet of the Committee."

"O, by all manner of means," said the Irishman, sitting down demurely at the board, and twirling his thumbs; "it puts me in mind of the way his honour set us to play when we were children—"

"I have here a letter from number three," Allen began, as if all had been silence, "who has prosecuted his journey successfully as far as Halifax, from whence he hopes to transmit, in a post or two, a sum nearly as large as was contributed by that place to the Bradford strike. It will gratify you, I am sure, to know with how much friendly anxiety our fellow-labourers watch the result of our present noble struggle; and I trust you will agree with me that their suggestions are entitled to our respectful attention. Dooley, be so good as read the letter to the Committee, while I look what must be brought forward next."

"With raal pleasure, Mr. Secretary; but first I'll take lave to wet my throat with a little ale or spirits. It's dry work reading and advising, and a clear sin to keep so many men shut up on a summer's day with not a drop to help their wits."

"Whatever is ordered is at your own cost, remember," said Allen; "and I would recommend your going elsewhere to refresh yourself. Meanwhile, will some one else have the goodness to read the letter now under consideration?"

After much complaint and discussion, Dooley was prevailed on to be quiet and let the business go forward. Having first loaded Allen with abuse and then with praise, he tried to behave well, much in the same way as if his priest had put him under penance.

The letter in question and some others having been discussed and dismissed with due decorum, a member brought before the notice of his fellow-workmen a calumny which he believed had been widely circulated, and which was likely to impair the credit of the association, and thus to deprive them of the countenance of their distant friends and of all chance of reconciliation with the masters. It was said and believed—

A push at the door. "Who is there?"

"Only Tom Hammond."

"Learn what he wants."

Tom Hammond only thought he would look in and see whether it was a full committee-day, and how they got on: which thought only occasioned the door to be shut in his face and the delivery of an admonition to go about his own business and leave other people to manage theirs in quiet.

"Well; what was this libel?"

It was said that the Committee had taken upon themselves to go round as inspectors, and to examine the work done by all members of the Union, and determine whether the price given for it was fair or not. Allen thought it incredible that any of the masters could have given heed to so absurd a report; but if one instance could be brought of its having been actually believed, he would be the first to propose some measure of effectual contradiction.

Clack would wish that the secretary was somewhat less inclined to make light of the information brought to the committee by some who were as likely to know what was going forward as himself. The association was not to lose its character because its secretary chose to laugh at the foul calumnies circulated against it, and which seemed anything but laughable to those who had the honour of the Union really at heart. And so forth.

The secretary begged to explain that nothing was further from his intention than to risk the good name of the association; and he must further assert that no man breathing had its honour more at heart than himself. He need but appeal to those who had heard him say but just now—And so forth.

The result was a resolution that a paper should be drawn up and presented to the masters, containing an explanation of what the office of this committee consisted in; *viz*.:—not in determining the value of work and the rate of wages, but in managing the affairs of the turn-out after the strike had been actually made; in collecting and distributing money, and conducting the correspondence and accounts.

While Allen was consulting his companions about the wording of this letter, the rub-a-dub of a drum, accompanying shrill piping, was heard approaching from a distance, and presently the sounds of merriment from without told that Bray was among the smokers on the outside. Sometimes a rumble and screech seemed to show that the unskilful were trying his instruments, and then it appeared from the heavy tread and shuffling of feet that some were dancing hornpipes under his instructions. Dooley soon started up.

"Let us have Bray in here. He'll put a little life in us, for all this is as dull as sitting at a loom all day. We make it a point of honour, you know, not to trample on a fallen man. We let Bray come and go as if he was still one of us, poor cratur."

"Wait till he comes," said Allen. "He is thinking no more of us at this moment than we need think of him."

Dooley returned to his seat with the mock face of a chidden child, and walking as softly as if he trod on eggs, twirling his thumbs as before. He had not long to wait for his diversion. Bray suddenly made a lodgment in the window, sitting astride on the sill with his drum balanced before him and playing with all his might, so as almost to deafen those within. When he saw the vexed countenances of two or three of the men of business, he ceased, dropped into the room, rolled his drum into a corner, flung his belled cap behind it, and said,—

"Don't scold me, pray. I'll make it all up to you. I'll have bars put up at the windows at my own cost to prevent any more idle fellows dropping in upon you when you have made all safe at the door. Moreover, I will give you the benefit of my best wisdom at this present time. What's the matter in hand?"

The Committee found their advantage in the consideration which made them admit Bray to their councils, though he had no longer any connexion with their affairs. His natural shrewdness and travelled wisdom were valuable helps upon occasion. When the terms of the disclaimer were agreed upon, Bray told them he had something of importance to say, and he should say it out as plainly as he had heard it, since he hoped they were all men, all possessed of resolution enough to bear what might be said of them, and to surrender their own gratification for the public good.

Clack was the first to give a vehement assent. With his hand on his heart, he protested that he would take his heart in his hand and give it to be toasted at the hangman's fire, if it would do the cause any good. All with different degrees of warmth declared their readiness to sacrifice or to be sacrificed. Allen's assent was given the last and least confidently, though without hesitation. He had inwardly flinched on first hearing Bray's portentous words, but the recollection that he had already devoted himself, restored his firmness and prepared him for whatever might be coming. He would have flinched no more, even had Bray's story concerned himself instead of another.

"I have been a pretty long round this morning," said Bray, "and among other places to Middleton, and there some good fellows and I had a pot of ale. Who should come in there but a traveller who deals, I am told, with several firms in this place. Well; he heard us talking about the strike, and not liking, seemingly, to overhear without speaking, like a spy, he joined in with us, and talked like a very sensible man,—more so than I should have expected, considering how much he has clearly been with the masters."

"You never miss a stroke at your old enemies, Bray."

"As long as they are enemies to me and such as me, I shall give them a hit at every turn. Well; this gentleman told us that he could speak to the dispositions of the masters, if any one could; and he was positive that if the men would take one step, they would soon have overtures from the masters. 'If,' said he, 'they will prevent Clack from having anything to do with their strike, the masters will begin to come round from that moment.'"

"Turn *me* out!" exclaimed Clack. "Prevent *my* having anything to do—"

Bray pursued as if Clack were a hundred miles off. "They think that fellow, says he, a vulgar speechifier that knows nothing about the matter in dispute, and is only fit to delude the more ignorant among the spinners and to libel the masters. Send him back into the crowd where his proper place is, and then you will see what the masters have to say to the Committee."

Allen endeavoured to stop remarks which it must be painful enough to Clack to hear under any form, and which were made needlessly offensive by Bray, who was rather glad of the opportunity of giving a set down to the mischief-maker. Clack was necessarily soon stopped also by general consent. He raged and vowed revenge in such a style that it was plainly right to dismiss him now if it had not been so before. He could no longer be trusted with any degree of power against the masters, if the Committee wished to preserve their character for impartiality. As soon as he could be persuaded to leave the room to have his case considered, it was agreed to recommend him resign, if he wished to avoid being regularly deposed at the next public meeting. He preferred the appeal to the public; and his companions could only hope that the masters would hear of what passed, and would take the will for the deed.

It was next proposed by a member of the Committee that a sum of money should be presented to Allen in consideration of his services; and he had the pain of hearing himself lauded at the expense of Clack, according to what seemed the general rule, to admire one man in proportion to the contempt with which another was treated. If Rowe was railed at, Wentworth was praised; if Clack was complained of, Allen was immediately extolled. Being aware of this, Allen would have declined the gift, if for no other reason than that a fit of generosity might be transient; but he had other reasons for refusing to listen to all mention of a gift. He chose to keep his disinterestedness beyond all question; and he feared that the funds were about to decline on the whole, though liberal contributions were looked for from particular places.

To stop further argument, which he intended should be unavailing, he returned brief thanks to his companions and broke up the Committee.

Chapter VIII: A Tete-a-Tete

It was the policy of the Committee to hold the public meetings of the workmen on pay-days, in order that they might appear on the green refreshed and in good spirits, and thus give the masters the most favourable impression possible of their resources and of the vigour with which they meant to maintain the strike. This arrangement had not the effect of raising the spirits of the leaders. Pay-day was an anxious and painful day to them. In addition to all the sad stories of distress which they must hear, and the discontent which they must witness, there was perpetual dread of the fund appearing to decline, and of the confidence of the people being therefore shaken. It was frequently necessary to borrow money,—sometimes as much as a hundred pounds at a time,—on the security of what was to come in during the next week; and even those least disposed to foresight could not help asking themselves and each other what was to be done next time, if the remittances of the week should not superabound.

Allen was turning these things over in his mind as he proceeded to the Spread-Eagle on the morning of the day when Clack was expected to be dismissed from the Committee by the public voice.

News was afloat which did not tend to cheer his spirits, though he thought he discerned in it a sign that the measures already taken concerning Clack were prudent. Ann Howlett, Clack's betrothed, had been taken up on a charge of breach of contract, and had been committed to prison by the magistrate; and if it was indeed necessary to propitiate the masters by sacrificing him, it was well that the sacrifice was offered by the committee before the arrest of the woman instead of in consequence of it. A more painful piece of intelligence followed. Immediately after this arrest, a carrier, who was conveying work into the country for Mortimer and Rowe, was attacked on his way out of the town, his cart ransacked, himself beaten, and the work carried off in triumph. Ten or twelve men had been concerned in the outrage; and it was acknowledged that they belonged to the Union; but Allen in vain attempted to learn who they were. His integrity was so well known, that it was understood that he would deliver the offenders up to justice, be they who they might; and therefore, though many knew, no one would tell. Mute signs and obscure hints conveyed that Clack headed the enterprise; but nothing in the shape of evidence was offered.

Mr. Rowe was standing at his window when Allen's gossips left him to pursue his way. The gentleman threw up the sash, looked cautiously up and down the street, to ascertain whether he was observed, and then mysteriously beckoned to Allen to come into the house.

"What do you want with me, sir?"

"I want a little conversation with you, that's all. Can't you come in for a quarter of an hour?"

"If I could find any one to take my place at the board," replied Allen, who thought that some overture might be coming. "If you will let me step to the Spread-Eagle or write a note, I am at your service."

The plan of writing a note was preferred, on condition that Allen should not say whence or why he wrote. He saw that the gentleman glanced over his shoulder, to see whether he kept his word, and turning sharp round, held up the paper in Rowe's face, saying,

"There is honour on the part of us men, I assure you, sir, whatever suspicion there is on the part of you gentlemen. Read the note, if you please."

Rowe did as he was desired, disclaiming suspicion, of course, and getting entangled in a complimentary speech which Allen listened to very quietly, waiting, with his arms by his side, for the end of it.

As an ending did not come readily, however, the gentleman broke off in order to send the note. He gave a penny to a child in the street to carry the note to the Spread-Eagle, and run away directly without saying where he came from; and then returning, made Allen sit down and take a glass of ale,—particularly fine ale,—such capital ale that the gentleman often indulged himself in a draught with a friend.

When nothing more remained to be said about ale, Mr. Rowe sighed, and observed what a pity it was that people should fall out to their mutual injury, and that those who had power to reconcile differences should not endeavour to do so.

Allen asked what party was meant by this description.

"You," replied Rowe, shaking him warmly by the hand. "You must know, Allen, that you can do what you please in the Union; and I only wish you knew how the masters look up to you, and respect your manly, moderate conduct. Any proposition from you would meet with attention from both parties; if you would—"

"I beg pardon, sir; but you forget that my propositions are before the masters already, and do not meet with attention. My propositions are those adopted by the Union—"

"Yes, yes; I know well enough what they are; but you must bring forward something new. Is there nothing else you can propose that we can support without going from our word?"

"Just tell me plainly," said Allen, "since you seem to like plain speaking: will you yourself make a concession about raising the wages to a middle point, if we yield some of our demands of equal importance?"

"Why, you see," replied Rowe, edging his chair closer, and filling Allen's glass, "I don't want to come forward the first in this kind of thing. Indeed, as a junior partner, I ought not so to commit myself. I can't be the first, you see; but I have no objection to be the second. Yes, you may, between you and me, depend upon my being the second."

"Between you and me!" exclaimed Allen, laughing. "That leaves me nothing to propose to the meeting. See now how they would laugh at me!—'My fellow-workmen, I propose that we should lower our demands because a person (I am not at liberty to say who) offers, between himself and me, to yield in part after others have yielded.' Why, sir, they would jeer me off the stand, or bid me say to their concealed opponent, 'Thank you for nothing. If others have yielded first, we shall owe nothing to you.'"

"Well, but, Allen, you don't seem to me to know the difficulty I am in, if you use my name. You don't know how unpleasant—"

"Pardon me, sir, I do know. You and I are neither of us men of nerve, Mr. Rowe, and so far, you have chosen your listener well. Clack would have laughed in your face, by this time, and been half way to the Spread-Eagle to tell the people there all that you have been saying; but I have so far a sympathy with you that I know the misery of looking round and seeing entanglement with one party or another on every side—blame from one or another sure to come. I know the longing to be somehow out of the scrape, the shrinking back with the hope of keeping out of sight, the dread of every one that comes near lest some new difficulty should be arising. I can pity you, sir, for all these feelings, for I have felt them myself."

"Have you? have you indeed?" replied Rowe, grasping his hand again. "What a sad thing it is for you, then, to be a leader of a turn-out."

"I am of a different opinion, sir. Because these feelings are natural to some persons, it does not follow that they should be indulged. It will not do to indulge them, sir, believe me. We have our duties as well as men of our make on the field of battle; and we must surrender ourselves, like them, to our duties, or be disgraced in our own eyes. Happen what will within us or without us, it is for you and me to speak out, to act openly, and bear the consequences. You will excuse my freedom."

Another grasp of the hand, with a speech about the secretary's integrity; upon which Allen rose, saying,—

"Then as we are of one mind, sir, suppose we go together to the meeting, and say what we have to say there, instead of shut up in this parlour. I believe I can promise you a courteous hearing."

"O no, no; that is quite out of the question. I have no offer, you know, to make on behalf of the masters,—nothing to say that I should think of occupying the meeting with."

"Then you can have nothing to say to me, sir, since, as an individual, I have no power to negotiate. Good morning, Mr. Rowe."

"Stay a moment, Allen. You understand that the men are not to know of this interview; and it is of more importance still that the masters should not. Promise me, Allen."

"I can promise no such thing," said Allen, returning from the door. "I regard your consent to be the second to raise wages as a concession, and I was going to report it to Mr. Wentworth."

"For God's sake don't!"

"I must," said Allen, firmly; and all entreaty, all reproach, was in vain.

"At least, don't give up the name. The fact will do just as well without the name. Give me your word to conceal the name till you see me again."

Out of pure compassion, Allen yielded thus far. Mr. Rowe accompanied him to the house-door, harping upon "the name, the name," till Allen turned round to say gravely,

"A promise once given is enough, sir, between honest men. I have given you my word."

"True, true, my good friend. It is only a trick I have got of repeating my sentences."

And the gentleman shut the door behind his guest, feeling very like a child who has persuaded her maid not to tell her governess who broke the china cup; knowing all the time that the mishap must come to light, and trembling every time any one goes near the cupboard.

Chapter IX: A Public Meeting

"How much did you fall short to-day?" inquired Allen, as he joined in with a group of committee-men going to the meeting.

"Sixty pounds; but we shall make it up before three days are over, depend upon it; and, besides, the masters will yield as soon as Clack is done for, you'll see. Wentworth is before us, going to the meeting. But what have you been about Allen, playing truant on pay-day?"

"Preaching fortitude and giving a fillip [encouragement] to the faint-hearted."

"As Christian a duty as feeding the hungry and easing the poor," observed a companion. "If Allen is absent from a good deed, you may be sure he is doing a better."

There was no part of Allen's duty that he disliked more than opening the weekly meetings. The applause discomposed him. He could not, like Clack, make a deprecating flourish of the hands, or shake his head modestly, or look round with a proud smile. He was very apt to fidget, and swing his hat, and make a short, ungraceful bow. As soon as he found this out, he adopted one posture, from which he determined not to move till the thing was over. He folded his arms and dropped his head upon his breast, and so stood as if facing a gust of wind, till the clapping had sunk into silence.—This day, the clapping on his appearance was twice as long and twice as vehement as usual, Clack's former popularity being transferred to himself. Mr. Wentworth appeared in time to share his honours, and to relieve him from applause, which seemed as if it would never end. Clack would fain have appropriated both series of cheers; but he could not manage it. As soon as he began to bow and look flattered, there arose cries of "Off, off!" which strengthened into groans when he attempted to brave them. With a nervous sneer, the orator observed to those within hearing that his time would soon come, when he would carry off more cheers than any of them.

"Better put yourself under Allen's wing, if you want to be clapped," observed Mr. Wentworth. "I conclude it was because I stood next to him that they cheered me to-day, instead of groaning, as they did a week ago. We must submit to be beholden to Allen— hey, Clack?"

With a look of ineffable contempt, the orator withdrew as far as he could from Allen, without going out of sight, while Mr. Wentworth sat down to take a pinch of snuff on the edge of the waggon in which the speakers were stationed.

The object of the meeting was to obtain the opinions of the people on certain questions to be proposed; and, in order to put Clack out of the pain of suspense, his affair was the first brought on. Allen expressed himself in the most moderate terms he could devise, saying that it sometimes happened that the usefulness of an individual was not in proportion to his zeal in the cause he had espoused, or to his desire to fulfil its duties, especially where the likings of two opposite parties had to be consulted; that it so happened, in the present case, that the individual in question did not possess the confidence of the masters, and that his remaining a member of the Committee might therefore prove an obstacle in the way of an amicable agreement. It was for the meeting to declare whether they were willing to take the chance of an accommodation by naming some substitute for Clack, who might be equally energetic in their service, and more agreeable to their employers. After a pause, and with evident effort, he added, that if the conduct of the person in question had been, in all respects, such as the Union could approve, it would have gone hard with the committee before they would have sanctioned his removal from office; but, as it seemed too evident that the cause had received injury by his means in ways which he might be spared the pain of pointing out, they might consider themselves relieved from the perplexity of reconciling consideration for the individual with a regard to the interests of the body.

A hubbub ensued; a strong party of Clack's friends raising shouts on his behalf, while opposing cries rose on all sides of "Down with the blusterer!" "Who waylaid the carrier?" "He is none of us. The Union keeps the laws." "Law and concord! No Clack!"

Quiet was restored on Mr. Wentworth's rising to explain that his being present was not to be considered as a sign that the masters would yield on Clack's dismissal. He had no authority to confirm any such belief.

Applause,—and Clack doomed by an overwhelming majority; whereupon his supporters made their way to the waggon, agreed with him that the meeting was not worth addressing, even if he *had* been allowed to speak; and carried him off on their shoulders to fish for popularity in the streets of Manchester, while the meeting conducted its affairs as well as it could without him. So ended that matter, except that somehow Clack and his party were forestalled in their return into the town, and the walls everywhere presented, conspicuous in white chalk, the phrase which still rang in their ears, "Law and Concord! No Clack!" An extraordinary number of little boys too seemed to have taken the fancy to mimick the action of weaving, with arm and foot, crying at the same time

> "Clickity, clickity, clack,
> Lay him on his back!
> Clickity, clickity, clack,
> Away let him pack!"

Far more decorous was the meeting in their rear, while the queries were dismissed, each in its turn.

"The case of Ann Howlett being admitted by all parties to be a hard one, (her contract being for wages which would not support her,) was her breach of contract sanctioned by the Union?"

Shouts of "No; we would have helped her to perform it!"

"If this breach of contract had been sanctioned by the Union, was it thought lawful revenge for the committal of Ann Howlett to way-lay the carrier and strip his cart?"

Groans, and shouts of "No revenge!"

Some one near the cart having spoken to Allen, he put the question,—

"Supposing this attack to have no connexion with Ann Howlett's affair, does the Union sanction forcible attempts to prevent work being carried into the country?"

Answer, "No. Law and Concord for ever!"

"If the men abide by the law, and the masters are found disposed to concord, will the Union be disposed to concession?"

Mixed cries, the most distinguishable of which was, "Stick by the Union! The Union for ever!"

Mr. Wentworth and Allen exchanged nods, as much as to say, "You see"—"Yes, I see."

"Supposing the Union to be preserved entire, are its members disposed to any concession in respect of wages?"

Cries of "Equalization!"

"An equalization is, as the Committee knows, indispensable; but the point on which the Committee has not yet received your instructions is whether that equalization may be fixed below the highest rate, *viz.*, that which Elliott is now giving?"

The answers were at first hesitating, then confused, so that no one prevailed.

"Don't press for an answer yet," said Mr. Wentworth. "I may tell them something which may help their judgments."

Way was made for Mr. Wentworth, and he presented himself to speak.

"Before you put this question to the vote, let me just mention a circumstance or two that you may not be aware of, from your having been lately out of communication with the factories. There are few things that we hear more of than of the changes that all mortal things are liable to; and these changes affect the affair we have in hand, like all other affairs. We are told that every one rises from sleep in the morning a different man from him who lay down at night; there having been a waste and repair of the substance of which the bodily man is composed. In the same manner, you may find that your strike is a different thing to-day from what it was at its beginning. Some of its parts have fallen off, and others have been added. Whether your body, having undergone this change, be the more vigorous, like a man refreshed with sleep, you know better than I. But further, whenever you return to your work you may find a factory a very different place on re-entering from what it was on your leaving it. There has been much waste, I fear, without any repair. You know what kind of waste I refer to. You have heard of large orders, which we have been unable to execute, having been sent to Scotland and elsewhere. You know that much of our capital, which ought by this time to be returning to us again, has been for many weeks locked up in our stocks of raw material. You know that the expense of keeping on our establishments has not been repaid by the production of goods for the market; or the cost of maintaining ourselves and our families, by the profitable employment of our time and our wits. We have been consuming idly, and so have you; and thus there must needs have been great waste.—And what is it which has been thus wasted? The fund which is to maintain you; the fund out of which your wages are paid. Your strike has already lasted long enough to change our ground of dispute. You will find that the question with the masters now is, whether fewer of you than before shall be employed at the same wages, or fewer still at higher wages, or as many as before at lower wages than you have yet received. Keep on your strike a little longer, and the question will be, how many less shall be employed, at how much less. Keep it on long enough, and the question will be entirely settled; there will be no wages for anybody. Do you understand me?"

The speaker took snuff while the murmur of disapprobation went round, and then continued.

"I do not suppose, any more than you, that we shall come to this pass, because your capital must be exhausted sooner than ours, and then you must have bread, and will come to us for work before our fund for wages is all wasted away; but the nearer you drive us to this point the more injury you do yourselves. Let me hear your objection, friend," he continued to a man in the crowd who looked eager to speak. "Where do you think me wrong? You acknowledge that a strike is a bad thing, but sometimes necessary to obtain a good one. Refusing wages altogether for a time, is to be the means of securing better afterwards. Do I understand you right? Why, that would be very true if you had the power or were in the habit of keeping workmen and wages in proportion to each other. If the masters had more capital than was necessary to pay you all at the rate you have hitherto received, you might gain your point by a strike, not as you sometimes do now, just for a little time till the masters can shake themselves free of their engagement,—but permanently. But this is not the case. The masters' capital does not return enough to pay you all at the same rate you desire. If they are to keep their capital entire, you must either take less wages, or fewer of you must take wages at all. If you will all have the wages you desire, the capital which pays them wastes away, and ruin approaches. This is the worst event that could happen, as I am sure we shall all agree. Your alternative, therefore, is to withdraw a portion of your people from taking wages, or all to take less than you are striking for. You are not satisfied yet? (speaking to the same man.) Well, let me hear. There are places where there are no strikes, because the workmen get as high wages as they wish for? Very true; there are such places, and London is one; concerning which I heard, the other day, a case in point.

"The money wages of skilled labour in London were higher from 1771 to 1793 than was ever known. They had been raised because prices were high. They were afterwards somewhat lowered; but as prices fell in a greater proportion after the war, the real wages of skilled labour are at present higher than they had ever been. They cannot be lowered while, as at present, there is an occasional deficiency of labour, since the men would strike when most wanted by the masters, and the loss thus caused would be greater than the gain of giving lower wages. In London there are two seasons in every year; a slack season in which many workmen remain unemployed; and a busy season in which they work over hours, because there are not hands enough. Now, here, you see, lies their advantage; in the supply of labour being limited. If it was the case with them, as with you, that some of their class always remained unemployed, the unemployed would undersell the busy, and wages would fall. Then, as here, there would be strikes; and then, as here, strikes would be of no avail. Where there are permanently fewer workmen than are wanted the men hold the power. Where there is the exact number that is wanted, the power is equal, and the contest fair. Where there are more than are wanted, even to the extent of three unemployed to a hundred, the power is in the masters' hands, and strikes must fail. Must there not be a larger surplus of unemployed labour than this in our neighbourhood, and elsewhere, since wages are fallen too low to enable the labourer to do more than barely exist? Allen, is there a silk small-ware weaver present, do you suppose? They have just struck, I find."

Proclamation was made for a silk small-ware weaver, and several held up their hands. In answer to questions, they stated that within two years their wages had been reduced forty-five per cent. Two years before, common galloon weaving[1] was paid at the rate of 1s. 10d. per gross; it was now reduced to 1s. 4d. per gross; and it was for an addition of 2d. per gross that the men struck: little enough when it is considered that, in the winter season, a weaver cannot average more than twelve gross per week. As he has to pay for the hire of his loom, for winding, for candle-light, and other expenses belonging to his work, he has left only about 8s. a week for himself and his family.

"Could so dreadful a reduction have ever taken place," continued Mr. Wentworth, "if you had not undersold one another? And how are the masters to help you if you go on increasing your numbers and underselling one another, as if your employers could find occupation for any number of millions of you, or could coin the stones under your feet into wages, or knead the dust of the earth into bread? They do what they can for you in increasing the capi-

---

1 A galloon is braid or trimming of worsted (wool) or silk.

tal on which you are to subsist; and you must do the rest by pro-portioning your numbers to the means of subsistence. But see how the masters are met! In Huddersfield the masters are doing their utmost to extend their trade; but the multitudes who are to subsist by it increase much faster. There are now thirteen thousand work-people in that place who toil for twopence half-penny a day. At Todmorden, the most skilful work fourteen hours a day for the pit-tance of one shilling. In the fair county of Kent there are thirty thousand who earn no more than sixpence a day. Compare this state of things with the condition of skilled labour wages in London, and see how much depends on the due proportion of labourers, and the capital by which they are to be fed. Would you could be convinced that your strike, besides occasioning vexation and ill-will between the two parties, besides inflicting distress upon yourselves, and inconvenience upon your employers, cannot but be worse than in vain!"

During the last few sentences, several persons had been engaged in conference with Bray, who leaned over a corner of the waggon to hear what they had to say. He now came forward and placed himself beside Mr. Wentworth, observing that all that had fallen from the gentleman seemed pretty true and reasonable as far as it went, but that it did not at all explain what course the people had now to pur-sue. It was poor comfort to tell the people that wages could not be any higher on account of their numbers, since it was not in their power to lessen those numbers.

"It is not with the view of giving present comfort," replied Mr. Wentworth, "that I represent what appears to me to be the truth: for alas! there is but little comfort in the case any way. My object is to prevent your making a bad case worse; and if it were possi-ble, to persuade you not to prepare for your descendants a repeti-tion of the evils under which you are yourselves suffering. All that you can now do, is to live as you best may upon such wages as the masters can give, keeping up your sense of respectability and your ambition to improve your state when better times shall come. You must watch every opportunity of making some little provision against the fluctuations of our trade, contributing your money rather for your mutual relief in hard times, than for the support of strikes. You must place your children out to different occupations, choosing those which are least likely to be overstocked; and, above all, you must discourage in them the imprudent, early marriages to which are mainly owing the distresses which afflict yourselves and those which will for some time, I fear, oppress your children.

You ask me what you must do. These things are all that I can suggest."[1]

"But these things, sir, will not guard our children any more than ourselves from the fluctuations in trade you speak of."

"But they will prevent those fluctuations from being so injurious as they now are. The lower wages are, the more are such fluctuations felt. In India, where an average day's wages are only three-pence, the people live in the poorest possible manner,—such as the poorest of you have no idea of. Any decrease of wages, therefore, makes the more weakly of the labourers lie down and die. In Ireland, where the average is five-pence a day, there is less positive starvation than in India, but more distress on a fall of wages, than in England. In England, such fluctuations are less felt than in old days, when the people knew nothing of many things which you now call necessaries. The better the state of the people, the better able are they to stand against the changes to which all trades are liable; but the worst of it is that we are all too little inclined to foresee the effects of these changes, and to provide for them; and when we experience the necessary consequences of a change which took place twenty years before, we are apt to suppose these consequences arise from something amiss at the present time. When a demand for any article of manufacture makes labour unusually profitable, labourers provide for a great decline of wages in future years, by bringing up large families to the same employment. During many years, that is, while their children are growing up, they feel no ill effects, and suppose that all is going on right. When a decline of wages comes, they suppose it happens from some new circumstance, and not from their own deed in over-stocking the labour market. Again; it must be some time before the effects of a decline in lessening the supply of labour are felt. A part of the population perishes slowly from want and misery, and others are made prudent in respect of marriage; but by the time these checks are seen to operate, a new period of prosperity has arrived, which is ascribed by the people to accident. It is this impossibility of making the supply of labour suit the demand at a moment's notice, which makes fluctuations in trade so sensibly felt, for good or for evil, by the labourer. Since he cannot, as you say, Mr. Bray, diminish the number of workmen when trade is slack, and if he wished his descendants not to be plunged into degradation by extreme pover-

---

1   This expository conversation reflects Martineau's study of the population doctrines of Thomas Malthus.

ty, he will do what in him lies to prevent population from increasing faster than the capital which is to support it."

Mr. Wentworth was encouraged to pursue his argumentative manner of speaking by the attention of the people near the waggon. Some of them had become a little tired of the weekly meetings at which their orators had said the same things over and over again, and were pleased to be reasoned with by one whom they esteemed, and to obtain, by these means, a better insight into their affairs than was given them by leaders who were all of one party. The more the present meeting assumed the character of a conference, the more eagerly the most thinking men in the crowd pressed towards the waggon, and cheered the questions and replies. Those on the outskirts, who were more fond of noise and display, were at liberty to come and go as they pleased; to listen to Mr. Wentworth, or to follow Clack.

Bray now observed that population must increase rapidly indeed, as it had outstripped the increase of capital in the cotton manufacture. He believed so rapid an increase of capital had never been known before. To this Mr. Wentworth replied by asking of the crowd whether there was any one among them who had known James Hargraves [sic].[1] An old man stept forwards and said that he was a native of Blackburn, and had been accustomed, as a boy, to frequent Hargraves' workshop; that he remembered seeing the carpenter busy about his invention, and his own delight at having the design of the spinning-jenny explained to him by the inventor; he saw directly how eight threads could be spun instead of one, and thought it a very fine thing, and had little notion how soon it would be so much improved upon as that a little girl might work one hundred, or one hundred and twenty spindles. When was this? Why, a few years after the old king George began to reign; in 1767, he believed.

"When that king came to the throne," observed Mr. Wentworth, "the whole value of the cotton goods manufactured in this country was only 200,000l. a year."

"There were very few people employed in it then," interrupted the old man. "We had no factories and no towns full of cotton-spinners and weavers. My father used to take his work home to his own cottage, and grow the flax that was then used for warp in his own garden, and set my mother to card and spin the raw cotton for the

---

1 James Hargreaves (d. 1778) invented the earliest spinning machine capable of spinning multiple threads simultaneously; a precursor of the more elaborate "spinning jenny."

weft.[1] This, and getting the warp from Ireland, was the way till Arkwright's spinning frame came into use."[2]

"Then was the time," said Mr. Wentworth, "that the people in China and in India had no rivals in the market for whatever was made of cotton. We owe it to these machines, and the mule-jenny, and the power-loom that came in afterwards, that though we have to bring our cotton from thousands of miles off, and though the wages in India are, as I said, only 3*d.* a day, we have beaten them in the competition, and can carry back their cotton five thousand miles, made into a cheaper fabric than they can afford. Such powers as these must make our capital grow; and the fact is that the cotton manufacture is the chief business carried on in the country, and that it has enabled us to sustain burdens which would have crushed any other people. Instead of 200,000*l.*, the annual produce of the manufacture is now more than 36,000,000*l.* We have no means of knowing how few persons were employed sixty years ago; but it is reckoned that the manufacture now affords subsistence to more than 1,400,000 persons. This enormous population has arisen naturally enough from the rise of the manufacture; but your present condition shows that it has already gone too far; and it rests with yourselves to determine whether the evil shall be found to have increased fifty years hence. And now Allen, you know the reason of the clause I added to your query in the arbour."

"Will our trade go on increasing?" was the next question asked.

"I hope and trust that it will, as we have got the start of our competitors abroad; but it will probably increase at a slower rate; and a succession of strikes may prove its destruction."

Here the speaker abruptly ceased, and nothing could induce him to say more. He let himself down from the waggon, and quietly made his way through the crowd, thinking perhaps that the people would draw their inferences from what he had said more freely in his absence.

The substance of Mr. Wentworth's argument, and especially the last words he spoke, left Allen and others thoughtful. They would not, on the impulse of the moment, advise a compromise with the

---

1 *warp ... weft*: threads stretched lengthwise on a loom to be crossed by weft creating woven fabric.
2 Sir Richard Arkwright (1732-92) invented the spinning jenny, which expanded on Hargreaves' invention. The innovations of Hargreaves and Arkwright transformed spinning and weaving from a cottage to a factory industry, radically altering England's social and economic frameworks.

masters; but appointed another general meeting for the next day, to take into consideration some matters of important concern.

One matter of important concern was taken into immediate consideration, however. As soon as Allen had turned his back, some members of the committee recalled the crowd for a few minutes, related how Allen had, from time to time, refused money in compensation for his services, and moved that a suit of clothes should be voted to him. This was a present which he could not refuse, if given under colour of enabling him to appear more respectably as their advocate before the masters, and would serve to make a proper distinction between such a sound friend to their cause as Allen, and such a frothy fellow as Clack. The motion was carried by acclamation; and as all Allen's scruples were so forestalled as that he could not decline the gift, he was, before nightfall, clothed in a suit which must mark him out at meetings as leader of the Union proceedings.

Chapter X: Hope Declining

Alas! what is so fleeting as popularity! Allen's was in great part gone before morning. Some mischievously disposed persons, who had marked what impression had been made on the mind of the secretary by Mr. Wentworth's speech, and who had afterward ascertained that he wished to propose a compromise with the masters, took upon themselves to make known that the favourite secretary turned tail and meant to betray the cause. A general gathering about the waggon of all who scorned to be betrayed was advised, in order to keep his friends at a distance and to raise a hiss with the more effect. When, confident of his reception, Allen advanced with a smiling countenance, in order to express his gratification at the mark of esteem he had received, he was startled by a burst of groans and hisses. For a moment he looked about him to see if Clack or any other unpopular person was standing near; but signs not to be mistaken convinced him too soon that he was the object of the people's dislike. He coloured scarlet, and was about to cover his face with his hands, but checked himself, and, by a strong effort, stood it out. Those who were near him saw how the papers in his hand shook; but his countenance was fixed and his attitude firm. After many vain attempts to make himself heard, he stripped off his new coat, folded it up and placed it in the hands of the committee-men near, and sent a messenger home for his working dress. This he communicated to the meeting the first moment that they would let him speak. He would not accept any gift from those to whom his services were no longer acceptable. He was ready to resign office,—an arduous office, which they no doubt remembered had been forced upon him,—as soon as they should direct him into whose hands he should deliver his papers. In the meanwhile, he would proceed with their business, forgetful of all personal considerations.

All propositions, whether made by himself or others, tending to a compromise, were rejected, and the meeting, after a stormy discussion, in which no point was settled, broke up. The whole affair put Clack and his friends in glee, and filled wiser people with grief and apprehension of the consequences.

The first consequence was that all the children were turned off. The masters were bent on bringing the affair to a close as speedily as possible; and, being disappointed in the hope that the men would propose a compromise, endeavoured to drive them to it.

This was thought by some parents far from being the worst thing that had happened. While the Committee shook their heads over this weighty additional item of weekly charge, many tender mothers stroked their children's heads and smiled when they wished them joy of their holiday, and bade them sleep on in the mornings without thinking of the factory bell.—It was some days before the little things got used to so strange a difference from their usual mode of life. Some would start up from sound sleep with the question, "Father, is it time?" Some talked in their sleep of being too late, and went on to devour their meals hastily, as if their time was not their own.—It would have amused some people and made others melancholy to watch the sports of these town-bred children. One little girl was seen making a garden;—that is, boring a hole between two flints in a yard with a rusty pair of scissors and inserting therein a daisy which by some rare chance had reached her hands. Others collected the fragments of broken plates and teacups from the kennels,[1] and spread them out for a mock feast where there was nothing to eat. The favourite game was playing at being cotton-spinners, a big boy frowning and strutting and personating the master, another with a switch in his hand being the overlooker, and the rest spinners or piecers, each trying which could be the naughtiest and get the most threats and scolding. Many were satisfied with lolling on the stairs of their dwellings and looking into the streets all day long; and many nursed their baby brothers and sisters, sitting on the steps or leaning against the walls of the street. Hannah Bray, when not abroad with her father, took pains to stir up her little neighbours to what she called play. She coaxed her father into giving them a ball, and tried

1 Gutters.

to teach the children in the next yard to play hide and seek; but she often said she never before saw such helpless and awkward people. They could not throw a ball five feet from them, or flung it in one another's faces so as to cause complaints and crying-fits. In hiding, they always showed themselves, or came out too soon or not soon enough, or jostled and threw one another down; and they were the worst runners that could be conceived. Any one of them trying to catch Hannah looked like a duck running after a greyhound. Hannah began with laughing at them all round; but observing that her father watched their play with tears in his eyes, she afterwards contented herself with wondering in silence why some children were so unlike others.

The affairs of all concerned in the strike looked more and more dismal every day. There were more brawls in the streets; there was less peace at home; for none are so prone to quarrel as those who have nothing else to do, and whose tempers are at the same time fretted by want. All the men who were prone to drink now spent hour after hour at the alehouse, and many a woman now for the first time took to her "drop of comfort" at home. Many a man who had hitherto been a helper to his wife and tender to his children, began to slam the door behind him, after having beaten or shaken the little ones all round, and spoken rough words to their trembling mother. While she, dashing away her tears, looked for something to do, and found one thing that she would wash if she had fuel and soap, and another that she would mend if she had material and cotton.—Now was the time to see the young woman, with the babe in her arms, pushing at the curtained door of the dram-shop,[1] while her husband held it against her,—he saying,— "Well, I tell you I'm coming in five minutes; I shan't be five minutes,"—and she plaintively replying, "Ah, I know, you always say so."—Now was the time to see the good son pacing slowly to the pawnbroker's to pledge his aged mother's last blanket to buy her bread. These were the days when the important men under the three balls[2] civilly declared, or insolently swore, that they could and would take no more goods in pawn, as their houses were full from top to bottom, and there was no sale for what they had encumbered themselves with. Never before had they been so humbly petitioned for loans,—a mother shewing that her winter shawl or her child's frock would take very

1   A dram-shop is a bar or gin-shop.
2   Three balls are the conventional symbol of a pawn shop, where one can sell one's belongings for ready cash in the hope of redeeming them in better economic times.

little room,—or a young girl urging that if a pawnbroker did not want her grandmother's old bible he could get more for it at a book-stall than she could. These were the times for poor landlords to look after their rents, and for hard landlords to press for them. These were the days for close scrutiny to be made by the Union Committee whether men's wives were really lying-in,[1] and whether each really had the number of children he swore to; and, therefore, these were the times when knaves tried to cheat and when honest men were wounded at having their word questioned. Now was the time when weak-minded men thought themselves each worse off than his neighbour. Many landlords were pronounced the hardest that ever owned two paltry rooms; many an applicant was certain the committee had been set against him by some sneaking enemy. In the abstract it was allowed, however, that the sneakers had the most to bear. Hare, for one, was in the depth of distress. Opposition was made, week after week, to his having any relief from the committee because he was not a hearty member of the Union; and on one occasion, when he had with the utmost difficulty obtained an extra shilling for his lying-in wife, and had failed in his plea that he was dunned [billed] for rent, he found on returning home that his landlord had sent in the officers during his absence, who had taken away all the little he possessed, but the mattress on which his wife lay. It was laid on the floor, the bedstead being gone; and the children and their mother were left crying within four bare walls.—Allen, to whose knowledge this hard case was brought, could do little to relieve it; but he almost succeeded in convincing his nervous wife that their own sufferings were light in comparison. Yet they had many painful sacrifices to make,—the more painful to Allen because his wife was not convinced that they were necessary. She urged that he might now ask for some of the money the committee had formerly offered him, since his services had not been repaid even in empty good-will, to the degree that he deserved. It was his duty, she thought, to demand more than the common weekly allowance; and the least he could do for his children was to take the suit of clothes back again which he had thrown away in a pet. Failing in her arguments, she had recourse to two measures,—one of action and the other of persuasion. She went secretly to the Committee, and asked in her husband's name for the

1   Lying-in refers to the period of a woman's confinement during childbirth and recovery.

clothes, which she sold on her way home, trying to persuade herself that she was only doing a mother's duty in providing her children with bread; and then she assailed her husband on the subject of taking work at the master's prices. She knew that he now wished for a compromise and thought the strike had been continued too long, and she would not see he was bound to wait till the Union viewed the matter as he did. She thought it very cruel to talk of honour, and very absurd to plead duty when he knew that his family were in want, and could not deny that it was not by his own choice that he had filled so conspicuous a station. It made Allen very miserable to hear her talk in this manner, sobbing between almost every word she said; especially when little Martha looked wistfully from one to the other, not understanding the grounds of the dispute, but hoping that it would end in father's leaving off walking about the room in that manner, and in mother's stopping her sobs, and in there being something better than those nasty potatoes for dinner. Once or twice she tried to make her bulfinch sing so loud that they could not hear one another speak; but this did not do, for her mother twitched off her apron and flung it over the cage, so that the poor bird cowered down in a corner for the whole day afterwards.

One morning Allen had persuaded his wife that he was immovable, and that the best thing she could do was to go out and buy some potatoes with what money they had, he came and leaned over the table to see Martha feed her bird.

"You are as fond of that bird as ever, Martha."

"Yes,—and I have so much time to teach him things now."

"Had you rather play with him or be at the factory all day?"

"I don't know. My knees are so much better since I have been home, and I like playing with Billy; but mother has got to cry so lately; and, father, we are all so tired of potatoes, we don't know how to eat them."

"Poor child! I wish we could give you anything better. But, Martha, do you think you could bear to stay at home without Billy?"

Martha's countenance fell.

"You see, my dear child, we have sold almost everything we have; and when we can scarcely get food for ourselves, it does not seem to me right to keep animals to feed. This was why I sold the dog so many weeks ago."

"But, father, it is only just a halfpenny now and then. Mother has always found me a halfpenny now and then for Billy."

"A halfpenny is as much to us now, child, as a guinea is to some people; besides we could get money by Billy. Ah! I knew it would make you cry to say so."

And he left her and walked about the room in the way which it always frightened Martha to see. She sobbed out a few words—

"I can't—I can't help crying, father, but I don't mean—I wish you would take Billy and sell him."

"Listen to me, my dear child," said Allen sitting down by her, and putting his arm round her waist. "You were always a very good little girl in working industriously as long as you had work. Now you cannot earn money by working, but you can get some by giving up your bird. Now, you know I always tried to make you as comfortable as I could when you earned money, and I promise you, that I will do the same if you will let me sell your bird. The very first money that I can properly spare, when better days come, shall go to buy a bird, and this very bird if we can get it back again."

Martha thanked him, and said the bird should go for certain; but if this very bird could not be got back again, she would rather have a triangle like Hannah's, and then, she thought, they might all grow rich. Allen smiled and said they would see about that when the time came; in the meanwhile, if Billy was to go, the sooner the better, and all the more as she had just cleaned the cage; and he took his hat.

Martha struggled with her tears, and asked if she might go too. Her father thought she had better not; but she said nobody could make Billy sing all his songs so well as herself; so her father kissed her, and let her follow him down stairs, asking Field's wife who happened to be in good humour, to have an eye to the children till their mother came home.

It was a sad trial for Martha to hear the bird fancier speak slightingly of her pet, and remark that the cage was very shabby. She had a great mind at first to make Billy seem dull, which she knew how to do; but remembering that this would punish nobody but her father, she put away the evil thought, and made Billy sing his best songs in his clearest tone. The bargain was made; her father bade the bird-fancier pay the money into her hand, and whispered that he wished he had anything which would sell for so much. When they were on the threshold, she once more turned round. The man was twirling the cage in a business-like manner, between his hands. "O, once more!" cried Martha, running back. Once more Billy fluttered at the sight of her, and put to his beak between the wires to meet her lips; and then she went away without looking back any more. Every day for the next fortnight, however, little Martha lingered about the bird-fancier's door, doing all she could without being observed, to set Billy singing. One day she was remarked by her parents to be very silent; and after that she went out less. She had missed Billy, though his empty cage still hung in the shop; and having made bold to ask, had found that he was sold to a country customer; really gone for ever. This hope destroyed, Martha tried to comfort herself, as she had proposed, with visions of a triangle.

Chapter XI: Final Deliberation

The spirits of the people were sunk, not only by poverty, but by a more bitter disappointment than had attended any former strike. The Combination Laws having formerly been the great object of dread and hatred, it had been too hastily supposed that the repeal of these laws would give all that was wanted; whereas the repeal only left the people free to make the best bargain they could for their labour, without its having any thing to do with the grounds of the bargain. The repeal could not increase the supply of capital, or diminish the supply of labour; it could not therefore affect the rate of wages.

One more event was looked to with hope; the arrival of the delegates who had travelled in search of support. They had remitted money as they had received it, and the remittances had fallen off much of late; but it was still hoped that the messengers might bring such assurances of sympathy and support, as might justify the people in holding out a little longer. These men, who returned nearly all at the same time, were met some miles out on the road, greeted with cheers, carried to the Committee-room, and with difficulty left alone with the Committee to tell their business.

These men brought advice and intelligence so various as might have perplexed the most discerning and prudent of all managers of public affairs. There were exhortations from some places to hold out to the very last shilling; and from others to retreat, while retreat could be managed with honour. Some distant friends gave them a kindly warning to look for no more contributions from that quarter; and others were sorry to send so little at present, but hoped to raise such and such sums before they should be much wanted. Some sent word that it had always been a bad case which they could not in conscience support, while so many more promising needed help; others declared that if ever there was a righteous cause, this was it, and that they should brand with the name of traitor the first who quailed. While the members of the Committee sighed and inquired of one another what they were to think of such opposite advice, and each delegate was vehement in urging the superior value of that which he brought, Allen proposed that they should abide by the advice of the London delegates, who had been in communication with persons who understood more of the matter in hand, than any who occupied a less central situation. All agreed to this, and the consideration of the matter was deferred till the next morning, when the delegates were expected to have arrived from London.

Every member of the committee was in his place the next morning, and the expected messengers appeared at the foot of the table, and delivered in their report, which was brief enough. Their London friends believed their strike to be in a hopeless condition, and advised their making the best terms they could with their masters, without any further waste of time and capital. Not that all combinations were disapproved of by their London advisers; there were cases in which such union was highly desirable, cases of especial grievance from multiplication of apprentices, or from unfair methods of measuring work, or from gross inequality of wages, &c.; but for a general and permanent rise of wages, no strike could ultimately prevail, where there was a permanent proportion of unemployed labour in the market. A proportion of three per cent of unemployed labour must destroy their chance against the masters.

"Just what Wentworth told us," observed a committee-man. "Pray did you inquire whether it is possible to get a rate of wages settled by law?"

"Of course, as we were instructed so to do; and the answer is what you probably expect,—that unless the law could determine the amount of capital, and the supply of labour, it cannot regulate wages. The law might as well order how much beef every man shall eat for his daily dinner, without having any power to supply cattle. If there be not cattle enough, men cannot have law beef. If there be not capital enough, men cannot have law wages."

"Besides," observed the other delegate, "wages-laws involve the same absurdity as the combination laws we are so glad to have got rid of. Every man who is not a slave has a right to ask a price for his labour; and if one man has this right, so have fifty or fifty thousand. What is an innocent act in itself, cannot be made guilt by being done by numbers; and if Government treats it as guilt, Government treats those who do it as slaves. Government then interferes where it has no business. This was the argument in the case of the combination laws, and it holds in this case too: Government is neither buyer nor seller, and has nothing to do with the bargain; and having nothing to do with it, could neither pass a just wages-law, nor enforce it when passed, any more than in the case of the combination laws, which we all know to have been unjust and perpetually evaded."

As it was now clear that the turn-out must come to a speedy end, the committee decided to waste no more time in discussion, but to proceed to immediate action. Allen begged to produce the accounts, which were balanced up to the present day, and the sight of which would, he thought, quicken their determination to let all get work who could. He had for some time found it difficult to get a hearing on the subject of the accounts, as his brethren were bent on holding out, and would listen to nothing which opposed their wishes; but they were now completely roused. "How much have we left?" was their first question.

"Left!" exclaimed Allen. "You know I have been telling you for this fortnight past that we are deficient 70*l*., without reckoning the bills for advertisements, which had not then come in, and which, I am sorry to say, swell the amount considerably."

This declaration was received with murmurs, and on the part of some, with loud declarations that there must have been mistake or bad management.

Allen passed his hand over his forehead, while enduring the bitter pang caused by this outcry; but he recovered himself instantly.

"There are the accounts." he said. "See for yourselves whether there has been any mistake, and bring home to me, if you can, your charge of bad management. You pressed the task upon me in the first instance against my will; you referred it to my disinterestedness to resume it, when, fearing that I had lost the confidence of the people, I would have resigned it. At your call, I have done my best, and —this is my reward!"

There was cry of "Shame, shame!" and two or three friends rose in turn to say for Allen what he was too modest to say for himself; that the unthankful office had been repeatedly forced upon him, because there was no other man who could discharge it so well; that he had never been detected in a mistake, never found in the rear of his business, never accepting fee or reward, never—

This eulogium was interrupted by objections. He *had* erred in involving the Union with the editor of a newspaper, who now unexpectedly brought an enormous charge for the insertion of notices, intelligence, &c., which it had been supposed he was glad to print gratuitously. Allen *had* also claimed fee and reward in a way which, to say the best of it, was shabby.

Allen calmly related the facts of the transaction with the editor, leaving it to his judges to decide whether the misunderstanding arose from carelessness on his part, or from some other cause. As to the other charge, what fee or reward had he taken?

"The clothes, the clothes!" was the cry. "To send for them privately to sell, after pretending to give them back in the face of the people. Fie! Shabby!"

Allen looked on his thread-bare dress with a smile, supposing this a mistake which a moment would clear up. He went to the press belonging to the committee, where the clothes had been deposited, and flung open the doors. He looked very naturally surprised at their having disappeared, and turned round with an open countenance to say,

"I see how it is. Some dishonest person has used my name to obtain possession of the clothes. I give you my word of honour that I have never seen the clothes, or known that they were not here, since the hour that I gave them back in the face of the people."

All believed him, and some had consideration enough to command silence by gesture; but before it could take effect, the fact was out, that Allen's own wife was the "dishonest person." While he silently walked to the window, and there hid his face in his hands, his friends called on business which attracted attention from him. It was pay-day, and what was to be done? What funds were in hand?

Allen returned to his seat to answer this question: and, as all were just now disposed to do as he pleased, he carried his point of honesty, and obtained authority to lessen the allowance one-half, and give advice to every applicant to attend the afternoon meeting for the purpose of voting for the dissolution of the strike.

Of these applicants, some were glad, and some were sorry to receive the advice of the pay-master; but there was a much greater unity of opinion about the reduction of the allowance. Some murmured, some clamoured, some silently wept, some sighed in resignation; but all felt it a great hardship, and wondered what was to become of them either way, if it was true, as Mr. Wentworth had said, that the wages-fund of the masters and the Union-fund of the men were wasting away together. Some were ready with bad news for Allen in return for that which he offered to them.

"You will be worst off, after all, Allen; for there is not a master that will give you work."

"Did you hear, Allen, what Elliott said about you? He hopes you will go to him for work, that he may have the pleasure of refusing you."

"Mortimer has got a promise out of his cowardly partner, that he will not let you set foot on the premises, Allen, on account of the part you have taken."

"They say, Allen, that you are a marked man in Manchester, and that no master in any trade will take you in among his men. What do you think of doing, I wonder?"

This question Allen could not have answered if he had wished it. It was again put to him by his wife, who waited for him in the street to tell him through her tears all the evil-bodings which a succession of Job's comforters had been pouring into her ears since the news of the probable dissolution of the strike had got wind. "What do you think of doing, I wonder?" was still the burden of her wail.

"Do you know that man?" replied her husband, pointing to a wasted and decrepit man who was selling matches; "that man was once a well-paid spinner. He lost his health in his employment, and now, at forty years of age, is selling matches from door to door. He has submitted to God's will. I too will submit to sell matches, if it be God's will that I should lose my good name as innocently as that man has lost his health."

"I told you how it would be. I told you—" cried Mary.

"I too foresaw it, Mary, and prepared myself for much;—but not for all."

He reproached her no further for the injury she had done to his good name than by declaring his unalterable will that not an article should be purchased by her beyond a bare supply of daily food till the clothes were brought back again and restored to the Committee, or their full value, if they could not be recovered.

Chapter XII: Hope Extinct

There had been a lingering hope among some who would fain have stood out longer, that this day's post would have brought the wherewithal to build up new expectations and prolong the struggle. The wiser ones had resolved that not even the receipt of 200*l.* should shake their determination to return to work; but there was no question about the matter, for no money came.—A prodigious amount of business was done in the few hours preceding the final meeting. The masters met and settled that they would give no more than the medium wages,—that is, the rate given by Wentworth; Elliot carelessly consenting to lower his. Rowe was consulted only as a matter of form, and the other firms had to make slight differences or none at all. They agreed to yield the point of their men belonging to the Union, since it appeared vain to contest it while of importance, and needless when not so.—The men settled that they must agree to a medium rate of wages, and make what they could of having obtained an equalization, such as it was, and of being permitted to adhere to the Union.—Clack agitated for his own private interest,—to get himself appointed to some salaried office in the Union, as he was no more likely to obtain employment from the masters than Allen.—So much was settled beforehand as to leave little to be done at the meeting but to make a public declaration of agreement.

With dark countenances and lagging steps the people came—not in proud procession, with banners and music and a soldier-like march, but in small parties or singly, dropping into the track from by-streets and lanes, and looking as if they were going to punishment rather than to consultation. There was a larger proportion than usual of ragged women and crying babies; for, as the women had been along opposed to the strike, they were sensible of a feeling of mournful triumph in seeing it dissolved. Bray was present, without his pipe and his bells, for this was no time for lively music; but he carried his drum to be used as a signal for silence if the speakers should find any difficulty in obtaining a hearing. He beat a roll between each proposition submitted and agreed to; and thus did his last service to the turn-out he had watched from its commencement.

Proposed:—That as the masters are represented to be inclined to concession, the men shall do their part towards promoting an adjustment of their differences, agreeing to take such and such a rate of wages, provided that the masters pay all alike, and that the men be not disturbed in their peaceable adherence to the Union.—Agreed.

Proposed: that the men shall set apart a portion of their weekly earnings, as soon as able to do so, and in proportion to the size of their families, in order to liquidate the debt incurred on account of the strike now about to be closed.—Murmurs.

Allen came forward to state the gross amount of subscriptions and expenses, intimating that the account-books would be left at the Committee-room for one month, open to the inspection of all who could prove themselves to belong to the Union. It would be seen through what unavoidable circumstances a debt had been incurred, and how essential it was to the honour of the body that it should be liquidated as soon as possible.

No reasonable exception could be made to any of the items of expenditure. The people could only wonder that there should be such crowds of children to receive pay, so many lying-in women to be relieved, so many sick persons to be aided, and so much to pay for printing and advertising. They could not deny that the expenses of the Committee had been very small.

This explanation finished, Allen's part was done. He had neither faults of his own nor favours of theirs to acknowledge. He spoke not of himself, but, when he had rendered his account, gravely made his bow and retired.

Clack then came forward, and, supported by a powerful party of friends near the waggon, succeeded in obtaining the public ear. With more success than delicacy, he enlarged upon his public services, pleaded his betrothment to one who was now suffering under the persecution of the masters, as a title to their support, as well as the certainty that he should not again be employed by any firm in Manchester. He declared that were it only through zeal for their rights, he would marry Ann Howlett as soon as she came out of prison—

"If she will have you," cried somebody; and the crowd laughed.

Clack repeated his declaration without noticing the doubt, and moreover declared his willingness to travel into every county in England, Scotland, and Ireland, in behalf of the Union. He boasted of his connexions in all places, and pointed out the wisdom there would be in employing him as a missionary of the Union, in preparation for any future struggle.—This proposal went a degree too far in impudence, or Clack might, perhaps, have gained his object; for he seemed to have recovered his hold on the people in proportion as that of better men had been weakened. A plain statement from the Committee that, as they were in debt, they had not power at present to appoint a missionary, served, however, to disappoint Clack's hopes. He skilfully laid hold of the words "at present," and left it an understood matter between himself and the people that the office was to be his by and by.

Within half an hour, not a trace of the meeting was left but the trampled grass and the empty waggon. The people seemed to try who could flee the fastest, some to obtain the first access to the masters, some to get out of sight of a scene which had become disagreeable and some few to talk big at the Spread-Eagle of what might have happened if this cowardly Committee would but have stood out a little longer.

Allen's steps were directed to Mr. Wentworth's counting-house. "I will ask work of him and of him only, in this line," thought he. "If I fail, I must take to some other occupation. They can hardly be all shut against an honest man."

"I am sorry for you, Allen," was Mr. Wentworth's reply when, with some difficulty, Allen had made his way through a crowd of people on the same errand with himself. "But you shall pronounce upon the case yourself. I can employ now only two-thirds of the number who turned out from me. Of these, at least half left me unwillingly, and have therefore the first title to employment; and the rest have worked for my firm for many years. At the best, I must refuse many whose services I should be glad to keep; judge then whether I can take a stranger, be he who he may."

Allen bowed and had no more to say.

"If the firm you worked under cannot take you on, I fear you have little chance, Allen; for all are circumstanced like myself, I believe."

Allen shook his head, and would trespass no longer on Mr. Wentworth's time.

In the street he met Bray, who was looking for him to say farewell, while Hannah was doing the same to little Martha. Where were they going, and why so soon?

There was nothing to stay for now, Bray thought; for he had no liking to see honest men stand idle in the labour-market, except by their own choice. Choice made the entire difference in the case. As for where he was going,—he and Hannah must find out where people were most fond of street music and dancing, and would pay the best for it. And this put him in mind of what he had to say. He was much obliged as Hannah herself, and more, by the hospitality with which she had been received at Allen's house; but his friend could not suppose he meant his daughter to be any charge upon the family in times like these. On this account, and for old friendship's sake, and from the sympathy which one proscribed man should feel for another he hoped Allen agreed so far as to defer saying much about it till better times should come. He only just told Bray that the bank note was most acceptable at present for a very particular purpose, wrung his friend's hand, and ran home to fetch his wife, that the suit of clothes might be rebought without loss of time. They proved a dear bargain; but that was a secondary consideration, poor as Allen was. He went to rest that night, satisfied that his honour was redeemed, and that his wife would scarcely venture to put it in pawn again.

His wife said to herself that she had no idea he could have been so stern as he was all this day; she scarcely knew him for William Allen.—Many people made the same observation from this time forward. His sternness only appeared when matters of honour were in question, and no one who knew by what means he had been made jealous on this point wondered at the tone of decision in which a once weak and timid man could speak. But there were other circumstances which made them scarcely able to believe him the same William Allen. He no longer touched his hat to the masters, or appeared to see them as they passed. He no longer repaired to the

Spread-Eagle to hear or tell the news, or to take part in consultation on the affairs of the workmen of Manchester, though he was ever ready to give his advice with freedom and mildness when called upon. He stated that he was a friend to their interests, and therefore anxious to avoid injuring them by being one of the body. He would not even represent his children, who grew up one after another to be employed in the factories, while their father toiled in the streets with his water-cart in summer and his broom in winter; enduring to be pointed out to strangers as the leader of an unsuccessful strike, as long as his family were not included with himself in the sentence of proscription.

When will it be understood by all that it rests with all to bring about a time when opposition of interests shall cease? When will masters and men work cheerfully together for their common good, respect instead of proscribing each other, and be equally proud to have such men as Wentworth and William Allen of their fellowship?

Summary of Principles illustrated in this volume

COMMODITIES being produced by capital and labour, are the joint property of the capitalist and labourer.

The capitalist pays in advance to the labourers their share of the commodity, and thus becomes its sole owner.

The portion thus paid is WAGES.

REAL WAGES are the articles of use and consumption that the labourer receives in return for his labour.

NOMINAL WAGES are the portion he receives of these things reckoned in money.

The fund from which wages are paid in any country consists of the articles required for the use and consumption of labourers which that country contains.

THE PROPORTION OF THIS FUND RECEIVED BY INDIVIDUALS MUST MAINLY DEPEND ON THE NUM-BER AMONG WHOM THE FUND IS DIVIDED.

The rate of wages in any country depends, therefore, not on the wealth which that country contains, but on the proportion between its capital and its population.

As population has a tendency to increase faster than capital, wages can be prevented from falling to the lowest point only by adjusting the proportion of population to capital.

The lowest point to which wages can be permanently reduced is that which affords a bare subsistence to the labourer.

The highest point to which wages can be permanently raised is that which leaves to the capitalist just profit enough to make it worth his while to invest his capital.

The variations of the rate of wages between these extreme points depending mainly on the supply of labour offered to the capitalist, the rate of wages is mainly determined by the sellers, not the buyers of labour.

Combinations of labourers against capitalists (whatever other effects they may have) cannot secure a permanent rise of wages unless the supply of labour falls short of the demand;—in which case, strikes are usually unnecessary.

Nothing can permanently affect the rate of wages which does not affect the proportion of population to capital.

Legislative interference does not affect this proportion, and is therefore useless.

Strikes affect it only by wasting capital, and are therefore worse than useless.

Combinations may avail or not, according to the reasonableness of their objects.

Whether reasonable or not, combinations are not subjects for legislative interference; the law having no cognizance of their causes.

Disturbance of the peace being otherwise provided against, combinations are wisely therefore now left unregarded by the law.

The condition of labourers may be best improved,—

1st. By inventions and discoveries which create capital.

2nd. By husbanding instead of wasting capital:—for instance by making savings instead of supporting strikes.

3rd. BY ADJUSTING THE PROPORTION OF POPULATION TO CAPITAL.

Cousin Marshall

[Poor law reform was central to the period's reform discourse, resulting in the controversial New Poor Law of 1834. Poor law debates reflect, on the one hand, the need to modernize official policy on treatment of the poor and, on the other hand, bureaucratic resistance to changing the system that had been in place since the reign of Elizabeth I.[1] In keeping with the period's prevailing emphasis on individualism, morality, and independence through self-help, poor law reform required a dramatic shift in the public's attitudes about poverty—away from the assumed inevitability of dependence on public assistance and toward the moral imperative that the able-bodied poor must help themselves, thus eliminating or at least minimizing the problem of their maintenance.

Perhaps the most significant shift in perspective was the challenge to the assumption that the poor deserved perpetual help, and that help was to be provided by those who worked for a living. This arrangement aroused deep resentment in workers who found that the more industrious and prosperous they were, the higher the poor-rates they were required to pay, making their own economic progress impossible. Among the poor, the system served to encourage marriage and procreation as well as idleness, since in any event their maintenance was guaranteed by the parish, leaving them little incentive to work. The parish system was "relied upon as an unfailing resource, to which every one clung, and from which every man considered he had a right to obtain the supply of every want, even although it were caused by his own indolence, vice, or improvidence" (Nicholls 229).

In poor law reform debates, the terms *deserving* and *undeserving* poor were common currency, as the distinction between chronic exploitation of the system and temporary emergency assistance became the defining terminology of the New Poor Law debates in the early 1830s. The science of political economy exposed the more insidious effects of charity which, many believed, actually created more problems than it solved. Political economy also revealed that unemployment and poverty were not always due to human irresponsibility but, rather, to the natural fluctuations of the marketplace. By associating poverty with an idea of immorality seemingly inher-

---

1   Elizabeth I, Tudor (1533-1603), daughter of Henry VIII; queen of England 1558-1603.

ent in the poor, the landed gentry, the middle-class *nouveaux riches*, and the political hegemony all denied culpability for this new economic power imbalance created by industrialism.

Opposition to poor law reform reflects another sort of power imbalance in its bid to preserve the charity system that kept the suffering masses subservient, immobile, and dependent. The old paternalistic system of charity and "the dole" disabled the threat of a mass uprising, while reform critics like Martineau argued against charity in favor of liberating the poor through teaching them to be self-sufficient. According to this perspective, paupers were corrupted by the system that fostered their dependence rather than their autonomy; further, because the "settlement" laws required people to live in the parish of their birth and not relocate, even to find work, paupers had no incentive to seek work elsewhere and were content to live off the parish.

Martineau's treatment of poor-law issues and her emphasis on the morality of self-help—seen especially in the character of Cousin Marshall, who embodies dignity through independence, despite her desperate poverty—rehearses the primary points in poor law debates. The tale dramatizes the problem presented by four children orphaned by a tragic fire. Cousin Marshall can only afford to support two children and reluctantly sends the others to the dreaded workhouse. Over time, her worst fears are confirmed when she learns that this catch-all institution that houses the dregs of humanity—criminals, prostitutes, thieves, murderers, unmarried mothers, and those incapacitated by infectious (including venereal) diseases—is not a safe-haven for the "deserving" poor driven to the workhouse by temporary tragedy but an insidious concentration of social depravity capable of contaminating the innocent. A related theme involves Mr. Dale, a prosperous, hard-working farmer driven to ruin by excessive rate-paying, demonstrating how charity and institutional relief compromised the subsistence fund by compelling productive citizens to maintain the unproductive, in the process driving themselves into poverty.]

Chapter I: A Very Hot Morning

The gray light of a summer's morning was dawning on the cathedral towers of the city of _____, when Mr. Burke, a surgeon, returned on horseback from the country, where he had been detained by a patient till past midnight. It was Sunday morning, and he was therefore less surprised than grieved to see what kind of people they were who still loitered in the streets, and occasionally disturbed the repose of those who slept after their weekly toils. Here and there lay on a door-step, or in the kennel, a working man, who had spent his week's wages at the alehouse, and on being turned out when the clock struck twelve, had sunk down in a drunken sleep. Farther on were more of the same class, reeling in the middle of the street, or holding by the walls of the houses, with just sense enough to make their way gradually homewards, where their wives were either watching anxiously, or disturbed with miserable dreams on their account. The sound of the horse's hoofs on the pavement roused the watchmen, of whom one rubbed his eyes, and came out of his box to learn the hour from the church clock, while another began to make a clearance of the tipplers [drinkers], bidding them move on with threats which were lost upon their drowsy ears. One of these guardians of the night, however, was too far gone in slumber to be roused like the rest. Perhaps his own snoring prevented his hearing that any one passed by. Mr. Burke tickled this man's ear with his riding whip, and asked him the meaning of certain clouds of dun smoke which were curling up, apparently at some little distance, between the gazers and the pale eastern sky. The watchman's wit served him just so far as to suggest that there ought to be no smoke in that direction at this hour of a Sunday morning, and that he supposed smoke must come from fire. Upon this hint, Mr. Burke rode off at full trot, through such byways as would lead him most directly to the spot. Before he got there, however, his fears were confirmed by the various methods in which information of a fire is given. Rattles were sprung in quick succession, shouts and whoops were echoed from street to street, a red blaze was reflected from every chimney, and glittered like the setting sun on the windows of the upper stories, and the clangor of bells followed in less time than could have been supposed possible. Window after window was thrown up, as Mr. Burke passed, and night-capped heads popped out with the incessant inquiry—"Fire! Where?"

This was what Mr. Burke was as anxious as any one to know, and he therefore increased his speed till he arrived on the spot, and found that it was not a dwelling-house, but a large grocery warehouse, that was in flames. Having satisfied himself that no lives were in danger, and that every one was on the alert, he hastened homewards to deposit his horse, and quiet his sister's alarms, and returned to give assistance.

When he came back, two or three engines were on the spot, but unable to work from a deficiency of water. The river was not far distant; but so many impediments arose from the disposition of some of the crowd to speculate idly on the causes of the fire, and of others to bustle about without doing any good, that the flames were gaining ground frightfully. As more gentlemen arrived, however, they assisted Mr. Burke in his exertions to form two lines down to the river side, by one of which the full, and by the other the empty buckets might be passed with regularity and speed. Meanwhile, the crowd felt themselves at liberty to crack their jokes, as nothing but property was yet at stake.

A child clapped its hands in glee, as a pale blue flame shot up where there had been no light before.

"That's rum," said a man. "If there be raisins beside it, 'tis a pity we are not near enough to play snap-dragon."

"There will be a fine treat for the little ones when all is cool again," observed another. "A fine store of lollipops under the ruins. Look how the hogsheads of sugar light one after another, like so many torches!"

"They say tea is best made of river water," said a third; "and it can't but boil in such a fire; so suppose you fetch your tea-service, neighbour."

"Rather tea than beer," replied another. "Did you taste the beer from the brewery fire? Pah! 'Twas like what sea-water will be when the world is burnt."

"I missed my share then," answered the neighbour; "but I got two or three gallons of what was let out because the white-washer's boy was drowned in it. That was none the worse, that I could find out. My wife was squeamish about it, so I had it all to myself. Heyday? what's this about? Why, they won't let a man look on in peace!"

The constables were now vigorously clearing a space for the firemen, as there was some apprehension that the flames were spreading backwards, where there were courts and alleys crowded with dwellings of the poor. The fear was soon perceived to be too well founded. From an arched passage close by the burning building there presently issued a half-dressed woman with two children clinging to her, a third girl shivering and crying just behind, and a boy following with his arms full of clothes and bedding. Mr. Burke was with them instantly.

"Have the houses behind caught fire?"

"Ours has, sir; and it can't be saved, for there is no way to it but this. Not a thing could we get out but what we have on; but, thank God, we are all safe!"

"O mammy, mammy!" cried the elder girl, "she has not been out of bed this week, sir. She'll die with cold."

Mr. Burke had observed the ghastly look of the woman. He now bade her compose herself, and promised that the children should be taken care of, if she would tell him where she wished to go. She answered doubtfully that her sister lived in the next street.

"O, not there, mother!" said the boy. "Let us go to John Marshall's."

" 'Tis too far, Ned. My sister will surely take us in at such a time as this. Lord have mercy! The flames dizzy one so!"

And the poor woman fell against the wall. Mr. Burke raised her, and bidding Ned go before to show the way, he half led and half carried her the short distance to her sister's house, the little ones running barefooted, holding by the skirts of his coat. On their way, they met a man whom the children proclaimed with one voice to be John Marshall.

"I was coming to you," said he, supporting the widow Bridgeman on the other side. "This is a sad plight I see you in, cousin; but cheer up! If you can get as far as our place, my wife bids me say you will be kindly welcome."

Mr. Burke thought the nearest resting-place was the best; and Marshall yielded, hoping the sister's door would be open, as it ought. It was but half open, and in that half stood the sister, Mrs. Bell, arguing with Ned that the place was too small for her own family, and that his mother would be more comfortable elsewhere, and so forth. Mr. Burke cut short the argument by pushing a way, and depositing his charge upon the bed within. He then gave his name to the amazed Mrs. Bell, desired her to lend the children some clothing, and to keep her sister quiet till he should come again, sent Marshall for his wife, who would apparently nurse the widow Bridgeman better than her own sister, and then returned with Ned to see if any of the widow's little furniture could be saved. Before they reached the spot, however, the tenement was burnt to the ground, and the two or three next to it were pulled down to stop the fire, so that nothing more was to be done.

The widow seemed at first so much revived by the treatment which Mr. Burke ordered, and her cousin Marshall administered, that there was room for hope that the shock would leave her little worse than it found her; and the benevolent surgeon went home at six o'clock to refresh himself, bearing tidings to his sister, not only that the fire was extinguished, but that it appeared to have done no irreparable mischief beyond the destruction of property. He was not fully aware, however, in how weak a state his patient had previously been.

"Mammy!" said little Ann Bridgeman, who sat on a low stool, with a blue apron of her aunt's over her shoulders, her only covering except her shift, "Mammy, there goes the church bell."

"Hush!" said Jane, the eldest, who was more considerate.

"Mammy is awake," persisted Ann, looking again into the curtainless bed to see that the widow's eyes were open. "Do you hear the bell, mammy? And we cannot go to church."

"'Tis a strange Sunday, indeed, my child," replied the mother. "When I prayed last night, after all our work was done, that this might be a day of rest, I little thought what would happen."

Her cousin, Mrs. Marshall, came to her and begged that she would try to rest, and not to trouble herself with uneasy thoughts.

"My mind is so tossed about!" replied the poor woman. "It distracts me to think what we are to do next. And there sit the poor children without so much as a petticoat to wear; and the room is all as if the fire was roaring about me; and a letter from my husband, the only one I ever had, that I thought to have carried to my grave with me, is burned; and I might as well have saved it, if I had had a minute's thought; and—"

The sick woman burst into a hysterical cry which shook her frame so, that her cousin began to think how she could calm her. She ventured on a bold experiment when she found that her patient's talk still ran upon the letter, and that the consolations of Mrs. Bell, who now came to the bedside, only made the matter worse.

"Well now, I wonder," said Mrs. Bell, "that you should trouble yourself so about a letter, when you will be sure to remember what is in it. One would think it was a bank note by the way you cry after it."

"A bank note!" cried the poor woman. "I would have set light to my house with a handful of bank notes, if I had had them, sooner than lose that letter; and yet nobody would think so by the way I left it behind me. There it was in the box with my rent, and with my mother's gold thimble, nigh at hand as I got out of bed, and I might just as well have saved it. O Lord! What a wretch I am!" she cried. "Take the children away! Don't let them come near me any more. Lord forgive me! Lord have mercy upon me!" and she raved fearfully.

"She's out of her senses," said Mrs. Bell, "and all for that trumpery letter. I'll make her believe we have found it."

"And so make her worse than ever when she discovered the trick," said Mrs. Marshall. "No, that won't do." And she turned to the sick woman,—"I say, Mary, you would not mind so much about the letter if you were to see your husband very soon, would you?"

"Surely no," replied the widow, looking perplexed, but immediately calm. "But my husband is gone, long ago, is not he? But perhaps I am going too. Is that what you mean, cousin Marshall?"

"I don't know whether you be or no, Mary; but you have no strength for raving as you did just now. If you wish to live for your children's sake, you must be quiet."

"I was thinking a deal about dying last night, and what was to become of the children; but I forgot all about it to-day. Poor things! They have no friends but you two," looking from Mrs. Bell to her cousin Marshall. "You will see to them, I am sure. You will not cast them out upon the world; and depend upon it, it will be repaid to you. I will pray God day and night, just as I would here, to watch over them and reward those that are kind to them; particularly whichever of you takes Sally; for I am much afraid Sally will go blind." As she gazed earnestly in the faces of her relations, Mrs. Bell tried to put her off with bidding her make her mind easy, and trust in Providence, and hope to live. Her cousin Marshall did better.

"I will take charge of Sally and of one of the others," said she. "I promise it to you; and you may trust my promise, because my husband and I have planned it many a time when we saw what a weakly way you were in. They shall be brought up like our own children, and you know how that is."

"God bless you for ever, cousin! And as for the other two—"

"Leave that to me," replied Mrs. Marshall, who saw that the patient's countenance began to resume its unsettled expression. "Leave it all to me, and trust to my promise."

"Just one thing more," said the widow, starting up as her cousin would have retired. "Dear me! How confused my head is,—and all because you have moved the bed opposite the window, which my head never could bear. Listen now. In the cupboard on the left side the bed,—at least, that is where it was,—you will find a japanned box that I keep my rent in. At the bottom of that box there is a letter—"

"Well, well, Mary. That will do by-and-by."

"Let me finish, cousin. Give that letter to Ned, and bid him keep it, because—"

"Aye, I understand. Because it is his father's writing, and the only one you ever had."

"Why, you know all about it!" exclaimed the widow, smiling, with a look of surprise. "I did not know I had ever told anybody. Well, now, I can't keep awake any longer; but be sure you wake me in time in the morning. I must be up to wash the children's things for they want them sadly."

She dropped asleep instantly when her cousin had hung a shawl at the foot of the bed to hide the strange window. Ned had gone some minutes before for Mr. Burke, who pronounced, on seeing her, that she would probably never wake again. This proved true; and before night she was no more.

The fire created a great sensation in the city. The local newspapers described it as the most awful that had occurred in the place within the memory of man; and the London prints copied from them. Strangers came in from the country to visit the smoking ruins, and the firm to whom the warehouses belonged were almost overwhelmed with sympathy and offers of assistance. Mrs. Bell was disposed to make a profit out of all this. She would have stationed Ned, in a tattered shirt, on the ruins of his mother's dwelling to beg, and have herself carried about a petition in behalf of the orphan children. The funeral, at least, ought, she thought, to be paid for by charity; but there was no moving the Marshalls on any of these points. They were so sure that the widow would have died at all events, in a very short time, that they could not see why the fire should throw the expense of her funeral on the public; and even Mrs. Bell could not pretend that anything of much value had been lost in the fire except the rent, which would never be called for. The Marshalls countenanced Ned's dislike to go near the idle boys who were practising leaping on the ruins, and found it a far more natural and pleasant thing to dress the little Bridgemans in some of their own children's clothes and take them home, than to appeal to strangers on their behalf.

"You may do as you please, neighbour," cried Mrs. Bell, after an argument upon this subject. "If you choose to burden yourselves with two children in addition to your own five, it is no concern of mine; only don't expect me to put any such dead-weight upon my husband's neck."

"Your husband earns better wages than mine, Mrs. Bell."

"And that is what makes me wonder at your folly in not sending the children to the workhouse at once. No need to tell me what a little way a man's wages go in families like yours and mine."

"You have a good deal of help in other ways to make out with, indeed, neighbour," observed Mrs. Marshall. "You have found the gentry very kind to you this year; so much so that I think the least you can do is to keep these children from being a burden on the rates, for the little time till they can shift for themselves.—I believe you bought neither coals nor blankets last winter."

"Bless your heart, cousin, the coals we got did not last half the winter through; for my husband likes a good fire when he can get it, and always expected to find one in the grate when he came home from the Leopard, however late at night it might be; and I had to sell one of the blankets presently. The other, on the bed there, is the only one we have till winter, when I hope to get a new one, if the ladies are not too particular about my having had two already. But, really, it tries one's patience to wait upon them ladies. Do you know I am disappointed again about the bag of linen against my confinement.[1] I may be down any day now, and every bag is engaged, so that they can't promise with any certainty. So I must just take my chance for getting through somehow."

"And how is your baby provided?"

"O, they gave me a few trifles for it, which will do till I get about again, and can carry it to show how poorly it is off."

"Well," said Mrs. Marshall, "I do wonder you can bear to live from hand to mouth in that way. You got your first set of baby-linen at the same time that I did, and with your own money; and why yours should not have lasted as well as mine, I can't think. Mine are not all worn out yet, and I always managed to replace, by timely saving, those that were. However, if you can't clothe your own children, I don't wonder so much that you will not feed your sister's. Poor things! Must they go to the workhouse?"

"Unless you choose to take them all, cousin. So wonderful a manager as you are, perhaps you might contrive it."

Mrs. Marshall shook her head mournfully. She had not lodging room for more than two girls among her own, and could not have engaged that her husband's rent should be ready if more than two in addition were to share their daily meals. As it was, they must give up one dish of meat a week, and make some other reductions of the same kind.

"Better ask the gentry to help you, at once," said Mrs. Bell; "but I suppose you are too proud?"

---

1   Mrs. Bell accepts coal and blankets from the parish, although her husband has money to spend regularly in pubs. She complains that the parish refused her a new set of baby linen for her impending childbirth. That parish charity provides fuel, blankets, and baby clothes to people as improvident as Mr. Bell and as productive (in terms of prolific child-bearing) as Mrs. Bell illustrates the attitudes fostered by charity among the poor, many of whom felt that the parish "owed" them a subsistence.

"We will try what our own charity can do before we ask it from those who have less concern in the matter," said Mrs. Marshall. "There is one thing I mean to ask, however, because I cannot anyhow get it for them myself; and that is, to have them taught like my own children. Poor Sally must learn to knot while she has some eyesight left."

"Which of the others do you mean to take?" enquired Mrs. Bell, as if quite unconcerned in the matter.

Mrs. Marshall called in the four children from the next room to consult them, to her cousin's utter amazement. She told them the plain truth,—that she had promised their mother to take charge of two of them, and that one of the two should be Sally; that the other two must live in the workhouse till they could earn their own subsistence; and that she wished them to agree with her which had best remain with her and Sally. Ned looked at his aunt with tears in his eyes; to which she answered by promising to see him sometimes, and to bring him some gingerbread when she had a penny to spare. Ned, who was too old to be spoken to in this way, brushed his sleeve across his eye, and observed to cousin Marshall that Jane had better go with him to the workhouse, because she was the oldest and would be soonest out of it, and because Sally liked to have little Ann to do things for her that she could not see to do herself. Cousin Marshall was quite of this opinion; and so the matter was settled.

A long private conversation followed after Mrs. Bell had left the room; if conversation it might be called which consisted of sobs and tears on the part of the children, and exhortations and pity on that of their friend.

"Remember, Ned," said she, "the one thing you must be always thinking about after you go into the workhouse is how soon you can get out again. It is God's will that has taken your mother from you, and that has made your relations poor, and so we must try and not think your lot a disgrace; but it will be a disgrace if you stay long. Keep this up in Jane's mind too, for I am afraid of her forgetting it, as she is rather giddy.—I am not sorry, Jane, to see you cry so much, because I hope it will make you remember this strange day. I have heard of workhouse frolics, my dear. Never let me hear of them from you. You will have a service, I hope, in a few years, and you must try to make yourself fit to live with a different sort of people from those you will find in the workhouse."

Mrs. Bell, who had come back in time to hear the last few words, began to tell all she had heard about the pleasant kind of life people might lead in a workhouse if they chose; but her cousin cut her short by bidding the children take leave at once.

Few events wrung tears from this stout-hearted woman; but she kept her apron to her eyes the whole way home, and could not speak to any body all day.

Chapter II: An Interior

Miss Burke had gone into the country the morning after the fire, and remained some weeks. When she returned, she inquired of her brother what had become of the family who had been burnt out. She was an occasional visitor at the workhouse school, and besides knew some of the elderly paupers, and went to see them now and then.[1] Her visits were made as disagreeable as possible by the matron, who hated spies, as she declared, and had good reasons for doing so; many practices going forward under her management which would not bear inspection. She was sometimes politic enough to keep out of sight, when she was aware that something wrong had already met the lady's eye; but she more frequently confronted her near the entrance with such incivility as might, she hoped, drive her away without having seen anything. The master was an indolent, easy man, much afraid of the more disorderly paupers, and yet more of his wife. He seldom appeared to strangers till called for; but was then quite disposed to make the best of everything, and to agree in all opinions that were offered. There was little more use, though less inconvenience, in pointing out abuses and suggesting remedies to him than to his wife; yet Mr. Burke and his sister conscientiously persevered in doing this,—the gentleman from the lights he obtained in his office of surgeon to the workhouse infirmary, and the lady, from her brother's reports and her own observations.

Miss Burke's first inquiry at the workhouse gate was for nurse Rudrum. The porter's office consisted merely in opening the gate; so that when the lady had entered the court, she had to make further search. The court was half-full of people, yet two women were washing dirty linen at the pump in the midst. Several men were seat-

---

1 Miss Burke's character represents the practice of "female philanthropy" or "benevolence" popular throughout the 19th-century. Middle- and upper-class women could not work for remuneration without losing their class status; therefore, women like Miss Burke did volunteer work, usually some form of social or religious work, as an alternative to either being confined at home or losing caste by working for pay.

ed cutting pegs for the tilers and shoemakers, and others patching shoes for their fellow-paupers; while several women stood round with their knitting, laughing loud; and some of the younger ones venturing upon a few practical jokes more coarse than amusing. At a little distance, sat two young women shelling peas for a grand corporation dinner that was to take place the next day, and beside them stood a little girl whose business was apparently to clean a spit on which she was leaning, but who was fully occupied in listening to the conversation which went on over the pea-basket. This group looking the least formidable, Miss Burke approached to make her inquiry. Being unperceived, the conversation was carried on in the same loud tone till she came quite near, when one of the young women exclaimed,

"I don't want to hear any more about it. I wonder you had the heart to do it."

"To do what?" asked Miss Burke. "Something that you do not look ashamed of," she continued, turning to the first speaker.

"Lord, no," said the girl with a bold stare. "It is only that a young mistress of mine, that died and left a child a week old, bade me see that it was taken care of till her husband came back, who was gone abroad; and I could not be troubled with the little thing, so I took it direct to the Foundling Hospital;[1] and I heard that the father came home soon after, and the people at the hospital could not the least tell which was his child, or whether it was one that had died. I kept out of the way, for I could not have helped them, and should only have got abused; for they say the young man was like one gone mad."

"And was it out of your own head that you took the child there, or who mentioned the hospital to you?"

"I knew enough about it myself," said the woman with a mean-

---

1 Foundling Hospitals accepted unwanted and orphaned infants and children, particularly those of unmarried mothers. Although designed to prevent abandonment and infanticide by providing an alternative resource, the system was abused by parents who could, but found it inconvenient to, maintain their children. Foundling children were rarely adopted, and the system was notorious for its poor quality care. Critics of the system, like Martineau, argued that Foundling Hospitals in effect encouraged adults to be improvident about procreation, since they could assume that any children resulting would be provided for by the hospitals. Although an idea based on benevolent intentions, in practice the system was fraught with problems.

ing laugh, "to manage the thing without asking any body. It is a fine place, that Foundling Hospital, as I have good reason to say."

"Pray find the matron," said Miss Burke to the little spit-cleaner, who was listening with open mouth; "and ask whether Miss Burke can be admitted to see nurse Rudrum. I think," she continued, when the little girl was out of hearing, "you might choose your conversation better in children's company."

"And in other people's company too," said the other sheller of peas. "I've not been used to such a place as this, and I can't bear it."

"You'll soon get used to it, Susan, my love," replied the bold one.

"Where do you come from, Susan, and why are you here?" inquired Miss Burke.

With many blushes, Susan told that she was a servant out of place, without friends, and with no one to give her a character [reference], her last master and mistress having gone off in debt and left her to be suspected of knowing of their frauds, though she had been so ignorant of them as not to have attempted to secure her own wages. It was a hard case, and she did not know how to help herself; but she would submit to any drudgery to get out of the workhouse.

"And who are you?" said the lady to the other. "Are you a servant out of place too?"

"Yes."

"And without a character?"

"O yes, quite," said the woman with a laugh. "It is well for me that there are some places where characters don't signify so much as the parson tells us. Susan and I are on the same footing here."

Susan rose in an agony, and by mistake emptied the shelled peas in her lap among the husks.[1]

"There! Never mind picking them out again," said the other. "If I take such a trouble, it shall be for my own supper, when the rest are done."

"So you really think," said Miss Burke, "that you and Susan are on the same footing because you live under the same roof and sit on the same seat? I hope Susan will soon find that you are mistaken."

At this moment appeared Mrs. Wilkes the matron, shouting so that all the yard might hear.

"Is it nurse Rudrum you want? She is out of her mind and not

---

1 Susan represents a single woman of the "deserving" poor. She is a respectable woman who has fallen on temporary hard times; she resists being linked with the degraded characters she is forced to associate with in the workhouse.

in a state for prayer. Gentlefolks are enough to send poor people out of their minds with praying and preaching."

"I am not going either to pray or preach," replied Miss Burke; "and you well know that it is some years since nurse Rudrum was in her right mind. I only ask the way to her."

"Yonder lies your way, madam. Only take care of the other mad people, that's all."

Surprised and vexed to perceive Miss Burke persevering in her purpose, notwithstanding this terrifying warning, she continued,

"Remember, if you please, that the doctors don't allow their patients to be made methodists[1] of; though God knows how many are sent here by the methodists. You'll please to take it all upon yourself, ma'am."

Miss Burke, not seeing how all this concerned herself and nurse Rudrum, who were about equally far from methodism, pursued her way, as well as she could guess, to the right ward.—She could not easily miss it when once within hearing of nurse Rudrum's never-ceasing voice, or the tip tap of her ancient high-heeled shoes, which she was indulged in wearing, as it was a fancy not likely to spread. Nurse was employed as usual, pacing to and fro in the ward appropriated to the harmless insane, knitting as fast as her well-practised fingers would go, and talking about Jupiter.[2]

"Miss Burke, I declare," cried she, as soon as her visitor appeared. "You are welcome, as you always are—always very welcome; but," and she came nearer and looked very mysterious, "you are come from them people at a distance, I doubt. Now don't deny it if you be. If they have practised upon me, you didn't know it; so no need to deny it, you know."

"I am come from Mr. Earle's nurse; and Mr. Earle sent his love to you, and hopes you will accept some tea and sugar; and the young ladies will come and see you when they visit me, and in the meanwhile they have sent you a Sunday shawl."

A dozen curtseys, and "My duty to them, my duty and many thanks; and I dare say it is because they are so sorry about them

---

1 Methodism is a protestant sect based on the teaching of theologian John Wesley (1703-91). A dissenting sect, early methodism was distinguished by public, outdoor meetings led by "lay" preachers who were thought to engender fanaticism.

2 Nurse Rudrum illustrates the stereotype of the domestic worker or governess who becomes deranged as a result of long years of labor for little pay. For this category of workers, old age and declining health left no choice but the workhouse, where they were confined without treatment.

people at a distance that practise upon my ancle, without so much as shaking their heads."

"O, your ancle! I was to ask particularly how your ancle is. You seem able to walk pretty briskly."

"That's to disappoint 'em, you see," and she laughed knowingly. "I only tell *you*, you know, so you'll be quiet. They can't touch me anywhere else, because of Jupiter in my cradle."

"What was that, nurse?"

"O that was when they made me a watch-planet; and a fine thing it was to keep me from harm,—all except my ancle, you see. It was Jupiter, you know; and I feel it all over me now sometimes,—most in my elbows. It was only Jupiter; none of the rest of them. That was my mother's doing; for Jupiter is the most religious of all the planets."

And so she ran on till her visitor interrupted her with questions about some of her companions in the ward.

"Ay—a queer set for me to be amongst, a'n't they? That poor man! Look at his sash;" and she giggled while she showed how a poor idiot was fastened by a leathern belt to a ring in the wall. "He spins a good deal as it is; but if he could walk about, he would do nothing. He has no more sense than a child, and people of that sort are always for tramp, tramp, tramping from morning till night, till it wearies one's ears to hear them."

And nurse resumed her walk. When she returned to the same place, she went on,—

"If these people could be made to hold their tongues, they would be better company; but you never heard such a clatter; they won't hear one speak. That girl sings to her spinning-wheel the whole day long, and she has but one tune. They say I am growing deaf; but I'm sure I hear that song for ever, as much when she is not singing as when she is. But do you think that I am growing deaf, really now?"

Miss Burke could only say that when people got to nurse's age, and so on.

"Well now, 'tis only because of Jupiter,—listening as a watch-planet should, you know. You should have heard his music last night;—that that I used to sing to the little Earles, when master Charles was afraid to go to bed alone because of the ghost-story I told him; and I put him to bed in Miss Emma's room for once, and nobody knew: so don't tell my mistress, for she never forgave such a thing."

Miss Burke smiled and sighed; for this master Charles was now a man of forty, and Mrs. Earle had been in her grave nearly twenty years. As the visitor was about to take leave, nurse laid her hand on the lady's arm, drew up her tight little person to its best advantage, and gravely said,

"One thing more, Miss Burke. You will give me leave to ask why I am detained in this place, among idiots and dolts that are no companions for me? This is a poor reward for my long service, and so you may tell Mr. Earle."

"We hoped you had everything comfortable, nurse. You always seem in good spirits."

"Comfortable! You mean as to tea and sugar and shawls; but what is that compared with the company I keep? The Earles don't know what they miss by what they do. Many a time I would go and see them, and carry them a piece of gingerbread, if I was not prevented."

"Well, nurse, you shall come and see them at our house by and by. In the meanwhile,—you know the boys in the yard are very rude, and they are too apt to teaze old people. We think you are more comfortable out of their way."

Nurse still looked haughty and dissatisfied.

"Besides," continued Miss Burke, "watch-planets are not common, you know; and who knows how they might be treated in the world?"

"True, true, true," cried the delighted old woman. "There are but two in the world besides me, and they are at Canterbury, where my mother lived nurse twenty years. 'Tis only them that study the stars that bow before watch-planets. Well! We shall all study the stars up above, and then will be the time for us watch-planets."

So saying, nurse Rudrum returned to the track she had worn in the floor, and Miss Burke heard the well known pit pat all the way down stairs.

The lady now turned into the school, where she was equally welcome to mistress and scholars, especially after an absence of some duration, as now. The mistress, Mrs. Mott, was not exactly the person the ladies would have appointed to the office, if the choice had been left to them; but, all things considered, the appointment might have been worse filled. Mrs. Mott, a starched, grim-looking personage, had kept a dame school in a village for many years, during which time she had acquired a very high opinion of herself and her modes of tuition;—an opinion which she continued to instill into the guardians of the poor, by whom she was appointed to her present office; their choice being also aided by the consideration that Mrs. Mott must have parish assistance at all events, and might as well do something in exchange for it. The ladies who interested themselves about the children, seeing that the choice lay between having no school at all and having Mrs. Mott for a schoolmistress, made the best of the latter alternative.

When the lady entered, Mrs. Mott was doing what she rather prided herself upon,—carrying on two affairs at once. She was fixing work for the girls,—plying her needle as fast as possible—and leading a hymn which the children sang after her, kneeling on their benches, with their hands clasped before them, and every little body rocking from side to side to mark the time. When it was over, and the children scrambled down into their seats, a universal grin of pleasure greeted Miss Burke from her old acquaintance, and a stare of wonder from the new comers who yet knew her only by reputation. Mrs. Mott, meanwhile, went on drawing out her thread most indefatigably, and murmuring as if under some emotion.

"Good morning, Mrs. Mott. It is sometime since I saw you last."

"Time, madam! Ay: time is given, time is given where all else is given. 'Tis ours to seize it ere it flies."

"How are your family, Mrs. Mott? I hope your sons are doing better."

"Son, madam, son! I suppose you don't know that the Lord has made choice of Jack?"

Miss Burke was much concerned; and tried to hear the story notwithstanding a hubbub at the bottom of the school, which at length roused the teacher's wrath.

"Tommy bit Jemmy," was the reply of twenty little voices to the inquiry of what was the matter.

"Tommy is a bad boy and must be punished," was the verdict; and the sentence speedily followed. "We are going to prayers, and I will have no disturbance while prayers are going on; but I will have justice. So, as soon as prayers are over, Jemmy shall bite Tommy in whatever part he chooses."

Miss Burke considered how she might best interfere with the process without setting aside the mistress's authority. She waited till prayers were over, and then called the two boys before her. She represented to the sobbing culprit the enormity of biting human flesh, and then asked Jemmy if he had any urgent desire to bite Tommy.

"I don't want to bite him, unless I'm bid," was the reply.

"Very well; then, suppose you forgive him instead. This will make him very careful not to hurt you another time. Will it not, Tommy?"

Tommy agreed, and words instead of wounds were exchanged.

The next inquiry was for the Bridgemans. Ned was called out of the ranks of departing schoolboys, and Jane was sent for, being detained from school this day to help to prepare for the corporation dinner. On her appearance, she was recognized as the cleaner of spits, who had listened so eagerly to the praises of the Foundling Hospital. Miss Burke told them how she had heard of their circumstances, and her intention to visit them from time to time. She asked them if they were happy.

"Yes, ma'am," replied Jane, readily; "a deal happier than we thought."

Ned, however, only bit his lip to keep back his tears. Miss Burke framed her speech to suit both.

"You know," she said, "that we all consider that you are here only for a time, and we trust a short time. It has pleased God to take from you your natural protectors and teachers; and children like you must be taken care of, and taught, before you can find a way in the world. But, if you choose, you may soon make yourselves fit for a better and a happier place than this; and the more cheerfully you set about it, Ned, the more quickly you will learn. You, Jane, should seek out the more sober and quiet young women to talk to, instead of listening to the foolish gossip that goes on in the yard. Has Susan been kind to you?"

"She always keeps by herself when she can, ma'am."

"She will be kind to you, however, I am sure, if you deserve it; and I believe she can teach you many things you will like to learn."

In order to unloose Ned's tongue, the lady made several inquiries about their comforts. They had nothing to complain of but that they did not like milk-broth, which composed their dinner twice a week, and that the workhouse dress was very hot and heavy. The first evil could not be helped—the other seemed very reasonable; and Miss Burke determined to urge an objection to it through her brother, as it appeared that a thick woollen dress was the most liable to dirt of any that could be fixed upon, and the most unseemly when worn into holes; besides this, the children were exposed to colds from the temptation to throw off the dress when heated, and from exchanging it for their own old clothes on Sundays and holidays. Jane had, as her brother declared, been scarcely ever without colds since she entered the workhouse, as cousin Marshall had been kind enough to provide her with a complete suit on her entrance, which Jane was fond of wearing whenever she went to church, or to the gardens, or—"

"To the gardens! What gardens?"

The public tea-gardens, where the girls and boys were treated very often on Sundays, sometimes under guidance, and sometimes without any. Jane was very eloquent in describing these frolics, and others which took place within the walls.

Miss Burke had little hope of counteracting such influences as these by an occasional visit; but she now said what she thought most likely to impress the mind of the poor girl, and then proceeded to find Susan, in order to recommend Jane to her care.[1] She was glad to see Wilkes, the master, unaccompanied by his wife, and conversing with a gentleman whom she knew to be one of the visitors. Before she reached them, she perceived that Ned was following her with a wistful look.

"Have you any thing more to say to me?" she inquired.

"Only, ma'am, that perhaps you may know when we may get out. I should like to see the time when we shall get out."

"I wish I could tell you, my dear boy; but I can only guess, like you. I guess it will be when Jane is fit for service, and you for labour in the fields or elsewhere."

"I can labour now," said the boy, brightening. "If they would try me, I am sure I could dig all day."

"Be patient, Ned; and then, if you turn out a clever workman when the right time comes, who knows but you may not only keep out of the workhouse yourself, but prevent somebody else from coming in?"

Ned smiled, pulled his forelock, and went away cheered.

Mr. Nugent, the visitor, met Miss Burke with an observation on the improvement of work-houses which rendered them accessible to female benevolence; whereas they were once places where no lady could set her foot. Miss Burke gravely replied that there was much yet for benevolence to do. The necessary evils of a work-house were bad enough; and it was afflicting to see them needlessly aggravated,—to see poverty and indigence confounded, and blameless and culpable indigence, temporary distress, and permanent destitution, all mixed up together, and placed under the same treatment. These distinctions were somewhat too nice for the gentleman's perceptions; at least, while announced in abstract terms. He stood in an attitude of perplexed attention, while Wilkes asked whether she would have the paupers live in separate dwellings.

Miss Burke observed that the evil began out of the workhouse; and that the want of proper distinctions there made classification in the house in imperative duty.

---

1   Miss Burke's concern reflects a prominent stereotype about the moral contamination of work-houses. Jane is young and impressionable, vain and silly, and thus especially vulnerable to unsavory influences likely to corrupt her morals.

"We are too apt," she said, "to regard all the poor alike, and to speak of them as one class, whether or not they are dependent; that is, whether they are indigent or only poor. There must always be poor in every society; that is, persons who can live by their industry, but have nothing beforehand. But that there should be able-bodied indigent, that is, capable persons who cannot support themselves, is a disgrace to every society, and ought to be so far regarded as such as to make us very careful how we confound the poor and the indigent."

"I assure you, ma'am," said Wilkes, "it grieves me very much to see honest working men, or sober servants out of place, come here to be mixed up with rogues and vagabonds."

"But they are all indigent alike," observed Mr. Nugent, "or your honest labourers would not have to come here."

"All indigent certainly, sir; but not all alike. We have had cottagers here for a time, after losing cows and pigs by accident; and even little farmers after a fire on their premises; and labourers, when many hundreds were turned off at once from the public works. Now, this sort of indigence is very different from that which springs out of vice."

"It seems to me," said Miss Burke, "that as wide a distinction ought to be made between temporary and lasting indigence, and between innocent and guilty indigence, within the work-house, as between poverty and indigence out of it; and as the numbers are, I believe, very unequal, I should think it might easily be done. I suppose, Mr. Wilkes, those who require permanent support, the invalids and the thoroughly depraved, are few in comparison with those who come in and go out again after a time."

"Very few indeed, ma'am. Mr. Nugent knows that our numbers are for ever varying. One year we may have seven hundred in the house, and another year not so much as three hundred. It seems to me the surest way of making the industrious into vagabonds, and the sober into rogues, to mix them all up together; to say nothing of the corruption to the children."

"I heard the other day," said Mr. Nugent, "that few of the children who have been brought up here turn out well. But it can't be helped, madam. The plan of out-door pay[1] must have its limits, and our building a new house for the moral or immoral, is out of the

---

1 Out-door pay is similar to modern-day welfare in that it was government assistance to the poor who live independently of the workhouse.

question in the present state of the funds. The rate[1] has increased fearfully of late, as your brother will tell you. I confess I do not see what is to become of the system altogether, if we go on as we have been doing for the last five years."

Miss Burke observed that she was far from wishing to urge any new expenses. She rather believed that much money would be saved by enabling the industrious to pursue their employments undisturbed, and by keeping the young and well-disposed out of the contagion of bad example. She pointed out the case of Susan as one of great hardship, and that of little Jane as one of much danger. Wilkes confirmed the fact of Susan being a good girl, and a well-qualified servant, and told that the other woman had been discharged from various services for theft and other crimes.

Mr. Nugent, who, in the midst of his talk about improvement, disliked trouble and innovation, related that an attempt at classification had once been made by building a wall across the yard, to separate the men and women; but that the wall had been pulled down in a riot of the paupers, after which it was considered too formidable an undertaking to rebuild it.

Miss Burke thought, on her way home, that classification must begin among the guardians of the poor, before much reformation could be looked for. The intrepid and active among the gentlemen, if separated from the fearful and indolent, might carry the day against the ill-conducted paupers; but such a result was scarcely to be hoped while the termagant Mrs. Wilkes monopolized all authority within the walls, and the majority of the guardians insisted on the let-alone plan of policy being pursued; a plan under which everything was let alone but the rates, which increased formidably from year to year.

Chapter III: Tea and Talk

Mr. Burke came in earlier than usual this evening, the first time since his sister's return that he could enjoy her society in peace. When he arrived wet and chilly from a stormy ride, and found a little fire, just enough for a rainy summer's evening, burning brightly in the grate, the tea apparatus prepared, his slippers set ready, his study gown awaiting him, and a pile of new medical books laid within reach, as

---

1 Rate refers to the tax paid by wage-earning citizens to support the poor and maintain the workhouse.

if to offer him the choice of reading or conversation, he wished within himself that Louisa would leave home no more till he was married, if that time should ever come. This wish was pardonable; for he was, to use his own expression, so accustomed to be spoiled by his sister that he scarcely knew what comfort was while she was away.

"Any notes or messages for me, Louisa?" he inquired, before resigning himself to his domestic luxuries.

"Alas, yes!" she replied, handing him two or three from their appointed receptacle.

"These will all do to-morrow," he cried; "so make tea while I change my coat," a direction which was gladly obeyed. On his return he flung the books on a distant table, stretched himself out with feet on fender, coaxed his dog with one hand, and stirred his steaming cup with the other.

"I wish I were a clergyman," were his first words.

"To have parsonage comforts without getting wet through in earning them, I suppose," said Louisa, laughing.

"You are far from the mark, Louisa."

Louisa made many guesses, all wrong, about capricious patients, provoking consulting physicians, unpaid bills, jealous competitors, and other causes of annoyance.

"No, no, dear. It is a deeper matter than any of these. The greatest question now moving in the world is, 'What is charity?'"

"Alas, yes! And who can answer it? Johnson gave a deficient answer, and Paley[1] a wrong one; and who can wonder that multitudes make mistakes after them?"

"A clergyman, Louisa, a wise clergyman who discerns times and seasons, may set many right; and God knows how many need it! He will not follow up a text from Paul with a definition from Johnson and an exhortation from Paley. He will not suppose because charity once meant alms-giving, that it means it still; or that a kind-hearted man must be right in thinking kindness of heart all-sufficient, whether its manifestation be injurious or beneficial. He will not recommend keeping the heart soft by giving green gooseberries to a

---

1 St. Paul (d. AD 67), a Christian apostle and author of several epistles in the Bible. Samuel Johnson (1709-84), poet and essayist, compiler of the first English-language dictionary. William Paley (1743-1805), a theologian and philosopher who studied the history of the gospels and natural theology.

griped[1] child,—as he might fairly do if he carried out Paley's principle to its extent."

"A professional illustration," replied Louisa. "You want me to carry it on unto the better charity of giving the child bitter medicine. But, brother, let the clergyman preach as wisely and benignantly as he may, why should you envy him? Cannot you, do not you, preach as eloquently by example?"

"That is the very thing," replied her brother. "I am afraid my example preaches against my principles.—O, dear, if it was but as easy to know how to do right as to do it!"

"What can have wounded your conscience to-day?" replied Louisa. "You are generally as ready in applying principles as decided in acting upon them. What can have placed you in a new position since morning?"

"Nothing: but my eyes are more opened to that in which I already stood; and really, Louisa, it is a very questionable one. I will tell you.—I am a medical officer of various charities which would be good if benevolent intention and careful management could make them so, but of the tendency of which I think very ill. The question is, whether I am not doing more harm than good by officiating at the Dispensary and Lying-in Hospital,[2] while it is clear to me that the absence of these charities would be an absence of evil to society?"

"You must remember, brother, that your secession would have no other effect than to put another medical officer in your place. I am afraid you are not yet of consequence enough," laughing, "to show that these institutions must stand or fall with you."

"That argument of yours, Louisa, has done long and good service to many a bad cause. I can allow it no more weight with me than with a discontented Catholic in good old Luther's days. No: my plea to my own doubts has hitherto been that my office gave me the opportunity of promoting my own views both among the benefactors and the poor; but I begin to think I may do so much more

---

1 Intestinal illness.
2 A Lying-in Hospital specializes in childbirth. Mr. Burke's concern is similar to that of critics of Foundling Hospitals: that is, because the poor are perpetually provided for, literally from the cradle to the grave, they have no incentive to be economically independent or self-sufficient, or to curb family size. In effect, those who work—the "rate-payers"—cannot themselves afford to go to dispensaries or hospitals, so long as they are paying benefits for the unemployed and indigent poor.

effectually by resigning my office in those charities which I consider to be doing harm, openly stating my reasons, of course."

"Have you long meditated this, brother?"

"Yes, for several months; but a particular circumstance has roused my attention to-day. These anniversary times always disgust me,—these stated periods for lauding the benevolent and exhibiting the benefited. I am sure the annual dinner would be better attended by the subscribers to the Dispensary, for instance, if the custom of parading round the room as many of the patients as could be got hold of were discontinued. But it is the matter of fact of the Report, and the way in which it is viewed by the patrons, that has startled me to-day. I was referred to, as usual, by the secretary and one or two more for information respecting certain classes of patients, and I was shown the Report which is to be read after dinner to-morrow. You will scarcely guess what is the principal topic of congratulation in it."

"That Lord B_____ takes the chair to-morrow, perhaps? Now, do not look angry, but let me guess again. That the subscriptions have increased?"

"Aim in an opposite direction, and you will hit it."

"That the funds are insufficient? Can this be it?"

"Just so. The number of patients has increased so much, that a further appeal is made to the public in behalf of this admirable charity, which has this year relieved just double the number it relieved ten years ago."

"I thought," said Louisa, "that its primary recommendation, ten years ago, was that it was to lessen the amount of sickness among the poor."

"True," replied her brother; "and upon this understanding many subscribed who are now rejoicing over the numbers of the sick. If the plague were to visit us, they might see the matter in its right light. They would scarcely rejoice that five hundred more were brought to the pest-house daily."

"But how comes the increase?" inquired Louisa. "I understand it in the case of the Lying-in Charity, which seems to me the worst in existence, except perhaps foundling hospitals: but this is different."

"From all other institutions, it is to be hoped," interrupted her brother. "It is dreadful to see the numbers of poor women disappointed of a reception at the last moment, and totally unprovided. The more are admitted, the more are thus disappointed; and those who are relieved quit the hospital in a miserable state of destitution."

"Probably, brother. What else could be expected under so direct a bounty on improvidence—under so high a premium on population? But how do you imagine the number of sick increases so fast? Are your Dispensary patients in due proportion to the general increase of numbers in the place?"

"Alas, no! They are much more numerous. Not only do numbers increase very rapidly; but from their increasing beyond the means of comfortable subsistence, the people are subject to a multitude of diseases arising from hardship alone. It would make your heart ache if I were to tell you how large a proportion of my Dispensary patients are children born puny from the destitution of their parents, or weakly boys and girls, stunted by bad nursing, or women who want rest and warmth more than medicine, or men whom I can never cure until they are provided with better food."

"How you must wish sometimes that your surgery was stocked with coals and butcher's meat!"

"If it were, Louisa, the evil would only be increased, provided this sort of medicine were given gratis [free], like my drugs. There is harm enough done by the poor taking for granted that they are to be supplied with medicine and advice gratis all their lives: the evil is increasing every day by their looking on assistance in child-birth as their due; and if they learn to expect food and warmth in like manner, their misery will be complete."

"But what can we do, brother? Distress exists: no immediate remedy is in the hands of the poor themselves. What can be done?"

"These are difficulties, Louisa, which dog the heels of all bad institutions.—We must do this. We must make the best of a vast amount of present misery, thankful that we see at length the error of having caused it. We must steadily refuse to increase it, and employ all the energies of thinking heads and benevolent hearts in preventing its recurrence, and shortening to the utmost its duration. Here is ample scope for all the tenderness of sensibility which moralists would encourage, and for all the wisdom which can alone convert that tenderness into true charity."

"What should be our first step, brother?"

"To ascertain clearly the problem which we are to solve. The grand question seems to me to be this—*How to reduce the number of the indigent?* Which includes, of course, the question, How to prevent the poor becoming indigent?"

"If this had been the problem originally proposed, brother, there would have been little indigence now: but formerly people looked no farther than the immediate relief of distress, and thought the reality of the misery a sufficient warrant for alms-giving."

"And what is the consequence, Louisa? Just this: that the funds raised for the relief of pauperism in this country exceed threefold the total revenues of Sweden and Denmark. Ay; our charitable fund exceeds the whole revenue of Spain; and yet distress is more prevalent than ever, and goes on to increase every year. The failure of British benevolence, vast as it is in amount, has hitherto been complete; and all for want of right direction."

"Well, brother, how would you direct it? How would you set about *lessening the number of the indigent?*"

"I would aim at two objects: increasing the fund on which labourers subsist, and proportioning their numbers to this fund.— For the first of these purposes, not only should the usual means of increasing capital be actively plied, but the immense amount which is now unproductively consumed by the indigent should be applied to purposes of production. This cannot be done suddenly; but it should be done intrepidly, steadily, and at a gradually increasing rate. This would have the effect, at the same time, of fulfilling the other important object,—that of limiting the number of consumers to a due proportion to the fund on which they subsist."

"You would gradually abolish all charitable institutions then—O no! Not all. There are some that neither lessen capital nor increase population. You would let such remain."

"There are some which I would extend as vigorously and perseveringly as possible; viz., all which have the enlightenment of the people for their object. Schools should be multiplied and improved without any other limit than the number and capabilities of the people."

"What! All schools? Schools where maintenance is given as well as education?"

"The maintenance part of the plan should be dropped, and the instruction remain."

"But, brother, if one great evil of gratuitous assistance is that the poor become dependent upon a false support, does not this apply in the case of a gratuitous education?"

"The time will come, I trust, Louisa, when, the poorer classes will provide wholly for themselves and their families; but at present we must be content with making them provide what is essential to existence. To enable them to do this, they must be educated; and as education is not essential to existence, we may fairly offer it gratis till they have learned to consider it indispensable. Even now, I would have all those pay something for the education of their children who can; but let all be educated, whether they pay or not."

"The blind, and the deaf and dumb, I suppose, among others?"

"Yes; and in these cases I would allow of maintenance also, since the unproductive consumption of capital in these cases is so small as to be imperceptible, and such relief does not act as a premium upon population. A man will scarcely be in any degree induced to marry by the prospect of his blind or deaf children being taken off his hands, as the chances are ten thousand to one against any of his off-spring being thus infirm. Such relief should be given till there are none to claim it."

"I heard the other day, brother, of a marriage taking place between a blind man and woman in the asylum at X_____."

"Indeed! If anything could make me put these institutions on my proscribed list, it would be such a fact as that. The man could play the organ, and the woman knit, and make sash-line, I suppose?"

"Just so; and they could each do several other things, but, of course, not those common offices which are essential to the rearing of a family. It struck me immediately as a crime against society. Well—what other charities should stand?"

"Whatever else I resign, Louisa, I shall retain my office at the Casualty Hospital.[1] I hope this kind of relief will be dispensed with in a future age; but the people are not yet in a condition to provide against the fractures, wounds and bruises which befall them in following their occupations. This institution may rank with Blind Asylums."

"And what do you think of alms-houses for the aged?"

"That they are very bad things. Only consider the numbers of young people that marry under the expectation of getting their helpless parents maintained by the public! There are cases of peculiar hardship, through deprivation of natural protection, where the aged should be taken care of by the public. But the instances are very rare where old people have no relations; and it should be as universal a rule that working men should support their parents, as that they should support their children. If this rule were allowed, we might see some revival of that genial spirit of charity and social duty among the poor, whose extinction we are apt to mourn, without reflecting that we ourselves have caused it by the injudicious direction of our own benevolence.—This reminds me of the Bridgemans. Mark how those poor children are disposed of. Two are taken care of by distant relations who have never in their lives

1 A Casualty Hospital is similar to a present-day hospital emergency room.

accepted charity, except the schooling of their children. A nearer relation, who has, to my knowledge, uselessly consumed many a pound of the charitable fund, sends the other two to the work-house."

"A case very appropriate to what you have been saying, brother. But how is poor Sally? Can nothing save her sight?"

"Nothing, I fear. I have already spoken of her case to several governors of the Blind Asylum, where I hope she may be received on the first vacancy. The Marshalls are too sensible, I am sure, not to see the advantage of getting her placed there; and it may be the means of releasing one of the others from the workhouse."

Louisa now related her morning's adventures. Her brother smiled as he warned her that she would, no doubt, be pronounced an eccentric young woman by Mr. Nugent, and declared that he thought her in the way to be admirably disciplined, between the railings of Mrs. Wilkes, the rude wonder of the paupers, and the more refined speculations of those who had different notions of charity from herself.

Louisa considered that an important constituent of charity was its capability of "bearing all things." She blushed while she described to her best friend the little trials she was exposed to in her attempts to do good. Abuse from beggars she little regarded, as it was the portion of all who passed along the streets of this ill-regulated city without giving alms; much harder things to bear were the astonishment of her fellow-members of the school committee at her refusing to sanction large gifts of clothing to the children; the glances of the visitors of the soup and blanket charities, when she declined subscribing and yielding her services; and above all, the observations of relatives whom she respected, and old friends whom she loved, on the hardness of heart and laxity of principle shown by those who thought and acted as she did.

"Laxity of principle!" exclaimed her brother. "That is a singular charge to bring in such a case;—as if less vigour of principle was required to reflect on the wisest, and to adopt unusual, methods of doing good than to let kindly emotions run in the ruts of ancient institutions! I should say that the vigour of principle is on your side."

"Better make no decision about it, brother. It is not the province of charity to meddle with motives, whatever its real province may be.—But about your medical offices;—it seems to me that you must resign them, thinking as you do."

"And then what a hard-hearted, brutal fellow I shall be thought," said her brother, smiling.

"No, no: only an oddity. But the speculations upon you may prove good for the cause of charity."

"It shall be done, Louisa; and that as soon as we have determined on the best manner. I shall give up the Dispensary and the Lying-in Charity, and keep the Casualty Hospital. As for the Workhouse Infirmary—"

"Ay; I was wondering what you would say to that."

"I like it no better, but considerably worse, than many others; but it stands on a different footing, inasmuch as it is established by law; and it seems to me that I must follow other methods of abolition than that of withdrawing my services. There is no place of appeal for such an act, as there is in the case of a voluntary charity."

"There is little enough that is voluntary in this case, to be sure, brother. Such complaints about the rate from the payers! Such an assertion on the part of the poor of their right to a maintenance by the state! Whence arises this right?"

"I do not admit it," replied her brother. "Those who do admit it, differ respecting its origin. Some assert the right of every individual born into any community to a maintenance from the state; regarding the state and its members as holding the relation of parent and children. This seems to me altogether a fallacy; originating in benevolent feelings, no doubt, but supported only by a false analogy. The state cannot control the number of its members, nor increase, at its will, the subsistence-fund; and, therefore, if it be engaged to support all the members that might be born to it, it would engage for more than it might have the power to perform.—Others, who admit this in the abstract, plead for the right of the indigent of Great Britain to a maintenance from the state, on the ground of the disabilities to which the poor are peculiarly liable in this country, from the aristocratic nature of some of our institutions, the oppressive amount of taxation, and its pressure upon the lower classes. I admit a claim to relief here; but the relief should not be given, even could it be effectual, in the shape of an arbitrary institution like that of our pauper system. The only appropriate relief is to be found in the removal of the grievances complained of; in the modification of certain of our institutions; in the lightening, and, yet more, in the equalization of taxation.—Mark what a state we have arrived at from our mistaken recognition of this *right* to support! Though the subsistence-fund has increased at a rapid rate within a hundred years, through the improvements introduced by art and civilization, the poor-rate has, in that time, increased from five or six hundred thousand pounds a-year to upwards of eight millions!"

"Some say," observed his sister, "that it is not the recognition of the right which has caused the mischief, but the imperfect fulfilment of the original law. You know better than I whether this is true."

"It is clear," replied her brother, "that neither the letter nor the spirit of the original law was adhered to; but it is also clear that, in that law, the state promised more than it could perform. Did you ever read the famous clause of the famous 43d of Elizabeth?[1] No? There lies Blackstone.[2] I will show it you."

"But first tell me what state the poor were in when that act was passed."

"For the credit of Elizabeth's government, it is certainly necessary to premise what you inquire about.—From the year 597, that is, from Pope Gregory's time, tithes paid to the clergy were expressly directed to be divided into four parts, as Blackstone here tells us, you see; one part for the bishops, one for the clergyman, incumbent, or parson; one for repairing and keeping up the church; and one for the maintenance of the poor."

"But do the clergy pay a fourth part of their tithes to the poor?"

"O no," replied her brother, laughing. "That troublesome order was got rid of many hundred years ago; and so was the clause respecting the share of the bishops; so that tithes became, in a short time, a very pretty consideration. Well; though some notice of the poor was occasionally taken by the legislature, no complaints of their state made much noise till Henry VIII. suppressed the monasteries [1536-40]. These monasteries had supported crowds of idle poor, who were now turned loose upon the country; and with them a multitude of vagabond monks, who were a nuisance to the whole kingdom. It became necessary to stop the roaming, begging, and thieving, which went on to the dismay and injury of all honest people; and for this purpose, the famous act of Elizabeth was framed [43rd statute]. This statute enacts, 'That the churchwardens and overseers shall take order, from time to time, (with the consent of two or more justices,) for setting to work the children of all such whose

---

1 The 43rd statute of Elizabeth I, also called the Poor Law Relief Act of 1601. The statute established parishes as the overseers of the poor and empowered them to collect poor rates for their maintenance, levied on the able and employed according to their income. The more one earned, the more one was required to pay, making it impossible to "get ahead" financially.

2 Sir William Blackstone (1723-80), a British legal scholar who wrote *Commentaries on the Laws of England* (4 vols., 1765-69).

parents shall not be thought able to keep and maintain their children; and also for setting to work all such persons, married or unmarried, having no means to maintain them, and using no ordinary or daily trade to get their living by; and also to raise, by taxation, &c., a convenient stock of flax, to set the poor on work; and also competent sums of money for and towards the necessary relief of the lame, impotent, old, blind, and such other among them, being poor and not able to work.' You see how this is aimed at vagabonds as well as designed for the impotent. Many a monkish bosom, no doubt, heaved a sigh at the mention of 'a convenient stock of flax.'"

"Surely, brother," said Louisa, "the state promises by this act just what you said no state could fairly promise, without having the control of its numbers; it promises to support all its indigent members."

"It does; and it promises another thing equally impossible of fulfilment. Here is an engagement to find employment for all who would not or could not procure it for themselves. Now, as the employment of labour must depend on the amount of the subsistence-fund, no law on earth can enforce the employment of more labour than that fund can support."

"Then this promise has not been fulfilled, I suppose?"

"Many attempts have been made to fulfil it, all of which have had the effect of diverting industry from its natural channel, and taking the occupation of the independent laborer out of his hands to put it into that of the pauper. This is so ruinous an operation, that the wonder is how the pauper system has failed to swallow up all our resources, and make us a nation of paupers."

"In which case," observed Louisa, "the state would be found to have engaged to maintain itself in a pauper condition. What a blunder! Twenty-four millions of paupers are bound by law to maintain twenty-four millions of paupers!"

"This is the condition we shall infallibly be brought to, Louisa, unless we take speedy means to stop ourselves. We are rolling down faster and faster towards the gulf, and two of our three estates, Lords and Commons, have declared that we shall soon be in it;—that in a few more years the profits of all kind of property will be absorbed by the increasing rates, and capital will therefore cease to be invested; land will be let out of cultivation, manufactures will be discontinued, commerce will cease, and the nation become a vast congregation of paupers."

"Dreadful! Brother, how can we all go quietly about our daily business with such a prospect before us?"

"A large proportion of the nation knows little about the matter;

some hope that fate, or Providence, or something will interfere to save us; others think that it is no business of theirs; and those whose business it is are at a loss what to do."

"But how long has there been so much cause for alarm?"

"Only within a few years. Thanks to the ungracious mode of executing the law, it effected less mischief during a century and a half than might have been anticipated. When persons could be relieved only in their own parishes, and when that relief was given in a manner which exposed the applicant to a feeling of degradation among his neighbors, few asked relief who could by any means subsist without it. Work-houses, too, were regarded as odious places, and to the workhouse paupers must go, in those days, if out of employ; and all who had any sense of comfort or decency delayed to the very last moment classing themselves with paupers. So that, up to 1795, the state was less burdened with pauperism than, from the bad system it had adopted, it deserved."[1]

"What makes you fix that precise date?"

"Because in that year a change took place in the administration of the poor-laws, which has altered the state of the country disastrously. There was a scarcity that season, and consequently much difficulty with our paupers, among whom now appeared not only the helpless, but the able-bodied, industrious men, who could no longer maintain their families. It was most unfortunately agreed by the county magistrates, first of Berkshire, and afterwards of other parts of the middle and south of England, that such and such ought to be and should henceforth be the weekly income of the labouring poor; and a table was published, exhibiting the proportions of this income according to the size of families and the price of bread."

"But how could that mend the matter?" exclaimed Louisa. "These magistrates and the public could not increase the quantity of bread, and where was the use, then, of giving money? It was merely taking bread from those who had earned it, to give it to those who had not."

"Just so; but these magistrates did not happen to view the matter as you do; and we have great cause to rue their short-sightedness.—

---

1   The Speenhamland System, implemented in 1795, offered poor relief according to family size. Although well-intended (like most such schemes), in practice the system diminished wages, increased poor rates, and left little incentive for self-sufficiency, as subsistence was always guaranteed. The system was replaced by the Poor Law Amendment Act of 1834, passed after the events of this tale.

Mark how the system has worked!—All labourers are given to understand that they ought to have a gallon loaf of wheaten bread weekly for each member of their families, and one over; that is, three loaves for two people, and eleven for ten. John comes and says that his wife and four children and himself must have seven loaves, costing twelve shillings; but that he can earn only nine shillings. As a matter of course, three shillings are given him from the parish.— Next comes Will. He has a wife and six children, and must have nine loaves, or fourteen shillings and eightpence. He earns ten shillings, and receives the rest from the parish. Hal is a vagabond whom no capitalist will admit within his gates. Work is out of the question; but his family must be fed, and want eight loaves: so the parish pays him thirteen shillings and eightpence."

"So that, in fact," observed Louisa, "eleven loaves are earned by these three families, and the twelve still deficient are taken from other earners. How very unjust! How very ruinous! But does this kind of management still go on?"

"Universally in the agricultural counties, with such slight variations as are introduced by local circumstances.—Great allowance must be made for the pressure of difficulties at the time when this system was adopted; but the system itself is execrable, however well-meaning its authors. The industry of the lower classes has been half ruined by it, and their sense of independence almost annihilated. The public burdens have become well nigh overwhelming; and the proportion of supply and demand in all the departments of industry is so deranged that there is no saying when it can be rectified."

"It is rather hard upon the poor," observed Louisa, "that we should complain of their improvidence when we bribe them to it by promising subsistence at all events. Paupers will spend and marry faster than their betters as long as this system lasts."

"It makes one indignant to see it," replied her brother. "I am now attending an industrious young man, a shopkeeper, who has been attached for years, but will not marry till his circumstances justify it. He has paid more to the rates every year; and half a dozen vagabond paupers have married in his parish during the time that he has been waiting."

"All these things, brother, bring us round to the question, what are we to do?"

"You must enlighten the children in your school, and all the poor you have any influence over, Louisa. As for me,—it is unnecessary to open my lips upon it to my country patients, for I seldom enter a farmhouse without hearing complaints of the system. But our towns are too quiet about the matter. General, calm, enlightened deliberation is required, and that without loss of time.—I am prepared with testimony respecting the increase of sickness and mortality which accompanies the augmentation of the poor-rate. Most happy should I be to have the opportunity of delivering it."

"Our wise men," said Louisa, "must start afresh the old question, and the nation must gather round them to be taught anew, '*What is Charity?*'"

Chapter IV: Pauper Life

No one could pass the gates of the workhouse on pay-day without seeing how much misery existed among the claimants of out-door relief; but few could guess, without following these applicants to their homes, how much guilt attended, not only their poverty, but the advancement of their claims;—guilt which would never have been dreamed of unless suggested and encouraged by a system which destroys the natural connexion between labour and its rewards.[1]

Mrs. Bell's husband was now out of work, after having earned and regularly spent twenty-five shillings a week for many months. His third child had died after a long illness, and one which had proved expensive to the parish, from whence this family now derived four and sixpence a week. Mrs. Bell, who always went herself to receive the weekly allowance, lest her husband, through his dislike of the business, should not "manage it cleverly," took credit to herself for having given notice that the doctor need not take any more trouble about her poor boy, as he was past hope and nothing more could be done for him; but she omitted to state the reason of his being past hope, (viz., that he was dead,) because it would have been inconvenient to give up the allowance received on his account. So no doctor came to ask awkward questions, and the money was a great comfort indeed. Mrs. Bell had truly managed the whole matter very "cleverly." She got another blanket, even out of due season, because the boy was apt to be cold at night. The Sick Poor Society allowed

---

1 Martineau refers to the "undeserving poor" who deliberately cheat the system. Mrs. Bell, for example, collects an additional stipend from the parish, including medicine and fuel, for one of her children who has died. Martineau implies that the administrators of the system are as much to blame for such abuses as the perpetrators themselves for not ascertaining the legitimacy of regular claims upon the system's resources.

her a certain sum weekly as long as the child lived; and two or three kind neighbors gave her leave to call at their houses when they had a wholesome joint for dinner, to carry away a slice and vegetables for the patient; and if all these desired her to call on the same day, she managed to borrow a couple of basins and obey directions; for though the patient could not eat three dinners at a time, nor perhaps even one, there were others in the house who liked savoury meat, and it was only returning their thanks for the "nourishing cordial" in poor Bob's name. Then came the lamentations over the impossibility of burying him decently, and the thanksgivings for a half-crown here and there for the purpose; and then hints about any old rag of black, and the pain to maternal feelings of having no mourning for so dear a child; and the tears at sight of the black stuff gown, and the black silk bonnet, and the black cotton shawl,—all so much too good for her before they were put into her hands, but pronounced rusty, rotten old rubbish when surveyed at home. Then came the commands to the children to say nothing about Bob unless they were asked, and the jealousy of that prying, malicious old widow Pine, who peeped through her lattice a full hour before she should properly have awaked, and just in time to see the coffin carried out of the yard. Lastly, came the subtraction of poor Bob's parish allowance from the rest before the money was delivered into her husband's hand. The early waking of widow Pine, and the use she might make of what she saw, no mortal could prevent; but all that devolved upon herself, Mrs. Bell flattered herself that she had "managed very cleverly."

One day when she was going to the workhouse for her allowance, her husband accompanied her part of the way. Widow Pine was before them in the street, stepping feebly along, supported by a stick in one hand and by the wall on the other side.

"She'll trip over the tatters of her gown," exclaimed Bell. "Poor old soul! She is not fit to walk the streets,—bent double, and ready to be knocked down by the first push. She will not trouble the parish long."

"She will die in the streets," replied his wife, "and with bad words in her mouth. She is for ever prying about people's affairs, and saying malicious things of her neighbors. The old hypocrite! She sits see-sawing herself, and drawling hymns while she combs her grey hair that never was cut, and all the while pricking up her ears for scandal."

"You and she never had much love to lose," replied Bell, obeying his wife's motion to cross the street to avoid passing at the widow's elbow. She saw them, however, and sent her well-known piping after them, striking the pavement with her stick, to attract the notice of the passers by.

"I wish you joy of your blue gown, Mrs. Bell! 'Tis no great thing to lose a child that comes to life again every parish pay-day!"

"Never mind the old wretch," said Bell. "By the by, I have observed you put off your black sometimes. What is it for?"

"The officers are so quick-sighted about a new gown. They might take off some pay if they knew I had a friend that would give me a gown; and it really is a rag not worth disputing about."

The husband was satisfied, but much annoyed with the abuse that came from over the way.

"I'll crush you yet!" railed the old woman. "I can, and I will, such a pack of knaves and liars as you are! You'll soon hear from the parish, I warrant you! You'll soon be posted for cheats!"

"I say, goody, hold your foul tongue, or I'll correct you as you little think for," said Bell.

"You! What harm can you do me, I wonder?—you that are lost, and I a holy person."

"A holy person! How do you mean holy?" asked Bell, laughing.

"How do you mean holy! Why, sure of heaven, to be sure. I'm sure of heaven, I tell you, and you are lost! God has given me nothing else, for a miserable life I've had of it; but he has given me grace, and is not that enough?"

"You must keep it close locked up somewhere, for never a one found out you had it," said Mrs. Bell. "I doubt the Talbots that have been so kind to you have never seen much of your grace."

"Kind to me! The proud, mean, slandering folks! You little know the Talbots if you think they can be generous to anybody. They'll meet you hereafter when I shall be in a better place!"

"That is pretty well," said Bell, "when you have had bed and board, clothes and comfort, from that family from your youth up. Suppose I tell them what you say, neighbour."

"As you please. It is only what I have told them myself. I shall look to hear you curse them soon, Mrs. Bell, for they have been told how you take parish money for your dead child. So you got a blanket to keep the boy warm? He's in a hot place now,—a little unregenerate devil as he was! If he was not to be saved, you are well off to be rid of him so soon."

The husband and wife quickened their pace till they got out of hearing, the one full of disgust, the other of the fear of detection. She was anxious to receive her money before the widow should arrive;

but there was already such a crowd about the gates that she saw she must wait long for her turn.

Two of the paupers had secured a seat on the door-step of an opposite house: the one, a well-known beggar, whose occupation had never been effectually interfered with by the police; the other, a young man, who was jeered at as a stranger by some who weekly resorted to this place. One gave him joy of his admission to the pauper brotherhood; another asked how he liked waiting on the great; a third observed that he could not judge till he had waited two hours in the snow of a winter's noon.

"Never fret yourself for their gibes, Hunt," said Childe, the beggar. "You are more in the way to do well than you have been this many a day. You may make what you will of the great, if you do but know how to set about it."

"I'm glad to hear it," said Hunt, fidgeting about in a state of great agitation. "I'm sure the rich know well enough what to make of us. Not a word do we ever hear from them about our right to be kept from starvation; and they expect us to be wonderfully grateful for a parish dole, while they cut off a pound of meat a week from every poor soul's allowance within yonder walls, and advise us to mix rye with our wheaten bread.—'Tis true, as I'm alive! A man told me so just now as he came out of yonder gate."

"Well; let us get the pound of meat for our share if we can. I'll bet you a wager, Hunt, I'll get a shilling a week more out of them for this very prank of theirs."

"Done!" cried Hunt. "I bet you a penny roll they will be too sharp for you."

"A penny roll!" exclaimed Childe. "A pint of wine is the lowest bet I ever lay, man. A pint of red port to be paid to-night. Come!"

"You might as well ask me to bet a diamond," said Hunt, laughing bitterly. "How am I to get port wine?"

"I'll show you when our business here is done," said Childe. "Your father was my friend, or I should not open my confidence so easily. But just attend a minute at that fat woman's elbow, will you? Just to screen me a bit. There; that will do. Don't look round till I bid you."

When Hunt had permission to look round, he scarcely knew his companion. Childe had slipped off his worsted stocking and bound it over his forehead and chin, so as to look very sickly. He sprinkled a few grains from his snuff-box into his eyes, so as to look blear-eyed, and forthwith set himself to tremble all over, except his right arm which appeared stiff.

"I have had a slight stroke of palsy this week, you see," said he. "I can just get abroad to show that I must have another shilling a week.—Hang it, Hunt, it is not worth the trouble for such a trifle, if it was not for the bet!"

Hunt thought a shilling a week no trifle, and wondered how Childe came by such mighty notions.

"Because I've an *e* at the end of my name, man, that's all. That little letter makes a great man of me. It is worth house and board and tobacco and clothes to me for the whole of my old age. You think I am mad, I see; but, hark'ee! Did you never hear of Childe's Hospital?"

"Yes; near London. Is not it?"

"Yes; and I have the next turn there, and a merry life I make of it till I get in, fearing that the confinement may be rather too close for my liking. However, it is not a thing to be sneezed at. The money gathers so fast that 'tis thought we Childes shall have silver spoons by the time I enter the brotherhood. I like gentility, and I would give up a little roving for the sake of it."

"But how had you the luck to get on the list?" inquired Hunt. "Who befriended you?"

"Lord bless you, how little you know about such things! 'Twas I befriended the trustees, not they me. They are beholden to me for saving them the trouble of searching farther for a Child with an *e* at the end of his name. None others will do by the terms of the bequest, which is for the support of thirteen aged men of the same name with the pious founder.—A deal of pride in his piety, I doubt, Hunt.—Well: the funds have grown and grown, and the trustees can't use them up any how, though their dinners and plate and knick-knackeries are the finest of the fine, I'm told; and the thirteen aged men have all they ask for. You should see what a figure I cut on the list of candidates,—alone in my glory, as they say;—'honest industry'—'undeserved poverty'—'infirmities of advancing years,' and so forth. I wonder they did not make a soldier or a sailor of me at once,—'to justify their choice,' as they finish by saying. Why, man, you look downright envious!"

"I wish any great man of the name of Hunt had endowed an hospital," sighed Hunt; "but I am afraid there would be too many claimants to give me a chance."

"To be sure. There's not one in ten thousand meets with such luck as mine. Bless you! There would be a string of Hunts a mile long, in such a case."

And the beggar threw himself back, laughing heartily; but suddenly stopped, saying,

"Mercy! How nearly I had lost my bet! People in the palsy do not laugh, do they?"

"When do you expect to get into this hospital?" inquired Hunt, who could think of nothing else; "and how do you keep yourself so sleek meanwhile?"

"I shall depart to that better place when any one of the old pensioners departs to a better still," replied the beggar; "meanwhile, I grow fat in the way I will show you presently. Now for it. It is our turn. Do you keep just behind me and see how I manage."

The method was worth watching. Childe won his way slowly among the groups, preserving his paralytic appearance wonderfully, and exciting the compassion of all who took notice of him.

"And who may you be, friend?" inquired the officer, as Childe approached the counter where the pay was being distributed. "Bless me! Childe! My poor fellow, how you are altered! You have had a stroke, I am afraid?"

"If it's ordained that the grasshopper must become a burden," said Childe, mumbling in his speech, "we must submit, and be thankful to have lived so long. But you will not refuse me another shilling, sir."

The officer was about to comply, when an assistant who stood by him remarked that the applicant looked wonderfully ruddy for a paralytic man, and that his eyes were as bright as ever. Hunt, who stood behind, jogged his arm, from which the stick immediately fell. Childe appeared to make several ineffectual efforts to pick it up, and looked imploringly towards the people behind him, as if complaining that they pressed upon him. The officer spoke sharply to Hunt,—

"Pick up the man's stick, you brute! You knocked it out of his hand, and you stand staring as if you liked to see how helpless he is.—You observed, John, his right arm is quite useless. Give him another shilling."

Hunt wished he had abstained from his practical hint. Before he could state his case, a woman got the officer's ear.—Sarah Simpson, spinster, by name and title. She was a clean, tight little body, poorly dressed, and sickly in appearance. She appeared excessively nervous, her eyes rolling and her head twitching incessantly. She pleaded for more pay, saying that she had a note from one of the guardians respecting it: but for this note her trembling hands searched in vain, while she was pushed about by the people who still continued to fill the room.

"Make haste, good woman," said the officer. "We can't wait on you all day."

At this moment, the poor creature turned round and swore a tremendous oath at a man who had taken upon him to hurry her.

"Upon my word, that is pretty well for a spinster!" observed the officer. "If you are not satisfied with your pay, madam, I would recommend your going into the workhouse. You have nobody dependent on you, I believe, and I should think the workhouse a very proper place for you."

"She has been there already," said the assistant. "Her tongue put me in mind of that. The master tells me such oaths were never heard within the walls as this woman's."

"Mercy, gentlemen, what did I say?" asked the poor creature, whose eyes now rolled frightfully. "I am not myself at times, gentlemen, when I'm hurried, gentlemen. I have such a—such a—such a strife and strangling here," she continued fretfully, tearing open her gown, and shaking herself like a passionate child.

"Well, well, that's enough of your symptoms; we are not your doctors," said the assistant; "take your money and make way."

In a hurried manner she closed her gown and drew back, forgetting her money, which however Hunt put into her hand.

"Only two shillings!" exclaimed the poor creature, returning timidly to the counter. "A'n't I to have what the gentleman recommended, then, sir?"

"You are to have no more money, so let us have no more words," said the officer. "You have your full share already."

Mrs. Bell, whose period of waiting seemed coming to an end, advanced to say that Sarah Simpson was subject to flights at times, when she did not know what words came out of her mouth; but that she was a humble, pious Christian as could be.

"I am afraid your recommendation is not worth much," observed the officer. "Let us see.—Your husband, yourself, and how many children?"

Mrs. Bell, suspecting herself suspected, hesitated whether to say four or five. She shaped her answer dubiously,—

"Four and sixpence a week is what we have had, sir."

"How many children?" thundered the officer.

"Four," admitted the terrified Mrs. Bell, who was glad to get away with three and sixpence, and a rating from the men in authority, accompanied by sneers and jests from the hearers. On her way home she laid the entire blame on the ill-nature of her neighbors, especially on the spite of old widow Pine.

Hunt obtained a small allowance, and left the place, grumbling at its amount and at the prospect of having to spend it all in wine to pay his wager. Childe, however, gave him his first lesson in the mysteries of begging. Under the pretence of sport, he practised the art for the first time in a street on the outskirts of the city, through which many gentlemen passed in their way home to dinner from their counting-houses. Hunt was astonished at his own success, and began to calculate how much alms might be given away in a year in this single street, if he and Childe had the begging department all to themselves. It might be enough, he thought, to enable them to set up a shop.—When the parish clock struck eight, Childe came to him and said it was near supper-time. Hunt was glad of it, for he was very hungry, having had nothing since morning. Childe begged pardon for the freedom of calling him a fool, but could not conceive why he had not taken a chop in the middle of the day, as it was his custom to do: it was sticking rather too close to the main chance to sit without food from morning till evening for fear of missing a monied passenger.

Hunt followed his tutor to a public-house in the heart of the city, called the Cow and Snuffers. Hunt had supposed this house too respectable to be the resort of beggars; but was informed that the fraternity thought nothing too good for them when their day's business was at an end, and the time of refreshment was come; not as it comes to poor artizans in their sordid homes, but rather to convivial men of wealth.

"Stay!" said Childe, as they were about to enter the house. "How much can you afford to spend? Five shillings, I suppose, at the least.—Never start at such a trifle as that, man! You will make it up between four and five tomorrow afternoon."

Hunt had not intended to beg any more; but he deferred the consideration of the matter for the present, and followed Childe to a small room upstairs, furnished with washing apparatus, and with a wardrobe well stocked with respectable clothing. Three or four persons were already in this room dressing, their beggar apparel being thrown into a corner, and looking-glass, brushes, and towels, being all in requisition. Hunt was declared, after a brushing, to be presentable without a change of apparel, especially as he was a stranger. Childe was about to open a door on the same floor, when a waiter stopped his hand and intimated that they must mount higher, as the room in question was occupied by the monthly meeting of the Benefit Club.[1] The cloth was laid upstairs, and it was hoped the apartment might be found quite as comfortable.

On the question being put to the vote among the beggars already assembled, it was pronounced an intolerable nuisance to be turned out of their apartment regularly once a month by these shabby fellows, who were always thinking how they should save money instead of spending it. The landlord was rung for, and requested to intimate to the workpeople that a large convivial party desired to change rooms with them. The landlord objected that the apartment had been positively engaged from the beginning by the club, and he could not think of turning them out. Being assailed, however, by various questions,—how he could bring the two companies into comparison?—whether he could honestly declare that the custom of the club was worth more than a few shillings in the year?—and, lastly, how he would like to lose the patronage of the beggars' company?—he consented to carry a message—the answer to which was a civil refusal to budge. Message after message was sent in vain. The club, having ascertained that there were unoccupied rooms in the house which would suit the purpose of the other party as well, very properly chose to keep the landlord to his engagement.

"It's monstrous, upon my soul!" cried a lady beggar, making her entree with a curtsey, which she had first practised on the boards of a barn, when personating Juliet,—"it is really monstrous to be poked into an attic in this way;—and to miss the view of the cathedral, too, which is so attractive to strangers!"

The appearance of this lady suggested a last appeal.

"Tell them," said Childe, "that there's a lady in the case,—a lady who is partial to the view of the cathedral."

The club sent their compliments, and would be happy to accommodate the lady with a seat among them, whence she might view the cathedral at leisure, while they settled their accounts.

---

1 Working-class members of Benefit Clubs invested regular subscriptions as a form of unemployment insurance. In times of need, workers drew on this insurance in order to maintain their families and stay "off the dole." Originally small and local, with meetings held in inns or pubs (18th century), the clubs eventually became national orders with chapters meeting in lodges (19th century). Discipline was strict and proper behavior among members enforced, demonstrating the clubs' desire for respectability and official approval. Similar to the Freemasons, meetings were highly secretive and elaborately ritualized. Benefit Clubs were also called "box clubs" or Friendly Societies.

The club were pronounced ill-mannered wretches, and the representations of the landlord about the probable overroasting of the geese were listened to. Supper was ordered. Roast goose top and bottom;—an informality for which apology was made to Hunt, on the ground that the company liked nothing so well as goose in the prime of the pea-season;—abundance of pease; delicate lamb chops and asparagus, and so forth. Hunt had never before beheld such a feast.

"It will be long enough," observed a junior member, "before those shabby fellows below treat themselves with such a set-out as this. I never liked their doings when I was an operative: I was one of the other sort."

"What other sort?"

"One of the good livers, and not one of the frugal. I and some friends of mine used to sup something in this fashion when we earned near three guineas a week. We used to get our fowls from London."

"Bravo! And what made you leave off trade?"

"I was turned off in bad times, and I shall tell you no more; for I hate to think of that winter of cold and water-gruel. My nose was positively frost-bitten, and my stomach like a wet bladder most part of the twenty-four hours. Pah! It was horrid."

"You would have exchanged conditions with one of the frugal at that time, probably?"

"Why, I did envy one his bit of fire, and another his mess of broth; and the next winter I may envy them again, for I hear the magistrates have got scent of me; but no more of that now.—Miss Molly, your very good health! May I ask what you have done with your seven small children?"

"Left some of them on the bridge, and the rest in the Butchers'-row, with directions where to find me when the halfpence grow too heavy for them. I hope it is going to rain so that they will get little; for I don't want to be bored with the brats any more to-night."

"They must be quite too much for you sometimes."

"Hang it! They are. It is all I can do to remember their parentage, in case of its being convenient to return them. Two of them are getting to a troublesome age, now,—so impertinent! I must really get rid of them, and borrow another baby or two."[1]

---

1   Molly is the proprietor of a baby-farm. Parents pay her in advance to feed and clothe and look after their children; instead, she squanders the money on her own pleasure and leaves the children to their own resources. The practice was notorious for the high mortality rate among baby-farm children and was eventually declared illegal.

"Gentlemen," said Childe, when the cloth was drawn and the door closed behind the waiter, "we have long wanted a general-officer in our company, and I flatter myself I have found one who will fill the department excellently, if he can be induced to join us. Hunt, what say you? Will you be one of us?"

Hunt wished to know what would be expected of him.

"The fact is," said Childe, "I took a hint during my travels last year, which is too good to be let drop. General Y_____, whom, as a boy, I used to see reviewing the troops, gamed and drank himself down into pauperism, and I met him last year walking the streets, not begging, but taking a vast deal of money; for it was whispered who he was, and everybody gave him something. 'Tis a case of the first water, you see, and it is a pity not to profit by it. You will find your part very easy. You have only to let your beard grow a little, and walk barefoot and bareheaded, buttoning your coat up to your chin in the way of military men, and as if to hide the want of a shirt. You must look straight before you as if you saw nobody, and keep your left hand in your bosom and your right by your side. You will find many a shilling put into it, I expect, and very little copper.—If you think it as well to vary the story, we can make you an admiral, with some resemblance to a pig-tail; but you are hardly round-shouldered enough for a seaman, and there is something in the upright military walk that catches the eye better."

Hunt had some scruples of conscience, which were discovered and combated with wonderful address by his tutor. The argument which proved finally successful was, that if he believed he had a right to comfortable support, and could not obtain it either by work, or by allowance from the public fund, he must get it in any way he could.—Nobody inquired whether this permission was to extend to thieving, in case the gentry should take it into their heads to leave off giving alms; nor did any one trouble himself to consider where, short of murder, the line was to be drawn in the prosecution of this supposed right. Hunt had some confused notion that the act of *begging* is inconsistent with a claim of *right*: if he changed his petition into a demand, the act became one of highway robbery; between which and petty larceny and burglary, there are only degrees of the same guilt: there must be some flaw in this reasoning, since the gallows stood at the end of it. It might have been proved to him that, if he had the supposed right to support, he was now about to urge it in the wrong quarter; and that, therefore, no species of begging is defensible on this very common plea. It might also have been proved that the right itself is purely imaginary; but he was now in a company whence it was most convenient to banish all questions of right except those involved in the settlement of bets, and of precedence in taking the chair.

There was much laughter at the sober folks below; the murmur of whose business-like voices rose occasionally during a pause, and who were heard descending the stairs before the clock struck ten. The waiter just then came up with a fresh supply of gin, Miss Molly having an inclination for another glass.

"How much do those people spend each time, pray?"

"Twopence a-piece, and a shilling over."

In reply to the mirth which followed, Childe pointed out that the very object of their meeting was the promotion of frugality; and that his only wonder therefore was, that they did not meet somewhere where they need spend nothing at all.

The waiter, who had looked grave during the laugh, now observed that the members of the club drank so little because they had something better to do. They read the newspapers, and took an important part in elections, and had the satisfaction of helping one another in many ways. He could speak to the satisfaction of being a member of one of these clubs, and the pride he felt in it. There was no occasion to fear any magistrate or constable living, or to have anything to do with the parish; and they were, moreover, prepared so as to be at no man's mercy in times of trouble and sickness; and when they were past work, there was a fund to go to, over which they held a right; and this, in his opinion, was worth more than jollity with want in prospect. The man was ordered away, and threatened with being thrown out of the window for his impertinence, and a riotous chorus was struck up on his disappearance; but there were, possibly, others besides Hunt, who sighed at his words, before they began to sing in praise of gin and revelry.

Chapter V: Cousin Marshall's Charities

Marshall was a member of the benefit club which met at the Cow and Snuffers. He had followed his father's advice and example by enrolling his name in it while yet a very young man; and he was now every day farther from repenting that he had thus invested the earnings of his youth. His companions, who knew him to be what is commonly called 'a poor creature,' smiled, and said that his club served him instead of a set of wits. He was not a man whose talents could have kept him afloat in bad times, and his club served admirably for a cork-jacket. His wife, who never seemed to have found out how much cleverer she was than her husband, put the matter in a somewhat different light. She attributed to her husband all the respectability they were enabled to maintain, and which concealed from the knowledge of many that Marshall earned but moderate wages from being a slow and dull, though steady workman. She gave him the credit, not only of the regularity of their little household, (which was, indeed, much promoted by the sobriety of his habits,) but of the many kindnesses which they rendered to their neighbours,—from sending in a fresh egg to an invalid next door, to taking home two orphans to be maintained. If it had not been for her husband's way of storing his earnings, as cousin Marshall truly observed, these offices of goodwill would have been out of the question; and this observation, made now and then at the close of a hard day's work, when Sally was trying to knit beside him, dropping, unperceived, as many stitches, poor girl! as she knitted, and when little Ann was at play among his own children before the door, made the slow smile break over his grave face, and constituted him a happy man.

Sally's eyes grew daily worse. Mrs. Marshall had long suspected, but could never make sure of the fact, that she injured them much by crying. As often as Sally had reason to suppose she was watched, she was ready with the complaint "My eyes always water so;" and how many of these tears came from disease, and how many from grief, it was difficult to make out. She was seldom merry, now and then a little fretful, but generally quiet and grave. Her great pleasures were to sit beside cousin Marshall, on the rare occasions when she could turn out all the little ones to play, and mend clothes of an afternoon; or to forget how old she was growing, and be taken on John Marshall's knee, and rest her aching forehead on his shoulder when he had an evening hour to spare. From the one she heard many stories of her mother as a girl no bigger than herself; and from the other, tidings of Ned and Jane, when, as often happened, John had been to see them. Mrs. Marshall now began to intersperse frequent notices of the Blind Asylum in her talk, trying to excite poor Sally's interest in the customs, employments, and advantages of the place; and she gave her husband a private hint to do the same, in order to familiarise the girl with the thought of the place she must shortly go to. John obeyed the hint; but he did it awkwardly. Whatever was the subject now started in his presence, it always ended in praises of the Blind Asylum, and declarations how much he should like to go there if it should please the Almighty to take away his eyesight. Sally was not long in fathoming the intention of this. At first she pressed down her forehead closer when John said 'a-hem' on approaching the subject; but soon she slid from his knee, and went away at the first sign.

"I think, John," said his wife, one evening when this happened, "poor Sally has heard enough for the present about this Asylum. It pains her sadly, I am afraid; but the time must be at hand, for she is very nearly blind now; and as to a vacancy, some of the people are very old."

"I was going to say, wife, one of them is dead, and Sally can be got in on Saturday, as Mr. Burke bids me tell you. I met him to-day, and that was his message."

Cousin Marshall's thoughts were at once painfully divided, between satisfaction at having Sally thus comfortably provided for, and the sorrow of parting with her; between the doubt how her clothes were to be got ready, and the dread of telling the girl what was to come to pass. She decided on sending her to bed in the first place, in order to hold a consultation in peace; so she went in search of her, led her up herself to the little nook which had been partitioned off for her as an invalid, helped her to bed, instead of letting Ann do it, swallowed her tears while hearing the simple prayer she had taught her, kissed her, and bade her good night.

"Cousin Marshall," said the little girl, after listening a minute, "what are you doing at the window?"

"Hanging up an apron, my dear, to keep the morning sun off your face."

"O, don't do that! I don't see much of the light now, and I like to feel the sun and know when it shines in."

"Just as you like. But what are you folding your clothes under your head for? You shall have a pillow. O yes; I have a pillow—I'll bring it."

Sally nestled her head down upon it as if for comfortable repose, while her cousin went down to meditate on her concerns. It was settled between the husband and wife, that either Ned or Jane should be immediately taken home in Sally's place, and that circumstances at the workhouse should determine which it should be.

Mrs. Marshall was wont to sleep as soundly as her toil and wholesome state of mind and conscience deserved; but this night she was disturbed by thoughts of the disclosure she must make in the morning. She scarcely closed her eyes while it was dark, and after it began to dawn, lay broad awake, watching the pink clouds that sailed past her little lattice, and planning how the washing, ironing, and preparing of Sally's few clothes was to be done, in addition to the day's business. Presently she thought she heard the noise of somebody stirring behind the little partition. She sat up and looked about her, thinking it might be one of the many children in the room; but they were all sound asleep in their wonted and divers postures. After repeated listenings, she softly rose to go and see what could ail Sally. She found her at the window; not, alas! watching the sunrise—for no sunrise should Sally ever more see—but drying her pillow in its first rays. The moment she perceived she was observed, she tossed the pillow into bed again, and scrambled after it; but it was too late to avoid explanation.

"It grieves me to chide you, my dear," said cousin Marshall; "but how should your eyes get better, if you take no more care of them? Here is your pillow wet through, wetter than it could have been if you had not been crying all night, and you are looking up at the flaring sky, instead of shutting your poor eyes in sleep."

"If I sleep ever so sound, cousin, I always wake when the sun rises, and I try sometimes how much I can see of him. It was scarce a blink to-day; so you need not fear its making my eyes ache any more. They never will be tried with bright light again! It is little more than a month since I could see yon tiled roof glistening at sunrise, and now I can't."

"That is no rule, my dear; the sun has moved somewhat, so that we can't see it strike straight upon it. That tiled roof looks blue to me now, and dull."

"Does it indeed?" cried Sally, starting up. "However, that is no matter, cousin; for my eyes are certainly very bad, and soon I shall not be able to do anything."

"O, but I hope you will soon be able to do more than ever I have been able to teach you. If you have not me beside you to take up stitches in your knitting, you will learn not to let them drop; and that is far better. And you will make sashline, and the more delicate sort of baskets; and you are better off than most at their first going into the Asylum, in having learned to wash a floor neatly, and to join your squares by the feel, almost as well as we that can see. Miss Burke could scarcely believe you were Sally, the first day she came, you were washing the floor so nicely."

Sally would have smiled at the compliment, but that she was too full of panic about the Asylum.

"But, cousin," she said, "it will be all so strange! I don't know any of the people, and I shall have no one to talk to. And that brown stuff dress, and little black bonnet, and the white handkerchiefs, all alike! I don't like to wear a charity dress. I remember—"

Before Sally could relate what it was that she remembered, her cousin stopped her with a gentle rebuke. She did not mind what Sally said about the place and the people being strange; it was natural, and it was an evil soon cured, and she hoped there would be less to teaze the girl in the Asylum, than among the rough children at home; but she could not see what reason there was for so much pride as should disdain to wear a charity dress. Sally explained that it was not pride exactly; but she remembered how she and her sisters used to stare at the pupils of the Blind Asylum, as they met them going to church, and how she got out of the way in a great hurry, and followed them to see how they would manage to turn in at the gate; and sometimes when the master was not observing, she would look quite under their bonnets, without their finding it out, to see what their countenances were like. She should not like now to have anybody do the same to her. It was in vain that her cousin reasoned, that if she did not know it, it would not signify. The bare idea made her cry again as if she could not be comforted.

"You did not think at those times, Sally, of doing as you would be done by. If anybody had told you then that you would be one of those pupils, you would have left off following them. But it seems to me that blind people remember as soon as any body to do as they would be done by; and so I hope you will find. I have often been in that Asylum, and it cheers one to see how cheerful the people are. 'It is God's will,' they say, when one asks them about their blindness. They are always ready with the word, 'It is God's will.' And it is not the word only, for they make the best of His will. If they make any little mistake, or do any little mischief unawares, they are thankful to be set right, and seem to forget it directly. But I hope you need not go there, Sally, to learn to say, cheerfully, 'It is God's will.'"

Sally tried to stop her tears.

"And as for doing as you would be done by," continued cousin Marshall, "now is your time. You have always found my husband tender to you, have not you?—and little Ann ready to guide and help you? Well, you don't know the concern John would feel, if he saw you leave us unwillingly, and I am afraid we could scarcely pacify Ann; but if you go with a steady heart and a cheerful face, they will see at once what a fine thing it is for you to be got into such a place. Just think now, if it was Ann instead of you, how would it make you most easy to see her?"

"O, cousin Marshall, I will try. Many's the time I have been glad it was not Ann. But when—when?"

Her cousin told her directly, that she was to go in the next day but one, so that she would soon be settled now, and find her lot come easy to her. After talking awhile longer with her so as to leave her quite composed, and bidding her go to sleep, as it was far too early to get up yet, she left her, and set quietly about her business, keeping on the watch to prevent husband and children making any noise in dressing, that Sally might sleep, if possible, into the middle of the day. One object in beginning her toil so early, was to have time to go to the workhouse, in the afternoon, with the news of the release of one of the children there.

On entering the workhouse, she heard more news than she came to tell. A service had been obtained for Jane at farmer Dale's a little way in the country, whither she was to be removed next market-day. Immediately on the announcement of the plan, Ned had disappeared, and had not been heard of since.[1]

Jane seemed to regard this event but little, so occupied was she with making up her mind whether on the whole she liked the change or not. It was a fine thing, she supposed, to be out of the workhouse; but there would be an end of workhouse frolics, and perhaps harder toil than she had been accustomed to. On cousin Marshall's inquiry, whether she had not earned a little money to carry away in her pocket, she replied that she had been obliged to spend it as fast as earned. How? Chiefly in buying a dinner every Monday when she could; for she could never abide milk-broth; and the rest went for a better bonnet for Sundays, the one she brought with her being too shabby to wear at church and the gardens.

"Church and the gardens!" exclaimed cousin Marshall, very sternly. "It is mostly vain and dainty girls like you, Jane, that come to learn how welcome milk is to an empty stomach, and that are kept away from church, to say nothing of the gardens, for want of decent covering. It is a great misfortune, Jane, to be a parish girl, but it is a far greater to forget that you are one."

There was much matter of concern for John when he returned from work this night, in speculating upon where poor Ned could be, and upon what would become of Jane, with her very handsome face, her bold manner, and her vain and giddy mind. The good couple hoped she was going to a hard service, where she would be out of the way of temptation.

---

1 As a workhouse inmate, Ned was not permitted to leave the institution without official permission. In effect, he is now a criminal of sorts, having left the workhouse on his own initiative.

Chapter VI: Parish Charities

John Marshall ran no great risk in offering to take his oath that poor Ned was after no harm. He was the last person in the world likely to plan mischief, or to wish to be idle with impunity. The fact was that he had long been uneasy on Jane's account, seeing that she was not steady enough to take care of herself; and the idea of being separated from her, added to the disgust of his pauper situation, which he had been bred up to detest, was too much for him. He had absconded with the intention of finding work, if possible, in or near Titford, the village where farmer Dale lived. For the sake of leaving his pauper dress behind him, he chose Sunday for the day of departure, and stole away from church in the afternoon. He had but threepence in his pocket, one penny of which went for bread that night, when he had walked two-thirds of the distance, and found a place of rest under a stack. Another penny was spent in like manner at the baker's shop at Titford, on his arrival there at ten on the Monday morning. He found a stream at which to refresh himself; and then, trying how stout-hearted he could make himself, inquired the way to farmer Dale's, peeped through the farm-yard gate, and seeing a woman feeding the fowls, went in, and asked for work.

"We have nothing to spare for strangers," said she. "We must give more than we can afford to our own people."

"I ask no charity," said Ned. "I ask for work."

"Where do you come from?"

"From a distance. No matter where."

The woman, who proved to be Mrs. Dale, was afraid he had run away from his parents and was a naughty boy. Ned explained that he was an orphan, and only desired that it should be proved whether he was naughty or not, by setting him to work, and trying whether he did not labour hard and honestly. Had he any money? He produced his penny. How did he get it? He earned it. Why not earn more in the same way? It was impossible. What could he do? He thought he could do whatever boys of his age could generally do. How would he manage if he could not get work here? He would walk on till he found some. Begging by the way, Mrs. Dale supposed. No, he never begged. Where did he sleep last night? Under a stack. Further back than this it was impossible to gather any information of his proceedings. Mrs. Dale went in search of her husband, to plead for the boy,—a thing which she would not have done, unless she had been particularly interested in the lad; for farmer Dale had grown sadly harsh of late about beggars and idle people. He proved so on this occasion; for instead of hearing what Ned had to say, he made signs to him over the fence to be gone, and when the poor lad lingered, shook his fist at him in a way so threatening, as to show that there was no hope.

Ned went to two more places with no better success. One large establishment remained to be tried; and, disheartened as he was, Ned determined to apply; though it was hardly to be expected that the master of such a place would take up with such a laborer as he. He resolved to make his application to no one but the master himself, and sat down to wait patiently for a good opportunity, which occurred when the gentleman came home to dinner, and his wife met him at the gate of the flower-garden. Ned followed, and respectfully urged his petition. Long and close was the examination he underwent, before the gentleman, equally struck with his reserve on some points and his openness on others, resolved to give him a trial. Ned was well satisfied with the offer of twopence that night, and of fourpence a day afterwards, as long as he should pick up stones and do inferior work of other kinds to the satisfaction of his employer. Mr. Effingham, for that was the gentleman's name, would not allow him to spend his third penny for his dinner; but ordered him a slice of bread and meat from the kitchen; after eating which, Ned set to work with a grave face and a lightened heart.

On receiving his twopence, he was asked where he meant to lodge. He did not know; but if there was any empty barn or shed where he might lay down a little straw, he would take it as a favour to be allowed to sleep there till he should have saved a few pence to pay for a lodging. He was taken at his word, and for a month slept soundly in the corner of an old barn, his only disturbance being the rats, three or four of which were frequently staring him full in the face when he woke in the morning.

After a few days, he began to linger about farmer Dale's premises, at leisure times, in hopes of ascertaining whether Jane had arrived, but could see nothing of her, and did not choose to inquire, knowing that after once having met her they could frequently exchange a few words without incurring the danger to himself in which he might be placed by asking for her. He was beginning to fear that the plan might be changed, and that Jane was not coming at all, when he heard tidings of her in a way that he little expected.

He was working in the field one day, when the bailiff approached, accompanied by farmer Dale. They were discussing the very common subject among farmers of the inconveniences of pauper labour.

"Don't you find these parish children a terrible plague?" inquired

Dale. "They are the idlest, most impudent people I ever had to do with."

"It is just the same with us," replied the bailiff, "the men being quite as bad as the boys, or worse. How should it be otherwise when they do not work for themselves? One may see the difference by comparing this boy here with his neighbours. Ned is a hard-working lad as can be, and gives no trouble."

Ned turned round on hearing this and made his bow. He smiled when the bailiff went on to say,

"He is not a parish boy, but was taken on against my wish because he wanted a living, and work, work, was all his cry. It was very well he came, for we find it does not always follow that a great many labourers do a great deal of work. This lad does nearly as much as two parish boys, as I told them the other day; and I am sorry I did, as I fear it has made them plague him instead of mending themselves."

"I cannot see," said Dale, "what is to become of us farmers if these infernal rates are to go on swallowing up our substance, and putting us at the mercy of our own labourers. There is a piece of land of mine up yonder that I make a pretty thing of; and I cannot touch it, because the tithe and the poor-rate together would just swallow up the whole profit."

"What a waste it is," rejoined the bailiff, "when a subsistence is wanted for so many!"

"And then I don't know that we gain anything by employing paupers and paying their wages out of the rates; for they just please themselves about working, and when they are paid, say to my face, 'No thanks: for you must pay us for doing nothing, if you did not for doing something.' I had words like that thrown in my teeth this very morning by a parish girl we have taken, and who seems to have learned her lesson wonderfully for the time she has been with us. Says she to my wife, 'What care I whether I stay or go? The parish is bound to find me.' It will be something more of a punishment soon, perhaps, to be sent away, for she seems to like keeping company with the farm-servants very well;—a flirting jade! With a face that is like to be the ruin of her."

Ned felt too sure that this must be Jane.

"I would pack her off before worse came of it," said the bailiff.

"I shall try her a little longer," said Dale: "there is no knowing whether one would change for the better. In my father's time, or at least in my grandfather's, a man might have his choice among independent labourers that had some regard to character, and looked to what they earned; but now the case is quite changed, except in the neighbourhood of flourishing large farms where the poor-rate is a very trifling concern. One may look round in vain for the cottagers one used to meet at every turn: they have mostly flocked to the towns, and are sent out to us again as pauper-labourers. There are more labourers than ever; more by far than we want; but they are labourers of a different and a much lower class."

"And the reason is evident enough," replied the bailiff. "Proprietors have suffered so much from the burden that is brought upon the land by cottagers' families, that they let no cottages be built that are not absolutely necessary. In towns, the burden is a very different thing, as land is divided into such small portions, and the houses built upon it let so high, that the increase of a rate does not balance the advantage; to say nothing of its being divided among so many. The consequence is that the overflow from the villages goes into the towns, and the people come out into the country for work. If it were not for the poor-rate, we should see in every parish many a rood[1] tilled that now lies waste, and many a row of cottages tenanted by those who now help to breed corruption in towns."

"And then," said Dale, "we might be free from the promises and cheats of overseers. God keep me from being uncharitable! But upon my soul, I am sick of having to do with overseers. One undertakes to farm the poor; and then it would make any heart ache to see how they are treated, while he pockets every penny that can be saved out of their accommodation. Another begins making himself popular with pretending to reduce the rate; and then, the most respectable of the paupers pine at home without relief, while we are beset with beggars at every turn. The worst of all is such a man as our present overseer, who comes to taunt one with every increase of the rate, and to give hints how little scruple he should have in distraining for it. And this is the pass we shall all come to soon, unless I am much mistaken."

"As for beggars," replied the bailiff, "one would wonder where they come from. They swarm from all quarters like flies on the first summer day."

"One may see what brings them," said Dale, with a bitter laugh. "The flies come in swarms when there is a honey-pot near; and the beggars are brought by your master's charity purse. I reckon, from

---

1 A *rood* is alternately a unit of linear measure (5-7 meters) or a unit of land measure equal to 1/4 acre.

what I have seen here, that every blanket given away brings two naked people, and every bushel of coals a family that wants to be warmed."

The bailiff, instead of defending his master, laughed significantly, and led the way onwards, leaving Ned to meditate with a heavy heart on as much as he understood of what they had been saying.

Chapter VII: What Comes of Parish Charities

It was not long before Ned accomplished an interview with his giddy sister, and bitterly was he disappointed at her appearing not altogether glad to see him. Each time that they conversed, she seemed more constrained, and insisted further on the danger of his being discovered and incurring the displeasure of the superiors of the work-house. Ned would listen to no hints about going up the country or back into the town: he chose to remain where he could keep an eye on Jane, and where moreover his own labour supplied him with necessaries, and enabled him to lay by a few pence now and then. The first of these reasons for keeping his place was soon removed, to the dismay and grief of all connected with Jane.

After having tried in vain for a fortnight to catch a sight of her, and afflicted himself perpetually with the thought of her depression of spirits the last time they met, Ned took the resolution of walking up to farmer Dale's door and asking to speak to Jane Bridgeman. The farmer happened to be within hearing, and came forward to give the answer.

"Bless me, is it you? After the character your master gave me of you, I should not have thought of finding you asking after Jane Bridgeman. But you are all alike, paupers or no paupers, as long as there are paupers among us to spread corruption. Off with you, if you want to find the person you ask for! She is not here, thank God! And never shall she enter these doors again. It was a great folly ever to take her in, only that another might have been as bad.—Where is she?—Nay; that is no concern of mine. I suppose she will lie in in the workhouse she came from; but whether she went straight there, or where she went, I neither know nor care. Off with you from my premises, if you please!"

And the farmer shut the door in Ned's face. His wife had more compassion. She saw Ned turn red and pale and look very wretched, and she knew him for the same lad who had many months before asked work in a tone that pleased her. She now went out at the back gate, and met him in the farm-yard. Ned at once owned, in answer to her enquiries, that Jane was his sister, and by this means learned much of her history. She had never settled well to her business from the day of her arrival, and had seemed far more bent on being admired than on discharging her duty. Her mistress was pleased to observe, however, after a time, that she grew graver in her deportment, though she became more careless than ever about her work. It was true, she forgot everything that was said to her, and gave much trouble by her slovenliness; but she no longer smiled at compliments from the farm-servants, or acted the coquette in her necessary intercourse with them. Mrs. Dale thought her patience with the girl strangely rewarded when Jane came one day to give her warning that she wished to leave her present service at the earliest term. She would neither give a reason nor say where she meant to go. When the day arrived, she waited till her master went out, and then appeared, to bid her mistress farewell. In answer to repeated questions about where she was going, she at length sank down on a chair, sobbed convulsively, and owned that she had neither protection nor home in prospect; that she had been cruelly deceived, and that she meant to find some hiding-place where she might lie down and her shame die with her. It was some time before she would give any hint who it was that had deceived and who seduced her, and she never revealed his name; but Mrs. Dale believed it to be a pauper laborer who had disappeared a few days before, probably to avoid being obliged to marry Jane when their guilt should be discovered. On ascertaining that the girl had relations, Mrs. Dale recommended that she should go to her cousin Marshall, open her whole heart to her, and follow her advice as to what should next be done; but Jane's sobs became more violent than ever at this suggestion. "They will tear me to pieces!" she cried. "They will never put up with disgrace; and I am the first that has disgraced them. I can never look cousin Marshall in the face again!"—Neither would she go to the workhouse. She loathed the idea of Mrs. Wilkes as much as she dreaded that of cousin Marshall; and Mrs. Dale was much perplexed, not daring to keep her another day, and not choosing to turn her out wholly destitute. After a long conversation, which served to soften the poor girl's heart and win her confidence, Mrs. Dale proposed a plan which was adopted,—that she should write a letter to cousin Marshall, urging that what was done could not be undone, and that the most likely way to make Jane's penitence real and lasting was to look to her present safety instead of driving her to desperation. Mrs. Dale expressed in very strong terms her concern that the respectability of the family should have been thus stained; and took the liberty of declaring her admiration of the parental kindness with which the poor orphans had been treated, and her earnest wishes that it might be better rewarded in the instance of the others than in that of poor Jane. With this letter in her hand, Jane was put into the carrier's cart, leaving as a last request to Ned that he would not follow her or give up his place on her account; and, partly for his sake, she promised that no persuasion should prevent her going straight to her cousin Marshall's and following the advice of her friends in every particular. Mrs. Dale had since ascertained that she was received at her cousin's; and had remained in their house up to the last market-day, when the inquiry was made; but the farmer's wife did not know what sad circumstances the family were in when Jane arrived to add to their sorrow.

John Marshall had died after a few days' illness; and it was on the very night of his funeral that Jane alighted at his widow's door. Her first feeling on hearing of the event was joy that one person the less,—and he one whom she much respected,—would know of her disgrace. The next moment she felt what a wretch she must be,—what a state she must be reduced to,—to rejoice in the death of one who had been like a parent in tenderness, where no parental duty enjoined the acts of kindness he had done. She hastily bade Ann not tell her cousin of her arrival, and said she would beg a shelter for the night at her aunt Bell's; but she was told that aunt Bell was in great distress too, and could not possibly receive her; so there was no escape, and Jane was led in, trembling like a criminal under sentence, and pulling her cloak about her, to meet the kind-hearted cousin who had never frowned upon her. Her agitation was naturally misunderstood at first; but, after some time, her refusal even to look up, and the force with which she prevented their relieving her of her cloak made her cousin suspect the fact, and dismiss the young people, in order to arrive at an explanation.—She could not read the letter, and Jane would not hear of Ann being called in to do it, but made an effort to get through it herself. Cousin Marshall said nothing for some time; not even the thought which was uppermost in her mind,—how glad she was that the fact never reached her husband's ear! At last, she merely assured Jane that she should be taken care of, and advised her to go to bed, and leave everything to be settled when there had been more time for thought.

"I cannot go," said Jane, "I will not leave you while you look so cold upon me, cousin."

"I will go with you, then," said Mrs. Marshall calmly. "We must have the same bed, and I am ready."

"You said you forgave me," cried the weeping Jane; "and I am sure this is not forgiving me. I never saw you look so upon anybody!"

"I never had reason, Jane; nobody belonging to me ever had to make such a confession as yours to-night. I pity you enough, God knows! For you must be very miserable; but I cannot look upon you as I do upon your innocent sisters; how should I?—Poor Sally! I remember her great comfort about being blind was that it was not Ann; and if you have any comfort at all, I suppose it must be that."

"Indeed, indeed, I had rather be anybody than what I am. I had rather be drowning this minute, or even on the gallows: I had rather die any how than be as I am. I hope I shall die when my time comes."

Cousin Marshall quietly represented the sinfulness of this thought, and Jane tempted her to say more and more, being able to bear anything better than the silence of displeasure. What, her cousin asked, could bring her to this pass? What madness could make her plunge herself into this abyss of distress after all the warning and watching, all the—But it was foolish to say more, Mrs. Marshall continued, when she might be led to say what would do no good and would be therefore unkind.

Jane would not let it drop. She laid much of the blame on the workhouse, where it was a common boast among the women how early they had got married, being so far better off than honester people that they need not trouble themselves about what became of themselves and their children, since the parish was bound to find them. It was considered a kind of enterprise among the paupers to cheat their superiors, and to get the girls early married by rendering marriage desirable on the score of decency, and of the chance of a man being able to support his children hereafter. Jane's leading idea was the glory of getting married at sixteen; and the last thing she thought of was the possibility of being deceived; and now that her intended husband was gone nobody knew whither, she was as much astonished and terrified at her own position as any of her friends could be. This explanation caused some inward relentings towards her; but cousin Marshall thought it too early yet to show them; and to avoid the danger of doing so, insisted on both going to bed, where neither of them slept a wink or exchanged a word during the whole night.

Before morning, Mrs. Marshall had arranged her plan. Jane's arrival was on no account to be mentioned, and she was to be kept entirely out of sight for the three months which were to pass before her confinement. By these means, the persecution of parish officers might be avoided, and an opportunity afforded for observing whether the shock had really so sobered Jane as to render her more fit to take care of herself than she was before. If she appeared truly penitent, Mrs. Marshall would try to obtain a service for her at some distance, where her disgrace would not follow her, and would also take charge of the infant, with such help as Jane could spare out of her wages; and then the parish need never know anything about the matter. Jane was most happy to agree to these terms, and settled herself in this bedroom for three long months, intending to work diligently for her infant, and to take all the needle-work of the family off her cousin's hands, with as much of the charge of the children as was possible within so confined a space. What more she wanted of exercise was to be taken with Mrs. Marshall very early in these spring mornings, before their neighbors should be stirring. The young people were so trained to obedience, that there was no fear of their telling anything that they were desired to keep to themselves.

Things went on as quietly as could be looked for in such unhappy circumstances. No difficulties arose for some time, and Jane had only to struggle with her inward shame, her grief at witnessing Ann's sorrow, her terror at the risks which must be daily run, and her inability to get rest of body or mind. She could scarcely be persuaded to come down in the evening when the door was shut and the window curtain drawn: she started at every noise, and could not get rid of a vague expectation that her lover would find her out and come to comfort her;—an expectation which made her turn pale whenever she heard a man's voice under the window, or a tap at the door below. Besides these fears, circumstances happened now and then to try her to the utmost.

Early one morning, before Jane was up, and while Mrs. Marshall and her young people were dressing, a step was heard slowly ascending the stairs, the door opened, and Sally appeared with a smiling countenance and the question,

"Are you awake yet, cousin Marshall, and all of you?"

Mrs. Marshall made a sign to the children by putting her finger on her lip, and pointing to Jane. She had no intention that Sally should be made unhappy by knowing the truth at present, and was besides afraid to trust her with such a secret among her companions at the Asylum, who were all accustomed to have no concealments from one another.

"Why don't you answer?" said Sally, groping for the bed. "I do believe you are all asleep, though I thought I heard you moving, and the door was on the latch below."

"We are all awake, my dear, and one or two gone out; but we are surprised to see you so early. What brings you at such a time, and who came with you?"

Sally explained that the ward of the Asylum in which she worked was to be whitewashed this day; and she and a few others whose friends lived near had leave to enjoy a long holiday. Three of them had taken care of one another, the streets being clear at this hour; and she had found her way easily for the short distance she had to come alone. While she spoke, Jane was gazing at her, tearful, and longing to throw herself on her sister's neck. The temptation became almost irresistible when Sally, feeling for a place on which to sit down, moved herself within reach.

"Take care where you sit, my dear," said Mrs. Marshall. "Here, I will give you a seat on my chest."

This chest was directly opposite the bed, so that Jane could see the face under the black bonnet, and convince herself that the old womanish little figure in brown stuff gown and white kerchief was really the sister Sally she had last seen in blue frock and pinafore. During the whole day, Jane sat on the stairs behind the half-shut door, listening to Sally's cheerful tales about the doings at the Asylum, and to her frequent inquiries about both her sisters, and trembling when any of the little ones spoke, lest they should reveal her presence. Many perplexing and dangerous questions too were asked.

"Which of you sighs so? I should not ask if it could be you, cousin; but it comes from the other side."

Again, when Jane's dinner was being carried to her.

"Ah, we are not allowed to move at dinnertime, happen what will: and you used not to let us either; and now Ann has gone upstairs twice since we sat down." Again,

"I have leave to knit what I please on Saturdays; so I am knitting a pair of mittens for Jane, against she comes to see me, which I hope she will one day; but be sure you none of you tell her about the mittens. I spoiled two pair in trying, and she would be so sorry to know how I wasted my time and the cotton."

"Poor dear!" said Mrs. Marshall at night, when Sally was gone; "it seems wicked to take advantage of her infirmity to deceive her; but it is all for her good, placed where she is by her blindness. It would be far more cruel to tell her all, when it may be that she need never know it."

Jane took all this upon herself; but, while she blamed herself for having caused this new practice of concealment, she was far more grieved at it in John Marshall's case. She did not strictly owe any confidence to Sally, but she did to John Marshall; and the idea that he had left her the same blessing with the rest of her family when he died, gave her far more pain than any tears or reproaches from Sally could ever do.

One Sunday, when cousin Marshall had gone to church in the morning with her family, and left her house apparently shut up, as usual; and when, moreover, it was so fine a day as to have taken almost all the neighbors from their homes, Jane came down to prepare the dinner, feeling quite secure from interruption. She was standing kneading the dumplings, when a noise was heard outside and she had but a moment's time to escape upstairs before her aunt Bell lifted the latch and entered. Seeing the dough on the board and nobody there to knead it, she naturally proceeded to the bedroom, where she found Jane on the bed with coverings thrown over her. Questions and explanations followed.—How long had Jane been unwell, and did she expect to go back to her place when recovered? Why did she not let her aunt know of her arrival? Though, to be sure, there was no use in expecting help from her, distressed as she was. Jane was really glad to turn the conversation away from her own troubles to those of Mrs. Bell, who was, as she herself said, as good as a widow, her husband having absconded. Dear! Had not Jane heard of it? He had been advertised by the overseers in the newspapers, and a great fuss had been made about it; but, for her part, she was convinced it was the best thing he could do for her and the children, to go and find a settlement in a distant parish, leaving his family to be provided for by his own. Where had he gone?—Why, supposing she knew, was it likely she should tell before the year was out? However, he had made all safe by not giving a hint in which direction he should travel. Jane asked what was the necessity of keeping the secret for a year? He would surely be out of reach before the year was over, if at all. Mrs. Bell laughed and said she saw Jane did not know how to get a settlement; and explained to her that her husband's aim was to obtain a claim on a distant and prosperous parish, which must be done either by living forty days on an estate of his own, worth thirty pounds, or in a rented tenement of the yearly value of ten pounds, or by serving an apprenticeship, or by going through a year's service on a yearly hiring as an unmarried man. This last was, of course, the only means within his power; and to make sure of it, it was his part to keep, to himself, whence he had come, and that he had a wife and family; and her's to remain ignorant whither he had gone, and not to inquire for her husband for a year at least.

"Do you call this a cheat, my dear?" she went on. "Lord! What a tender conscience you have! It is no worse than what is done every day. Would you think it such a very wicked thing now,—suppose a young creature like you should have happened to have a misfortune, and should wish her infant to have a settlement in a particular parish,—would you think it such a very wicked thing to hide yourself and keep your condition a secret from the officers till your child was born?" And Mrs. Bell looked inquisitively in her niece's face.

"That would be telling no lie," replied Jane, her face making the confession which she kept her tongue from uttering.

"Well; and whose fault is it, my dear, that lies are told about the matter? If the laws put such difficulty in the way of getting relief, we are driven to tell fibs; for relief we must have."

Mrs. Marshall, who had overheard some of the conversation, and now came to Jane's assistance, observed that the fault seemed to her to be in the laws giving relief at all. Mischiefs out of number came of it, and no good that she saw. The more relief the law gave, the more it might give, to judge by the swarms of paupers; and all this made it the more difficult for honest and independent folks to get their bread. She thought her own experience, and Mrs. Bell's together, might be enough to show how bad the system was.

"Mine, I grant you," cried Mrs. Bell; "but what have you had to do with it? You, that pride yourself on never having touched a penny of parish money."

"Thanks, under God, to my husband, cousin Bell, we have been beholden to nobody but ourselves for our living. We have never had to bear the scornful glance from the rate-payers, nor the caprice of the overseer, nor any of the uncertainty of depending on what might fail us, nor the shame of calling our children paupers.—I say these things freely, cousin Bell, because I know you have been too long used to them to mind them.—We have never crossed the threshold of the workhouse on our own account; nor ever been driven to expose our want when it was the greatest; or tempted to fib by word or act to get more than our share of other people's money. Yet, the worst things we have suffered have arisen out of these poor laws; and the worst thing about them is, that those suffer by them who desire to have nothing to do with them. They prevent people going where their labour is wanted, and would be well paid, and keep them in a place where there are far more hands than there is work for. Honest, hard-working men, like my husband, have always felt the hardship of either being obliged to stay where wages were low from the number of labourers, or to give up their settlements for the chance of work in some other place."

"He had better have run off by himself, and left his settlement to you and the children," observed Mrs. Bell.

"John Marshall was not the man to do that, cousin. But, as I was saying, many a time when we were brought very low, so much so that my husband had not had his pint, nor the children anything but bread for a week, and less of that than they could have eaten,—at many such times we have been told of this parish and that parish where there was plenty of work and good wages, and have had half a mind to go and try our fortune; but we always remembered that so many more needy people would be likely to do the same, that it would soon cease to be a good parish, and we might have left a place where we were known and respected, for what would prove to be no good. I have heard that these favourite parishes are seldom long prosperous under the best management, for paupers contrive, by all sorts of tricks, to get a settlement in them."

"Well; that makes an end, however, of your complaint of there not being labour where labour is wanted."

"Indeed it does not, cousin Bell; for they are mostly idle men and cheats that wander about making experiments on such places. Sober, good labourers, would be much more ready to go where they are wanted, if it were not for the fear of losing their settlements. Such end, as my husband did, by staying in their own parish to have their labour poorly paid, and to see rogues and vagabonds consuming what would have added to their wages, if labour had been left to earn its due reward."

Mrs. Bell did not care about all this; all she knew was that people must live, and that she and her family could not have lived without the parish, and a deal of help besides.

"The very thing I complain of most, cousin Bell, is, that those who have the relief are those that know and care the least about the matter. It is they that are above taking the relief that have good reason to know, and much cause to care, that their labour cannot be properly paid, and that their children cannot have a fair chance in the world, while the money that should pay their wages is spent without bringing any more gain than if it was thrown into the sea. It is because such as you, cousin Bell, care about nothing but getting relief, that such husbands as mine lose their natural rest through anxiety, and pinch themselves and work themselves into their graves, and die, not knowing but their families may come to be paupers after all.—I am warm, cousin, but you'll excuse me; nothing chafes me so easily as thinking of this; the more from remembering nearly the last words my husband spoke. 'I hope,' says he,—but I thought there was little hope in his tone, or in his face,—'I hope you and yours will be able to keep free of the parish. Get the boys into my club, if they live to be old enough; and then they will keep their mother and sisters free of the parish.'—I thank God! We can get on at present; but I sometimes think some of us will end our days in the workhouse, if idle and needy people go on to increase as they do, and to eat up the substance they never helped, as we have done, to make."

"It will be some time yet, cousin Marshall, before your boys can belong to the club."

"Yes; but in the meanwhile there is the Savings Bank, where the girls can put their little savings as well as the boys. Not that they have done anything in that way yet, except my eldest and Ann. But the others are earning their own clothes."

Mrs. Bell asked Jane whether it was not a nice thing for her sister Ann to have a little money in the bank ready for such occasions as Jane's present illness? She supposed Jane was now using it up; and to be sure it was a charming thing to have such help at hand. Mrs. Marshall, who knew that one of Jane's griefs was depriving Ann of her little store, saved her the pain of replying by inviting Mrs. Bell down to dinner.

At the close of the meal, Mrs. Bell cast a longing eye on the few fragments she had left. Her children had only a crust of bread to eat this day; and she complained much of the hardships they were reduced to, showing how her only gown was wearing out, and relating that it was ruinous work to do as she was doing now, pawning her blanket in the morning to release her gown, and the gown in the evening to release the blanket. Cousin Marshall was grieved for the children, but, charitable as she was known to be, she offered no help. She had nothing to spare, and had done her utmost in giving a hearty dinner; and, if she had had the means, she would have bestowed them where they might have afforded real relief, which no charity ever did to Mrs. Bell.

This woman seldom visited her neighbors without leaving them cause to wish that she had stayed away. This was the case in the present instance. She whispered her suspicions of Jane's situation, either to the parish officers, or to some one who carried it round to them; and the consequence was that the poor girl was hunted up, taken before a magistrate to be sworn, and removed to the workhouse to abide her confinement. In return to her bitter reproaches the next time they met, Mrs. Bell laughed, and said she thought she had done them all a great kindness.—Cousin Marshall ought to be very glad to be relieved of the charge, and Jane would be sure of a husband if her lover could be found up. Jane's views had, however, been altered by her intercourse with Mrs. Marshall. She would much rather have gone to service and tried to atone for what was done, than remain to be the pauper-wife of a man who had cruelly deceived her,—who would not marry unless he could be caught,—and who, being an unwilling, would be probably an unkind, husband. Her good cousin feared something worse for her than the misery of her lot: she feared that this misery might drive her to habitual vice; and that her re-entrance into the workhouse might prove the date from which she would become a castaway from her family for ever.

Chapter VIII: What is Charity?

Ned heard of Jane's return to the workhouse, and of her confinement, from Mr. Burke, who attended Mr. Effingham's family, and who recognized, to his great surprise, Ned Bridgeman in the boy who one day opened the gate for him, and followed to hold his horse. Whenever he came, from that time forward, he inquired for Ned, and was ready to make the wished-for reply to the customary petition, not to tell the officers or anybody belonging to them, where he was, but just to inform cousin Marshall and his sisters that he was well, and likely to go on earning a living. It was in vain to reason with him, that the parish could desire nothing more than that he should maintain himself, and that the officers would be glad to leave him unmolested. He had eloped, and was possessed with the idea that he should be carried back whence he came; and had, moreover, such a horror of the place and people connected with his short period of pauperism, that he longed above all things to keep out of sight of the one, and be forgotten by the other. The pauper labourers who worked with him in the field, discovered something of this, and amused themselves by alarming him with dark hints, from time to time, that some danger impended. They were not over-fond of him, harmless and good-natured as he was. The bailiff was apt to hold him up as an example to them in an injudicious way, and Ned's horror of pauperism,—his pride, as his companions called it,—was not exactly the quality to secure their good fellowship. They teased the boy sadly, and Mr. Burke thought he looked more and more grave every time he saw him. The gentleman was not, therefore, much surprised when he was told one day that Ned was missing, nor did he give much heed to the remarks on the unsteadiness of the boy who had twice absconded. On finding that, so far from having done anything dishonest, Ned had left nearly half-a-crown of his savings in Mr. Effingham's hands, Mr. Burke made inquiry into the circumstances, and found that, as he suspected, Ned had been assured that the officers were after him, and so cruelly taunted with his sister's shame, that it was no wonder he had gone farther up the country, where he might work in peace, if work was to be found. Nothing could be done but to take charge of his money, and invest it where it might increase till the owner should be forthcoming to claim it. So Mr. Burke pocketed the two shillings and fourpence half-penny as carefully as if it had been a hundred pounds, and saw that it was placed in the Savings Bank with Ann's, and made as light as he could to the family of the fact that he no longer knew where the lad was; adding that Ned was a boy whom he would trust all over the world by himself, and prophesying that he would re-appear some day to be a credit and a help to his orphan sisters.

On one occasion when Mr. Burke was entering the village of Titford, he overtook Mr. Effingham walking slowly with his head bent down, and his hands in his pockets. He looked up when greeted by his friend, who accosted him with—

"I am afraid you are to be one of my patients to-day, to judge by your gait and countenance. What can be the matter? No misfortune at home, I hope?"

"No; but I have just heard something that has shocked me very much. There is an execution[1] at Dale's."

"How hard that poor man has struggled!" observed Mr. Burke. "And has it even come to this at last?"

"Even so; and through no fault of his own that I can see. They are distraining for the rate."

"Ay, that is the way, Effingham. Thus is our pauper list swelled, year by year. It grows at both ends. Paupers multiply their own numbers as fast as they can, and rate-payers sink down into rate-receivers. This will probably be Dale's fate, as it has been that of many little farmers before him. And if it is, he will only anticipate by a few years the fate of others besides small farmers, of shopkeepers, manufacturers, merchants, and agriculturalists of every class; always providing that some radical amendment of the system does not take place."

"God help us!" cried Effingham. "If so, our security is gone, as a nation, and as individuals."

"At present, Effingham, the security of property is to the pauper, and not to the proprietor, however rich he may be. The proprietor

---

1 An execution is a bankruptcy, which Dale was forced into due to excessive rate-paying.

is compelled, as in the case before us, to pay more and more to the rate till his profits are absorbed, and he is obliged to relinquish his undertakings one after another; field after field goes out of cultivation, his capital is gradually transferred to his wages-fund, which is paid away without bringing an adequate return; and when all but his fixed capital is gone, that becomes liable to seizure, and the ruin is complete. There is no more security of property, under such a system, than there is security of life to a poor wretch in a quicksand, who feels himself swallowed up inch by inch. The paupers meanwhile are sure of their relief as long as the law subsists. They are to be provided for at all events, let what will become of other people. While Dale has been fretting by day, and tossing by night under the burden of his cares, his pauper labourers have been supporting a very different kind of burden,—the burden of the pauper song,

> 'Hang sorrow and cast away care,
> The parish is bound to find us!'"

"This very security of property, which is the most precious of an independent man's rights," said Effingham, "seems to be the most pernicious thing in the world to the indigent. One may fairly call it so in relation to them, for they seem to consider the produce of the rate as their property."

"It is really so," replied Burke. "They know it to be the lawful property of the pauper body, and that the only question is how it is to be distributed? As long as they know this, they will go on multiplying the claims upon it till nothing is left with which to satisfy them."

"It is very odd," said Effingham, "that none of the checks that have ever been tried have done any good; they seem rather to have made the matter worse."

"I do not think it strange, Effingham. None of the remedies have struck at the root of the evil, and none could therefore effect lasting good. The test is just this: do they tend to lessen the number of the indigent? Unless they do this, they may afford relief to a generation, or shift a burden from one district to another, or from one class of producers upon another; but they will not improve the system. Look at the experiments tried! First, paupers were to wear a badge, a mark of infamy. Of course, the profligate and hardened were the readiest to put it on, and those who had modesty and humble pride refused it, and obtained help only through the compassion of overseers, who evaded the regulation so perpetually, that it was abolished as useless. While it lasted, profligate pauperism increased very rapidly. Next came the expedient of workhouses, in which the poor were expected to do more work, and be fed less expensively, than in their own houses. But here again the rogue and vagabond class reaped the advantage, the houses being detested by the sober and quiet; and the choice of the latter to pine at home, rather than be shut up in a workhouse, occasioned a diminution of the rate for some time; but that time has long been over, and now the maintenance of a pauper costs three or four times as much in a workhouse as out of it, there being no inducement to the paupers to work, and but little to their managers to economise. And this is just what any one might have foretold from the beginning, if he had seen what experience has plainly taught us, that indigence must spread while numbers increase, and while the subsistence-fund, on which they are to be supported, is consumed unproductively."

"But why unproductively?" said Effingham. "I cannot help thinking that there must be some mode of management, by which manufactures might be carried on by paupers with pretty good success?"

"Suppose it to be so, according to what I imagine you to mean by success,—suppose a certain quantity of produce to be achieved and disposed of,—this is in itself a great evil. Capital raised by forcible means, arbitrarily applied, and made to bring a return from an artificial market, can never be so productive as if it found a natural channel; and its employment in this artificial manner is a serious injury to individual capitalists. In the neighbourhood of a workhouse where work is really done a manufacturer, while paying to the rate, bitterly feels that he is subscribing the means by which his trade is to be stolen from him. It is adding insult to injury to set up in the faces of rate-payers workhouse manufactures, which are to have a preference in the market to their own. In all these cases, however, the object fails. To all remedies yet tried, the same fundamental objection applies: they all encourage the increase of population, while they sink capital. What we want is the very reverse of this,—we want a reproduction of capital with increase, and a limitation of numbers within a due proportion to this fund."

"What do you think, then, of the methods proposed for the amelioration of the system?"

"Which? There are so many."

"The cottage system,[1] for one."

---

1   The cottage system was designed to provide each pauper family with its own cottage and small plot of land (rather than housing them collectively in workhouses), in the hope they would become economically self-sufficient.

"It will not bear the test. Under no system does population increase more rapidly;—witness Ireland; and in addition to the worst evils that afflict Ireland, we should have that of a legal claim to support, which effectually prevents the due improvement of capital. Cottages would prove no better than workhouses, depend upon it."

"Well, then, what do you think of assessing new kinds of property?"

"Worse and worse! This would be only casting more of our substance into the gulf before its time. It would be helping to increase the number of paupers; it would be encouraging the unproductive consumption of capital; it would be—"

"Like pouring water into one of your dropsical patients," said Effingham, smiling.

"Just so, Effingham; and it needs no great skill to foresee the result in both cases."

"Then there are Benefit Clubs," replied Effingham. "Some think that if they were made obligatory by law, they might soon supersede the poor-rate. What do you think of them?"

"No man approves such societies more than I, as long as they are voluntary; but fellowship of this kind would lose its virtue, I doubt, by being made compulsory. There are no means that I know of, of compelling a man who will not earn to store his earnings; and the frugal and industrious will do it without compulsion, as soon as they understand the matter: so that in fact the worst classes of society would be left as free to roam, and beg, and steal, as if the institution did not exist."

"But Friendly Societies and Benefit Clubs will bear your test. They tend to the increase of capital, and, by encouraging prudence, to the limitation of numbers."

"True; and therefore I wish they were in universal operation among the working classes; but this must be by voluntary association. It will be a work of time to convince our whole population of their advantages; and even then the less industrious part will rather depend on the poor rate, if it still subsists. We must have recourse to some speedier method of lessening our burdens, giving all possible encouragement to Friendly Societies in the mean time."

"What method? It seems to me that relief is already given in every possible way."

"Ay; there is the mistake, Effingham. People think they give relief in giving money."

"I seldom give money," replied Effingham.

"No; but you give what money will buy, which is, begging your pardon, worse than ineffectual. Now, if you have no objection, I should like to know how much you spent on coals and blankets the first Christmas you settled here, and how much last year?"

"I began with devoting five pounds a year to this purpose; but it increased sadly. I stopped short two years ago at twenty pounds; but it grieved me to the heart to do so, for more objects remain now unsupplied than I supplied at first."

"Probably; and are these new applicants strangers from other parishes brought round you by your bounty, or are more of your near neighbours in a condition for receiving charity?"

"Dale reproaches me with having brought an inundation of paupers from a distance; but really our own population has increased wonderfully."

"And the more support you offer them, friend, the more surprisingly they will increase, if there can be anything surprising in the case. Surely you do not mean to go on giving coals and blankets?"

"What can I do? You would call me cruel to withdraw the gift, if you could see the destitution of the poor creatures. I am completely at a loss how to proceed. If I go on, poverty increases; if I stop, the people will freeze and pine before my eyes. What a dilemma!"

"Much like that of government about its pauper subjects. I should recommend the same method to both."

"To fix a maximum, I suppose; to declare the amount beyond which relief shall not be given? I have tried that, and it does not succeed. Twenty pounds a year is my maximum, and is known to be so; but every one hopes to have a portion of it, and reckons upon his share nearly as confidently as if all were sure of it."

"Of course; and there is the additional evil of admitting the principle of a claim to support, which is at the bottom of the mischief.— No; to fix a maximum is to unite the evils of the maintenance and the abolition of the pauper system; and both are bad enough singly. If I were you, and if I were the government, I would immediately disavow the principle in question, and take measures for ceasing to act upon it. If I were you, I would explain to my neighbours that, finding this mode of charity creates more misery than it relieves, I should discontinue it in the way which appears to inflict the least hardship. I would give notice that, after the next Christmas donation, no more coals and blankets shall be given except to those aged and sickly people who at present look for them; and that no new applicants whatever shall be placed on the list, the object being to have the charity die out as soon as possible."

"But I shall be railed at wherever I turn my face. I should not wonder if they pull my house about my ears. They will rob my poultry-yard, and burn my ricks. They will—"

"Very like the situation of government!" exclaimed Mr. Burke. "The very same difficulties on a smaller scale. Friend, you must bear the railing for a time, since it comes as a natural consequence of what you have already done. I am sure so benevolent a man as you would rather endure this personal inconvenience than add to the misery around you. You are capable of heroism in retrieving a mistake, Effingham. As for your house and other property, you must take measures to protect it. You must firmly and gently repress tendencies to violence which arise, as you now perceive, from an error of your own."

"I will consider, resolve, and act; and that without delay, for the evil is pressing," said Effingham.

"I wish government would do the same," replied Mr. Burke. "We hear much of consideration, but the resolve is yet to be made; and how long the act may be in following, it is impossible to guess. Meanwhile, we are going headlong to ruin as fast as you would do if you answered all the petitions for charity which would be brought upon you by unbounded readiness to give. Your private fortune would be gone in a twinkling, and so will vanish our national resources."

"What period would you fix for abolishing the rate?"

"The best plan, in my opinion, yet proposed, is this:—to enact that no child born from any marriage taking place within a year from the date of the law, and no illegitimate child born within two years from the same date, shall ever be entitled to parish assistance. This regulation should be made known, and its purpose explained universally; and this, if properly done, might, I think, prevent violence, and save a vast amount of future distress. The people should be called together, either in their places of worship or elsewhere, in such a manner as to attract the whole population to listen, and the case should be explained to them by their pastors or others. It is so plain a case, and so capable of illustration, that I see no great difficulty in making the most ignorant comprehend it."

"And yet the details are vast."

"Vast, but not complicated; so the whole might be conveyed in a parable which any child can understand. I think I dare undertake to prove to any rational being that national distress *cannot* be relieved by money, and that consequently individual distress cannot be so relieved without inflicting the same portion of distress elsewhere. A child can see that if there is so much bread in a country and no more, and if the rich give some of the poor two shillings a day that they may eat more bread, the price of bread may rise, and some who could buy before must go without now. Since no more bread is created by this charity, the only thing done is to take some of it out of the reach of purchasers to give it to paupers."

"True: the only real charity is to create more bread; and, till this can be done, to teach men to be frugal of what they have.—I happen to know a case which illustrates your doctrine. Owen, who lives in this village, earned ten shillings a week before the last scarcity. He bought eight shillings' worth of flour for his family, and had two to spare for other necessaries. During the scarcity he received fourteen shillings a week from his parish, in addition to the ten he earned; but the price of corn had risen so much that he now gave twenty-two shillings out of his twenty-four for the same quantity of flour; so that he had still two shillings left for other necessaries; and thus was no richer with twenty-four shillings than he had been with ten."

"If there had been many such cases," observed Mr. Burke, "the price of corn would have been even higher than it was. The best charity to the public as well as to this man would have been to teach him that he had better look after other kinds of food, and not insist on such an abundance of flour. Do not you think he could have understood this? And if he could, why should not his brethren understand the state of the pauper system, and be brought to acquiesce in the measures now necessary to be taken?—If the regulation I have described had been made when first proposed, there would have been much less difficulty than now. If not done now, there is no saying how soon it may be out of our power to do anything. We are now borne down, we shall soon be crushed, by the weight of our burdens."

"We must hasten to give our testimony," said Effingham: "I, by withdrawing my donations, and declaring why; you, by—but you have given yours, I suspect. I see now the reasons of your resigning your offices at both the charitable institutions where I and others took so much pains to get you in. I was more than half angry at it when I thought of our canvass, and all the disagreeablenesses belonging to it;—and all done and endured for nothing. But I see now how it is. I can only hope that your going out of office may do more good than your going in; and what more can I say?"

"Nothing more gratifying to my self-complacency, I am sure," said Mr. Burke, smiling, "I have had my recompense already in finding that many more than I expected attend to my reasons, and take them into consideration as a matter of real importance. My hopes sometimes mount so high as to flatter me that all Great Britain may soon be effectually employed upon the problem—HOW TO REDUCE THE NUMBER OF THE INDIGENT."

Chapter IX: Cousin Marshall's End

It was some years before any tidings came of Ned that could be depended upon. At length a countryman called on the widow Marshall one market-day, saying that he had had a world of trouble in finding her out in the small place she had got into outside the city, but was determined not to meet Ned Bridgeman again without having seen her and delivered Ned's packet into her own hand. Mrs. Marshall had nobody living with her now but her youngest daughter, who happened not to be at home at this hour; and as Mrs. Marshall could not read, she was obliged to wait till evening to know what was in the letter, and what the guinea was for which the packet contained. She obtained great satisfaction from the countrymen concerning Ned, sent him her love and blessing, and the promise of an answer to his letter when there should be an opportunity to sending one, which might happen by means of the present messenger within six months. Many times before the evening did cousin Marshall open the letter, and examine it, and admire as much of it as was apparent to her; viz. the evenness of the lines and the absence of blots. The guinea, too, was a very good sign. The letter proved that his workhouse schooling had not been lost upon him; and the money, that her methods of education had taken effect. Her answer, written down by her daughter, was as follows:—

"Dear Ned, Your letter was very welcome to us, since you could not come yourself. I do not wonder you met with hardships and difficulty in settling. Such is the way with many people in these days who wish to be beholden to nobody; but such generally meet with their deserts at last, as I am glad to hear you have. We have put your guinea into the Savings Bank for you, my dear boy, as, thank God! we none of us want it at present, and there was half-a-guinea of yours there before. Now I dare say you are wondering how it came there? It was the half-crown of wages you left behind you at Titford that Mr. Burke took care of, and it has grown into half-a-guinea by not being touched, which I hope will be good news to you. I quite approve your wish about the Friendly Society, knowing how my husband did the wisest thing in belonging to one, and at times could have got through in no other way. There is nothing about your sisters that should give you any scruple. Sally, poor thing, is very contented in the Asylum; and, as the people there are fond of her, has fewer troubles than many that have their eyesight. I have not seen so many tears from her since she went in as when my Susan read your letter to her, and she sends you her love. Ann is pretty well off in service, having nothing to complain of but her mistress's temper, with which she will contrive to bear, I hope, for she has a sweet one of her own. She will write to you herself, and tell you as much as we know about Jane, which is but little, and that little very sad. She is quite lost, I fear; but you may depend on my keeping my eye upon her. I thank you, my dear boy, for your questions about me and mine. My children have all left me but the one that holds the pen, and she is going to marry too. I hope she will have an easier life than her sisters, who are much put to it with their large families. I begin to feel myself growing old when I see so many grandchildren about me; and perhaps it is owing to that that I feel far more troubled about how their parents are to get through than I ever did for John Marshall and myself, when we had another little family added, as it were, to our own eight. But God preserve me from failing in my trust!—trusting as I wish to do, not to other people's charity, but to one's own labour and thrift, which has His blessing sooner than the other. Many a merciful lesson has been given me about trusting,—one since I had your letter. On Saturday, my eldest grandson and daughter were both out of work. Today is Monday, and they have each got a place. Indeed God Almighty is very good to us. But Susan is tired, not having kept up her schooling, I am afraid, so well as you. However, it looks a long letter, though I have many more things to say to you if you were here. Old as I call myself, I may see you on this side the grave, or will try to think so till you say not. Till then, I send you my love and blessing, which I hope you know you have had all this long while."

The close of cousin Marshall's very long life was not altogether so serene as the character of its days of vigour might seem to deserve. Her children were so burdened with families of their own that they could offer no further assistance than that she should lodge with them by turns. She was positive, however, in her determination to live alone; and a small room in a poor place on the outskirts of the city was her dwelling. In one way or another she earned a little matter, and lived upon it, to the astonishment of some who received twice as much from the parish and could not make it do. Her adopted children found the utmost difficulty in making her accept any assistance, clearly as it was her due from those to whom she had been a mother in their orphan state. It grieved Ned to the heart to see her using her dim sight to patch her cloak for the twentieth time, when he had placed at her disposal the guinea and half, with all that had accumulated upon it, in the Savings Bank.

"Not yet. When I want it. I can do for myself still," were always her answers; and though, without consulting her, he laid in coals and bought clothes for her during the two only visits that he was able to make to that neighbourhood, and though these presents were, after some scruple, accepted, he never could prevail upon her to use the little fund during his absence for her daily comforts. She was somewhat unpopular among her neighbours, who did not relish her occasional observations on the multiplication of alehouses, or her reports of what a comely, robust man her John Marshall was, for all he had seldom a pint and pipe to refresh himself with when his days' work was done. Nobody was more openhearted and sociable; but he could not afford both ale and independence,—to say nothing of charity; and everybody knew he was a father to the orphan.—The neighbours observed that he was certainly very kind to the parish; but that, for their parts, they could not afford to give charity to the parish. It was more natural for the parish to give to them. Such degeneracy as this roused cousin Marshall to prophesy evil. She was rather too ready with her forebodings that those who thus spoke would die in the workhouse, and with her horror at the warning seeming to create no alarm. But what roused her indignation above everything was the frequent question how, after all her toils and savings, she was better off than her cousin, Mrs. Bell? Mrs. Bell had never more heard of her husband, and had at length been taken into the workhouse with her family; of whom one daughter had followed Jane's example, and gained her point of a pauper marriage; one son was an ill-doing pauper-labourer; and another, having been transported for theft, was flourishing at Sydney, and likely to get more money than all cousin Marshall's honest children put together. Mrs. Bell was proud of this son's prosperity, and would not have been sorry to hear any day of the other getting transported in like manner.—Now and then it occurred to cousin Marshall that there was little use in answering those who could ask such a question as wherein she was better off than Mrs. Bell; but it oftener happened that her replies were given in a style of eloquence that did not increase her popularity.—Death came at last, in time to save her from the dependence she dreaded, though not from the apprehension of it. In crossing her threshold, one winter's day, with her apron full of sticks, she tripped and fell. She seemed to sustain no injury but the jar; but that was fatal. She survived just long enough to see the daughter who lived in the neighbourhood, and make a bequest of her Bible to one child, her bed to another, her few poor clothes to a third, pointing out the corner of her chest where was deposited the little hoard she had saved for her burial.

"God has been very good to me and mine," she said. "They tell me I have not always said so; but I meant no mistrust. I may have been too much in a hurry to go where 'the wicked cease from troubling and the weary are at rest:' but it is all right now that I am really going at last. Thank God! I can say to the last that He has been very good to me."

She left her blessing for every one by name, and died.

Mr. Burke met the funeral train coming out of the churchyard, and immediately knew Ned, long as it was since they had met.

"Your cousin Marshall's funeral!" he exclaimed. "My wife and Louisa and I inquired for her in vain, a long while ago, and supposed she had been dead some time. She must have been a great age."

"Eighty-one, sir."

In answer to Mr. Burke's inquiries how she had passed her latter days, and in opposition to Ned's affectionate report of her, a neighbour observed, with a shake of the head, that she was awfully forsaken at times.

"It was but the day before she died, sir, that she complained that the Almighty had forgotten her, and that she was tired of looking to be released."

Ned brushed his hand across his eyes as he observed that her neighbours were not capable of judging of such a woman as cousin Marshall, and not worthy to find fault with what she let fall in her dark moments.

"My wife said at the time, however," replied the man, "that it would be well if a judgment did not come upon her for such words; and, sure enough, by the same hour the next day she was dead; and not in a natural way either."

Mr. Burke smiled at Ned, who gravely observed that his cousin had lived too late to be done justice to. By what he had heard her tell, he judged that a hundred years ago she would have been honoured and tended in her old age, and saved all she had suffered from fear of the parish, and have had it told on her tombstone how many children she had bred up by her industry. It would not be difficult, for that matter, to put up a tombstone now; but where would be the use of it, unless it was honored? The want lay there.

"I hope," said Mr. Burke, "that we may as reasonably say that your cousin lived too early as that she lived too late. The time will come, trust me, when there will be an end of the system under which she has suffered. It cannot always be that the law will snatch the bread from the industrious to give it to the idle, and turn labour from its natural channel, and defraud it of its due reward, and authorise the selfish and dissolute to mock at those who prize independence, and who bind themselves to self-denial that they may practise charity. The time will come, depend upon it, when the nation will effectually take to heart such injustice as this. There is much to undo, much to rectify, before the labours of the poor, in their prime, shall secure to them a serene old age; but the time will come, though by that day yonder grave may be level with the turf beside it, and there may be none to remember or speak of Cousin Marshall."

Summary of Principles Illustrated in this Volume

In a society composed of a natural gradation of ranks, some must be poor; i.e. have nothing more than the means of present subsistence.

Any suspension of these means of subsistence, whether through disaster, sickness, or decrepitude, converts the poor into the indigent.

Since indigence occasions misery, and disposes to vice, the welfare of society requires the greatest possible reduction of the number of the indigent.

Charity, public and private, or an arbitrary distribution of the subsistence-fund, has hitherto failed to effect this object; the proportion of the indigent to the rest of the population having increased from age to age.

This is not surprising, since an arbitrary distribution of the subsistence-fund, besides rendering consumption unproductive, and encouraging a multiplication of consumers, does not meet the difficulty arising from a disproportion of numbers to the means of subsistence.

The small unproductive consumption occasioned by the relief of sudden accidents and rare infirmities is necessary, and may be justifiably provided for by charity, since such charity does not tend to the increase of numbers; but, with this exception, all arbitrary distribution of the necessaries of life is injurious to society, whether in the form of private almsgiving, public charitable institutions, or a legal pauper-system.

The tendency of all such modes of distribution having been found to be to encourage improvidence with all its attendant evils,—to injure the good while relieving the bad,—to extinguish the spirit of independence on one side,—and of charity on the other,—to encourage peculation, tyranny, and fraud,—and to increase perpetually the evil they are meant to remedy,—but one plea is now commonly urged in favour of a legal provision for the indigent.

This plea is that every individual born into a state has a right to subsistence from the state.

This plea, in its general application, is grounded on a false analogy between a state and its members, and a parent and his family.

A parent has a considerable influence over the subsistence-fund of his family, and an absolute control over the numbers to be supported by that fund; whereas the rulers of a state, from whom a legal provision emanates, have little influence over its subsistence-fund, and no control whatever over the number of its members.

If the plea of right to subsistence be grounded on the faults of national institutions, the right ought rather to be superseded by the rectification of those institutions, than admitted at the cost of perpetuating an institution more hurtful than all the others combined.

What, then, must be done to lessen the number of the indigent, now so frightfully increasing?

The subsistence-fund must be employed productively, and capital and labour be allowed to take their natural course; i.e. the pauper system must, by some means or other, be extinguished.

The number of consumers must be proportioned to the subsistence-fund. To this end, all encouragements to the increase of population should be withdrawn, and every sanction given to the preventive check; i.e. charity must be directed to the enlightenment of the mind, instead of to the relief of bodily wants.

If not adopted speedily, all measures will be too late to prevent the universal prevalence of poverty in this kingdom, the legal provision for the indigent now operating the extinction of our national resources at a perpetually increasing rate.

Sowers not Reapers

[The theme of delayed marriages introduced by Martineau in "Weal and Woe in Garveloch" resurfaces in this tale that contrasts the fates of Mr. and Mrs. Kay, whose marriage and parenthood are severely compromised by poverty, with that of Mary Kay and her suitor, Chatham, who delay their union, no doubt disheartened by the exhibition of suffering daily unfolding before their eyes. But the romance between Chatham and Mary Kay, though charming, is secondary to the tragic example of the Kays' marriage. Drought and famine add to the poverty endured by this family, as does the alcoholism of Mrs. Kay. The most notorious example of working-class exploitation is in the scarcity and exorbitant expense—due to the Corn Laws—of solid food, like bread and meal, and in the comparative cheapness and availability of gin and opium.

Although substance abuse is assumed to prove the inherent immorality of this class, Martineau demonstrates that the tragedy of those who starve in the foremost industrialized nation in the world is far more complex than generally assumed. As the tale unfolds, Mrs. Kay is revealed to be an alcoholic who has given her portion of food to her hungry family for so long that she is starving to death of malnutrition. Rather than a moral issue, Mrs. Kay's condition is rooted in a common, and insidious, medical practice: during childhood, she was regularly dosed with laudanum[1] to keep her quiet. Indiscriminate use of drugs and alcohol by physicians and parents thus comes under Martineau's scrutiny, as does the systematic starvation of the working classes resulting from the Corn Laws.

Alcohol and alcoholism raised a variety of issues in industrial society. As a sanitation issue, what moderns might term the *indiscriminate* use of alcohol during the period proves to be rooted in both custom and in the new social problems resulting from industrialization. Alcohol served as a painkiller in surgery, in dentistry, and during childbirth and was used not only to treat but to prevent disease and infection. In terms of the sanitation problems created by rapid urbanization and industrial pollution, alcohol was believed to offer protection from bad air and water, so that even an ordinary

---

1 Laudanum is a tincture of opium dissolved in alcohol. The solution was highly addictive, and long-term use compromised, rather than aided, the health problems it was designed to cure. Ironically, it was the remedy most frequently prescribed, even for such ordinary childhood "behavior problems" as teething and colic.

glass of water had its "purifying" measure of alcohol added to it. Socially, alcohol use among the lower classes mitigated the hopelessness of their lives, while the lively atmosphere of the public houses and gin shops provided an irresistible contrast with the damp and dark, odorous and airless hovels in which they lived. So widely and unquestioningly was alcohol use accepted among all classes that it was the teetotalers and temperance reformers who were viewed as radicals to be ostracized and ridiculed. Drinking also served to emphasize class distinctions: regarded as a moral failing among the poor, alcohol use among the middle and upper classes symbolized taste, breeding, and socio-economic privilege.

"Sowers not Reapers" confronts such class bias by presenting alcoholism as symptomatic of broader cultural problems rather than evidence of poor character or immorality. Indeed, Mrs. Kay proves herself to have superior character by overcoming her addiction, although too late to prevent her death from malnutrition. In this tale, the Corn Laws (enacted in 1815, repealed in 1846) provide the political framework contributing to widespread alcoholism among the poor. The most immediate beneficiaries of the Corn Laws were those who had the political power to enact them in the first place: the aristocracy or landed gentry. Thus was agricultural profit privileged over the subsistence concerns of the poor and over considerations of competitive trade in the industrial sector. One of Martineau's most uncompromising tenets was that protectionist tariffs represented blatant government intervention in private sector economy. For her, the repeal of the Corn Laws in favor of a Free Trade policy was not only in the best interests of England but also in the interests of international relations. "Sowers not Reapers" is one of the earliest of Martineau's writings on the topic, which she periodically revisited until the Corn Laws' repeal in 1846. Repeal was not only a resounding defeat for the ruling class: it also evidenced an unprecedented alliance between the middle and lower classes that dramatized the shift in the balance of power initiated by the 1832 Reform Bill.

Nearly twenty years after the publication of this tale, Florence Nightingale wrote to Martineau of her admiration for the writer's compelling treatment of alcoholism in the character of "the drinking woman," Margaret Kay. Other themes presented in "Sowers not Reapers" include machine-breaking and other mob violence; midnight "drills" and "raids" on grain stores organized by starving workers; bureaucratic paranoia, seen in Chatham's arrest and imprisonment for treason; and the unexpected economic effects of the Corn Laws on the landed gentry.]

Chapter I: Midsummer Moonlight

The nights of a certain summer of the present century would scarcely have been known for nights by those sober people who shut themselves in as it grows dark, and look out in the morning, perceiving only that the sun is come again. During the nights we speak of, repose did not descend with the twilight upon the black moors of Yorkshire, and the moon looked down upon something more glittering than the reflection of her own face in the tarns of Ingleborough,[1] or in the reaches of the Wharf and the Don. Some of the polished and sharpened ware of Sheffield[2] was exposed to the night dews in the fields, and passed from the hands of those who tempered to the possession of those who were to wield it.

Others were also abroad, with the view of relieving their hardships instead of seeking to avenge them. The dwellers on high grounds were so far worse off than the inhabitants of the valleys, that they could not quench their thirst, and lost in sleep their weariness and their apprehensions of hunger. During the day, there was drought within, and the images of drought without;—hay dried before it was mown; cattle with their tongues hanging out, panting in the parched meadows; horses lashing madly at the clouds of flies that descended upon them as they stooped to the slimy pools which had still some moisture in them; wells with cracked buckets and dangling ropes; and ditches where there was an equally small probability that children would find weeds and be drowned in the search. During the night, when some of these spectacles were hidden, it was necessary to take the chance of preventing a repetition of them on the following day; and those who had cattle growing lean, children growing fretful, and no remaining patience with a dry well, bore with the weariness of night-watching in the hope of relieving the more urgent evil of thirst.

On the night when the midsummer full moon gradually emerged from the partial eclipse caused by the smokes of Sheffield, and shone full on the hill-sides to the west, two women were sitting near a spring which had rarely, till lately, failed to bless the stony region in which it was wont to flow. They came to watch for any gush or drip which might betoken the fall of showers somewhere among the

---

1 A tarn is a small lake or pool in the mountains. Ingleborough is a mountain in the Yorkshire Dales.
2 Sheffield is a city in south Yorkshire known for producing cutlery.

hills; and patient would their watch have appeared to an observer. The one sat on the stone fence which separated the road from a field of drooping oats, and never moved, except to cast a frightened look around her when an unseasonable bleat proceeded from the restless ewes on the moor, or the distant foundry clock was heard to strike. Her companion sat, also in silence, on the edge of the dry cistern where her pitcher rested, and kept her eyes fixed on the fitful lights of the foundry from whose neighbourhood she had come.

"I have been thinking, Mary," said Mrs. Kay, leaving her seat on the wall, and speaking in a low voice to her sister-in-law,—"I have been thinking that my husband may, perhaps, come round for us when his hours are up at the foundry, instead of going straight home. I wish he may; for I declare I don't like being out in this way, all by ourselves."

Mary made no answer.

"It is all so still and unnatural here. There's the foundry at work, to be sure; but to see the tilting-mill standing, all black and quiet, is what I never met with before. We may see it for some time to come, though; for there seems a little chance of a sufficient fall to touch the wheel at present. Do you think there is, Mary?"

Mary shook her head; and Mrs. Kay, having examined the spring with eye and ear, stole back to her former seat.

After looking into the field behind her for some time, she came again to say,—

"My husband talks about the crops, and the harvest being at hand, and so on; but I do not see what sort of a harvest it is to be, unless we have rain directly. What a poor-looking oatfield that is behind the wall! and there are none any better on these high grounds, as far as I can see."

"There would be some chance for the low grounds, if the springs would flow," answered Mary.

"Why, yes. My husband was telling me that there is a corner left of one of Anderson's meadows down below, where the grass is as fresh and sweet as if there had been forty-eight hours' rain. It was but a corner; but there was one of the little Andersons, and his sister, raking up the grass after the mower, and piling their garden barrow with it, to give to their white pony. Even Anderson's beasts have been foddered, as if it was winter, for this fortnight past."

Mary nodded, and her sister proceeded.

"I wonder how many more improvements of Anderson's we shall see after this next bad harvest; for bad it must be now. It seems to me that the less his land yields, the more he lays out upon it."

"The less it yields, the more he wants, I suppose."

"Yes; but it is an accident its yielding so ill for three years together; and where he gets the money, I don't know, except that bread has been dear enough of late to pay for any thing."

"That's it, to be sure," said Mary.

"Dear enough for any thing," repeated Mrs. Kay. "When I used to have my fill of meat every day, I little thought that the bread I ate with it would grow scarce among us. No rise of wages, such as the masters make such a complaint of, can stand against it."

Mary shook her head, and there was a long pause.

"I'll tell you what, Mary," resumed the chief speaker, after a time, "there would be much more pleasure in talking with you, if you would talk a little yourself. It sets one down so not to know whether you are listening to what one says."

"I always listen when I am spoken to," replied Mary; "but people are not all made talkers alike."

"Why, no, that they certainly are not. My husband laughs, and says what a pretty dull time you and Chatham must have of it, when you are out walking on Sundays. You will both get all you want to say in a week said in five minutes. Well, I don't wonder at your not answering that; but you will not be offended at a joke from your own brother; and you know he does not think the worse of Chatham for keeping his thoughts to himself, and—Mercy! what did I see over yonder!"

And in her hurry Mrs. Kay pushed the pitcher, which Mary caught before it went rattling down among the stones. She sat very quietly, watching the motions of a number of men who were crossing a gate from one field to another as some distance, and who seemed to be making for the road.

"Mary! Mary! what shall we do if they come here?" asked the trembling Mrs. Kay.

Mary rose and took up her pitcher, observing that they might sit safe enough in the shadow of Warden's mill, just to the left; and then they might have another chance for the spring as they came by on their way home. Mrs. Kay could scarcely be persuaded that going home would be perfectly safe as soon as it was daylight, and that the men who had evidently been out at drill would be dispersed by dawn.

The women crept along, under the shadow of the wall, and then quickly crossed the broad strip of moonlight which lay between them and the mill. Before they reached the steps, which happened to be on the shadowy side, Mrs. Kay was nearly unable to walk, and her terrors were not lessened by the apparition of a person standing on the first stage, and looking down on them from the top of the long flight of steps.

"Sit still," said Mary, beginning to ascend, till she saw that Warden, the miller, was coming down to inquire their business. She then briefly explained what brought them upon his property.

"So you are looking for water," he replied, "and I am looking for wind. For three weeks there has not been a breath, and not a steady breeze since long before that. The bakers are calling out upon us so as to keep us out of our beds, watching for any rack[1] in the sky that may betoken a coming wind."

"And have you ever seen, sir, such a sight as sent us here?" inquired the trembling Mrs. Kay. "Such a sight as there is in the fields there?"

"What, the nightly drill? O yes, many a night, though they may not be aware who has been overlooking them. They have never come near enough on light nights for me to pick them out by their faces, so that there is no occasion for me to take any notice; but I mark how they get on in shouldering their pikes and learning to obey orders. Here, as I stand by the fan-wheel, I hear the word of command quite plain through the still air; and once they came upon this very slope. It was too dark a night for them to see me; but I heard them stumble against the very steps you are sitting on, Mrs. Kay."

"How long do you suppose it is to last, Mr. Warden?"

"Till prices fall, or the people have burned a mill or two, perhaps. 'Tis a happy thing for you and yours, Mrs. Kay, that Oliver's foundry does not come under the ban. There it blazes away, night and day, and I hear no curses upon it, like what are visited upon the mills. It is well for you and yours that Kay has to ladle molten metal instead of having to manage machinery. I hope ye is well, Mrs. Kay?"

Mrs. Kay did not answer, and was found to be in no condition for dialogue. Fear and fatigue had overpowered her, and she could only lean, faint and sobbing, against the rail.

"She is not strong," observed Mary. "Do you happen to have any thing in the mill to revive her? My pitcher is empty."

Warden fanned her with his hat, having no other means of refreshment in his power; and he carried on the conversation with Mary while doing so, that the poor woman might have time to recover herself. It was not merely machinery that was the object of the trained bands, he observed. In many parts they had pulled down corn stores;

---

1 Drifting clouds.

and it was rumoured that Kirkland's granaries were threatened by the very people who were now near them. If they really entertained the idea that it was a public injury to have a stock of corn laid by while the price was high, it was no wonder that they were angry with Kirkland, as well as with some people that had much more credit, without having done and suffered so much to get it. He should like to know what the country was to do without such men as Kirkland, when there had been three bad harvests following one another?

"Your mill would stand idle if there was not corn brought from here or there," observed Mary. "But are those people that we saw bound for Kirkland's granaries? I should be sorry to think that they were about any mischief."

"They could be about little but mischief at this time of night, and with arms too; but it is full late, I fancy, to be going so far. It is said my father-in-law's threshing-machine is doomed."

"And what does he say to that?"

"O, he swears at the people because they can't be contented when he is. But, to my mind, it would not be so great a hardship this year as another, seeing how little corn there will be to thresh. Not that I approve such doings in any way; but when people are so badly off with the high price of provisions, and the uncertainty of peace, what can you expect?"

"You talked of noting faces; are there any of our people now in yonder fields, do you suppose?"

"Do you mean Sheffield people, or people of your village?"

"Why, either."

"There are undoubtedly many from about Stockport, and out of Leicestershire, who go the round to stir up discontent, and teach the drill. But it is said there are a good many neighbours of ours among them too. What is more likely than that those who have not had their fill in the day should turn out at night to something that may amuse them better than lying awake, or dreaming of cheap bread? This is just what you have been doing, you see; and what Mrs. Kay had better have let alone, it seems. Come, Mrs. Kay, how are you now? Able to walk, do you think?"

Quite able now to walk, and to ask a hundred questions on the way about the cause of the terror which had shaken her, and the probable duration of the hardship which had reduced her; on neither of which matters was much satisfaction to be gained from the miller.

The spring was still dry, but Mary chose to watch till the children came to take her place in the morning. The miller took charge of

Mrs. Kay till she was fairly within the light of the foundry fires, and then struck across the fields homewards, hoping that his mill would not again be the refuge of frightened women while he was on the spot.

Mary's watch was vain, and the more wearisome from her occasional fancy that it would not prove vain. More than once she was persuaded that she heard the trickling of water while listening intently after the moon had gone down; and when she fell asleep for a few moments, her thoughts were full of the hardship of having only one pitcher to fill when the water was overflowing every place. Not the less for this did she carry home this very pitcher, swinging empty at arm's length, when the village was up and awake, and the sun beating down hot upon the slippery turf, and glaring, reflected from the stone fences, upon the dusty road.

At the door she met a neighbour, Mrs. Skipper, the baker of the village, who supplied a use for the pitcher.

"Well, Mary Kay, and what's the news with you?"

"Nothing particular, Mrs. Skipper. Are you come to tell us again that bread is risen?"[1]

"Why, that I am, I'm sorry to say; and I wish you would change looks with me, Mary, and then people would not taunt me as they do, when I say that bread has risen."

"How would that alter the matter?"

"O, they talk about my being fresh-coloured, and all that, and say it's a sign that I live of the best, whatever I may charge to others. Just as if I made the bread dear, instead of the corn being as high to us bakers as to other people; and as if there was no assize of bread in London."[2]

"And as if you cared for being called handsome," added Kay from behind, having come to breakfast in the midst of the greeting.

"I think you are handsome—very handsome," said little John Kay, looking up earnestly into Mrs. Skipper's bonny face. She stooped down to give him a hearty smack, and promise him a halfpenny bun if he would come and see her.

"There now, master John, you well night made me spill my cider, boy. Here, Mary, hold your pitcher. Yes, it is for you—for all of you, I mean. You will give John a drop, I'm sure. Ah! I thought you would like it, now it is so difficult to get any thing good to drink. Do but

1   That is, "risen" in price.
2   In Mrs. Skipper's use of the term, an assize is a judicial statute regulating the control of commodities—here, the price of bread.

taste it, Mr. Kay. Is not it good? It was sent me by a cousin of mine, and I thought I would bring you some, especially as I had to tell you that the bread is risen again. It is nineteen-pence now! What do you say to that, Mary?"

Mary, as usual, said nothing. She did not find that speech mended matters of this kind; and besides, it was time she was setting about her task of purifying the distasteful water which they must drink, if they meant to drink at all, till the springs should flow again. She emptied the clear, fresh-looking cider into her own pitcher, and returned Mrs. Skipper's with a look which was less indifferent than her manner.

"What I say is," observed Kay, "that if bread is risen, our wages must rise. We are all of one mind about that—that a man cannot live for less than will keep him alive; to say nothing of his being fresh-coloured, Mrs. Skipper. We can none of us boast much of that."

"Well, how's your wife, Mr. Kay? She was but poorly, I thought, when I saw her two days ago."

"O, she is a poor thing enough. She was not much to boast of when she had an easy life compared with the present; and now she droops sadly. John can hardly call her very handsome indeed. Can you, John?"

"John, carry your mother a cup of cider, if she is awake," said Mary; "and tell her I am home, getting breakfast."

"There, that's right, Mary," said Mrs. Skipper. "You have such a way of telling giddy people what they should not say and do. I am going my ways directly, to leave you to yours. But send one of the children after me for a nice hot roll for your sister. The new bread is just coming out of the oven. And be sure you tell me whether she likes the cider, you know."

"And if she has not an appetite for the roll, we won't send it back, I promise you," said Kay. "She has got into the way of not touching her breakfast, lately; and the same thing cannot be said of me, when I have been busy casting all night. Somebody will eat your roll, and thank you for it."

"That means that I may send two; but—"

Kay protested, and Mrs. Skipper explained, and Mary announced breakfast.

"Breakfast, such as it is, Mrs. Skipper," observed Kay. "No disrespect to your bread! But time was when I could afford it newer, and plenty of it, and a bit of something to relish it. One does not relish it so well when one can't cut and come again, but may have just so much and no more."

Mrs. Skipper wished he could see what she saw of poor creatures that could get none,—not the smallest and driest loaf, to try whether they could relish it. If the potato crop failed, she did not know what was to become of them; or of herself either, if they went on to look in at her shop window. She had not the heart to draw the bread, with them looking on, and not stuff a bit into the children's mouths. And, dashing away the tears from her bright black eyes, widow Skipper hastened whence she came, hugging by the way the child who was sent to wait her pleasure about the roll.

Before sitting down to his scanty meal, Kay went to rally his wife about what she had seen and been alarmed at in her late expedition, and to advise her to cheer up, instead of giving way, as she seemed disposed now to do. She was up, but he supposed hardly awake yet; for she had not much to say, and seemed flurried, and not able to take exactly what he meant. He thought she had better have slept another hour.

Chapter II: A Harvest Eve

Mary rightly believed that there was a chance for the corn on the low grounds, if rain should speedily fall. By the time that the horned sheep of the western moors had cropped the last bite of juicy grass in the dells, they were gathered together by the shepherd to abide the storms which were gathering about the summits of Wharnside and Pennygant.[1] While they stood trembling and bleating in the rising blasts, the cattle in the vales left the muddy pools, and turned towards the shelter of the stooping and rustling trees; and many a human eye was raised to the whirling mills, whose inactivity had wearied expectation so long.

Neither the wind, nor the rain which followed, pleased every body, any more than any other wind and rain. Havoc was made by the blasts in Mr. Fergusson's young plantations, where a thousand saplings stood, dry enough for firewood, ready to be snapped by the first visitation of a gust. Trees of loftier growth strewed the Abbey lawn, and afforded matter of lamentation to the elder members of Mr. Fergusson's family, and of entertainment to the children, who watched for hours the operations of the woodmen in removing the fallen ornaments of the estate. Every washerwoman within some miles who happened to be pursuing her vocation that day, had to

---

1 Wharnside and Pennygant are mountains in Yorkshire.

mourn the disappearance of cap or handkerchief from the line or bush; and how many kitchen chimneys smoked, no chimney doctor near would have ventured to say. Meanwhile, the millers and their men bestirred themselves cheerily, as sailors do when the breeze freshens after a long calm; and careful housewives dislodged all unclean insects from their water tubs, and swept out their spouts in preparation for the first droppings. As might have been expected, the rain came, not in droppings, but in sheets. No woollen coat, woven or unwoven, saved the shepherd and his sheep from being drenched to the skin. Every tree became a commodious shower-bath to the horse or cow beneath it. Many an infirmity was exposed in thatch or tile which had never before been suspected; and everybody looked gloomy in Anderson's farm, (except the ducks,) from the apprehension that the meagre crops would be laid, past recovery. On the first cessation of the storm, matters did appear sad enough: in the villages, every thing smutted, from the smoke of the furnaces being beaten down; in the country, all brown and muddy-looking till the waters had had time to retire into the ditches, and the verdure to show itself; and even then, the straggling oats and prostrate wheat presented but a small improvement on their former appearance. Landlords and tenants crossed each other's path while taking their rounds, but could not agree as to the probabilities of the approaching harvest. Mr. Fergusson hoped that a day or two would make a great difference in the appearance of the fields; while Anderson was certain that it was too late for the crops to revive under the gentlest rain, and that they would prove to have been utterly destroyed by the flood which had swept down from the hills. Neither could establish his point till harvest came.

Then each proved to be right. On the high grounds, the produce was, in truth, scarcely worth carrying away, while in the vales there was better work for the harvest wain.[1] Even there, however, there were more gleaners than reapers;[2] and the artisans who came forth in the evening to see what had been done, agreed with the disappointed Irish, who must travel farther in search of harvest work, that the total crop would indeed turn out to be far below the average.

---

1 A wain is a farm wagon or cart.
2 To glean is to gather food from the fields left over after reapers have harvested a crop. Anderson's objection (306) is not to this common practice itself, but to the gleaners' stealing from his stores rather than gathering what had been left behind by the reapers.

The best of the harvest fields did not present the usual images of peace and contentment.

"Out, out, out!" cried Anderson, to a troop of boys and girls who had pressed in at his heels as he entered a field whence the sheaves were not yet carried. "How many times am I to have the trouble of turning you out, I wonder? Wait, can't ye, till the corn is carried?"

At the flourish of his stick the intruders took flight, and jostled each other at the gate, in their hurry to get out; but they returned, one by one, keeping in his rear, like a spider watching a fly, till they could stoop down behind a shock, and filch from the sheaves at their leisure. Following the example of the children, a woman dropped in at the gate, another entered from a gap in the fence, at a moment when the farmer had his back turned, while the heads of two or three men appeared over the wall. It was plain that the tenth commandment was not in the thoughts of any present, unless in Anderson's own.

"Here again, you rogue!" he cried, lifting up a boy by the collar from a hiding-place between two sheaves. "You are the very boy I told twice to go to the field below. There is plenty of room for you there."

"But there is no corn there, sir."

"Corn or no corn, there you shall go to be made an example of for pilfering from my sheaves. Here, Hoggets, take this lad down to the Lane field, and give him a good whipping in sight of them all."

"O, no, no! Mercy, mercy!" cried the boy. "Mother said I should have no supper,—father said he would beat me, if I did not make a good gleaning. I won't go, I tell you; I won't. O, sir, don't let him beat me! Ask father! I won't go."

Mary Kay came up to intercede. The boy was her nephew; and she could assure Mr. Anderson that John was told to go home at his peril without an apron full of corn.

"Then let his parents answer for his flogging, as they ought to do, for driving the boy to steal," said the farmer. "I am not to be encroached upon because they choose to be harsh with their boy; and I tell you, mistress, this pilfering must be put a stop to. This very season, when the crop is scanty enough at the best, I am losing more than I ever did before by foul gleaning. Let the boy's parents be answerable for the flogging he shall have. Hoggets, take him away."

"Had you not better send Hoggets to flog the boy's father and mother?" Mary inquired. "That would be more just, I think."

"O, do, sir, do!" entreated John; "and I will show him the way."

"I dare say you would; and this aunt of yours would find some excuse next for their not being flogged."

"I won't promise but I might," said Mary; "for they may have something to say about what has driven them to covet your corn. It is not the going without one supper, but the being supperless every night. Instead of a beating, once and away, such as they promised the poor lad, it is the scourge of want, sir, for week after week, and month after month."

"I am very sorry to hear it; and if they come and ask in a proper way, they may chance to get some help from me. But, as to countenancing my property being taken because they are poor, it would be a sin for their boy's sake, and for the sake of all the boys that would follow his example. So off with him!"

Mary was far from wishing to defend the act of pilfering from sheaves, and equally far from supposing that her brother and sister thought of any such mode of fulfilling their command when it was delivered to their boy. Mr. Anderson might be perfectly sure that Kay and his wife would not come and ask, in the "proper way" he alluded to, for what they were wearing themselves out in struggling to earn; and as for the boy, she believed she could answer for him that the being deprived of what he had gathered, or, at most, a private beating, would avail to make him observe other commands in endeavouring to fulfil those of his parents. Anderson still thought differently; and, perceiving at the moment half a dozen little heads peeping from behind so many shocks, was confirmed in his opinion that the boy must be flogged. Hoggets accordingly whipped up the little lad, slung him, screaming and writhing, over his shoulder, and disappeared behind the wall, while the farmer hunted out the other culprits, and sent them, for a punishment, to see their companion flogged in the field. Mary first detained them to see her restore John's handfuls of corn to the sheaves, and then went down to do the best she could for her poor little nephew in his agony.

She presently overtook him, and found that his agony was now of a more mixed character than she had expected. He was alternating between hope and fear. The quivering nostril and short sob told what his terror had been, while his raised eye, and efforts to compose himself, testified to his trust that he had found a deliverer. Two young ladies on horseback were talking with Hoggets, and looking compassionately on the culprit, while Hoggets touched his hat every instant, and had already lowered the boy from his disgraceful elevation. The Miss Fergussons only asked him to delay till they had overtaken Mr. Anderson, and endeavoured to procure pardon; and Hoggets thought it was not for him to resist the wishes of the ladies.

The whole matter was argued over again, and the farmer strongly urged with the plea that corn was more tempting to the poor than ever before,—the quartern[1] being now one shilling and eight-pence. The farmer thought that the stronger the temptation, the more exemplary should be the punishment. If he could supply every breadeater near him with abundance of corn, so as to obviate the temptation, he would gladly do so, as he held prevention to be better than punishment; but, as he had not this in his power, the best thing he could do was to discourage compliance with temptation. In this case, however, as the boy had been a good deal punished by exposure, and by being off and on in his expectations of being flogged, enough was done for example, and John might run home as fast as he liked.

"That will not be very fast," Mary observed, "since he is to be beaten at the end of his walk for bringing his mother's apron home empty. I have heard say, sir, by one that knows well, that our people are treated like this boy; brought low for want of food, driven to skulk and pilfer for it, and then disgraced and punished. But there is this difference, that you cannot prevent the want, and, in the case of the people, it might be prevented."

"Chatham put that into your head, I suppose. It is just like one of his sayings. But I wish he would not make the worst of matters, as if any thing ailed the nation more than there has been ever since people herded together with mischief-makers among them here and there."

Miss Fergusson hoped that there had not always been, and would not always be, such proceedings as some which were going on now. The coppice[2] field had been green and smooth as velvet the evening before, and this morning at daybreak it was brown and trampled. The skulkers and meditators of violence had been there; and the records of her father's justice-room would show that the disgrace and punishment spoken of by Mary were fast following the destitution which is the cause of crime. She hoped Mr. Anderson did not suppose that this was the natural state in which people will always live, while congregating for the sake of the advantages of society.

Anderson hoped that men would grow wiser in time than to set up midnight drills as a remedy for the distress which always occurs from time to time; and then Mr. Fergusson would have less dis-

---

1   Quartern, a quarter weight of a pound, ounce, peck, or pint.
2   Coppice or copse, a thicket of bushes or small trees.

agreeable justice-work to do. The ladies believed that the shortest
way to obviate the folly would be to obviate the distress; and, as they
moved on, were recommended to pray for a better harvest than had
this year blessed the land.

John had stolen away in advance of their horses. Finding that they
were proceeding to join their brothers, who had been grouse-shoot-
ing in the moors since daybreak, it occurred to the poor boy that by
following the track of the gentlemen, he might chance to pick up
something which would serve as a propitiation at home for his failure in the article of corn. It was possible that a wounded bird or two
might have been left by the sportsmen, and that those who could not
purchase bread might sup off game:—no uncommon occurrence in
a country when the tenants of a preserve are better fed than the
inhabitants of a village. Half resolving to try his fortune on the other
side of the hills, and never to face his parents again unless he could
find a black cock, John plunged into the moors, keeping the ladies
in view from a distance, as a sort of guide to the track that the sportsmen had been pursuing. He had not speed of foot to sustain, for any
length of time, his share of the race. The riding party disappeared in
the dusk; no living thing crossed his path, but many inanimate ones
put on the appearance of a fluttering bird to deceive the agitated and
hungry boy; and the breeze which stirred them did not cool his
brow. He could nowhere find a pool of water from which he might
drink. His legs bent under him; and at the thought of how far they
must yet carry him before he could reach shelter, north, south, east,
or west, he began to cry.

Tears do not flow long when they may flow freely. It is the presence of restraint, or the interruption of thought, causing the
painful idea to recur, which renders it difficult for a child to stop a
fit of crying. John had no such restraint, and was subject to no further interruption than the silent appearance of light after light in
the village below, and the survey of an occasional sheep, which
came noiselessly to look at him and walk away again. By the time
that the dew began to make itself felt upon his face, he was yawn-
ing instead of crying; and he rose from the turf as much from a
desire to be moving again as from any anxiety as to what was to
become of him this night. A manifold bleat resounded as he erected himself, and a score or two of sheep ran over one another as he
moved from his resting place, giving hope that the shepherd was at
no great distance. It was not long before he was seen through the
grey twilight, moving on a slope a little to the west; and, to John's
delight, he turned out to be an acquaintance, Bill Hookey, who

lived close by the Kays till he went upon the moors in Wilkins the grazier's service.[1]

"How late are you going to be out, Will?" was John's first question.

"As late as it be before it is early," replied Will. "Yon's my sleeping place, and I am going to turn in when I have made out what is doing on the river there. Look farther down,—below the forge, boy. They are quiet enough this minute, or the wind is lulled. When it blows again, you may chance to hear what I heard."

"But about sleeping," said John. "I am mortally tired, and I've a great way to go home. Can't you give me a corner in your hut till morning?"

"Why, I doubt there will be scarce room, for I promised two of my ewes that they should have shelter to-night; and this lamb is too tender, you see, to be left to itself. I don't see how they can let you be served."

John promised to let the ewes have the first choice of a snug corner, and to be content with any space they might leave him, explaining that he wanted to be abroad early to glean, and that it would save him a long walk to sleep on this side Anderson's fields, instead of a mile to the east of them. He said nothing at present about his hunger, lest it should prove an objection to his abiding in Will's company. The objection came spontaneously, however, into the mind of the prudent Will.

"I hope you've your supper with you, lad, or you'll fare hardly here."

"O, never mind supper," said John, brushing his sleeve across his eyes. "I have gone without often enough lately."

"Like many a one besides. Well, if you don't mind supper, so much the better for you. I have left but a scanty one for myself, I was so mortal hungry at dinner time; and there is no more bread and milk in the jar than the lamb will want."

"Can't I get some fresh sweet grass for the lamb that will do as well? Do let me! Pretty creature! I should like to feed it."

The offer was scornfully declined, and he was told that he might help any of the older lambs to graze, but that he must, at his peril, touch this particularly precious, newly-dropped lamb. John was more disposed to graze on his own account than to assist any creature in eating what he could not share. It next occurred to him to propose

---

1 A grazier is one who grazes or tends cattle or sheep to be sold at market.

a bargain. He thought it promised to be a cold night. Will agreed that it might be middlingly so. John had his mother's stout apron with him, and Will should be welcome to it to wrap the lamb in, if John might have some of the lamb's bread and milk. Will had, however, a provokingly comfortable woollen wrapper, one end of which was always at the service of the pet lamb for the time being. While the next mode of attack was being devised, the soft pacing of horses' feet on the turf, and the occasional striking of a hoof against a flint, were heard; and Will, offering an obeisance which was lost in the darkness, made bold to inquire what sport the gentlemen had had on the moors.

"Excellent sport, if we had bagged as many as we brought down," answered one of the youths: "but thieves seem to be as plentiful as furze-bushes hereabouts. There were so many loiterers about our steps that our dogs could not move quick enough when we brought down more than one bird at a time."

"There will be a savoury supper or two eaten to-night by those who sport without pulling a trigger," observed the other Mr. Fergusson. "But they are welcome to my share of the powder and shot they have helped themselves to."

John's heart swelled at the thoughts of how he should like to be a sportsman after this fashion, especially as the gentleman declared that he should have been welcome.

The ladies had paused to listen to another such sound from afar as Will had described. Many of the twinkling lights from the village had disappeared, and there seemed to be a great bustle below the forge, displayed as often as the big bellows exerted themselves to throw out a peculiarly vivid flame to light up the banks of the river. Will was of opinion that the people were in a hurry for their corn, and unwilling to await Kirkland's time for opening his granaries, and unlading his lighters.[1] There had been talk,—as he had overheard on the moors,—of going down the river to where the lighters took in their cargoes, and demanding the distribution of the corn upon the spot. Probably this was what was now being done at Kirkland's, instead of a few miles nearer the river's mouth.

"It is time we were off, if that be the case," cried one of the gentlemen. "Kirkland must not be borne down in this manner, for the people's sake any more than for his own. Come, Charles. The girls will be safe enough with Jackson. Let us run down to the village.

---

1 A lighter is a barge used to transport goods. Unlading is unloading.

Here, little boy! You know Anderson's? You know Mr. Anderson himself?"

John hung down his head, and acknowledged that he knew Mr. Anderson.

"Well, here is a shilling for you. Run to Mr. Anderson, and beg him from me to come down, with his steadiest men, if he has any, to Kirkland's premises, as fast as possible. Off with you! What are you waiting for?"

"If he should be gone already, sir?"

"Why, then, go and call your father, if your father is not an ass, like the rest of the people hereabouts."

John heard one of the young ladies check her brother for his expression, reminding him that nothing makes the ears grow so fast as the having an empty stomach; and the boy pondered for a moment whether his father's ears had lengthened since the time when the family had become subject to hunger. His hand involuntarily went up to the side of his own head; and then came the speculation whether he should offer Will a high price for the lamb's bread and milk on the spot, or wait to change his shilling at Mrs. Skipper's counter. A sharp rebuke from his employer for his delay sent him bounding down the slope, calling up his courage to face the farmer, and consoling himself with thoughts of real white bread, dispensed under Mrs. Skipper's bright smile.

Alas! Mrs. Skipper had no bright smile, this evening, even for John; much less for any one who had not so decided an opinion about her being very handsome. Anderson had looked full as grave as John expected, whether about the matter in hand, or the boy's past offence, was not clear; but the farmer's gravity was nothing to Mrs. Skipper's terror. She scolded everybody about her, ran from one neighbour to another for advice whether to barricade her windows, and could by no means attend to John's demand of a penny roll till he was on the point of helping himself; and, slipping the shilling into the till, Mrs. Skipper huffed him when he asked for change, and turned her back upon him so as to make him fear that he had made a more costly bargain, after all, than if he had bid for the lamb's bread and milk upon the moor. All this was not without cause. A friendly neighbour had come up from the river-side to warn her that it had been proposed by the people assembled round Kirkland's granaries, that, failing a supply of food from his stores, the hungry should help themselves out of the baker's shop. It seemed but too probable that the threat would be executed; for Mrs. Skipper found (and God forgive her, she said, for being sorry to hear it!) that Kirkland was prepared for the attack; having thrown open two granaries to show that they were empty, and promised that he had something particular to say about the wheat on board the lighters; something which was likely to send the people away as hungry as they came.

A champion soon appeared in the person of Kay, who was almost the only man of the village who was not engaged on the more important scene of alarm. Women came in plenty, and children stood, like scouts, in the distance; but the women were found to be very poor comforters, and the children ran away as often as they were wanted for messengers. Mary was there; and her indifference to the danger served almost as well as Kay's promised valour to restore spirits to Mrs. Skipper. It was something to do when the most valuable part of the stock was carried away to be hidden in some safe place, and the oldest loaves ostentatiously placed so as to be stolen first, to taunt Mary with her not caring for what happened to her friends, and looking as indifferent as if she came merely to buy a threepenny loaf. Mary made no reply; but her brother declared that he must just say for her, that if she was indifferent about other people's concerns, so she was about her own. There was Chatham, very busy down by the river-side, with everybody listening to him but the one who had the most reason to be proud to hear what he said; and Mrs. Skipper would see, when she was cool, that it was rather hard to scold Mary for being better able to give assistance than if she was subject to being heated like some people. Mrs. Skipper begged a world of pardons. She was not half good enough for Mary to care at all about her, and she was ready to bite her tongue out for what she had said. As Mary did not intimate any wish to this effect, however, no such catastrophe took place, and the necessary disposition of affairs proceeded quietly.

Mrs. Skipper had not to wait long to know her fate. Chatham came to tell her that the people had been exasperated by finding that there was no good corn for them on Kirkland's premises, and had gone on towards Sheffield, to burn or pull down a mill or two, it was supposed, as some faces well known at the midnight drill were seen among them. If the few who remained behind should come and ask bread of Mrs. Skipper, he advised her to give it without any show of unwillingness.

"Mercy on me! that will be hard work, if they look beyond the bread on the counter,—two days old," cried Mrs. Skipper. "Suppose they should get at the dough, what am I to do to-morrow? And the flour! There has not been time to hide half the flour! they will want to cut my head off every day for a week to come, if they strip me of my flour, and expect me to go on baking at the same price. O, Mr. Kay, what shall I do?"

"Do as dealers in corn in another shape have done, often and often," replied Chatham. "Bear your lot patiently as a dealer in that which the people want most, and in which they are most stinted."

Mrs. Skipper looked doubtfully at Mary for a further explanation of what it was that she was to do.

"Do you mean," asked Kay, "that they have stripped Kirkland of his corn, and expect him to sell more next week at the same price?"

"They would have done so, if Kirkland had had much wheat to part with. The trade of a corndealer, I have heard him and others say, has always been a hard one to carry on. All parties have joined against them, for as long as time as can be remembered."

"Ay; the farmers are jealous, I suppose, of their coming between them and the people, thinking they could get better prices if there was nobody to be served between them and their customers. And the people, in the same way, think that they must pay higher for their bread, to enable the corndealers to live."

"Forgetting that the farmers have something else to be doing than buying and selling corn, here and there, wherever it is wanted, and getting it from abroad when there is not enough at home, and government lets more come in. But it is not only the farmers and the people. The government used to punish the buying up of corn where it was plentiful, and selling it where it was scarce. Many a corndealer has been punished instead of thanked for doing this."

"I do not see why any man need be thanked for doing what answers best to his own pocket, as it certainly does to buy cheap and sell dear. But to punish a man for coming between the people and want, seems to me to be more like an idle tale than anything to be believed."

"Kirkland's father was taken up and tried for doing this very thing, not longer ago than a dozen years or so. The law was against him, (one of the old laws that we are learning to be ashamed of;) but it was too clear that he had done no harm, for anybody to wish that he should be punished. So they let him go."

"Who told you this?"

"Kirkland himself told us so, just now. He said he had rather be brought to his trial in the same way, than have the people take the matter into their own hands to their own injury. I thought it was very brave of him to say so at the moment."

"Why? Were the people angry?"

"Like to tear him to pieces."

"And he within their reach?"

"Standing on the plank between the lighter and the wharf."

"Ugh! And they might have toppled him into the water any minute!" cried Mrs. Skipper. "I am sure I hope they won't come near me."

"The most angry of them are gone on, as I told you," replied Chatham. "And that is well for you, perhaps; for never did you see angrier faces. They called out, two hundred voices like one, that it was a sin they should have to pay twenty pence for their quartern while he had a houseful of wheat stored up, and more coming."

"And so it is, if he can get more when that is done."

"That is the very thing he cannot be sure of doing, as he told these people they must know very well. No one can be sure beforehand when and how he may get in corn from abroad; and, at any rate, it cannot be had till it has grown monstrously dear at home; and so he insisted upon it that he was doing the wisest thing in selling his corn as others sell it, and no cheaper; that we may not eat it all up now, and starve entirely before the end of the winter."

"Well, I grumble as much as anybody else at our having to pay twenty pence for our loaf; begging your pardon, Mrs. Skipper, whose fault I know it is not. I, with a wife and children, can't reconcile myself to such a price. I grumble as much as anybody."

"So do I," said Chatham.

"Only you don't blame Kirkland."

"Kirkland can't help the grievance, any more than you or I; and I am sure he suffers enough by it. There is a loss of some hundred pounds by this one cargo. It is more than half spoiled."

"Spoiled! How?"

"The sea-water has got to it, and it is downright rotten."

"What a pity, when it is so particularly wanted! Such accidents signify twice as much at some times as at others; and that this should happen now—just when bread is at the highest! O dear! what a pity!"

"It would not signify half so much if there was more certainly coming, and the people knew what they had to depend on. But if more is ordered, it may come or it may not; and it may be in good time, or not arrive till the season is far advanced; and so much must be paid for shipping charges (always dear in autumn), that it may mount up as high as our own home supply, after all."

"What a worry Kirkland must be in!" observed Kay. "He is not one of the quietest at any time; and now, between hurrying his correspondents abroad, and finding his cargo spoiled at home, and having the people gathering about him with their clamour, he must feel something like a dog with a saucepan tied to its tail."

"Not like your master, Mr. Kay," observed Mrs. Skipper. "There is no law to meddle with his selling his brass abroad or at home, as he likes; and so he knows what to expect, and how to live with his neighbours; and has little to worry him."

"I beg your pardon, Mrs. Skipper. My master is prevented selling freely abroad and at home; and prevented by the same law that worries Kirkland. And the worry is great, I can tell you; though Oliver does not run about, losing his breath and fidgeting himself like Kirkland, but walks so solemn and slow, you might take him for a Quaker."

"Well, I thought, as his foundry is always at work, and people must have things made of brass, and nobody objecting,—I thought things went easily enough with Oliver."

"His foundry works at night," said Chatham, "and his metal runs as well at Christmas as at Midsummer; and yet Oliver's prosperity depends on rain and sunshine as much as if zinc and copper were sown in the furrows and came up brass."

"There, now," said Mrs. Skipper, "that is one of your odd speeches, Chatham. And Mr. Kay nods as if he knew what you meant."

"I have good reason to know," replied Kay. "I and my fellow-workmen must have higher wages when corn is scarce, and then Oliver must put a better price upon his brass, without either his or our gaining anything by it: and then—"

"O ay; there will be less brass bought; that is what you mean."

"Moreover, there are plenty of people abroad that want brass, and would take it if they could give us corn in exchange,—so regularly as that they and we might know what we are about. And so, as sure as sunshine or rain falls short, some of Oliver's furnaces die out: and as sure as Kirkland's corn-vessels might come and go, without let or hindrance, our foundry would send a light, night and day, over all the vale."

"That is the way Chatham's sayings come out," observed the widow: "but I think he might as well speak plain at once, and make no mysteries."

"I spoke plain enough about what was going to happen to you and your bread," said Chatham, "and now you will soon see whether it comes out true; for here is the street filling fast, I see."

"Poor souls!" cried the widow, having run out at her door to look. "They do not seem creatures to be afraid of, when one comes close to them;—so tired and lagging! I say, Dixon, won't you have something to eat after your walk? Smith, you look worse still, and I saw how early you were off to your work this morning, and you have a good way to go to supper. Try a roll, won't you? Come, that's right, Bullen, set to, and tell me if it is not good bread; and you, Taylor,—carry it home to your wife, if you scruple to eat it yourself.—Bless you, make no speeches! I only wish I had more; but this is all, you see, except the dough that is laid for the morning, and that belongs to my customers, not to me.—Well; I am pleased you like it. I would have thought to get in some cheese, if I had known, before the shop was shut, that you would be passing.—Never make such a favour of it. I'll ask the same of you some day. Or you will remember me when times mend with you.—Do look, Mr. Kay; if they be not going to cheer!—I never thought to live to be cheered.—Bless them! how hearty they are!"

And laughing, sparkling, and waving her right arm vehemently, the dame watched in their progress down the street the neighbours whose approach she had thought, an hour before, she could scarcely survive. Kay followed the munching groups, to see what they would do next; and Chatham drew Mary's arm within his own, to escort her home, leaving the widow to bolt herself in, and survey at her leisure her bare shelves, and sweep down her empty shopboard,—soliloquizing, as she went on,

"I forgot these little sweet-cakes, or some of the children should have had them,—for they are rather stale. It is well they did not press for the dough, for I don't believe I could have refused them anything at the moment,—and then what should I have said to the Fergussons' man in the morning?—Well; it does look forlorn, now it is all over; and it was but this morning that I refused to take Mrs. Holmes's ten-shilling bonnet because I thought I could not afford it; and now I have given away,—let me see how many shillings' worth of bread! Ugh! I dare not think of it. But it is done, and can't be undone; and besides I dare say they would have taken it, if I had not given it; and, as I bargained with them, they will do the same for me some day. Smith does look rarely bad, to be sure. I wish he be not going; though, if he be, it will be pleasant to think that one gave him a meal when he was hungry. Not that it won't be pleasant to remember the same thing if he lives. I wonder what his poor wife's expectation is concerning him. If she loses him, I hope she will find it no more of a trouble than I have done. So much less than I thought! I think poor Mrs. Kay droops almost as much as Smith. But there's no knowing. Those weakly people often live the longest;—except, to be sure, when they have got into a habit like hers. Not a word has her husband ever let drop about it. I wonder whether he knows as much as I do. He shall never hear a word of it from me, nor not even Mary, though I fancy she can't be blind. Catch Mary Kay blind to anything! For all she looks so dull and stony when she chooses, she sees as sharp as a hawk,—and has such a way of setting one down. She's a good creature too, with all she does for those children; and nothing could be more handy than she was about the bread to-night. I wish she might chance to look in in the morning, and give me more of her handiness, to help to make the place look a little less forlorn than it does with all these empty shelves. I was very hasty, to be sure, in emptying them; but, as the parson said on Sunday, God loves a cheerful giver. So now, I will cast a look to see if the dough is rising, and go to bed; for it must be full late, I am sure."

Chatham and Mary were meanwhile walking home, conversing after their fashion,—making six words do where others would use twenty. An incident occurred on which they understood each other without any words at all. A gleam of light fell across the street as a door on the shadowy side of the way slowly opened, to let out a woman, who walked along under the houses, slowly and with her head hung down. It was the door of the gin-ship that opened, and it would have been absurd to pretend not to know the woman. Mary instantly slackened her pace, and motioned to cross over to the dark side.

"She is steady enough," said Chatham. "She will get on very well by herself."

"To be sure she will. It is not quite come to that yet. But let her get home first, and not know that we have been following her. It is only merciful."

"She shall have mercy from me;—more perhaps than from those who are answerable for her failing and sinking as she does, poor soul!"

Mary consented to turn back to the end of the street, to give a little more time, and asked whether grindstone[1] cutting was not warm work in these sultry noons. She had learned all she wanted about grindstones by the time she could safely knock at her brother's door with the hope that there was somebody stirring within to open it.

"I say nothing about coming in to sit with you all till Kay comes, because—"

---

1   A grindstone is a rotating stone wheel for sharpening blades.

"I was not going to ask you to-night. Tomorrow evening, perhaps. Good night now. I hear her coming. Good night."

And Chatham was out of sight from within, before Mrs. Kay, her bonnet off, and her cap somehow not put on, opened the door, and left Mary to fasten it.

Chapter III: Fasters and Feasters

There were two opposite lights on the horizon that night, to those who looked out from the village. While the moon sank serenely behind the dark western hills, a red flame shot up, amidst volumes of wreathing smoke, in the direction of Sheffield. Some persons were trying the often-repeated experiment of gaining bread by the destruction of that by which bread is gained. A metal-mill was gutted, its machinery broken, and its woodwork burned, because the sea water had got to Kirkland's corn; and more mills were threatened in case the price of bread did not fall within a few days.[1] As no one could answer for the price of bread falling within the time specified, the only thing to be done was to take measures to avert the promised destruction. For this purpose, strict inquiries were made as to what the inhabitants of the district had been about the preceding evening; who had gone home from the harvest-field; who attended the arrival of Kirkland's corn; and how many there were who could give no good account of themselves. Early in the morning the officers of justice were abroad, and Mr. Fergusson and his sons were seen riding about, greeted not the less respectfully wherever they went from its being known that their object was to bring some of their neighbours to justice. Mr. Fergusson's character stood too high among his tenants to allow of their thinking the worse of him under any misfortunes that might happen. Let him do what he might in his character of magistrate, he was trusted to do what was right, as he showed himself, on all occasions, not only compassionate to the sufferings of the people, but as wise in discerning the causes of the suffering as anxious to relieve it when relief was in his power. Accordingly, hats were touched when he looked in the faces of those whom he met this morning, and ready answers given to his inquiries where the innocent were called upon to speak, and respectful ones from the guilty, when the necessity came upon them of making out a case. All

---

1   This represents an example of Luddism, peasant-organized uprisings aimed at destroying the machinery believed to create unemployment.

the complaisance that there was, however, was engrossed by the Mr. Fergussons. The constables got only sneers and short answers, and men and women looked suspiciously on one another all through the district, none knowing what a neighbour might have the power to tell. Perhaps so many cross words were never spoken in one day in the vale, as the day after the burning of Halsted's mill. "What do you look at me for? You had better look to yourself," was the common sentiment at the forge, in the field, and on the alehouse bench. As for the children, they were so perplexed with instructions what they were to say, that it was only to be hoped no one would ask them any questions.

It was not to be supposed that Mrs. Skipper could stay quietly at home while strangers were passing up and down the street about whom her journeyman could give her no information, and while reports were travelling round of one neighbour and another being compromised. She burst in at Kay's, just after he was gone to his work, when his wife was preparing to put away breakfast, and Mary was beating out the corn which she had gleaned the evening before, and which was destined to the mill this day.

"I have not brought you a hot roll this morning, Mrs. Kay; no, nor so much as a crust. I cannot afford any more of that at present; and so you will not look for it from me."

"What do you speak in that way to me for? I don't know what you mean," said Mrs. Kay, with an angry, puzzled stare.

"Nor I what you would be at, I'm sure," replied Mrs. Skipper. "One would not believe you were the soft-spoken Mrs. Kay, now-a-days. You can be sharper in your speech than ever I am, let me tell you."

"That is the more reason why you should be soft in yours," said Mary. "She has borne with you sometimes, when you have been better in health than she is now."

"Well; that is true: and she does look so poorly....Ah! now, there's master John coming out with a speech about my fresh colour again."

John was not thinking about anybody's colour. He wanted to know whether it was not true that he had had eleven-pence change from her the night before.

"To be sure you had, after taking a penny roll."

John called his mother to witness, that she might tell his father, that he was in possession of a shilling before the troubles began at Kirkland's; to say nothing of those farther on. His father had doubted his getting that shilling honestly, and had desired his mother to take possession of the eleven pence till the whole was unquestionably accounted for; and now John wanted his money back again. Mrs. Kay did not, however, heed his request; and the matter ended in Mary's persuading the boy that if he had the money by the time he was at liberty to go out, it would do very well, instead of pressing for it now that his mother was busy thinking of something else.

"Why, take care, Mrs. Kay!" cried her neighbour. "Your hand shakes so, you will certainly let the dish down, and that will cost you more than a meal of my best bread would have done. Well! that is a beautiful potato to have left among the peelings. And here's another! I wonder you let the children scatter their food about in that manner."

" 'Tis not the children," observed Mary. "They have not more than they are very willing to eat, poor things! Their mother has but little appetite, and she is apt to slip her food back into the dish, that it may not make her husband uneasy.—I want your help more than she does," she continued, seeing that Mrs. Skipper's officious assistance was obstinately refused by the poor woman. "Will you step behind, and help me to beat and winnow my corn, if you have a minute to spare?"

With all her heart, Mrs. Skipper, said; but she *had* an errand, though it was not to bring cider or hot bread. She had learned the secret of making potato-bread: not the doughy distasteful stuff that many people were eating, but light, digestible, palatable bread. She would not tell the secret to everybody,—giving away her own trade; but when she saw a family of old friends eating potatoes, morning, noon, and night, she could not help telling them how they might get something better.

Mary thanked her, and observed that she did not know how she could put her gleaned corn to a better use than in making the experiment of a batch of mixed flour and potato-bread.

"Ah! do; and I will treat you to the baking, and look well to it myself. For my credit's sake, you know; having set you to try. Come, let us have the corn beat out."

They went to the back of the house to thresh and winnow, and then the widow's first exclamation was about how sadly out of sorts Mrs. Kay seemed to be.

"These are not times for her," replied Mary. "They bear harder upon such as she was than upon anybody. Who could have thought, you know, when she was an only child, brought up delicately for a poor man's daughter, that she would come to loathe a potato breakfast, and have no other?"

"Bless you! I know," whispered the widow, with a wise look.

"People may take things over-night that leave them no sense, nor temper, nor appetite in the morning. My dear, I see how it is."

Mary was apparently too busy with the wheat to take any notice of this intimation. The next thing she said was,

"Where are all the potatoes to come from that will be wanted if people take to this new sort of bread? and indeed whether they do or not; for potatoes they must eat, either by themselves or made into bread. How are we to get enough?"

"The price is rising, they say; faster than the price of anything else, except corn: and if you go up yonder towards the moors, you will see what a quantity of new ground is being taken up for growing potatoes. I have had half a mind to try what I could do with a bit of a field myself. Anderson knows what he is about, generally; and what he tries in a large way might be safe for such as we in a small."

"I would not try," replied Mary.

"No, not if you were me, because you think I fly from one thing to another, and do myself harm."

"Besides," said Mary, attempting no denial, "how will it be with you next year, if there should chance to be a fine wheat and barley crop? People do not live on potatoes when they can get bread; and I am sure it is not to be wished that they should. I hope there will be much less demand for potatoes next year; and it is likely there will. We have had so many bad seasons, it cannot be long before a good one comes."

"And then what a pity it will be that so much money has been spent in fencing and managing these potato-grounds! It may chance to come to be worth while to turn the sheep on again. That *would* be a pity."

"Say rather it is a pity they were ever turned off. The land on the moors is much more fit for them than for us to feed off; and leaving them there would leave the money that is spent on the land (more than it is worth, if matters went on in their usual course) to be used in a more profitable way."

"In what way?"

"Why; take your own case. If you pay so much for hedging and ditching, and draining, and manuring the potato-ground you have a mind for, and the crop brings you no more next year than the same plot now brings as a sheep-feed, is not the money just lost that was laid out in making a field of it? My opinion is that it would bring less; and if it does not, it ought to do. Our people will be badly off indeed if food is so high next year as to make them take your potatoes at a price that would make your bargain a good one; and if they are obliged to do so, they will be eating up in those potatoes the money that should have set some of them to work at weaving or cutlery-employment. Better buy corn of Kirkland when we can, and let the sheep graze on."

"Ay, when we can. There is the very thing. If we could always do that, as much as we pleased, we should not spend much of our money on the moors; but it is because it is all a chance whether we shall be buying of Kirkland next year, that one thinks of taking the chance of potatoes selling well."

"I would not."

"No, not you. You would spend your money, if you had any, in a little bargain of grindstones, for the sake of a certain person."

"That would depend on the price of potatoes," replied Mary, smiling, "for they would depend on the price of corn; and on the price of corn mainly depends the cutlery trade; and where is the use of grindstones unless the cutlery business flourishes?"

"There is another thing to be looked to; and that is, that those you help in cutting grindstones do not get themselves into trouble;—ay, by being abroad at night, and having the constables after them in the day. I would have you consider that, my dear. Mercy! how frightened you look,—as white as my apron! Now, don't push me away because I let out a thing that made you frightened."

"Angry—very angry," said Mary.

"Not with me, to be sure; for I did not make it, be it true or not true; though I need not have cast it in your teeth as I did. It was Dick Rose told me; and he said he knew it from—"

"Do get me a little vinegar, Mrs. Skipper. I never pinched my finger so smartly before. I shall not be able to get my thimble on this week."

"Well, now, it was that made you turn white, while you pretended to be so angry with me that you made my heart beat in my throat. I shall know you now another time, mistress Mary."

"Not you," thought Mary, as her giddy companion bustled into the house for vinegar.

"I don't see your sister," said she, returning, "but I guessed where to look for the vinegar. Is the pain going? Well, only do you ask Dick Rose about how the folks were seen creeping out of the quarry, one by one,—those that worked there, and some strangers that came to visit them; and how—"

"I shall not ask Dick Rose any such thing, when there is a person that can tell me so much better," said Mary.

"Ay, if he will."

"John fetch me the large blue apron," cried Mary; "and bring out Nanny with you. I promised she should lend a hand, and see the chaff fly."

Before John could reach the door, a sharp scream,—the scream of a child,—was heard from within. Mary flew to see what had happened, but just as she was entering, her brother, seeing that some one was behind her, slammed the door in her face, and was heard to bolt it. Mrs. Skipper would not listen to what she had to say about the child having a fall, but exclaimed,

"Well, I should not have thought Mr. Kay could have behaved in that manner to you; and he looked at me quite fierce, so as I thought had not been in his nature."

And she stepped to the window to tap, and ask an explanation: but she caught a glimpse of something that quieted her, and sent her to stoop down over the wheat again, without looking at Mary, or speaking another word. Kay was carrying his wife up stairs. The helpless arm, hanging over his shoulder, was just visible, and the awe-struck children, suspending their crying, moved Mrs. Skipper to concern too deep to be expressed in her usual giddy speech.

"Which way are you going?" asked Mary at length. "I am off for the mill, as soon as I can get in to take the children with me."

"And I home; and you may depend on me, you know for what. My tongue does run too fast sometimes, I know; but you may depend on me, as it was only by a chance that I was here."

"Thank you!" replied Mary, warmly. "And I will take it kindly of you to show me the way about the bread, as soon as my corn is ground."

By the united resources of the children within, the door was unbolted, and the party allowed egress into the street, when Mrs. Skipper turned down, and Mary up; the children asking her, one to go out of the way for the sake of the pond on the heath, and another hoping to jump down five steps of the mill-ladder, four having been achieved last time. Mary would have been glad to forget their mother as easily as they.

When Warden saw her toiling up the slope on the top of which the mill stood, her bundle on her head, and a child tugging at each side of her gown, he civilly came down to relieve her, and told her that she was more welcome than on the occasion of her last visit. It was a fine breezy day, he observed, and perhaps she might like to look about her from the top of the mill, if she did not mind the shaking that there always was in a wind. Mary thanked him, but dared not leave the children, lest they should put themselves in the way of the sails. This difficulty was soon obviated by the miller's taking the girl upon his shoulder, and calling to his man to bring up the boy, and let him play among the sacks in the first story, or climb higher, as he liked.

"I suppose you saw the fire finely from here, if you chanced to be looking out last night," Mary observed.

"My man did, as he stayed to take advantage of the wind. He says it lighted up every turn of the river between this and Sheffield. You may see the smoke still, among the other smoke. Half the country has flocked there this morning, my father-in-law told me just now, as he passed on his way to pay his rent. It is a good time to choose to pay his rent, when every body is thinking of something else than emptying his pockets. Otherwise, it is not the safest and pleasantest thing in the world to be carrying money over the by-road between this and Fergusson's. Yonder he goes," continued the miller, stooping to the little girl whom he was keeping steady with his arm round her waist. "Yonder goes Mr. Anderson, on his black mare. You may see him trotting along the lane between those young oaks."

"He will come back slower in the evening, when he has left his money behind him," observed Mary.

"He will not wait till evening. He will just finish with the steward, and come home again, for the Mr. Fergussons are abroad over the country to-day; and besides, my father-in-law is wanted at home every hour of the day while the improvements are going on. Look how busy he is thereabouts."

"I see; they drive the poor sheep higher and higher up the moors, with their walls and their ditches."

"Yes, year by year. Before these many bad seasons, the sheep used to browse on this very slope where my mill stands. I used to come up among the bleaters every morning."

"You speak as if the bad seasons were the cause of the change."

"And so they are, mainly. Where numbers increase as they have done here in my time, more food will be wanted at all events, be the seasons what they may. But when the soil yields scantily, for years together, the inclosing will go on faster, from the cry for food. Yonder field, red even now with poppies, would never have been sown if the nine-acres in the bottom had yielded as they ought. The nine-acres used to yield as much as was reaped this year in itself and the poppy-field together."

"And there has been all the cost of taking it in besides."

"Yes; and my father-in-law does wisely to pay that cost (if he must pay it) before his rent is raised. He and the steward will have an argument about that rent to-day, I fancy. The lease will be up soon now, and rents are rising everywhere; and I suppose my father-in-law is content to let his mount up too. He would not otherwise be carrying on all these works."

"I wonder at his being content to pay more rent after so many short harvests."

"It is easier than after larger; for corn sells dear, more than in proportion to its scarcity. Nobody can tell you better than Anderson that a single short harvest makes a heavy pocket; much more a succession of short harvests."

"Till the poor get a-head of the rate-payers, I suppose,—no longer. When Mr. Anderson has to maintain half of us down in the village, because we cannot buy food, he will find us lighten his pockets as fast as bad years can fill them."

"The manufacturers must help him then. They must raise their people's wages—"

"And so must Anderson."

"They must raise their people's wages, and maintain the poor in the towns, and in the working villages."

"I wish the manufacturers joy of their good nature. They first pay dear for their own bread, and then pay dear for the labour which is to buy their workmen's bread, and then spend what profits are left in supporting those whose labour they cannot employ; and all to make Anderson's and other farmers' pockets heavy for a little while after bad seasons. I wish them joy of their patience."

"Anderson will want patience too, when his turn comes. Depend upon it, as soon as he gets fairly saddled with a high rent and high rates, there will come a fine crop or two to make prices as low in proportion as they now are high. He cannot bring down his men's wages all in a day; much less can the rates be disburthened at once; and so it will be well if he makes ready beforehand for such a change."

"I hope he does make ready; but what I see there looks little like it."

"What, you mean the bay-window and balcony now making to my house, and the shrubbery he is laying out. All that was no wish of mine, for I thought the white house looked very neat as it was before; and the bit of garden behind was as much as my wife and I had time to attend to. But her father liked that his daughter's house should be improving while he was adding so much to his own, and he made us accept of the alteration, whether we would or no. He said, that while he was sending my wife's sister to Paris, and bringing up her brothers to look higher than he once thought of for them, he could not leave her neglected, as if he was ashamed of her having married more humbly than the other girls will do."

"And his own house looks hardly like the same place. His having built up among all the rambling old parts gives it one face as a whole."

"Yes; three more bad years, and it will look like a gentleman's mansion. Yes, yes; these are the joyous rent-days, when the steward gets every farthing, and pretends to shake his head because it is no more; and when the farmers try to look dismal about the short crops, and then sing merry songs over their ale,—such of them as have not taken to port. Well, the millers' day will come in time, it is to be hoped."

"When will that be?"

"When the people are not setting their wits to work to make potato-bread, and eating every thing that grows rather than flour. We have had more going and coming, more watching and jealousy about waste, and more grumbling because we cannot grind for nothing,—more trouble of all sorts about a few trumpery bundles of gleanings this last week, than about fifty sacks when I first became a miller."

"I will give you as little trouble as I can with mine," said Mary; "but you must not call it a trumpery bundle, for it is worth much to me. If you knew how much, I might trust you not to waste any of it."

"You would not dream of my wasting, if you saw how carefully I look to every grain. Why, I drive away the very birds themselves, if they light when the sails stop at any time. We do not leave the sweepings to them and the wind, as we used to do, but sift them as a housemaid sifts for pins. That is the reason why I do not offer your young master a handfull for the pigeons, as I used to do."

"Don't think of it, pray. He is going to play with the ducks on the pond as we go home, and that will do as well: besides, I hear him laughing now, merry enough without the pigeons."

"Playing hide and seek with Jerry among the sacks, I fancy."

"Where he must have done playing for today," observed Mary. "How quiet every place looks for a working day!" she continued, giving one more glance round the horizon before she descended. "Except the sheep, creeping like mites on the uplands, and the labourers gathering like ants about the new inclosures, I see nobody stirring."

"I seldom see it so quiet, except on a starlight night, when there is no noise but the whizzing of the sails when they go by starts; or perhaps an owl from my gable. But you see the people in the quarries stick to their work, as if they had no share in what was doing last night." And the miller looked full at Mary as he spoke.

"I see a man or two with his pick in yonder stone-pit, hewing away as if nothing had happened. Cannot you see them? Well, it is a wonder your head has stood the shaking in this breeze for so long. Many people can fix their sight on nothing after the first two minutes."

Mary was determined to see more of the quarries before she went home than could be discerned from the mill-top. She let one child peep into the hopper to see how the corn ran down to be ground, and the other to exhibit his jump of five steps, with a topple at the end of it, and then walked quickly away towards the part of the heath where bilberries[1] were to be found, and where she thought she might leave her charges safely employed while she looked into the quarry to see whether Chatham was really there, and whether or not he had had any transactions with the constable since she saw him last.

Chapter IV: A Poor Man's Induction

It took but a little time to show the children how to find bilberries, and not very much longer to teach them not to eat what they found; after which Mary was at liberty to walk round to the mouth of the stone-quarry, beside which the fashioning of grindstones went on, in subservience to the cutlery business of Sheffield. She avoided the sheds where the sawing and smoothing proceeded, and looked only among the men who were excavating the stone. But few were at work this day; Chatham was one of them. He was engaged high up, with his face to the rock, and having no glances to spare for the scene below him, or for the narrow, rough path by which his present position must be attained.

Mary had never been here before, and she lingered in hopes that Chatham might turn, and encourage her to go on. She gathered rag-wort[2] from the moist recesses by the way, and paused to observe how the ivy was spreading over a portion of the stone face of the quarry which had been left untouched for some time, and to listen to the

---

1 Bilberries or blueberry, whortleberry (*vaccinium myrtillus*).
2 Rag-wort, genus *senecio*, with yellow flowers.

water trickling down among the weeds by a channel which it had worn for itself. As Chatham still did not turn, she proceeded to climb the path, being aware that children who were playing in the bottom had given notice of her presence, and that face after face peeped out from beneath the sheds to gaze, and then disappeared again. When at length she laid her hand on the arm of the toiling man, he started as if his tool had broken under his blow.

"Mary! what brought you here?"

"I heard that the constables were after you."

"So did I; and here I am, if they choose to come."

"And what next?"

"My words and deeds will be taken up against me, perhaps. Perhaps it may be found that I am a good friend to all the parties that were quarrelling last night. This last is what I wish to be."

"And trying to be so, you will get blamed by all in turn."

"By all at once, if they so please. As often as they choose to ask my opinion, as they did last night, they shall have it, though they themselves try to hoot me down. I do not want to meddle; but, being bid to speak out, I will speak, out of the fire or the water, if they bid me burn or drown. So it is not the notion of a constable that can frighten me."

"Out of fire or water, would you? Then much more would you speak in a moonlight field. O, tell me if you were there."

"How did you spend your thoughts, Mary, those nights that you sat by the spring, during the drought? What were you thinking about when your sister threw down the pitcher that you caught? That must have been a weary night to you both."

"You saw us! Then it is true; and you are one that hopes to get food by night-arming?"

"Not I. If the question of stinting food or getting plenty of it were waiting to be decided by arms,—the hungry on the one side and the full on the other,—I would take up my pike with a hopeful heart, however sorry I might be that blood should be shed in settling so plain a matter. But what could a little band of pale complainers do, creeping under the shadows of yonder walls, with limbs as trembling as their hearts are firm? How should they be champions of the right while they are victims of the wrong? They must be fed before they can effectually struggle for perpetual food."

"Poor wretches! they did look, it seemed to me, as if they had no life nor spirit in them."

"The spirit goes from the sunk eye to swell the heart, Mary; and those that have not strength of arm this day, may prove, many a day hence, what their strength of purpose has been. This is what the authorities ought to look to. Instead of scouring the country to wake up a wretch from the noon-day sleep which he seeks because he has had no morning meal, they should provide against the time when his arm will be strong to make his hungry dreams come true. Instead of carrying one man in disgrace from his loom, and another from the forge, and another from the quarry, to tell the old story—'We have been patient long, and can endure no longer,' our rulers should be satisfying themselves whether this is one of the stories which is to have no end. It cannot be very pleasing to their ears. The wonder is, that if they are weary of it, they go on from century to century to cry, 'Tell us this story again.'"

"They cannot yet be so weary of it as we."

"No; for they hear others in turn with it,—tales of victories abroad, and of rejoicings at home in places where no poor man sets his foot. Their painters show them pictures of jolly rent-days, and the music they hear is triumphant and spirit-stirring. If they go abroad in the day, they laugh to see their enemies made mirth of in the streets; and if at night, they glorify themselves and one another in the light of illuminations. Thus they can forget our story for a while."

"I would rather they should come here than go myself among them, to be the merriest of the merry."

"Ay; if we could set each of them down in this vale as one of ourselves, they would be surprised to find how dismal night-lights are when they shine upon scowling brows and hollow cheeks; and how little spirit war-music has when it cannot drown the moans of the famished, and the cries of mothers weeping for their children."

"It seems to me that their very religion helps to deceive them about us. Last Sunday, the clergyman looked comfortably about him, and spoke very steadily when he read about the springing corn in the furrows, and that the little hills rejoice on every side. I thought of the red poppies and the stones in Fergusson's new fields, and the scanty gleanings on the uplands, and my heart turned back from my Bible."

"It should not have done that, Mary. It is not that the Bible is in fault, but that some people read it wrong. There is never any day of any year when there are not springing grains and ripening harvests on God's earth."

"You ought to be able to speak to that, having gone so far round the world when you were a boy at sea."

"I can speak to it. If there are angels hovering over the fields, as 'tis said there once were, and if the earth lies stretched beneath them as in a map, they may point to one fruitful place or another, and never cease their song, 'Thou visitest the earth and waterest it. The pastures are clothed with flocks, and the valleys are covered over with corn. Thou crownest the year with thy goodness.'"[1]

"But of what use is it to us that there is corn somewhere, if we have it not? Are we to bless God that he feeds some people somewhere, while there are still poppies and stones where we look for bread?"

"You might as well ask 'of what use is the fruit on the tree to him who sits hungering at its foot?' And, 'is not a parched traveller to repine at his thirst, when a well is springing in the neighbouring shade?' What would you say to hungering and thirsty men like these?"

"'Bless God that there is fruit, and climb to reach it. Be thankful that there is water, and go down to take your fill.'"

"We are required by our rulers to do one half of this reasonable thanksgiving, and to forego the remainder. We are bidden to thank God for his gifts, but forbidden to reach and take.—How great is the folly of this, you would see at a glance, if you could go where I have been."

"To see how perfectly happy people are in the fruitful places, while so many are suffering here? To see how unequal is the lot of dwellers in different countries?"

"Not so; but worse. There is but too much equality in the lot of dwellers in fruitful and on barren soils; between those who are too many for their food, and those who bury their spare corn out of their way. If some were satisfied while others suffer, the sufferers might be the more patient because all were not afflicted like themselves; but it is when all suffer, and might yield mutual relief, if they were not prevented, that patience is impossible. I would ask no man to have patience with our state who had seen the state of many others, striving after patience as painfully as we."

"What others?"

"Why, there is the labouring man of Poland, for one. He creeps out of his log hut, shivering, half naked, in the first cold of autumn, to feed his pigs with the grain—"

"Grain! What sort of grain?"

"Wheat, or rye, as may happen; whichever happens to be rotting the fastest. Between him and the black forest on the horizon are

---

1   Psalms 65:9-11.

plains, stretching away for leagues upon leagues, some sprinkled with a few cattle, and some showing a stubble that you would be glad to have the gleaning of; and others lying waste, though richer as soil than many a field of Anderson's."

"O, but that is a shame, with the people so poor."

"It would make the people no richer to till those wastes, unless the crops could sell. The people there do not want food—"

"So I think, if they feed their beasts on wheat and rye."

"They want clothes, and good houses, and all that makes a dwelling comfortable; and yet, though our warehouses are overfull of broad cloth, and we could furnish twice as much metalwork as we do, if we had bread for the workmen, it is only by fits and starts that we will let Poland sell us corn, and clothe her sons. Then, again, near the Black Sea,—"

"Is that sea really blacker than other seas?"

"The sun glitters there as bright as on the heaving Indian bays, and it is as blue when the sky is clear as any tarn in yonder hills. God has done all to make it beautiful, not only from above, but by spreading fertile tracts all along its shores. If man would do his part, sending ships upon its bosom, and leaving no spot desolate around, it might be made the happy place that, in my opinion, the whole earth might be made, and will be, some time or other."

"The people are not happy there now, then?"

"Not what we should call happy, though they may like better than we should the flitting from plain to plain to gather corn, as bees flit from blossom to blossom for honey. They reap for three seasons from a field, and then move to another, leaving an exhausted soil and a desolate place behind them."

"We might teach them husbandry, if they would let us have some of the fruits of it."

"And then they might learn to live a little more like Christians than they do, and have some of the pleasures that we have, in the midst of all our hardships, in growing up from the state of brute beasts into that of thinking men. There are other parts,—in America,—where thinking men live who fret in the impossibility of making their children wiser and more civilized than themselves,—which should be every man's aim for his children. They can give them work,—but what is it all for?—food. They can give them wealth,—but what does it all consist of?—food. They can hold out a prospect of increase,—but of what?—food. They long for a thousand comforts, if they could but convert their corn into these comforts. They perceive that there are a thousand advantages and blessings over the sea, if they could but stretch out a long arm to throw corn into our lap, and reach home—things which we can now use no more than they, because we have too little bread, and they have too much. Though their sons are thus condemned to be clowns, and ours to be paupers, we must hope that they will learn from our follies so to deal together as that the clown may become a wise man, and the pauper take his stand on the rights of his industry."

"But why, if so many countries are fruitful, is England alone barren?"

"England is fruitful in corn; but yet more so in men, and in arts which she chooses to make barren of food. England has corn on her hills, corn in her valleys, corn waving over her plains; yet this corn is not enough, or not always enough, for the multitudes who gather together in her villages, and throng her cities, and multiply about her workhouses. If this corn is not enough, England's duty is,—not to starve hundreds, or half-starve thousands of her children, but to bring out corn from all the apparatus of her arts. She should bring out corn from her looms, corn from her forges, corn from her mines; and when more than all this is wanted, let her multiply her looms and her forges, and sink new mines from which other millions may derive their bread."

"You dig bread from this hard rock, I suppose, when you furnish grindstones on which the cutlery is to be prepared which may be exchanged with the Russian and the American for corn."

"I do: and to limit this exchange is not only to limit the comforts of us workmen, but to forbid that there shall be more lives in our borders than the fruits of our own soil can support. There is room for myriads more of us, and for a boundless improvement of our resources; these resources are forbidden to improve, and these myriads to exist. Whence rulers derive their commission thus to limit that to which God has placed no perceivable bound, let them declare."

"Then there are not too many of us, if all were wise."

"By no means. If all were permitted to be as happy as God bids them be, there would be neither the recklessness of those who multiply without thought, nor the forced patience of those who have a conscience and listen to it. If all were wise, they would proportion their numbers to their food; but then that food would not be stinted by arbitrary laws which issue in evil to all. Our rulers turn away, if perchance they see in the streets infants that pine for a while, only to die; and pronounce that such children should never have been born. And it may be true; but it is not for our rulers to pronounce, except with shame; for it is only while waiting for their becoming just that it behoves [behooves] the people to be as self-denying as they require."

"Strangers that pass this way for their pleasure," observed Mary, "wonder at the hardness of our shepherds in turning their tender lambs exposed upon the moors, where, if some thrive, many pine. Do not they themselves (as many of them as have to do with making laws) turn out the young of our cities into stony fields, where they pine like starving lambs? There is small use in pitying—small kindness in saying that such should never have been born, if there are indeed fields where for stones they may gather bread."

"When I see money buried in the furrows of such fields," replied Chatham, "I feel that it is taken twice from those whose due it is;—from the mechanic who, instead of standing idle, would fain be producing corn on his anvil; and from the spiritless boor abroad, who would as willingly exchange his superfluity to supply his need. When I see the harrow pass over such fields, I see it harrow human souls; and voices cry out from the ground, however little the whistling husbandman may heed them."

"The husbandman will not long whistle, if all must at length scramble for food. His turn to see his infants pine must come at last."

"At last! It comes early, for there are more to follow. There is the farmer to swear that it is hard upon him that his labourers must live, as it is upon his substance that they must live. Then comes she for whom the farmer labours in his turn. He complains that, let the sunshine be as bright, the dews as balmy as they may, he can reap scarcely half the harvest of his gains, and that he is pressed upon by the crowds who come to him for bread."

"He can hardly wonder at this, when it is he himself who forbids their going elsewhere. To what third party would he commend them?"

"Perhaps he would quote Scripture, as may be done for all purposes, and tell them that the clouds drop fatness, and bid them look up and await the promised manna. Till it comes, however, or till he and his tribe have unlocked the paths of the seas, he has no more right to complain of the importunity which disturbs him than the child who debars the thrush from its native woods has to be angry when it will not plume itself and sing, but beats against its wires because its fountain is no longer filled."

"I could not but think something like this when I saw even so good a man as our Mr. Fergusson on rough terms with some of the people he met on the way, when he went out to view the harvest-home."

"The harvest-home which used to be a merry feast when it was clear that its golden fruits were to be wealth to all! Now, there is no knowing what is to become of it; whether it shall be divided and consumed in peace, or scrambled for by men possessed by the demon of want, or burned by those who cannot share, and are therefore resolved that none others shall enjoy. It is said, and no one contradicts, that the harvest-moon rose clear, and lighted up alike every mansion and cottage in the dale; but I was abroad to see her rise; and I declare that with my mind's eye I beheld her eclipsed, shedding a sickly light, maybe, upon the manor and the farm, but blight and darkness into the dwellings of the poor."

"It has ever been God's hand that has drawn a shadow over sun and moon, but now—"

"Now man has usurped the office, and uses his power, not once and again to make the people quail, but day by day. To none is the sun so dark as to the dim-eyed hungerer. To none is the moon so sickly as to the watcher over a pining infant's cradle. Let man remove the shadow of social tyranny, let him disperse the mists which rise from a deluge of tears, and God's sun and moon will be found to make the dew-drops glitter as bright as ever on the lowliest thatch, and to shine mildly into humble chambers where those who are not kneeling in thanksgiving are blessing God as well by the soundness of their repose."

"Are those whom you meet at midnight of the same mind with you? Do they go to church on Sunday to bring away this sort of religion for the week?"

"They do not go to church,—partly because they know themselves to be squalid,—partly because, as you say, their hearts turn back from their Bible. They are slow to believe that their soul-sickness will be pitied somewhere, if not by man. They no doubt feel also some of the unwillingness of guilt; but I can tell,—I will tell those whom it may concern,—that the way to bring these men from their unlawful drill into the church aisle is to preach to them full, and not hungering, that God giveth to all living things food in its season. This, like all other words of God, is true; but with his vicegerents [deputies] rests the blasphemy if shrunken lips whisper that it is a lie.—Such sufferers, if they did make Sabbath, have not the leisure that I have to work out their religion by themselves, during the week, making it and toil lighten each other."

"So that is what you do in this place,—high up on the face of the stone, with no moving thing near you but these dancing weeds overhead, and no sound but the dull shock of your own blows! So your religion is what you think over all day!"

"In some form or other; but you know religion takes many forms;—all forms, or religion would be good for little. I am not always thinking of the church and the sermon; but sometimes of how I am to advise the people that come to me, and sometimes of what I could tell the powerful if I could get their ear; and oftener than all, Mary, of what was said between you and me the evening before, and what will be said this evening, and of what we may dare to look to in a future time."

"With so much to think about, you could do without me," said Mary, smiling. "You would hardly miss me much, if I was drowned to-morrow, till the country is quiet, and there is nothing more to be complained of."

"Meanwhile, Mary, you want nothing more, I suppose, than to clean trenchers and wash and mend stockings. To do this would make you perfectly happy for evermore, would it?"

"It is light work cleaning trenchers for a half-starved family," replied Mary; "and as for the stockings, the children are going bare-foot, one by one. So, no light jesting, Chatham; but tell me—"

"Who these men are just at your shoulder? They are constables, and come for me, I rather think."

"And what next?" inquired Mary, as she had done half an hour before.

"I know no more than when you asked me last; but I suppose they will either let me come back here to think over the matters we have been talking about, or put me where I may consider them at more leisure still, not having my tools with me wherewith to hew down stone walls. You well know, in that case, Mary, what I shall be thinking about and doing; and so you will not trouble yourself or be frightened about me. Promise me."

"Certainly: what should I be frightened about?" asked Mary, with white lips. "You cannot have done wrong,—you cannot have joined in—"

She stopped short, as the constable was within hearing. His office was an easy one, as Chatham cheerfully surrendered himself; and Mary turned to descend, as soon as he had flung on his coat and disposed of his tools. They were permitted to walk arm-in-arm, and to talk, if they chose to do it so as to be overheard. Not being at Liberty in heart and mind for such conversation as the constable might share, they passed in silence the groups of workpeople, some of whom grinned with nervousness or mirth, and others gazed with countenances of grave concern; while a very few showed their sympathy by carefully taking no notice of what must be considered the disgrace of their companion. In a little while, Mary was told she must go no farther; and, presently after, she was at the door of her own home, with a child in each hand,—one talking of bilberries, and the other telling a story of a duckling in the pool, which had billed a worm larger than it knew what to do with; and how it ended with dropping the worm in deep water, and, after a vain poke in pursuit of it, had scuttled after the rest of the brood. All this Mary was, or seemed to be, listening to, when her brother looked out from the door, and told her impatiently that he had been watching for her this half-hour. His wife was asleep at present; but he had not liked to leave her alone in the house, much as he wished to go out and see what sort of a net the constables were drawing in.

"Have you heard of anybody that they have taken?" he inquired.

"Yes."

"Well! Anybody that we know?"

"Yes; Chatham."

Kay looked at her for a moment, sent the children different ways, and then looked at her again.

"You are not down-hearted, Mary?"

"No."

"He will come out clear, depend upon it: my life upon it, it will turn out well. Oh! it will turn out a good thing,—a real good thing!"

"Everything does."

"Ay, ay, in the end; but I mean—But come, sit you down. I am in no hurry to go out; and I will get you something after your long walk."

"Pray do not; I do not wish it, indeed. I will help myself when I am hungry."

As she seemed not to want him, Kay thought perhaps he had better go. Before he closed the door behind him, he saw that Mary was taking a long, deep draught of cold water.

Chapter V: Taking Counsel

As there was sufficient evidence, in the magistrate's opinion, of Chatham's having been once present at the midnight drill, and active among the crowd by the river-side the night before, he was committed to prison, it being left to himself to prove, at the time of trial, for what purposes he had mixed himself up with the rioters. As he was a very important personage in his village, his jeopardy excited much speculation and interest. For the first two or three days, there was much curiousity among the neighbours to see Mary, in order to observe how she took it. Mary was somehow always busy with her sister and the children; but when a gossip or two had become qualified to testify to her aspect—that she looked just as usual,—and when the children were found to have nothing particular to tell about her, everybody was vexed at having been troubled on behalf of a person who was never put out, happen what might.

Times were so flat this autumn that there was abundance of leisure for talking about whatever might turn up, and no lack of tongues to treat thereof. Some of the foundry-men were turned off, as it had been necessary to raise the wages of those who remained. As there was no increase of business at the time this rise of wages took place, and as Oliver himself was living at largest expense as provisions became dearer, there was no alternative for him but to turn off some of his men, contract his business, and be as content as he could with smaller profits than he had ever before made. By the rise of wages, his remaining men were, for a short time, relieved from the extreme of misery they had endured in the interval between the great increase in the cost of provisions and the raising of their wages; but they were no richer than they had formerly been with two-thirds of the nominal amount of the present recompense of their labour. Want still pressed, and must still press, up to the point of Oliver having no more wages to give, unless the deficiencies of the harvest might be supplied by large importations from abroad. In the uncertainty whether this would be done, and with the certainty before their eyes that there had not been food enough in the country for three years past, Anderson and the neighbouring farmers took in more and more land, and flung about the abundance of money they received for their dear corn.

The circulation of this morsel of wealth, dwindling on every transfer, was easily traceable in a small society like that of the village. The waste could be detected in every direction, and the landlord stood marked as the focus of it. Whether Mr. Fergusson was the better for the waste incurred on his account was a separate question; and, till it was decided, he stood in a remarkable relation to the people about him: he was their injurer and their benefactor;—their injurer, in as far as he was one of the persons for whose sake a bad system was upheld;—their benefactor, in his capacity of a wealthy and benevolent resident among them. He was taunted with being the landowner, and was offered obeisance as Mr. Fergusson. All were complaining that he received an unconscionable share of the fruits of their labour; but there was not one who would not have grieved at any misfortune that might befall him. They talked loudly against him and his class for narrowing the field of their exertions, and praised the pains and good-nature with which he devised employment for those who were perpetually being turned out of work.

The fact that he must have supported these extra labourers as paupers, if he had not rather chosen to get some work out of them in return for the cost of their subsistence, made no difference in the kindness with which Mr. Fergusson attended to their interests, and endeavoured to preserve in them a spirit of independence till better times. The effort was vain under a system which authorized men to say that they had not surrendered their independence, but that it had been taken from them, and that those who took it away might make the best they could of its absence. Notwithstanding all that Fergusson could do, paupers increased in the parish; and while a few stout men, who were turned off from the various works in the neighbourhood, were taken on by Anderson, to try their hands at a new kind of labour, many more lay about asleep on the moors, or gathered in knots to gossip, in the intervals of being worse employed.

No place could be obtained for Kay's boy, John, who pleased himself with looking about him while he had no business to do, and amusing himself as he best could. The less objection was made to this at home, as it was hoped that his curiousity might now and then make him forget the time, and justify his going without a meal—a consideration which was becoming of more and more importance in Kay's family. It happened that Bill Hookey, the shepherd-lad, was one day leaning against the door of a cutler's workshop, when his old companion, John, ran up, pushing back his hair from his hot forehead.

"I'd be glad to be as cool as you," said John, "standing gaping here. I have been at the forge: crept in when they did not see me, and got behind the bellows. I gave them such a puff when they were not expecting it,—I nearly got flogged. They let me off for blowing for them till there was no more breath in my body than in the empty bellows. But I don't half like standing here: come to the other side; you will see just as well."

Bill stuck out his legs colossus-fashion, and yawned again.

"'Twas just where you are standing that Brett was when the grindstone flew; and those grindstones make ugly splinters, I can tell you."

"I a'n't afraid."

"No, because you've been in the moors all your days, and have not seen mishaps with grindstones and such. You should have seen

Duncan. The knife he was grinding flew up, and it was a done thing before he knew what he was about. the cut was only across the wrist; but the whole arm was perished, and good for nothing, just in that minute. The Duncans are all off to Scotland, with nothing to look to, after having had fine wages all this time—for he was a capital workman; but, as Anderson says, we have too many folks out of work here already to be expected to keep a Scotchman. What accidents do happen to people, to be sure!"

"Aye, they do."

"Then I wonder you put yourself in the way of one, when you would be quite safe by just crossing over."

"Oh! grindstones very often don't fly, nor knives either."

"But they very often do."

"He a'n't afraid," observed Bill, nodding towards the cutler.

"No, because he is paid high for the risk. Well, I wonder any wages will tempt a man to have such a cough as that. I suppose, however, he don't believe where it will end, as we do. I often think, if several were to take turns, and change their work about, there would be a better chance. If ever I am a cutler, I will try that way, if I can get anybody else of the same mind."

"Not you," said Bill; "you will do like the people before you."

"Perhaps I may, when the time comes. I may no more like to try my hand at a new thing than you. Have you asked anybody for work hereabouts?"

"The flock is all sold, higher up the country," replied Bill. "They would not let me stay on the walk when the flock was gone."

"I know that; and how you got it into your head that you might go on sleeping in the hut just the same when the place was a field as when it was a sheep-walk. They say they had to take you neck and heels to turn you out, if you would not have the roof down over your head. Why did not you bestir yourself in time, and get work from Anderson, before others stepped before you?"

"There are no sheep now for anybody to keep."

"Well; if you have no mind to do anything but keep sheep, cannot you go higher up, among the graziers, and offer yourself?"

"I don't know anybody thereabouts, nor yet the walks."

"No, nor ever will, of your own accord," thought John. "What would you be now, Bill, if you might never be a shepherd again?"

Bill only rubbed his hand over the back of his head, and shifted his weight from both legs to one. Few things could daunt John's love of talk.

"What became of the poor little lamb you were nursing that

night that I was on the moors? It was too tender, surely, to walk up into the hills with the rest."

"It be well if he be not dead by this time," replied Bill. "I carried him full two miles myself, and I told 'em how to feed him and when; and, for all I could say, they minded no more when he complained— O, they don't understand him no more than if he was a puppy-dog. When I bid him good-bye, he looked up at me, though he could scarce speak to me. He did speak, though; but he would not so much as look at the new shepherd, and if it was not for the ewe—"

"What's coming?" cried John, interrupting his companion's new loquacity. "Let us go and see. I dare say it is somebody fresh taken up. Do you know, I went to see Chatham's jail, the other day. Father locked doors against me because I came home so late; but I had a mind to see what sort of a place it was. I may be in it some day. I should not mind being anywhere that Chatham has been."

"You that can't stand being flogged!"

"Chatham is not going to be flogged. They say it will be 'Death Recorded.'"

"What's that?"

"Transportation."

"Why can't they say so at once?"

"I don't know: but they often speak in the same way. I have heard Chatham say that they talk of 'agriculture,' and nobody means just the same as they do by it. Some say 'tis farmers, and some say 'tis landlords, and some that 'tis having corn."

"I think it is keeping sheep."

"No, no; the Parliament does not meddle with keeping sheep. When they are asked to 'protect agriculture,' Chatham says, Anderson understands, 'take care of the farmer;' and Mr. Fergusson, 'have an eye to the landlords,' and all the rest of us,—except you, you say,—'let us have corn.'"

Bill yawned, and supposed it was all one. John being of a different opinion, and seeing that a very knowing personage of the village, who vouchsafed him a word or two on occasion, was flourishing a newspaper out of the window of the public-house, ran off to try whether the doubtful definition was likely to be mended by the wise men of the Cock and Gun.

He found that there was a grand piece of news going from mouth to mouth, and that everybody seemed much pleased at it. He did not know, when he had heard it, what it meant; but as the hand which held the newspaper shook very much, and two or three men waved their hats, and women came running from their doors, and even the little children clapped their hands and hugged one another, he had no doubt of its being a very fine piece of news indeed. Bill had slowly followed, and was now watching what John meant to do next.

"I don't believe they have heard it at the foundry yet," thought John. "I'll be the first to tell it them."

And off he ran, followed by Bill, and gradually gained upon by him. Now, Bill's legs were some inches longer than little John's, and, if he had the mind, there was no doubt he might be the first at the foundry to tell the news. This would have been very provoking, and the little runner put out all his strength, looking back fearfully over his shoulder, stumbling in consequence, and falling; rising as cold with the shock as he was warm when he fell, and running on again, rubbing his knee, and thinking how far he should be from hobbling like Bill, (with head hung back, bent knees, and dangling arms,) if he had Bill's capacity of limb. What Bill wanted was the heart to use his capacities. He soon gave over the race, even against his little friend John, first slackening his speed, and then contriving to miss the bustle both before and behind him by stopping to lean over a rail which looked convenient for a lounge.

John snapped his fingers triumphantly at the lazy shepherd-boy on reaching the foundry gate. He rushed in, disregarding all the usual decorums about obtaining entrance. Through the paved yard ran John, and into the huge vault where the furnaces were roaring, and where all the workmen looked so impish that it was no wonder he did not immediately discover his father among them. He nearly ran foul of one who was bearing a ladle of molten metal of a white heat, and set his foot on the exquisitely levelled sand-bed which was prepared to form the plate. Scolded on one side, jostled on another, the breathless boy could only ask eagerly for his father.

"Let go the lad's collar," cried one of the workmen to another, adding in a low voice, "'Tis some mishap about his poor mother. Can't ye help him to find his father?"

Kay was roasting and fuming in the red glare of one of the furnaces when his boy's wide eyes looked up in his face, while he cried,

"There's such news, father! The greatest news there has been this many a day, there's an Order in Council, father; and the people are all about the Cock and Gun, and the newspaper is being read, and everybody coming out of their houses. Only think, father! It is certainly true. There is an Order in Council."

"An Order in Council! Well, what of that? What is the Order about?"

"About? O, they did not say what it is about,—at least, nobody that I heard speaking. But I'll run back and ask, directly."

"You will do no such thing. You would bring back only half your story. What should a child know about an Order in Council?" he asked of his fellow-workmen, who began to gather round. "Can't one of you go and learn what it is he means?—for I suppose some news is really come; and I can't leave the furnace just now."

John slunk away mortified to a corner where he could spread wet sand, in case any passing workman should be bountiful enough to spare him the brimmings of some overflowing ladle. It was very odd that his father did not seem to understand his news when everybody, down to the very babies, seemed to be so glad of it at the Cock and Gun.

The messenger soon returned, and then the tidings produced all the effects that the veriest newsmonger could have desired. John ceased his sand-levelling to creep near and listen how there had been issued an Order in Council for opening the ports, and allowing the importation of foreign grain. There was a great buzz of voices, and that of the furnace was the loudest of all.

"Now you hear, lad," said one of the boy's tormentors. "The Order is for the importation of foreign grain."

"Just as if I did not know that half-an-hour ago," said John solemnly. "Why, I was at the Cock and Gun the minute after the news came."

And the lad rescued himself from the man's grasp; and went in search of some one else whom he might throw into a state of admiration. He met Mr. Oliver himself, saying,

"What is all this about? The people stand in the heat as if it was no more than a warm bath; and my work is spoiling all the time, I suppose."

"They are talking about the news, sir,—the great news that is just come."

"News? What news?"

"The King is going to unbar the forts [sic], sir; and he allows the importance [sic] of foreign grain."

"It is high time he should. Your father and I have seen the importance you speak of, this long while."

"I'll warrant you have, sir. And now, perhaps, father will let me go and see it, if you speak a word to him."

Mr. Oliver laughed, and told him he would probably see more of it than he liked as he grew up. John thought he had rather not wait till then to see the sight; besides that he thought it hardly likely that the King should go on unlocking forts [sic] all that time. The fort [sic] that he could just remember to have seen, when his grandfather once took him a journey, might, he believed, be unlocked in five minutes. The young politician proceeded on his rounds, hoping to find a dull person here and there, who had rather go on with his castings, and be talked to, than flock with the rest round the main furnace.

"Well, good fellows," said Mr. Oliver, "what is your opinion of this news?"

"That it is good, sir, as far as it goes; and that it will be better, if it teaches some folks to make such laws as will not starve people first, and then have to be broken at last."

"The laws chop and change so that it seems to me overhard to punish a man for breaking them," observed another. "That law against buying corn when it is wanted is bad enough in the best times, as we can all tell; but if you want damning proof, look to the fact that they are obliged to contradict it upon occasion;—not once only, but many times;—as often as it has wrought so well as to produce starvation."

Kay thought, that putting out a little temporary law upon a great lasting one, was like sending a messenger after a kite,—which proves it ill-made and unlikely to sustain itself. Somebody wondered what Fergusson would think of the news.

"What matters it to us what he thinks?" answered another. "He has stood too long between us and our food;—not knowingly, perhaps; but not the less certainly for that."

Mr. Oliver wished that his men could talk over their own case without abusing their neighbours. He would not stand and hear a word against Mr. Fergusson on these premises.

"Then let us say nothing about Mr. Fergusson, sir, for whom, as is due, I have a high respect. When I mentioned him, I meant him as the receiver of a very high rent; and I maintain that if we make corn by manufacturing, with fire and water, what will buy corn, we are robbed if we have not bread. Deny that who can."

And the speaker brandished his brawny arm, and thrust forward his shining face in the glowing light, to see if any one accepted his challenge. But all were of the same mind.

Mr. Oliver, however, observed that, though he had as little cause as any one to relish the disproportionate prosperity of the landlords in a time of general distress, he wished not to forget that they were brought up to look to their rent as he to look to the returns of his capital, and his men to their wages.

"That is the very thing I complain of," said Kay; "that is, I complain of the amount of rent thus looked for. In as far as a landowner's property is the natural fruit of his own and his ancestors' labour and services,—or accidents of war and state, if you will,—let him have it and enjoy it, so long as it interferes with no other man's property, held on as good a claim. But if by a piece of management this rent is increased out of another man's funds, the increase is not 'property,'—I take it,—but stolen goods. If a man has a shopkeeping business, with the capital, left him, the whole is his property, as long as he deals fairly; but if he uses any power he may have to prevent people buying of his neighbours, and thus puts any price he pleases upon his goods, do you mean to say that his customers may not get leave if they can to buy at other shops, without any remorse as to how the great shopkeeper may take such meddling with his 'property?' Give us a free trade in corn, and our landowners shall be heartily welcome to the best rents they can get. But, till that is done, we will not pretend to agree in making them a present of more of the fruits of our labour the more we want ourselves. The fruits of our labour are as much our property as their rents are theirs, to say the least; and if it was anything but food that was in question we would not be long in proving it; but food is just the thing we cannot do without, and we cannot hold out long enough to prove our point."

"They will find it all out soon," replied Mr. Oliver. "Whatever is ruinous for many of us must be bad for all; and such men as Fergusson will see this before long."

"They will not see it, sir, till they feel it; and what a pass *we* must have come to before they will feel enough to give up a prejudice some hundred years old!"

"Before we can ask them to give up the point entirely, we must relieve them of some of the taxes which bear particularly upon them. Their great cry is about the weight of their taxation. They must first be relieved in that respect."

"With all my heart. Let them go free of taxation as great folks, in the same way that my wife and Mary are let off free at cards on Christmas night, because they are women. This was the case with the old French nobility, I have heard. They paid no taxes; and so let it be with our landowners, if they choose to accept the favour of having their burdens borne by the sweating people to whom they would not own themselves obliged in respect of money matters if they met in the churchyard, though the time may not be far off when they must lie side by side under the sod."

"Their pride must be pretty well humbled before they would

accept of that kind of obligation. They had need go to church, in those days, to learn to bear the humiliation."

"Perhaps that is what they go to church for now, sir; for they are now taking much more from us than they would in the case I have mentioned. I don't say they all do it knowingly,—not half of them. There are many of our rich men who would be offended enough at being told, 'Your eldest son's bills at Eton were paid last year by contributions from three hedgers, and five brass-founders, and seven weavers, all of whom have families only half-fed.' 'Miss Isabella's beautiful bay mare was bought for her by the knife-grinder, who has gone to bed supperless, and the work-woman who will have no fire next winter, and the thirty little children who are kept from school that Miss Isabella's bay mare may be bought.' O yes; there are many who are too proud to bear this being said to them, true though it be."

"They would call you a leveller,[1] Kay, if they could hear you."

"Then I should beg leave to contradict them; for a leveller I am not.—I have no objection on earth to young gentlemen going to Eton, or young ladies riding bay mares, if these things are paid for by the natural rent which a free trade in corn would leave. If we have that free trade, and workpeople still go to bed supperless and sit up without fire, still let young gentlemen go to Eton, and young ladies ride bay mares. In that case, the landlords will be absolved, and the hardship must go to the account of imprudence in some other quarter. O, I am no leveller! Let the rich keep their estates, as long as they will let them find their own value in comparison with labour. It is the making and keeping up laws which make land of more and more value, and labour of less and less, that I complain of."

"But you did not really mean, Kay," said a bystander, "that you would let off every man that has land from paying taxes? It is the most unfair thing I ever heard of."

"It is unfair enough, but much less unfair and ruinous than the present plan. It is better worth our while to pay the landowners' taxes than to lose ten times the amount to enable the landowners to pay them; and that is what we are doing now."

"Ten times as much as the landlords pay in taxes?"

"Yes," replied Oliver. "We pay, as a nation, 12,500,000*l* more for corn than we should pay if our ports were open to the world. Of

---

1 A leveller is a political radical advocating religious tolerance and social equality through "levelling" the hierarchical class system.

this, not more than one-fifth goes into the pockets of the landown-ers, the rest being, for the most part, buried in poor soils. Now if the landlords pay one-half of this fifth in taxes, it is as much as their bur-den can be supposed to be. And now, which of you would not be glad to take his share of this one-tenth, to get rid of the other nine?"

"Every one of us would go down on his knees to pray the land-lords to permit us to pay their taxes, if we could but tell how to get at the gentlemen."

"The landlords would need no such begging and praying, I trust," said Mr. Oliver, "if they saw the true state of the case. I hope and believe they would be in a hurry to surrender their other tenth, if they could see at what an expense to the people it was raised."

Some heartily believed it, but Kay asked why the landowners did not see the state of the case;—a question which it was not easy to answer, unless it was that they did not attend to it. And why did they not attend to it?—attend to it, not merely so far as to sanction an Order in Council for the admission of food when the people were on the brink of starvation, but so as to calculate justly how much corn we grow, how many of our people are properly fed upon that corn, how we may most cheaply get more corn, and—(but that is a matter beyond human calculation)—how many more busy and happy people might live within our borders if we and the other parts of the earth had free access to each other. If our rich men once attended to this large question, they would see what we see; and see-ing, they would surrender, and—"

"And be far richer, as well as happier, than they are now. But, never fear! They will feel soon; and feeling helps seeing marvellously."

"It was found so in the case of the county on the exportation of corn. The landowning legislators thought they saw plainly enough, once upon a time, that it was a capital thing for all parties to give a present to every man who would sell corn abroad:—it would employ more hands in tillage than were employed before; it would secure a supply in case of scarcity; it would increase the value of landed property by causing the greatest possible quantity of land to be cultivated. This is what they saw in vision,—or rather through a pair of flawed spectacles. It ended in the labourers producing only half as much wealth in a forced tillage as they might have made in manufactures, if food had been free; in exposing us to the danger of famine, as often as the deficiency of the crops exceeded what we sent out of the country, (no other nation being prepared to send us corn in a hurry, as if we were regular buyers;) and lastly, in sending a great deal of capital out of this country into others where living was cheaper. At first, no doubt, tillage was brisk, and some of the objects seemed to be answered: but this that I have described was the end. Then the landlords saw, for the first time, that, in giving the bounty to our corn-sellers, they had been offering a bribe to foreigners to buy our corn cheaper than we could afford to sell it. A pretty bargain for us! So that pair of flawed spectacles broke to pieces on being examined, and—"

"And now they must break another pair before they will learn that they can see best with the eyes God gave them, if they will but put them to the right use. I am not for spectacles, unless there is something the matter with the eyes. And, in the same way, I am not for any man helping himself with the opinions of a class because he belongs to a class, unless he has such a faulty reason of his own that he would do worse if left to judge for himself. Let such of our landowners as are incompetent go on upholding the corn laws because their class has always done so; but let such of them as are men stand out, and judge for themselves, after looking the case plainly in the face. I am not afraid of what their judgment would be, especially as some of the richest and wisest have done so already. Honour be upon them!"

The men were perhaps the more disposed to give honour where honour was due from their notion of the smallness of the number of landowners in those days to whom they could award it. They gave three cheers to the Privy Council[1] for having issued the present Order; and to the few landowners who advocated a free trade in corn. That done, they began to inquire what this order was to do for them, and found that it would just serve to avert the starvation of the people, now, and might probably lead to the ruin of a good many farmers within a few months; which ruin must be ascribed, should it arrive, not to the Order in Council, but to the previous state of things which it was designed to repair. Prices had been rising so rapidly from week to week since the quarterly average had been taken, that there was no saying how far even oats might be out of the reach of the poorer classes, before the next quarterly average could be struck, and prices be proved to have risen to the point at which the law authorized the importation of corn. To save the people from perishing while waiting for the quarter to come round, this order was issued without leave of parliament; and, as it would

---

1 A Privy Council is a board of advisors to the monarch which makes recommendations on matters of state. An Order in Council bypasses and supercedes parliamentary legislation.

have the effect of lessening the general panic, in the first place, and also of bringing a large supply into the kingdom, the probability was that the farmers would find prices falling by spring-time, rapidly,—ruinously for them, calculating as they had done on high prices continuing till next harvest, and laying their plans of expense accordingly.

But all this would be a fine thing for Oliver, would not it?

In as far as cheaper living was a good to him and his people, and in as far as more manufactures would be wanted to go abroad, it would be a benefit; but fluctuations in the fortunes of any class of society,—be they farmers or any body else,—are bad for the rest of society. For every farmer that is ruined, the manufacturing and commercial world suffers; and Mr. Oliver would rather therefore,—not only that corn had not been so dear as it now was,—but that it should not be so cheap as it might now soon be, unless its cheapness could be maintained. Fluctuations apart, the cheaper the better; but it was a strange and unhappy way of going on, first to ruin one class by high prices, and then to ruin another by low prices.

All this was allowed to be very true; yet the substantial fact remained, that the day of the manufacturer and mechanic was probably approaching, and that a season of cheap bread was in prospect, let what might follow in its train in the shape of disastrous consequence.

This was enough to proceed upon in rejoicing, and when the furnaces had been duly fed, by strong and willing hands, and a few plates cast amid more talking than was usual during so nice an operation, Oliver's day-men turned out like school-boys on a holiday morning, and tried which could get first to the Cock and Gun. There they stood, regardless of the chill of the breeze after the heats of the foundry. How could they be sensible to it when they felt that the icy grasp of poverty on their heartstrings was relaxing, and the warm currents of hope had leave again to flow?

Kay was not one of the talkers at the public house. It was so long since he had had any pleasant news to carry home, that he was impatient to lose no time about it.

This was one of Mrs. Kay's dismal days. She seldom made any complaints; but there were times when the tears would run down her face for hours together, while there appeared to be no particular reason; and she sometimes said she could not account for it herself. On those occasions, she was not moody, or disposed to speak by signs rather than words, as was often her way; she would speak, and move about, and even try to laugh; but still the tears would run down, and she was obliged to give the matter up. Thus it was to-day, though Mary had not yet parted with the hope that, between them, they might stop the tears.

"Which way did John run?" asked Mary. "Did you happen to see, sister?"

"Down by the coal wharf, I think," she replied, speaking rapidly. "O yes, it must have been by the coal wharf, because—No; it was not; that was yesterday. It could not have been to-day, because his father bade him go up the lane to gather acorns for the pig. That I should have forgot it was yesterday he went to the wharf! But that is always the way with my head. It is so—"

"It will be better when you have tried the medicine from the dispensary a little longer. What a kind, pleasant gentleman that is at the dispensary! He told me he really believed you would be better directly, if—"

"I shall never be better,—never, head nor heart, till I see these poor children of mine—and my husband too—"

"Well, well: cheer up! They will be better fed soon, please God. Don't let that trouble you to night, when you feel yourself not strong."

"And there's Chatham too. That lies at my heart, Mary, more than you know. I must tell you so, for you have been a kind sister to me and mine."

"I should be sorry it should lie so heavy at your heart," said Mary, very quietly. "I thank you for him; but you must not make yourself unhappy about me. I am thinking your husband will be home soon. The sun has been down some good while."

After a silence, she went on:—

"You should have seen Betsy this morning, how prettily she made the bed, though she could scarce reach up to the bolster. Did you happen to look how she set about it?"

"No. I have been thinking, Mary, how completely you and I are changed. It is not so long since you used to check me for talking; or rather, I used to check myself, seeing that you were no talker. You used to say that people were not all made talkers alike; and you went up and down, and about the house, just like a dumb person, and sometimes looking as dull too. And now—I say, Mary, when I don't answer you, you must not always think that I am thankless. And I know what it must cost you to be for ever saying something cheerful and pleasant, when Chatham is in gaol, and the cupboard is so often empty, and I such a poor, good-for-nothing—No; no! Don't try to persuade me. I tell you I can't bear myself, and I don't ask you or any body to bear with me. Mercy! now here's my husband! and I in this condition."

"Heyday! it is time I was coming home, I see," cried Kay good humouredly, as he entered. "You too, Mary! Well, dear, you have cause, so don't turn away; I have only wondered to see none of this before; but I have something for you both. Something we have not had this many a-day. Something better than ever was in this or any other physic bottle," he continued, shaking the dispensary phial and telling the news.

Mary had no sooner made herself mistress of it than she disappeared, probably to devise the means of getting the intelligence conveyed to her lover. As soon as she was gone, Kay drew a chair beside his wife, saying,—

"Now we are alone, Margaret, and times are like to change, so as to give one the heart to speak, I have something to say to you."

"O, no, don't," cried she, starting up. "I know what you are going to say."

"You do not;" and he obliged her to sit down. "Don't tremble so, for I am not going to find fault with you in any way."

"Then you ought. I am a poor, lost—"

"Not lost, Margaret. We have all near lost ourselves in such times as we have had of late; except indeed Mary, who will never lose herself, it is my opinion. It has come across me, Margaret, that I may have hurt you sometimes, without thinking, with light talk when you had not spirits for it, (not that I had real spirits, for that matter,) and with saying silly things to Mrs. Skipper, and the like. Ah! I see you felt it so; and it is no wonder you should. But you may take my word for it, I think nothing of Mrs. Skipper, nor ever did. Only, one is driven on, one does not know how, to behave foolishly when one is near desperate at heart."

"And that's my fault."

"Not altogether. No! not by any means. There were many things besides—besides one—to make me unwilling to look back to the time when we used to walk in Fergusson's oak copse, and say—Nay, Margaret, if you cannot hold up your head in thinking of that time, where should you rest it but upon your husband's shoulder, as you did then? How can you turn away so, as if I was your enemy? Well, I turned away too from the thought of those days, knowing, all the while, that it was a bad sign to turn away."

"And to think of all that has happened since! Of all these children, and of my being such a bad mother—"

"It was the children I most wanted to speak about, especially

John. But come, now, Margaret, open your mind to me, and don't be afraid. It was want and downright weakness that first led you into it. Was not it?"

"O, it began long and long ago. When I was weakly as a girl, they used to give me things, and that was the beginning of it all.[1] Then when I grew weakly again, it seemed to come most natural, especially because it was cheaper than bread, and the children wanted all we could get of that."

"So, often when you have pretended to have no appetite, it was for the children's sake and mine. Well, I half thought so all the time."

"No, not often; only at the beginning. Afterwards it was true that I could not eat,—no, not if the king's dinner had been before me. I did try for long to get the better of the habit, and three times I thought I had; but a sinking came, and I could not bear it. That was twice; and the third time, it was your joking sharply about—but that was no reason. I don't mean to say it was. You don't know what the support is for the time, John, whatever comes after it. It raises one; and yet I remember times—many times—when I knew I could not speak sensibly if you spoke to me, and yet I prayed and prayed that I might die before the morning light."

"Does that mean that you were less afraid of God than of me?"

"No, I did not think of being afraid, exactly; but I wanted to be out of your way and the children's; and, for my own part, I should have been very glad to be at rest."

After a long pause, John resumed.

"You said you tried three times to leave it off. Do you think you could try again?"

"No, John, I do not think I could."

"Not for my sake,—as you say I drove you into it last time? Not for your own sake? for nobody knows but ourselves, I dare say. I have never breathed it, and Mary—"

"O, Mary has vexed me many a time,—taking such pains, and having so many reasons and excuses with the neighbours. Why,—do you suppose I never met anybody? And then there was the night that Mrs. Skipper, of all people in the world, gave me her arm. I was forced to take it, but—"

"Mrs. Skipper! Really! She never breathed a word. Depend upon it, she never told any body."

---

1 That is, childhood dosing with Godfrey's Cordial, a solution of laudanum designed especially for children.

"If she did not, I am sure I have told plenty of people myself: so don't say any more about it, John."

"I was just going to say, that now is the time for trying. We are going to have better living, I hope, which is what you will want; and I am sure Mary and I do not care what there is for us, if we could see you recover. If you will only give us the word, we will watch and watch, night and day; and you shall have all manner of help, and comfort, and no more thoughts of cruel joking, or of Mrs. Skipper. O, Margaret, try!"

"I am almost sure I cannot," muttered the poor woman; "but I will just try."

"Ah! do, and I should not wonder.—You talk of being at rest; and it may be a rest in this very room,—on that very bed, such as you little thought of when you wished your wish."

Margaret shook her head. "If I go on, I die; if I leave off, I die; it is all one."

"No, Margaret, it is not all one; for I have one more thing to say,—and the chief thing. The children do not fully understand yet, though I have seen John wonder-struck lately, and his aunt could not put him off."

"Why should she?"

"Just because neither she nor I choose that the children should grow used to see drunkenness before their eyes indifferently. I speak plain, because it is about those who cannot speak for themselves. Do you know now what I mean to say?"

"Go on."

"I mean to say, (and to do it too,) that as often as I see you not yourself, I shall tell the children, not that their mother is ill, or low-spirited, or any thing else,—but what is really the case. Now, Margaret, how will you bear this? Remember I shall really do it, from this day."

Margaret made no answer.

"You know I cannot let our children's morals get corrupted at home, and them ruined for here and hereafter by such a habit as this. I cannot, Margaret."

"No; you cannot."

"I am sure they have enough against them, at the best,—what with poverty, (temptation and no proper instruction,) and sometimes idleness, and sometimes over-work. They have enough before them at the best."

"They have."

"And who have they to look to but you and me? except Mary,

and she would not set against your example. It goes against my heart more than you know to say an unkind word to you, and always did, when I seemed cruel. But I can say what you will think cruel, and I must, unless you take my warning."

"You do not know—"

"Yes, I know, down to the bottom of my soul, what the misery was, and how many, many excuses there are for you. But the children do not know this, and there is no making them understand, and I must think of them first. If it was only myself, I think I could sit up with you all night, and shield you all day, and even indulge you with the very thing itself, when I saw you sinking for want of it. But, as it is, whatever I may do when the children are out of the way, I will do as I said when they are by."

"Do. I was not going to excuse myself when you stopped me just now,—but only to say you do not know how glad I should be to stop, if I could, though I shall never recover my head again now. It will go on roaring like the sea as long as ever I live."

"No, no. With good food, you know—"

"I shall never relish food more; but I will try; and do you do as you said. I am not sure how I shall mind it in such a case; I never can tell any thing beforehand now. But you know your part; and if I fall back, you must all mind me as little as you can."

"Only, don't think me less tender to you, Margaret."

"No: O, no; you have given me warning, you know."

"Your poor head! how it beats! You had better let me carry you to bed; you are not fit to sit up. Better let me lay you on the bed."

"Well, I can't go walking. This is the sinking,—now."

"And enough there has been to sink you. There! I'll stay beside you. Where's your apron to hang up before your eyes? Now, don't think of any thing but sleep."

"O, but then I dream."

"Well! I shall be here to wake you, in case of your starting. Only just give me the key of the cupboard, and do not ask Mary for it any more when I am away."

Chapter VI: Too Late

On a bright morning of the following May, the stroke of the wood-cutter's axe had resounded through Fergusson's woods from day-break till the sun was high. More than one fine young tree which had shaken off the gathered dews at the first greeting of the morning light, now lay prostrate, no more to be refreshed by midnight dews, no more to uprear its leafy top in the early sunshine. Such seemed to meet with little pity in their fall. The very men whose hands had felled them sat down on their horizontal trunks, and kicked the bark with their clownish heels, while they munched their bread and cheese. Children dropped into the green recess from all quarters, to pluck oak boughs and leaves from the fallen stem, wherewith to ornament their hats, and lead a procession to the neighbouring Whit Monday fair.[1] These trees should have flourished twenty, fifty, seventy years longer, if the affairs of their owner had gone on in a steady and natural course. When Mr. Fergusson had walked round his plantations to see these oaks put into the ground, his thoughts had glanced forward to the time when his descendants might give a last mournful look at the doomed trees, towering stately before their fall; and now he was compelled himself to sentence them to the axe before they had attained nearly the fullness of their massive growth. Frequent and sudden losses during the last few months, and the prospect of more had obliged Mr. Fergusson to collect all his resources, or surrender some of his domestic plans. He must sacrifice either a portion of his woods or the completion of the new buildings at the Abbey. His oaks must be felled, or his sons give up some of the advantages of education that he had promised them. It was found impossible to collect two-thirds of the rent due to him; and the condition of his farms foretold too plainly that further deficiencies would ensue. Poppies flourished more luxuriantly than ever this season among the thin-springing corn in Anderson's new fields. The sheep had returned to their old haunts, and could not be kept out by the untended walls and ricketty gates which reminded the passenger of the field of the slothful. When Mr. Fergusson was disposed to stop in his walks for purposes of meditation, he could hardly choose his station better than within sight of one of Anderson's enclosures when any rapacious sheep happened to covet what was within. It was a sight of monotony to behold one sheep after another follow the adventurous one, each in turn placing its fore-feet on the breach in the fence, bringing up its hind legs after it, looking around for an instant from the summit, and then making the plunge into the dry ditch, tufted with locks of wool. The process might have been more composing if the field had been another man's property,

---

1   In the Christian tradition, Whit Sunday is Pentecost, the seventh Sunday after Easter. Whit Monday fair drew the agricultural community together for exchanges of goods and celebrations.

or if the flock had been making its way out instead of in; but the recollection of the scene of transit served to send the landowner to sleep more than once, when occurring at the end of the train of anxious thoughts which had kept him awake. There was little sleepiness, however, in the tone with which he called his tenant to account for letting his property thus go to destruction. Mr. Fergusson was as near losing his temper as he ever was, when he pointed out to Anderson a ditch here that was choked up in one part and overflowing in another; a gate, whose stuffing of briars was proved a mockery by the meddling children who had unhooked it from its lower hinge, and the groping swine which enlarged the gap thus made; and the cattle-sheds, roofless and grass-grown, which should be either pulled down or repaired. Andersons' tone was also high, as he declared that a half-ruined man could not keep his farm in as thrifty a manner as a prosperous one; and that if, as soon as he began to improve the property he held, his funds melted away beneath the fluctuations of the corn-market, it was unreasonable to expect him to spend his capital in repairs till he should see whether government would or would not do something to protect agriculture from the consequences of vicissitude. Fergusson thought it useless to wait, on this ground. Government had been protecting agriculture for some hundreds of years, and yet fluctuations there had always been, and fluctuations there would always be, to judge by all experience. Anderson was not for this the less resolved to let his roofless cow-sheds and crumbling fences stand,—to be rebuilt if government should extend its protecting care,—to stand as monuments, if agriculture should be neglected.

Monuments of what?—Anderson was a proud man, building for his own and his family's honour and glory when he was in prosperity, and finding something to be proud of in adversity;—Anderson would therefore have replied—'monuments of injury.' Injury from an act of government by which the starving were rescued from destitution, and the oppressed allowed one more chance of the redemption of their fortunes. That act which all other classes received as one of tardy justice,—of absolute necessity,—Anderson complained of as an act of injury to himself, so deep that he left certain wrecks of his property to serve as tokens to a future race of the wrongs he had suffered.

And the fortunes of Anderson *were* injured,—and injured by the acts of government, though not, as his wisest friends thought, so much by the permission of importation as by the preceding restrictions. They rightly called his wrecks and ruins monuments of his ill-luck in speculation, as their poorer neighbours called them monuments of the injustice done to the productive classes by encouraging or compelling the disadvantageous investment of capital. Both parties were right: but Anderson was induced to speculate by acts of protection which failed in the proof; and the disadvantageous application of capital, originating in the same acts, issued in disaster to all parties. If the interests of Anderson were placed in apparent or real temporary opposition to those of his neighbours, the blame rested, not with him, but with the legislation which had interfered to derange the natural harmonies of social interests; which had impaired the loyalty and embittered the spirits of artizans, curtailed the usefulness and enjoyments of manufacturers, puffed up the farmer with the pride, first of ostentation and then of injury, and compelled the landowner to lay low his young woods before they had attained half their growth.

There was but little prospect of improvement in Anderson's affairs for a long time to come. There had been enormous importations of corn during the winter,—importations which in the end proved as ruinous to the corn-dealer as to the farmer at home. The bargain with foreign corn-growers having been made in a panic was agreed upon at a panic price. The foreigners had naturally laid heavy duties on corn, both because it was known how much the English wanted food, and because what they bought was not a surplus regularly grown for sale, but a part of the stock of the countries they bought of. In the midst of a panic, and in entire uncertainty how long the ports might be open, the corn importers could not possibly calculate how much would be wanted, any more than the people ascertain how much was brought in. While all were thus in the dark, prices fell in the home market, till wheat which sold at all sold at 50s. per quarter, and much was left which was not even bid for. The importer's foreign debts must, however, be paid. He was unwilling to warehouse his wheat, because there was promise of a fine home harvest for this year, and the perishable nature of his commodity rendered it unwise for him to store it against some future contingency. The only thing for him to do, therefore, was to obtain a drawback on what he had imported, and to export it at a lower price than he had paid for it, pronouncing himself and every body else a fool that had entered upon so ruinous a branch of commerce.

This resource of exportations would fail in Anderson's case, if his harvest should prove never so flourishing. The high average price at home, caused by dependence on home growth, disables the home producer for competition in a foreign market, even if the uncertainty of a sale attending so irregular a commerce did not deter him from the attempt. A capricious demand abroad is the necessary consequence of alternate monopoly and relaxation at home; and when to this uncertainty is added the impediment of a higher average price, and the disadvantage of the known desire of the seller to sell, so small a chance of remuneration is left, that Anderson could not look with any confidence to this mode of disposing of the superabundance of his next crop. No great increase of demand at home was to be expected in the course of one season, as people cannot eat much more bread immediately because there happens to be a good supply, however certain an ultimate increase of demand may be, as the consequence of a single fruitful year. All that Anderson could look forward to, therefore, was waiting in hope of future temporary high prices, unless, indeed, all parties should grow so wise as to agree upon a freedom of trade which should secure permanent good profits to the farmers. Meantime, as capital invested in agricultural improvements is much less easily withdrawn and converted to other purposes than capital applied in manufactures, it was but too probable that the profits of Anderson's prosperous years were buried in useless drains and fences, and in stony soils, while he was burdened with an increased rent and a family now accustomed to a lavish expenditure. It was to be feared that more of Fergusson's young oaks must be brought low to supply the deficiencies of the tenant's half-yearly payments to his landlord.

The woodmen who sat on the fallen trunks thought little, while enjoying their meal and their joke, of all that was included in the fact of these trees having fallen.

Some talked of the work done and to be done this day. Others had thoughts at liberty for the fair to which so many persons within view were hastening; and yet others had eyes wherewith to look beyond the green slope where they were sitting, and to mark signs of the times in whatever they saw;—the whirling mill, with one or two additional powdered persons on the steps, or appearing at the windows;—the multiplication of the smokes of Sheffield;—the laden lighters below Kirkland's granaries;—Anderson's fields, waving green before the breeze;—sheep and cows grazing where there was to have been corn;—and, above all, Chatham taking his way to the accustomed quarry, in a very unaccustomed manner.

"Do look at that fellow, walking as if he was mazed," said Jack to Hal. "He is not like one bound for the fair. He is on his way to work, seemingly; but what a lagging step for one going to his work!"

"Don't you see 'tis Chatham?"

"No more like Chatham than you. And yet it is,—yes,—that it is! You may know by the way his arm is stuck in his side. But that is not the gait Chatham used to have."

"No, because he never took such a queer walk before. Don't you know he has been between four walls all these many months, and has but just got out? I have heard a man say that knew well, that the blue sky is a new sky when you have been shut out from it for a long while: and the grass seems really alive; and as for such boughs as this that dance in the wind, you could almost think they were going to speak to you."

"Chatham seems to be fancying some such thing, he pays so little heed. If he is not going to pass without seeing us!—without once looking up into the wood! His thoughts are all in the middle of the vale. I'll step down, and have a chat with him."

Before the last mouthful was stuffed into the mouth of the speaker, however, in preparation for descending to the road, livelier sounds than any that it was in his power to make, roused Chatham from his reverie. A train of little boys and girls, who had disappeared a few minutes before, issued from the neighbouring sawpit, and from behind the piles of planks which lay around, their hats and bonnets stuck round with oak-leaves, and their procession of boughs arranged in boy and girl style. As each one scrambled out of the pit, there was a shout; as they ranged themselves, there was more shouting; and as they marched down the green slope on their way to the fair, there was the most shouting of all.

"I don't think Chatham seems to relish his walk so much as you thought for," said Jack to Hal. "He looks mighty melancholy."

"What! laughing at the brats. And look! he is nodding to one and another."

"Melancholy enough, for all that. For such a fine-made man, he is a hollow-faced, poor-looking fellow."

"Just now. When he has been three months at his work, you will see the difference."

"It is a lucky thing for him to have stepped into his work so naturally, as if he had only left it just from Saturday night till Monday morning. That is more than happens to many men who have been in prison. There was Joe Wilson never got the better of it, though he was only in a month. Not a stroke more of work did he get."

"Because his was for stealing, and nobody could trust him afterwards. In Chatham's case, no one thinks he did or meant any harm, considering what the pressure of the times was. And if the masters believed that he had really broken the law, they would have had no objection to take him on again, in consideration of the cause, which they view as in some measure their own, against the farmers and landlords. Chatham is pretty sure of work at all times; but if he had been the worst workman in all Yorkshire, he would have had plenty of masters courting him for having been punished for helping to bring in corn. It pleases him best, however, to be going back to his old perch, so as to get the matter dropped as soon as possible."

"Ay, ay, for more reasons than one."

"Not only for the sake of Mary Kay, but because the mischief that he wanted to set right is over. It cannot be said now that our people hereabouts want bread; and so the sooner all ill-will is forgotten, the better. Hoy, oy! how does your dame get you such a wedge of cold meat as that? She must be a thriftier body than mine."

"No thrift in the world served to get me cold meat six months ago; but times have changed since; and, as my wife says, it is mortal hard work I have to do here."

"Mortal hard work,—swinging your heels, and looking at people going to the fair! Mine is as toilsome as yours, neighbour; and yet I have only a lump of hard cheese with my bread, while droves and droves of bullocks and sheep are passing within sight to the fair, making one think of mottled beef and juicy mutton. I wonder when the day will come for the working man to have his fill of meat, like him that does not work."

"Chatham will tell you the very day;—whenever this vale, and all our other vales, are portioned out for the purposes they are most fit for,—the choice parts for corn, and the meadows for pastures, and the heights for sheep-walks, and so on; instead of our insisting on growing wheat at all costs, and so preventing our having as much meat and cheese and butter and milk as we should like. If we could get our corn where we please, we should soon find other food growing more plentiful."

"And a few things besides food. I suppose the Leeds[1] men would take off all the wool we could grow?"

"Yes; and without bating [excluding] an ounce of what they get already from abroad; for where we get corn, there we must carry cloth, among other things."

"And then we must get more houses run up for our new weavers. By the way, if our landlords let more land to be built upon, that

---

1   Leeds is a manufacturing city in West Yorkshire.

would fully make up for any difference from the fields being turned back into sheep-walks."

"And with a much better chance of the rents being paid regularly for ten years together;—which is no small consideration to such men as Fergusson just now. There's Chatham walking away without speaking to one of us. Call him; your voice is loudest. Well done! You make the very cows turn and low at us. He won't come. How he points towards his work, as much as to tell us we ought to be going to ours! All in good time, friend Chatham. We have not been shut up for months, with our hands before us, like you."

"Nor yet been much busier than he, for that matter. 'Tis a pity this fair did not fall on our idle time. There go the folks in a train, while we are dawdling here—"

"Then don't let us dawdle. Off with you, children! We are going to lop the branches, and you may chance to get an ugly cut if you don't keep clear of the hatchet. Come, neighbour."

"In a minute, neighbour. Bless us! look at that monkey, down in the road! How the creature dances, like any Christian! And the music sounds prettily, does not it? I am just like a child for wanting to be off to the fair. Who is that rogue of a boy plaguing the beast? I think it is John Kay."

"Not it. John is in your predicament,—can't go to the fair till night. It does seem hard to keep so young a lad sweating among those furnaces all the week, and on a holyday especially; but he is proud of being on full work, like a man, and left with the few in charge of the furnaces; and they say his parents have comfort of him, in respect of his carrying home his wages."

"That is very well; for they want all they can get, while that poor woman goes on pining as she does. She has got very feeble lately."

"And well she may, taking nothing stronger than tea, after having lived so differently. She made the change suddenly too. 'Tis not six weeks since I saw her as bad as she ever was,—trying to reach home."

"Ay; after striving and striving all the winter to get the better of it, poor soul! But that falling back seemed to be the finishing of her. She has never held up her head since, nor ever will, in my opinion, though she has more reason to hold up her head than for these five years past; as they say her family are for ever trying to make her think."

"Poor Kay finds full work and cheap food come too late for him; for whatever fails to do his wife good brings little comfort to him. For all he used to do in the way of light words and silly fun, he has made a good husband; and no man can be more down-hearted than he is to see his wife in this way. No: that is not his boy John below. He would not let him be abroad plaguing monkeys when he may be called for any minute to see his mother die.—Bravo, boy, whoever you be! Little John Kay could not have done the thing more cleverly."

"There runs the monkey! Look ye! Through the gap! over the slope in no time! He will be up in the tree before they can catch him. Did you ever see man in such a passion as his master? I don't wonder, having got within a mile of the fair, and full late too."

"Ah! but you missed seeing how the lad slipped the chain the very moment the man beat the poor animal over the nose. Trust the beast for running away at the first hint! A fine time it will take to get him back again!"

"Look at his red jacket, showing so unnatural on the tree top! Down he comes again. No, not he! it is only to get farther out on the branch."

"That is a marked tree that he is upon. Suppose we cut it down next. It joins no other, and monkey must come down with it or without it."

The harassed owner of the monkey received this proposal as a very bright thought. The monkey seemed to be of the same opinion, though not so fully approving of the idea. He chattered, screamed, whisked the skirts of his red coat, and clapped his paws together as he saw the workmen gathering round the tree with shouts, leaving neglected nice bits of food which monkey would fain have had the benefit of, and shaking their tools at him in token of what he had shortly to expect.

At the first shock, monkey became perfectly quiet, squatting with his fore paws clapped together, and looking down, like an amateur observer, on the progress of the work. In proportion as there was any movement below, he descended a little way, to look into the matter more closely, and then returned to his place on the fork of the branch. By the time it began to totter, a new ecstacy seemed to seize the beast. Again he mounted to the topmost bough that was strong enough to bear his weight; and when there, he again jabbered and screamed. Some thought this was terror at his approaching downfall, and others took it for delight at seeing the circle divide to leave room for the tree to fall. The master, however, believed that he saw some object which excited him on the road, which was hidden by the trees from less exalted spectators.

The master was right. There was a crowd gathering at a short distance, as was shortly made known by the busy hum which came upon the ears of those who were standing among the trees on the slope. From end to end of England was such a tumult of many voices heard when the news arrived which caused the present assemblage. The agricultural districts took it very quietly, to be sure; but the manufacturing towns and villages were all in a ferment throughout the island. Meetings were convened at the moment of the arrival of the newspapers; and while manufacturers assembled in town halls, or addressed the people from the balconies of inn-windows, workmen of all classes met on the green, in the moor, about the public house, or wherever they could most numerously collect, for the purpose of declaring their opinions to the government.

The intelligence which caused all this bustle related to what the House of Commons had been doing and planning about the corn-laws—a House of Commons which had the year before barely managed to retain the confidence of the manufacturing classes by throwing out the suggestion of a Committee of its own, that the prices to which corn must arrive at home before importation was permitted should be very much raised. A proposal like this, made at a time when the home price was at least 112s. per quarter, showed so determined an intention on the part of the proposers to render their country wholly self-dependent in the article of food, (i.e. to limit the population and wealth of the country to a certain bound, which should be agreeable to the landowners,) that the only chance the House of Commons had of preserving the allegiance of the bulk of the people was by rejecting the proposal; and the proposal had been accordingly rejected. The watchfulness of the people had not, however, been lulled. Their subsequent brief enjoyment of cheap food had strengthened their vigilance over the operations of the Commons' House; and they were the more intent as they knew that the landowners were suffering cruelly from the reduction of their rents and the deterioration of their estates; and that these landlords would probably attribute their losses to the late admission of foreign corn, rather than to the true cause,—the previous system of restriction. The event proved such vigilance to be very needful. The late fall of prices had disclosed an appalling prospect of the owners of land. They found that their extraordinary methods of legislation had exposed their country to a much more extensive dependence on foreign supplies than they had attempted to obviate, and that they had been working hard to reduce their own rents, and hurt their own estates, by the very means they had taken to enrich themselves. During such a remarkably fruitful season as the present (the natural follower of several bad seasons) the supply would be so plentiful as to cause the poorer soils to be thrown back into pasturage, the demand meantime increasing (as it had been for some time increasing) up to the maximum supply; so that on the first occurrence of a merely average season, the nation would be more dependent on a foreign supply than it had ever been before. Under this panic, the House voted a series of resolutions, declaring it expedient to let exportation alone, and to impose very high duties on importation. The news of the passing of these resolutions, and of the preparation of two bills founded upon them, was that which stirred up all England to remonstrance, and occasioned the Yorkshire graziers to leave their droves [herd] in the fair, and the corn-dealers to quit their resort in the market, to hear what would be said by the manufacturers who came forth from their desks, the artificers who poured in from the enjoyment of their holyday, and the country labourers who dropped down from among the hills, or converged to the point of meeting from the wide-spreading fields.

The day being warm and the road dusty, it was natural that the sounds of the wood-cutters' labour should suggest to the gathering crowd the idea of meeting on the grass, in the outskirts of Fergusson's wood. Mr. Fergusson and his sons were found in the fair, and they gave permission, and promised to come presently and hear what was going on. Chatham was met on the road, just about to turn up towards the quarry; but he was easily persuaded to go back and help; and the whole party was approaching when Monkey offered them his uncouth welcome from the top of the tree.

This tree was left slanting to its fall when the people began to pour in from the road, and to possess themselves of the trunks which lay about, in order to pile them into a sort of hustings.[1] The organ-man could find no one to assist him in catching his monkey, in case the rogue should vouchsafe to descend from his high place. Nobody could attend to the monkey now; and if he chose to run off from one side of the tree while his master was at the other, and lead the chase as far as Sheffield, he might, for any thing the woodmen seemed to care. Flinging down their tools, or resting them against their shoulders, they threw themselves along on the carpet of wild anemones which stretched beneath the trees; while the more restless mechanics flitted about among the stems, looking, with their smut-

---

1 A platform, often impromptu and temporary, from which political speeches or announcements are made.

ted faces and leathern aprons, very unnatural inhabitants of such a place. Long after Chatham and others began to enlarge upon the matter which had brought them together, the frowning brows and eager gesticulations of these men, as they talked low with one another, showed that they had their own thoughts, and were not met merely to have notions put into their heads.

"Is it possible to mistake what these men are thinking and feeling?" asked Chatham of Mr. Fergusson. "If the House of Commons could for once take their sitting here, with the Speaker on yon bit of grey rock, and the members on these trunks or on the flowery ground, like the Indians when they hold a council, they would legislate for these listeners after another fashion than they now do."

"Why so? I see, as well as you, that these men are thinking and feeling strongly; but are they thinking that which should change the policy of a nation?"

"That which will change the policy of a nation, though not so soon as if the National Council could for once come here to legislate. Friends!" he said to some near him, whose sudden silence called the attention of others beyond them,—"I am telling this gentleman that I believe there is one thought in the minds of us all, though that thought might be spoken in many ways. One might say, that he felt himself injured by the high price of bread last year, and another by the falling off of work—one might point to the grave of his spirit-broken brother, and another hold up before us his pining child—one might be angry with our masters for altering our wages, so that we never know what to depend upon, and another may be grieved that Anderson should have sharpened his speech, and that Mr. Fergusson should come among us with so grave a countenance as this; but there is one plain thought at the bottom of all this,—that the prime necessary of life is the last thing that should be taxed. I should not wonder if Mr. Fergusson himself agrees with us there."

"It depends upon what the object of the tax is," replied Mr. Fergusson. "If the corn-tax be laid on to swell the revenue of the state, I grant that it is the very worst that could be imposed; because, while it presses so heavily on all as to cramp immeasurably the resources of the nation, it presses most on those who have little but the prime necessary of life, and the harder in proportion as they possess little else."

"In what case will you then justify a corn-tax?"

"When it is laid on to balance an excess of taxes laid on the agriculturists over those laid on other classes."

A confusion of voices here arose, in cries of—

"We will take them on ourselves!"

"You and yours shall live duty-free, if you give us corn free."

"We pay your taxes many times over already."

"I will work one day in the week for you for nothing but a free corn trade."

"I will give you a share of my wages every Saturday night, and my vote, if you'll go up to Parliament, and speak our minds there."

And many a black hand was held out to see if Mr. Fergusson would say "Done." He did not quite say this, but he went on,—

"I am sure I can have no objection to a change in our system; for I have suffered as well as you."

"Ay, and you would make it up by having corn dearer than ever," cried one of the discontented.

"No, I would not, because I am convinced that this would only bring on a repetition of the same evils some time hence, and in an aggravated form. I dread, as much as you can do, further fluctuations of this kind, which have injured us all in turn. More bad seasons followed by plenty, with a fickle legislation, and those of you who have pined will die; the masters who have ceased to be rich will be ruined; the farmers who have now buried some of their capital will find that they have got back a part only to lose the whole; and, as for me and mine, I should expect the gates that are now unhinged to be broken up for fuel, and the stones of my crumbling fences to be used for knocking me off my horse. If in those days I should go abroad, it would be to rescue my life from your rage, and not, as now, to economise the income which I can no longer spend among you. No, no; we must have no more mismanagement like that which has well nigh ruined us all."

"What does he mean? Where is he going? Won't he live at the Abbey any more?" were the questions which went round, and caught Mr. Fergusson's ear.

"I told you," he said, "that we had all suffered in turn, though I am far from pretending that we have suffered equally. I assure you that I spend many an anxious day, and many a sleepless night, in planning how I may fulfil all my engagements as a member of society, and keep my promises to my children. These engagements were made when I was prosperous; and now I am no longer prosperous. My steward comes to me every quarter-day with a smaller handful of receipts, and a longer bill of arrears; and wherever I turn, I see with my own eyes, and find many comforters to tell me, that my property is wasting for want of care, and that I must sustain great losses hereafter for want of a small expenditure which cannot be afforded now. If I or my tenants could just spare a hundred pounds here, and fifty there, and two hundred somewhere else, it would save me a thousand or two that will have to be spent at last. But it cannot be done. My sons are entering upon a new stage of a very expensive but necessary education; and though my daughters have given up their usual journey to London, I have no hundreds to spare. My tenants cannot scrape their rent together, and it is folly to ask them for their fifties."

"The papers say you have lowered your rents."

"It is true that I have; and I am sorry the papers take upon themselves to praise me for it as an act of generosity. You all know now that I cannot get my full rents, so that I do not in fact give up any thing that I might have; and I consider it no more than justice to reduce the claims which I made when the farmers were in very different circumstances from those in which they are at present placed. I have no objection to the newspapers stating the fact, because it may lead others to follow my example, and may afford a useful lesson to all; but I do object to the act being lauded as one of generosity, as much as I should to the House of Commons being praised for giving up the bills now in question, in case the whole nation should prove to be of your mind about them."

"Very fair! very good! Spoken like one of the people!"

"I am one of the people,—taxed as one of the people, I assure you," continued Mr. Fergusson. "You offer,—very sincerely, I have no doubt,—to take the taxes of the landowners upon yourselves, in return for a free trade in corn. But you know perfectly well that such an arrangement cannot be made, even if we chose to accept your kind offer."

"Why not? What prevents, if we are all of a mind?"

Chatham thought that it would take so long to bring all people into one mind on the point that it would be a quicker and probably equally good method to allow such a duty on imported corn as would cover the landlords' peculiar liabilities. A small duty,—at the most 5s. or 6s. per quarter,—would be found sufficient, he believed, at the beginning; and such a duty as this would not materially impede importation. Under such a system of regular supply, pauperism would decrease, or ought to decrease, year by year; this would lessen the burdens of the agriculturalist, and open the way for a further reduction of the duty, which should expire when that equalization of taxation should take place which must arrive as nations grow wiser.

"Without committing myself as to the amount of duty," replied

Mr. Fergusson, "I may say that I should not object to some such plan as Chatham proposes: and I would insist that the duty should, above all things, be fixed. If a duty is imposed on the basis of the distresses of the country, it may be right enough that it should be graduated, the duty lessening as prices rise: but in the case of such a duty as Chatham advocates,—a mere set-off against our excess of taxation,—it should be so far fixed as that every one might know beforehand how it would operate, and all classes be able to make their calculations."

"Why, yes," said Chatham. "If any corn-tax is, generally speaking, bad, none can be so bad as one that makes twice as much uncertainty as there is occasion for. To impose a duty on the basis, as you say, sir, of the distresses of the country, seems an odd way of raising money for the state; and to make such a duty a gambling matter seems to me more odd still. In the case of such a graduated duty as you speak of, falling as home prices rise, the corn-dealer's business becomes an affair of gambling speculation. He sends for corn when wheat is at one price, and brings it in when wheat is at another. If the price has fallen, he has so much more duty to pay that the speculation may ruin him. If the price has risen, he may make enormous profits that he did not expect. I may say this much for the corn-dealer, as Kirkland is not here to speak for himself, that he had much rather pay a constant duty which would leave him no uncertainties to manage but the supplies of corn at home and abroad, than take the chance of enormous occasional profits at the risk of ruinous occasional loss."

"Ay, Chatham: there you come to a very important part of the question,—the uncertainty of supply. If you can answer for our having a regular and unfailing supply of food from abroad, when we have too little for our people at home, you can answer for more than the House of Commons can; for they adopt as their principle the safety of lessening our dependence on foreign countries for food."

"When they can answer for our having a regular and constantly increasing supply at home," replied Chatham, "I may perhaps yield the question to them. When you find any member of their committee who will tell me, at any seed-time, what will be the produce of an average sowing, I will consent to his making the nation depend on that produce. When you can bring me proof that the rich harvests of one district are not of use in repairing the deficiencies of a less favoured district, I will own it to be as safe to depend for supply on our own little island as on the collective corn districts of the globe. When you can convince me that we buy as advantageously by fits and starts as under a system of regular commerce, I will grant that regularly importing countries have not the steadiest market."

A listener observed that Kirkland had lately said, in reference to his having had to hunt up corn abroad during the scarcity, that there was a difference of ten per cent. between "Will you sell?" and "Will you buy?"

"Kirkland learned that saying from a greater man than any of us," observed Mr. Fergusson. "It was Franklin who said that true saying. But there are other uncertainties to be considered, besides the variations of the seasons. Clouds gather over men's tempers as well as over the face of the sky. Tempests of passion sweep away the fruits sown between nations in a season of promise. Springs of kindness are dried up, as well as fountains of waters. We have not considered the risks of war."

"Indeed but we have, sir," replied Chatham, "and we come to the conclusion that when we are at war with all the nations whom God has blessed with his sunshine and his rain, we shall not deserve to touch God's bounties, and it will be high time that we should be starved off God's earth. If we wanted to restrict our own trade, sir, instead of throwing it open,—if we wanted to forbid our merchants buying of more than one or two countries, we might believe that war would bring starvation; but never while our ships may touch at all ports that look out upon the seas."

"We do not grow half our own hemp," said a man with a coil of tow about his waist. "Has the British navy ever wanted for ropes? If our enemies at sea ever meant to hurt us, their readiest way would have been to stint us in cordage;[1] and, since they have not done it during all this war, it must be, I take it, because they can't."

"Certainly," replied Chatham. "In cases like these, Mr. Fergusson, our conclusions about the choice of an evil or a danger must be compounded of the greatness and of the degree of probability. Now here is, under the old restrictive system, a vast amount of certain evil, which you and the House of Commons seem to think little of, in comparison with a much greater evil which it is barely within the line of possibility to happen. Here are present labourers who have had their spirits bowed and their bodies worn by want, and who can look out from this green to the spot where their kindred are laid

---

1   Hemp (cannabis sativa) is cultivated for its tough fiber used in making rope and cloth (for sails). Tow is a rope made of hemp fiber. Cordage are lines used in the rigging of a sailing vessel.

under the sod, mown down by this sharp law like meadow flowers under the scythe. Here are present the gentle who have been made fierce, the once loyal who were made rebels,—ay, and the proudly innocent who have been disgraced by captivity—"

While Chatham stopped for breath, one and another cried out to Mr. Fergusson,

"If you think us rude in our speech to you, sir, you may lay it to the bread-tax." "Get the bread-tax taken off, and you will hear no more of the midnight drill." "Masters and men never would have quarrelled, sir, but for the bread-tax."

"From this place, you may see," Chatham went on, "not only poppies coming up instead of wheat, and stones strewed where lambs should have been browsing, but hovels with mouldering thatch where there should have been slated houses, and a waste wilderness stretching beyond where there might have been the abodes of thousands of busy, prosperous beings; and all through the pressure of restrictive law."

"And where there is not a waste, there will soon be a deserted mansion," added Mr. Fergusson. "I told you I was going away. My sons must finish their education abroad; and we all go together, that we may live within our means in a manner that we could not do at home. This is one consequence of the late fluctuations—"

"I can tell you, sir," said Oliver, showing himself from behind a knot of his own men,—"I can tell you another consequence that would have happened if the late fluctuation had not taken place. If prices had not fallen, and fallen just when they did, I must have gone abroad to live, where I might work to some purpose,—where my capital might have been employed in producing wealth, instead of being given to my workmen to buy dear food. Moreover, if prices now rise again so as to make you change your mind and stay, I must go; so it comes just to the question, which of us can best be spared?"

"If it comes to that," replied Mr. Fergusson, "It is clear that I can best be spared. Without saying anything about our respective characters and influence, it is plain that it signifies much less where I spend my revenue, than whether you invest your capital at home or abroad. If it must come to this, I am the one to go."

"And what but a bad state of the law could have brought the matter to this point?" said Chatham. "What greater curse need a nation have than a legislation which condemns either the rent-receiver or the capitalist to banishment?"

Oliver's men proceeded to agree in whispers that he was not in earnest about going abroad; that it was only said to make the landlord wonder, and put the question in a strong light. A man must suffer much and long before he would leave his own land, and the workmen that were used to his ways, and all that he had ever been accustomed to.

"True," said Oliver, overhearing their remarks; "and I have suffered much and long. It is true that banishment is the last attempt that many a man will make to improve his fortunes; but it is an attempt which must and will be made, if the fortunes of our manufacturers continue to decline. I know all that you can tell me about the hardship to the workmen who are left behind to be soon driven into the workhouse. I feel how I should grieve to turn you all off, and shut up my foundry; but it is one of the natural consequences of a legislation like that which we have lived under. If our manufactures remain unsold on account of the cost of feeding the labourers, it is certain that the manufacturers will carry their capital,—the subsistence-fund of the people,—to some cheaper land."

And how much was it supposed that the price of wheat would fall if the ports were opened? was the question proposed by the workmen, in their alarm at the idea of manufacturing capital being forced out of the country.

Six, seven, eight, or, at most, nine shillings, was the utmost fall, on the average of the last ten years, anticipated by Chatham, Oliver, and Fergusson,—a fall which, accompanied as it would be with regularity of supply, and freedom from panic and from the intolerable sense of oppression, would prove an all-important relief to the manufacturer and artisan, without doing the landlord and farmer any injury. Such a fall as this would drive out of cultivation none but the poorest soils, which ought never to have passed under the plough; there would be an end of the farmer's sufferings from vicissitude; and the small reduction of the landlords' rents would be much more than compensated by the advantages which must accrue to them from the growth of a thriving population within their borders.

Chatham observed that many might object to the estimate just given of the probable fall of price on opening the ports,—and it was indeed a matter which required large observation and close calculation; but he, for one, was not disposed to rest the question on probabilities of this nature, but rather on the dilemma,—"If the price of corn is heightened by the restrictive system, why should the nation be taxed for the sake of the landlords? if not,—why do the landlords fear a free trade in corn?"

"There is yet another consideration," observed Mr. Fergusson, "and a very important one, Chatham. You have said nothing of Ireland, while the fact is that Ireland sends us three times as much corn as she sent us ten years ago. There seems no reason why so fertile a country should not supply us with more and more till our prices fall the nine shillings per quarter we were talking, and even till we are able to export. What do you say to this?"

"That it is owing to the establishment of a free trade in corn between us and Ireland that we employ so much more than formerly of her industry, and enjoy so much more of its fruits. What has been proved so great a good in the experiment with one country, is the finest possible encouragement to extend the system to all. If you object, as I see you are ready to do, that this success with respect to Ireland renders a further emancipation of the trade unnecessary, I answer, that the corn-laws are by the same rule unnecessary,—an unnecessary mockery and irritation of the people. If they are not yet unnecessary because Ireland does not yet fully supply us,—in exact proportion as they are not unnecessary, they are hurtful. From this dilemma, Mr. Fergusson, you cannot escape, and you had best help us to press it upon the House of Commons. If you will join us, sir, in drawing up our address to Parliament on the principles we have been arguing about for this hour past, I rather think we ourselves may find, and may help to show the House, that landowners and their neighbours have the same interests, and are willing to be all happy together, if the legislature will let them. Whenever we see a wealthy and wise landowner taking up the question on its broad principles, and addressing the legislature, whether from his seat in the Lords or by petition to the Commons, as a citizen rather than as one of a protected class, I shall feel a joyful confidence that these broad principles will soon be recognized and acted upon by the loftiest members of the state."

"It is time," replied a voice from below, "for they have long been forced upon the lowliest."

"This is one of the deep things that is better understood by many an one that has never learned his letters than by some who are boasted of for their scholarship," observed another. "Wakeful nights and days of hardship drive some truths deep and firm into the minds of the veriest fool, which the wise man, in his luxury, finds it difficult to learn."

"You say truly enough that it is time," said a third, with sternness in his look and tone. "The charity comes too late which sticks bread between the teeth of a famished man; and the justice we seek will be a mockery if it does not come in time to prevent another such season of misery as we have endured, and as they threaten us with again. Yet they talk of playing the same game over again. Come, Chatham, make haste down, and draw up what we are to say, and let us sign before the sun goes down. We have not an hour to lose."

"Not an hour to lose, as you say, neighbour, when for many it is already too late. Mend the system as fast as you will, there is many and many a home where there will never be comfort more."

Several who were present knew that Chatham must be thinking of Kay's family when he said these words. He went on,

"You might as well hope to close up the clefts of yonder ash, and to make it rich with growing grafts, struck as it was by last year's lightning, as to heal the spirit of a man whose fortunes have been blighted by the curse of partial laws, and to repair his wrongs. For him it is too late. He stands the monument of social tyranny till his last hour of decay. For him it is too late; but not yet for others. There are thousands yet in infancy,—millions yet to be born whose lot depends on what is done with the corn-laws in our day."

"Mine and that of my descendants does," observed Oliver; "though, in one sense, it is also too late for me. I have lost my place in the market abroad; and for this my work-people are suffering and will suffer. But let no chance of recovery be lost through our delay. Come, Chatham; let us be gone, and give the people the opportunity of declaring their wishes before they disperse, and fancy that, because dispersed, they have no power. Let every man raise his voice so that the legislature may understand."

All present were so eager to do this that no leisure seemed to be left for the follies which usually lurk in some corners of all popular assemblies, from the largest to the smallest. No monkey tricks were played by any but the monkey, though country clowns and many boys were present. When the animal, after being well nigh given up in despair by his irritated master, made a sudden descent on the head and shoulders of a listener, he was very quietly delivered over to his owner to receive the chastisement which was prepared for him, and which no one troubled himself to turn round to witness. All were too busy watching Chatham writing with a pencil, and on paper furnished by Mr. Fergusson, who sat beside him on his woodland seat, now agreeing, now dissenting, but in no case desiring to hinder the full execution of the object for which his neighbours were assembled.

When a short petition to the Commons' House against the imposition of further restrictions on the foreign corn-trade had been drawn up, and fully agreed to by a large majority, it was carried away with all expedition to be copied and signed while the fair was yet thronged; and the wood was found by the noonday sun nearly as quiet as when visited by the midnight moon;—as nearly so as the blackbird and the linnet would permit.

Chapter VII: The Breaking Up

Kay was indeed one of the many to whom a temporary relief from the bread-tax came too late. Five years before, no man could be found more eager in the statement of his case of hardship: five months before, he had still some hope that a perpetuation of the then ample supply of food might yet avail to restore his domestic peace. His wife might struggle through her difficulties, and be once more a mother to his children, and in aspect and mind something like the woman he married. Now, however, all hope of this was over, and Kay had had no heart to attend the meeting in the wood, or to mix with his former companions more than could not be avoided. He went straight from the foundry to the side of his wife's chair, as long as she was able to sit up, and to nurse her when she at length took to her bed. He owed her the exemplary attention she received from him; for the same poverty which had seduced her into a fatal habit had embittered his temper, and they had need of mutual forgiveness. Since the noble effort each had made,—he to warn his children against her example, and she to break away from the indulgence which had become necessary,—neither had sinned against the other. No rough word was heard from his lips, and self-denial, by Mary's help, never failed. Mrs. Kay sank slowly and very painfully. She well knew that she must sink, either way, and to this she had no objection; but often and often, in the solitude of her daily sufferings and the restlessness of her nightly dozings, she thought that every body was hard upon her; that they might have let her sink a little more rapidly, and give her what she longed for. They did not seem to feel for her as she thought they might, or they would indulge her without letting the children perceive it. Mary must know sometimes, when she saw her very low, what it must be that she wanted; but instead of taking any notice, she only began to talk about any thing that would win away her mind for a while. Then all these secret complainings were thrust away as if they were suggestions of the devil, and a throng of reproachful recollections would come,— of her husband's patience in smoothing her pillow twenty times in a night, and holding her head for hours when her startings had frightened her; and of Mary's never seeming tired, with all that was upon her, or saying a word about what she gave up for her in keeping

Chatham waiting so long. She knew that it was only on her account that they were not married yet, and she hoped she should soon be under the sod, and no hindrance to any body; meanwhile, nobody but she would perceive, so much as Mary had to say now, and so cheerfully as she spoke, that she was giving up any thing for a sister who had deserved so little from her.

Mrs. Kay expressed all this so fully and forcibly to her husband one day, that he told Mary he really believed it would make all parties happier if she would marry Chatham at once. The affair was soon settled, and every body concerned was so evidently satisfied, that very few neighbours ventured to pronounce above their breath how shocking it was to marry from a house where there must soon be a death.

Mrs. Skipper, who had throughout been profuse of neighbourly attentions, came to sit with Mrs. Kay while the party were gone to church on the Sunday morning when the marriage took place. She was far from being the most considerate and judicious of nurses; but Mrs. Kay did not seem so alive to this as her husband and Mary, and appeared to like that she should occasionally supply their place. This morning she showed herself with eyes more red and swollen than a nurse should ever exhibit. Mrs. Kay directly perceived this.

"O dear, Mrs. Skipper, what has happened to you? I am sure some misfortune has happened. Tell me! Tell us at once."

"Why, love, 'tis no misfortune of mine particularly, but every body's misfortune."

"Why, that is worse still! Nothing has come in the way of the wedding?" And she tried to start up in her bed.

"Bless you, no! Lie still. The wedding is likely to go on well enough; and in my opinion it is high time they were off to church. No, no. It is only that the Fergussons are gone."

"Gone!" cried every voice in the house.

"Yes. Just slipped away quietly on a Sunday morning, when nobody was suspecting, that they might not have their hearts half broke, I suppose—"—A loud sob stopped the good woman's utterance.

"Well, I am sure, Mrs. Skipper, it gives us all much concern," said Kay. "They are good people,—the Fergussons,—and of great consequence to all the people about them: and it will be a sad thing to see the Abbey shut up, and the grounds left to themselves. It is not the less melancholy for our having looked forward to it this long while."

"Why no, but rather the more," said Chatham, "because we know what misfortune sent them away. When the wind has torn the linnets' nest, we know that they will fly away; and the wood will miss them the more, and not the less, for the fear that they will not venture to build in the same place again."

"And 'tis six years, come Michaelmas,"[1] said Mrs. Skipper, "that they have had hot bread from me every morning, except while they were just gone to London. They have been the best customers that ever I had, and now there is no knowing—They looked very grave, every one of them that I could see, as they whisked past. I wonder whether they saw how I cried. I hope they did. I am sure I don't care who saw, for I am not ashamed of being sorry for such as they."

"I thought they would have stayed till harvest," said Mary. "Such a beautiful harvest as it will be this year. I have been telling my sister, Mrs. Skipper, what a fine promising season it is. John and I shall manage a better gleaning this year."

"Why, yes, Mrs. Kay," observed the widow, "I could not help thinking, when I saw the sun shining, and the fields waving, and the people all abroad in their best, that it is hard upon you to be lying here, so dull, when you have not seen a green field, nor a number of people, for I don't know when. Well, I must tell you all about it, instead, when they are gone. Now, Mary, what are you going in that way for, as grave as a quaker, and more so than the quaker I saw married once? I know you have a gown more fit to be married in than that. Go and put it on in a minute,—your light green one, I mean, and I will lend you my pink handkerchief. I will step for it, and bring it before you have got your gown on. And you shall have this cap,— the ribbon is pink, you see; and my other better one will do just as well for me. Come! Make haste!"

Such was not Mary's will, however; and as her brother declared it quite time to be gone, she proceeded at once to the altar in her dark-coloured gown, thus leaving a fruitful topic for Mrs. Skipper to enlarge upon to her patient, as soon as the party had closed the door behind them. Before they went out, Mary offered a smiling hint to the widow not to cry any more about the Fergussons, or any thing else, if she could help it, while they were away; and to keep her charge as cheerful, if she could, as she had been for the last few hours; hours of more ease than she had known for some time past.

On their return, they found Mrs. Skipper,—not crying,—but in great trouble,—in far too deep a trouble for tears. She was leaning

---

1 September 29 is celebrated as the feast day of the archangel Michael.

over the bed, looking aghast, when Chatham and Mary entered, arm in arm, with Kay and his two elder children following.

"Why, Mrs. Skipper, what have you been doing to my wife?" cried Kay, seeing that the sick woman's eyes were fixed, and her whole countenance quite different from what he had ever seen it before.

"Nothing, Mr. Kay; but I thought you never would have come back. She took such a strange way the minute you were gone, I had the greatest mind to call you back."

"I wish you had," said Mary, who had already thrown off her bonnet, and was chafing the cold hands that lay helpless on the bed clothes.

"Ah! she has changed much within a few minutes too. Her hand lies still now; but I had to put it down several times. She kept stretching it out as if she thought to reach something; and I supposed she was thirsty, but—"

A mournful shake of the head from Kay stopped her. He said she had often done this when she was not quite herself.

"Yes: often and often," said Mary; "and I have seen her as bad as this before. Look, she is coming about. She sees us now."

"If she be not trying to speak!" whispered Mrs. Skipper.

Mrs. Kay spoke, but she was wandering. She told Mary that next Sunday should be the day for Chatham and her to be married as she herself should be buried out of their way by that time. Then perceiving Chatham, she tried to give him some advice incoherently, and far too painfully to be ever referred to after that day by any of them, about not letting his wife come to poverty,—extreme poverty; and about distrusting her in such a case, if she were an angel from heaven.

"For God's sake stop her!" cried Kay, taking a sudden turn through the room; and Mary stopped her by a kiss, though her own tears were dropping like rain. Mrs. Kay proceeded with her self-accusations, however, as long as she could speak at all; and the awe-struck children were taken out of the room by Chatham.

"No, no!" said Mary, whispering her emphatic contradictions into the ear of the dying woman, as soon as she could command her voice. "You have done the noblest—you have gone through the hardest trial—God will not forget your struggles as you forget them yourself. Your children shall never forget them. Well, well. It was suffering,—it was hunger that did all that! Don't dwell upon that! All that was over long ago; and now the pain is over,—just over; and we know what the promises are. If *we* deserved them as well—"

"Bless you! Bless you, Mary!" cried the husband, in a broken voice.

But the painful impression of his wife's words remained as strong as ever when the restless eyes were finally closed, and a faint smile rested on the lips whence the breath had departed. John was terrified by his father's manner of fetching him into the room, and saying, as he showed him the corpse,

"You heard her say that she had been wicked. You heard her say— but never mind all that. You will not know for this many a year how noble a woman your mother was, and what she did for your sake. And if I ever hear you say a word,—if I see you give the least look against her—"

John slunk away as Mary took her brother's arm, and led him beside Chatham, while she hung up a curtain before the bed, and made Mrs. Skipper somewhat ashamed of being so much less able to exert herself than the nearer connexions of the dead. The widow presently slipped out to consult with her neighbours on the necessary arrangements, and to express the most vehement admiration for the departed, while preserving the strictest honour respecting the particulars of the closing scene.

Since that day, the curse of the bread-tax has alighted again and again on that busy vale. Again has the landowner had the painful choice of sinking from his rank at home or going abroad to preserve it. Again has the farmer found himself, now marvellously rich, and now unaccountably poor. Again has the manufacturer repined at having to surrender his resources to support the burden of factitious pauperism,—to take too low a place in the markets abroad in order that his agricultural neighbour may be upheld in too high an one at home. Again has the corn-dealer staked his all upon the chances of man's caprice, with about as much confidence as he would upon the cast of the die. Again gloom has brooded over the dwellings of the poor, and evil passions have wrought there, in proportion to the pressure of want,—the main spring of the vast machinery of moral evil by which society is harrowed and torn. And as often as a gleam of hope and present plenty has visited the cottage of a long-suffering artizan, it has been clouded by the repinings of some neighbour whose adversity has been, by ingenious methods of misrule, made coincident with his prosperity. In this busy vale, as in every valley of England inhabited by thinking men, there is one question still for ever rising through the night air, and borne on the morning breeze,—"How long?"—and on many a hill there are thinking men to take up the inquiry, and echo "HOW LONG?"

Summary of Principles illustrated in this Volume.

As exchangeable value is ultimately determined by the cost of production, and as there is an incessant tendency to an increase in the cost of producing food, (inferior soils being taken into cultivation as population increases,) there is a perpetual tendency in the exchangeable value of food to rise, however this tendency may be temporarily checked by accidents of seasons, and by improvements in agricultural arts.

As wages rise (without advantage to the labourer) in consequence of a rise in the value of food, capitalists must either sell their productions dearer than is necessary where food is cheaper, or submit to a diminution of their profits.

Under the first alternative, the capitalist is incapacitated for competition with the capitalists of countries where food is cheaper: under the second, the capital of the country tends, through perpetual diminution, to extinction.

Such is the case of a thickly-peopled country depending for food wholly on its own resources.

There are many countries in the world where these tendencies have not yet shown themselves; where there is so much fertile land, that the cost of producing food does not yet increase; and where corn superabounds, or would do so, if there was inducement to grow it.

Such inducement exists in the liberty to exchange the corn with which a thinly-peopled country may abound, for the productions in which it is deficient, and with which a populous country may abound. While, by this exchange, the first country obtains more corn in return for its other productions, and the second more of other productions in return for its corn, than could be extracted at home, both are benefited. The capital of the thickly-peopled country will perpetually grow; the thinly-peopled country will become populous; and the only necessary limit of the prosperity of all will be the limit to the fertility of the world.

But the waste of capital caused by raising corn dear and in limited quantity at home, when it might be purchased cheap and in unlimited quantity abroad, is not the only evil attending a restriction of any country to its own resources of food; a further waste of capital and infliction of hardship are occasioned by other consequences of such restriction.

As the demand for bread varies little within any one season, or few seasons, while the supply is perpetually varying, the exchangeable value of corn fluctuates more than that of any article whose return to the cost of production is more calculable.

Its necessity to existence causes a panic to arise on the smallest deficiency of supply, enhancing its price in undue proportion; and as the demand cannot materially increase on the immediate occasion of a surplus, and as corn is a perishable article, the price falls in an undue proportion.

These excessive fluctuations, alternately wasting the resources of the consumers and the producers of corn, are avoided where there is liberty to the one class to buy abroad in deficient seasons, and to the other to sell abroad in times of superabundance.

It is not enough that such purchase and sale are permitted by special legislation when occasion arises, as there can be no certainty of obtaining a sufficient supply, on reasonable terms, in answer to a capricious and urgent demand.

Permanently importing countries are thus more regularly and cheaply supplied than those which occasionally import and occasionally export; but these last are, if their corn exchanges be left free, immeasurably more prosperous than one which is placed at the mercy of man and circumstance by a system of alternate restriction and freedom.

By a regular importation of corn, the proper check is provided against capital being wasted on inferior soils; and this capital is directed towards manufactures, which bring in a larger return of food from abroad than could have been yielded by those inferior soils. Labour is at the same time directed into the most profitable channels. Any degree of restriction on this natural direction of labour and capital is ultimately injurious to every class of the community,— to landowners, farming and manufacturing capitalists, and labourers.

Labourers suffer by whatever makes the prime necessary of life dear and uncertain in its supply, and by whatever impairs the resources of their employers.

Manufacturing capitalists suffer by whatever tends needlessly to check the reciprocal growth of capital and population, to raise wages, and disable them for competition abroad.

Farming capitalists suffer by whatever exposes their fortunes to unnecessary vicissitude, and tempts them to an application of capital which can be rendered profitable only by the maintenance of a system which injures their customers.

Landowners suffer by whatever renders their revenues fluctuating, and impairs the prosperity of their tenants, and of the society at large on which the security of their property depends.

As it is the interest of all classes that the supply of food should be regular and cheap, and as regularity and cheapness are best secured by a free trade in corn, it is the interest of all classes that there should be a free trade in corn.

Appendix A: Titles and themes of the *complete* Illustrations of Political Economy

[Each of the twenty-five numbers of the *Illustrations of Political Economy* features varied settings and aims to dramatize a broad range of political economy principles. In her *Autobiography*, Martineau outlined her method of composition for this series, which began with listing the principles she wished to illustrate; this list guided her fiction writing and appeared in didactic form as the "Summary of Principles Illustrated in this Volume" at the end of each tale. She then selected the geographical location, social situation, and character types that would best illustrate her points. The titles, in order of publication, and the general themes addressed by Martineau, are as follows.]

Title	Theme
Life in the Wilds	self-sufficiency, cooperation, survival, colonialism
The Hill and the Valley	industry, commerce, agrarianism, Luddism
Brooke and Brooke Farm	gentry, peasants, the enclosure of public land
Demerara	slavery on a West Indies plantation
Ella of Garveloch	Ricardian rent theory, economic self-sufficiency
Weal and Woe in Garveloch	corporate vs. cottage industries, Malthusian theory
A Manchester Strike	strikes and trade unionism, workers and manufacturers
Cousin Marshall	poor laws, charity, the "dole," work-houses
Ireland	poverty, famine, education, emigration
Homes Abroad	emigration as a solution to poverty
For Each and For All	class, art, and basic subsistence
French Wines and Politics	supply and demand, French Revolution

The Charmed Sea	exposé of Russian atrocities against the Poles
Berkeley the Banker, Parts 1 & 2	banking and counterfeiting
Messrs. Vanderput & Snoek	fortunes and misfortunes of "bills of exchange"
The Loom and the Lugger, Parts 1 & 2	promotes international free-trade
Sowers not Reapers	Corn Laws, poverty, and working-class alcoholism
Cinnamon & Pearls	imperialist exploitation in Ceylon
A Tale of the Tyne	urges alleviation of "press-gangs"
Briery Creek	supply and demand, communal net-working
The Three Ages	evolution of Britain's political economy
The Farrers of Budge Row	children forced to pay parents' debts
The Moral of Many Fables	compilation of Summary of Principles

Appendix B: Reform Era Documents

[The period of social reform reflected in the *Illustrations of Political Economy* raised issues that sparked lively debates among "lay" reformers as well as politicians and legislators. Further, this period marks an unprecedented expansion of the periodical press and a rise in literacy levels among the working classes, who increasingly had the means and the audience for voicing their concerns themselves. Periodicals such as the *British Labourer's Protector and Factory Child's Friend* gave voice to workers, employing the poetry and prose of adults as well as children. Social philanthropists like Peter Gaskell and James Kay-Shuttleworth published persuasive pamphlets expressing their concerns with what they viewed as radical shifts in social morality among the working classes as a result of industrialization. By extension, the generalized concern with morality was closely linked with physical living conditions, which were typically so squalid that alcoholism was a common solution to chronic hopelessness. Robert Macnish, in *The Anatomy of Drunkenness*, is particularly concerned with the erosion of the social fabric created by the drunkenness of women—wives, mothers, and wet-nurses—a phenomenon Martineau sympathetically dramatizes in the character of Mrs. Kay ("Sowers not Reapers"). Although Thomas Malthus's *An Essay on the Principle of Population* predates the era reflected in Martineau's series, this seminal text deeply influenced Martineau's thinking about the problems of social reform and their relation to population, while W. Cooke Taylor's *Factories and the Factory System* exhibits the wide-spread concern with the decline in morality fostered by the "indiscriminate" mixing of the sexes in the workplace. Each of these reform era documents participated in debates that were often divided along class and gender lines, but always directed at the masses or residuum, the working poor.]

1. Thomas Malthus, "Of Poor-Laws" *An Essay on the Principle of Population* (1798). Reprinted, London: J.M. Dent (1958)

Independently of any considerations respecting a year of deficient crops, it is evident that an increase of population, without a proportional increase of food, must lower the value of each man's earnings. The food must necessarily be distributed in smaller quantities, and consequently a day's labour will purchase a smaller quantity of provisions. An increase in the price of provisions will arise either from an increase of population faster than the means of subsistence, or from a different distribution of the money of the society. The food of a country which has been long peopled, if it be increasing, increases slowly and regularly, and cannot be made to answer any sudden demands: but variations in the distribution of the money of the society are not unfrequently occurring, and are undoubtedly among the causes which occasion the continual variations in the prices of provisions.

The poor-laws of England tend to depress the general condition of the poor in these two ways. Their first obvious tendency is to increase population without increasing the food for its support. A poor man may marry with little or no prospect of being able to support a family without parish assistance. They may be said, therefore, to create the poor which they maintain: and as the provisions of the country must, in consequence of the increased population, be distributed to every man in smaller proportions, it is evident that the labour of those who are not supported by parish assistance will purchase a smaller quantity of provisions than before, and consequently more of them must be driven to apply for assistance.

Secondly, the quantity of provisions consumed in workhouses, upon a part of the society that cannot in general be considered as the most valuable part, diminishes the shares that would otherwise belong to more industrious and more worthy members, and thus, in the same manner, forces more to become dependent. If the poor in the workhouses were to live better than they do now, this new distribution of the money of the society would tend more conspicuously to depress the condition of those out of the workhouses by occasioning an advance in the price of provisions.

Fortunately for England, a spirit of independence still remains among the peasantry. The poor-laws are strongly calculated to eradicate this spirit. They have succeeded in part; but had they succeeded as completely as might have been expected, their pernicious tendency would not have been so long concealed.

Hard as it may appear in individual instances, dependent poverty ought to be held disgraceful. Such a stimulus seems to be absolutely necessary to promote the happiness of the great mass of mankind; and every general attempt to weaken this stimulus, however benevolent its intention, will always defeat its own purpose. If men be induced to marry from the mere prospect of parish provision, they are not only unjustly tempted to bring unhappiness and dependence upon themselves and children, but they are tempted, without knowing it, to injure all the same class with themselves.

The poor-laws of England appear to have contributed to raise the price of provisions, and to lower the real price of labour. They have therefore contributed to impoverish that class of people whose only possession is their labour. It is also difficult to suppose that they have not powerfully contributed to generate that carelessness and want of frugality observable among the poor, so contrary to the disposition generally to be remarked among petty tradesmen and small farmers. The labouring poor, to use a vulgar expression, seem always to live from hand to mouth. Their present wants employ their whole attention; and they seldom think of the future. Even when they have an opportunity of saving, they seldom exercise it; but all that they earn beyond their present necessities goes, generally speaking, to the ale-house. The poor-laws may therefore be said to diminish both the power and the will to save among the common people; and thus to weaken one of the strongest incentives to sobriety and industry, and consequently to happiness.

It is a general complaint among master manufacturers, that high wages ruin all their workmen; but it is difficult to conceive that these men would not save a part of their high wages for the future support of their families, instead of spending it in drunkenness and dissipation, if they did not rely on parish assistance for support in case of accidents. And that the poor employed in manufactures consider this assistance as a reason why they may spend all the wages which they earn, and enjoy themselves while they can, appears to be evident from the number of families that upon the failure of any great manufactory immediately fall upon the parish; when perhaps the wages earned in this manufactory while it flourished were sufficiently above the price of common country labour to have allowed them to save enough for their support till they could find some other channel for their industry.

A man who might not be deterred from going to the ale-house from the consideration that on his death or sickness he should leave his wife and family upon the parish, might yet hesitate in thus dissipating his earnings, if he were assured that in either of these cases his family must starve, or be left to the support of casual bounty.

The mass of happiness among the common people cannot but be diminished when one of the strongest checks to idleness and dissipation is thus removed; and positive institutions, which render dependent poverty so general, weaken that disgrace which for the best and most humane reasons ought to be attached to it.

The poor-laws of England were undoubtedly instituted for the most benevolent purpose; but it is evident they have failed in attaining it. They certainly mitigate some cases of severe distress which might otherwise occur; though the state of the poor who are supported by parishes, considered in all its circumstances, is very miserable. But one of the principal objections to the system is, that for the assistance which some of the poor receive, in itself almost a doubtful blessing, the whole class of the common people of England is subjected to a set of grating, inconvenient, and tyrannical laws, totally inconsistent with the genuine spirit of the constitution. The whole business of settlements, even in its present amended state, is contradictory to all ideas of freedom. The parish persecution of men whose families are likely to become chargeable, and of poor women who are near lying-in, is a most disgraceful and disgusting tyranny. And the obstructions continually occasioned in the market of labour by these laws have a constant tendency to add to the difficulties of those who are struggling to support themselves without assistance.

These evils attendant on the poor-laws seem to be irremediable. If assistance be to be distributed to a certain class of people, a power must be lodged somewhere of discriminating the proper objects, and of managing the concerns of the institutions that are necessary; but any great interference with the affairs of other people is a species of tyranny, and in the common course of things the exercise of this power may be expected to become grating to those who are driven to ask for support. The tyranny of churchwardens and overseers is a common complaint among the poor; but the fault does not lie so much in these persons, who probably before they were in power were not worse than other people, but in the nature of all such institutions.

I feel persuaded that if the poor-laws had never existed in this country, though there might have been a few more instances of very severe distress, the aggregate mass of happiness among the common people would have been much greater than it is at present.

The radical defect of all systems of the kind is that of tending to depress the condition of those that are not relieved by parishes, and to create more poor. If, indeed, we examine some of our statutes strictly with reference to the principle of population, we shall find that they attempt an absolute impossibility: and we cannot be surprised, therefore, that they should constantly fail in the attainment of their object.

The famous 43rd of Elizabeth, which has been so often referred to and admired, enacts that the overseers of the poor "shall take order from time to time, by and with the consent of two or more justices, for setting to work the children of all such, whose parents shall not by the said persons be thought able to keep and maintain their children: and also such persons, married or unmarried, as, having no means to maintain them, use no ordinary and daily trade of life to get their living by; and also to raise weekly, or otherwise, by taxation of every inhabitant, and every occupier of lands in the said parish, (in such competent sums as they shall think fit,) a convenient stock of flax, hemp, wool, thread, iron, and other necessary ware and stuff, to set the poor to work."

What is this but saying that the funds for the maintenance of labour in this country may be increased at will, and without limit, by a *fiat* [decree] of government, or an assessment of the overseers? Strictly speaking, this clause is as arrogant and as absurd as if it had enacted that two ears of wheat should in future grow where one only had grown before....

...[E]very labouring man might marry as early as he pleased, under the certain prospect of having all his children properly provided for; and as, according to the supposition, there would be no check to population from the consequences of poverty after marriage, the increase of people would be rapid beyond example....

....A great part of the redundant population occasioned by the poor-laws is thus taken off by the operation of the laws themselves, or at least by their ill execution. The remaining part which survives, by causing the funds for the maintenance of labour to be divided among a greater number than can be properly maintained by them, and by turning a considerable share from the support of the diligent and careful workman to the support of the idle and negligent, depresses the condition of all those who are out of the work-houses, forces more into them every year, and has ultimately produced the enormous evil which we all so justly deplore; that of the great and unnatural proportion of the people which is now become dependent upon charity.

If this be a just representation of the manner in which the clause in question has been executed, and of the effects which it has produced, it must be allowed that we have practised an unpardonable deceit upon the poor, and have promised what we have been very far from performing....

My intention is merely to show that the poor-laws as a general system are founded on a gross error; and that the common declamation on the subject of the poor, which we see so often in print, and hear continually in conversation, namely, that the market price of labour ought always to be sufficient decently to support a family, and that employment ought to be found for all those who are willing to work, is in effect to say that the funds for the maintenance of labour in this country are not only infinite, but not subject to variation; and that, whether the resources of a country be rapidly progressive, slowly progressive, stationary, or declining, the power of giving full employment and good wages to the labouring classes must always remain exactly the same—a conclusion which contradicts the plainest and most obvious principles of supply and demand, and involves the absurd position that a definite quantity of territory can maintain an infinite population.

....If it be taught that all who are born have a *right* to support on the land, whatever be their number, and that there is no occasion to exercise any prudence in the affair of marriage so as to check this number, the temptations, according to all the known principles of human nature, will inevitably be yielded to, and more and more will gradually become dependent on parish assistance. There cannot therefore be a greater inconsistency and contradiction than that those who maintain these doctrines respecting the poor should still complain of the number of paupers. Such doctrines and a crowd of paupers are unavoidably united; and it is utterly beyond the power of any revolution or change of government to separate them.

2. "An Appeal of the Factory Labourers and their Children to the good Sense and Humanity of the Nation." *British Labourer's Protector and Factory Child's Friend* (1832–33): 238–41

Weary and worn down by the burdens of a life, which for us has little but pain and suffering, we call upon our fellow subjects for sympathy. Our labour is run down by the cruel spirit of competition, till it will yield many of us scarcely one half of the food required to keep soul and body together. Every moment of time that can be racked out of us, in our toil, is greedily demanded and of necessity given up to the vulture-spirit of gain. To cheapen the cost of production, machines have been invented and introduced for doing the work by the hands of our children, who are taken too early into the factories. Here they are immured, and kept to tasks of labour which are far worse than the horses of stage-coaches can endure. This you may know by observing that 10 miles a day for a year round is as much labour as can be got out of coach-horses, one with another, whereas our children, in attending some of the machines, actually walk as much as is equal to a distance of 14 miles in as many hours. This labour has frequently to be done in heat enough to stifle any one who is not used to it, where there is also the smell of oil and metal and the stunning noise of the machinery. Each of these, the doctors say, is hurtful to the health, especially in childhood. What then must they be to children of six, seven, or eight years old, who have to suffer them all? It is no wonder, then, that their little bodies become thin and sickly pale, that the bones of their legs and backs give way under them, that their senses are benumbed, and that they get their limbs entangled in the machinery, and cut and bruised, and sometimes torn off, from the stupor down to which they are brought by their excessive and unhealthy toil.

But these are the lightest of our evils. In an age which boasts of the great advancement of knowledge, we and our hapless children are shut out from any due share of its advantages. A constant addition to our toils and sufferings leads us to conclude that the increase of information effects no other purpose than that of giving a keener edge to the shears with which cunning and avarice fleece the multitude of labourers. Instead of imparting any of its benefits to us, knowledge has become as a wolf's den, set up in the neighbourhood of the sheep walks. We are always hearing of the decrease of labour which improvements in machinery are to bring about, and of the great advantage of multiplying productions.—We are prepared to prove that in every step of these vaunted improvements our hours of labour have kept increasing, our wages have diminished, and of that very clothing with which our industry burdens the markets of the world, we have not left, in many cases, what is necessary for the decent covering of our wives and children.

As to the pleasures of the mind, of which we have heard something, we know little of them, and our children are doomed to know nothing. Their bodily energies are exhausted, long before the end of their daily toil, and a sleep as heavy but less happy than the sleep of death, over-takes them as soon as it is brought to a close. Thus are they reduced to a state of mechanical existence, scarcely more intelligent than the machines which they have to watch, and all hope of cultivating their minds is taken away.

We are told that Christianity is part of the law of England, and that the protection and defence of helpless innocence is particularly due from a people who profess to believe the doctrine and example of the Lord Jesus. But of his command and precept, "suffer little children to come unto me," we see no other use, or invitation, than that which invites our little ones into the steam factories, there to be over-worked and half starved; perhaps to imbibe wasting disease, perhaps to be warped and deformed in their limbs, but certainly to be for ever bereft of the opportunity of acquiring the health, morals and intelligence by which people of other ranks are enabled to improve their lot in life.

We are told, that in this country every body is presumed to be present at the making of the laws—consequently, every one is bound by them, and ignorance is no excuse for breaking them. Yet we find that laws of increasing rigour are multiplying every day, which are to bind us who have neither voice nor influence in preparing them, and are utterly without either time or any other means for resisting the encroachments which we daily witness and feel on our common rights. For the right of life and health, and adequate provision of food for them and their infant children, who are able and willing to labour, have been declared common rights by the law of England.

In this deep state of calamity, and suffering from excessive labour, and low wages, from the wasting of our bodies, and the privation of almost every thing agreeable and consoling to our minds, from the premature misery and decay of the health and strength of our children, which has been and still is pushed to the whole extent of their ability to endure, we respectfully and loyally called upon the legislature to interfere, so as to effect some mitigation of the mighty evils which are crushing us to the earth, and grinding us to powder. We made no accusations against the masters, though it is known throughout the world that all those evils, and many more from which we suffer, are attributable to the reckless and wasteful spirit of competition of the master manufacturers in the home and foreign markets, and the greediness which leads them to filch from the proper wages of labour at home.

We asked for a law to prevent the masters from injuring and destroying the bodies of our children, at so early an age, and to give their minds some opportunity of sharing in that knowledge so boasted of, the want of which is charged against us and our offspring as a reproach and a crime. Many Gentlemen of the best rank, in the medical profession, came forward and vowed that such labour so continued, was in deadly opposition to the continuance of infant health and strength, and forbad the chance of a sound and able manhood. Crowds of witnesses came forward to prove that the Factory population are lessening in size, and that the strength and beauty of their appearance, which were remarkable thirty or forty years ago, have given way to sallow cheeks and unsightly forms, to dwarfish bodies, crooked limbs, anxious visages, and scrophulous complexions.

Many clergymen bore testimony, (for ever honoured be their names and memories!) that the ignorance of the Factory population, and the crimes to which it necessarily tends, were to be ascribed to the long hours of toil, and the tender years at which the children must be given up to *since the overseers will not relieve the sick and afflicted who keep their little children at home.*

These are the evils which we implored Government to relieve, and how are we answered? One of those who make profit of our incredible sufferings and hardships, got up in the House of Commons and moved an address to the Crown, praying for a Royal Commission to collect Evidence in favour of the countenance of our sufferings. In this we are supported by most of the members who are connected with manufacturers. These men, instead of displaying any compassion for the misery of the labourers, whose wrongs and injuries they seem to reckon as part of the contract of wage, treated the allegation as an affair *personally* offensive to themselves. One of the members reasoned upon the subject as if the labourers had taken up a most unwarrantable opinion as to their rights, in supposing that manufacturing profits and capital, were to be put to the last risk of inconvenience, to remedy the bodily afflictions and mental destitution of the labourers. Thus, as the Scriptures faithfully teach us, do riches harden new hearts, and those who make the laws, should be as fathers to the poor; when we ask for bread they give us a stone, and instead of a fish, a serpent.

We were told that the laws of England, were particularly favourable to the protection of life and liberty—and we had heard that overseers of the parish had frequently brought upon themselves, the magistrates, for their lawlessness in suffering even the *idlers* to perish. We hear now, with dismay and despair, that it is to be made a question, into which the Commissioners will be instructed to inquire, not whether our infant children can do this work and live, but whether or not it is better for them to endure those lingering and destroying tortures than *starve*, without having to endure them. So that by this assumption, the protection of the land is wholly taken away from our lives, and those of our innocent children; and they are demanded from us as a necessary sacrifice on our parts, to entitle us to the privilege of eating our daily bread. Nor is this all. For when we have made this horrible sacrifice of ourselves and our little ones, we do not get the compensation held out to us!

3. "The Factory Children." *British Labourer's Protector and Factory Child's Friend* (1831)

The following Lines are sent us from Glasgow, and are the effort of a very young Operative Spinner, who has shewn very laudable zeal in the cause of the Ten Hour Bill.[1]

THE FACTORY CHILDREN

All ye true born Sons of Freedom,
Hear the Factory Children's tale;
The long hours they have to labour,
Make their lips and cheeks quite pale.

Long they toil the whole week over,
Twelve and thirteen hours each day;
Food, their wages scarce will cover,—
A bare half-crown is all their pay.

Five o'clock they rise each morning,
The coldest day that e'er doth blow;
Shoe they cannot get—nor stocking,
To keep their cold feet from the snow.

At eight at night, when home returning,
Their limbs are frail, *their hearts are sore,*
To bed they go till early morning,
Rejoicing that their day's work's o'er.

Next morn at five, they go to work,
And scarcely ever break their fast;
Oft times I've heard them moan and say,
"I wish the Ten Hour Bill was past.

---

1 The Factory Acts regulated the employment of children in cotton manufacturing. The 1802 act limited children's workdays to twelve hours per day; the 1819 Act prohibited the employment of children under nine. Neither act provided for regulating officials; this was remedied by the 1833 Act, which allowed for special full-time inspectors to enforce the law. This act also reduced workdays to nine hours (ages 9-13) and twelve hours (ages 13-18).

"And then at night we'd go to school,—
"There we would learn to read and write,
"And speak against the sad misrule,
"Which robs us of our dearest right.

"'Tis shameful they should work us so,
"Like convicts banish'd o'er the sea;
"And why is this? I'd wish to know;
"Our fathers fought for Liberty!

"Our fathers fought for Briton's rights,—
"The broad-sword they did boldly wave,
"And we, their children, only want
"The *Ten Hour Bill*—that's all we crave."

Ye nobles, that are now to be
The rulers of this Christian land,
Pity the Slave of the Factory,
And take the Ten Hour Bill in hand.

O, for the sake of *Him* who said,
"Let little children come to me"—
Stand boldly forth and plead *our cause*,
And from such Slavery set us free!
—George McCallum, A Glasgow Factory "Laddie."
Glasgow, 14th January, 1833.

4. James Phillips Kay-Shuttleworth, *The Moral and Physical Condition of the Working Classes Employed in the Cotton Manufacture in Manchester*. London: James Ridgway (1832)

As competition and the restrictions and burdens of trade diminished the profits of capital, and consequently reduced the price of labour, the contagious example of ignorance and a barbarous disregard of forethought and economy, exhibited by the Irish, spread.[1] The colonization of savage tribes has ever been attended with effects on civilization as fatal as those which have marked the progress of the

---

1   The influence of Irish immigrants on British society was a popular scapegoat of social critics and reformists. For some, like Kay, working-class squalor stemmed less from industry and rapid urbanization than from the influx of an "inferior" race—like the Irish.

sand flood over the fertile plains of Egypt. Instructed in the fatal secret of subsisting on what is barely necessary to life, the labouring classes have ceased to entertain a laudable pride in furnishing their houses, and in multiplying the decent comforts which minister to happiness. What is superfluous to the mere exigencies of nature, is too often expended at the tavern; and for the provision of old age and infirmity, they too frequently trust either to charity, to the support of their children, or to the protection of the poor laws.

When this example is considered in connection with the unremitted labour of the whole population engaged in the various branches of the cotton manufacture, our wonder will be less excited by their fatal demoralization. Prolonged and exhausting labour, continued from day to day, and from year to year, is not calculated to develop the intellectual or moral faculties of man. The dull routine of a ceaseless drudgery, in which the same mechanical process is incessantly repeated, resembles the torment of Sisyphus[1]—the toil, like the rock, recoils perpetually on the wearied operative. The mind gathers neither stores nor strength from the constant extension and retraction of the same muscles. The intellect slumbers in supine inertness; but the grosser parts of our nature attain a rank development. To condemn man to such severity of toil is, in some measure, to cultivate in him the habits of an animal. He becomes reckless. He disregards the distinguishing appetites and habits of his species. He neglects the comforts and delicacies of life. He lives in squalid wretchedness, on meagre food, and expends his superfluous gains in debauchery.

[T]he population...is crowded into one dense mass, in cottages separated by narrow, unpaved, and almost pestilential streets; in an atmosphere loaded with the smoke and exhalations of a large manufacturing city. The operatives are congregated in rooms and workshops during twelve hours in the day, in an enervating, heated atmosphere, which is frequently loaded with dust or filaments of cotton, or impure from constant respiration, or from other causes. They are engaged in an employment which absorbs their attention, and unremittingly employs their physical energies. They are drudges who watch the movements, and assist the operations, of a mighty material force, which toils with an energy ever unconscious of

---

1   According to legend, Sisyphus of Corinth was doomed for eternity to push a boulder uphill, only to have it roll back down to the bottom, to be pushed up again and again. His example represents the futility of human endeavors.

fatigue. The persevering labour of the operative must rival the mathematical precision, the incessant motion, and the exhaustless power of the machine.

Hence, besides the negative results—the total abstraction of every moral and intellectual stimulus—the absence of variety—banishment from the grateful air and the cheering influences of light, the physical energies are exhausted by incessant toil, and imperfect nutrition. Having been subjected to the prolonged labour of the animal—his physical energy wasted—his mind in supine inaction—the artizan has neither moral dignity nor intellectual nor organic strength to resist the seductions of appetite. His wife and children, too frequently subjected to the same process, are unable to cheer his remaining moments of leisure. Domestic economy is neglected, domestic comforts are unknown. A meal of the coarsest food is prepared with heedless haste, and devoured with equal precipitation. Home has no other relation to him than that of shelter—few pleasures are there— it chiefly presents to him a scene of physical exhaustion, from which he is glad to escape. Himself impotent of all the distinguishing aims of his species, he sinks into sensual sloth, or revels in more degrading licentiousness. His house is ill furnished, uncleanly, often ill ventilated, perhaps damp; his food, from want of forethought and domestic economy, is meagre and innutritious; he is debilitated and hypochondriacal, and falls the victim of dissipation.[1]

These artizans are frequently subject to a disease, in which the sensibility of the stomach and bowels is morbidly excited; the alvine secretions are deranged, and the appetite impaired. Whilst this state continues, the patient loses flesh, his features are sharpened, the skin becomes pale, leaden coloured, or of the yellow hue which is observed in those who have suffered from the influence of tropical climates. The strength fails, all the capacities of physical enjoyment are destroyed, and the paroxysms of corporeal suffering are aggravated by the horrors of a disordered imagination, till they lead to gloomy apprehension, to the deepest depression, and almost, to despair. We cannot wonder that the wretched victim of this disease, invited by those haunts of misery and crime the gin shop and the tavern, as he passes to his daily labour, should endeavour to cheat his suffering of a few moments, by the false excitement procured by ardent spirits; or

1 Although he acknowledges that the women and children of the family endure the same challenges and hardships as the men, Kay does not extend the same concern for the quality of their lives that he does to men.

that the exhausted artizan, driven by ennui and discomfort from his squalid home, should strive, in the delirious dreams of a continued debauch, to forget the remembrance of his reckless improvidence, of the destitution, hunger, and uninterrupted toil, which threaten to destroy the remaining energies of his enfeebled constitution....

The greatest portion of these districts...are of very recent origin; and from the want of proper police regulations are untraversed by common sewers. The houses are ill soughed,[1] often ill ventilated, unprovided with privies, and in consequence, the streets which are narrow, unpaved, and worn into deep ruts, become the common receptacles of mud, refuse, and disgusting ordure....

Predisposition to contagious disease is encouraged by every thing which depresses the physical energies, amongst the principal of which agencies may be enumerated imperfect nutrition; exposure to cold and moisture, whether from inadequate shelter, or from want of clothing and fuel, or from dampness of the habitation; uncleanliness of the person, the street, and the abode; an atmosphere contaminated, whether from the want of ventilation, or from impure effluvia [toxic vapors]; extreme labour, and consequent physical exhaustion; intemperance; fear; anxiety; diarrhoea, and other diseases....

The state of the streets powerfully affects the health of their inhabitants. Sporadic cases of typhus chiefly appear in those which are narrow, ill ventilated, unpaved, or which contain heaps of refuse, or stagnant pools. The confined air and noxious exhalations, which abound in such places, depress the health of the people, and on this account contagious diseases are also most rapidly propagated there. The operation of these causes is exceedingly promoted by their reflex influence on the manners. The houses, in such situations, are uncleanly, ill provided with furniture; an air of discomfort if not of squalid and loathsome wretchedness pervades them, they are often dilapidated, badly drained, damp; and the habits of their tenants are gross—they are ill-fed, ill-clothed, and uneconomical—at once spendthrifts and destitute—denying themselves the comforts of life, in order that they may wallow in the unrestrained licence of animal appetite. An intimate connexion subsists, among the poor, between the cleanliness of the street and that of the house and person. Uneconomical habits, and dissipation are almost inseparably allied; and they are so frequently connected with uncleanliness, that we cannot consider their concomitance as altogether accidental....

---

1 Aired.

The poor laws provide, we fear, too frequently a plea for improvidence and idleness. When reckless of the future, the intelligence of man is confined by the narrow limits of the present. By that step he debases himself beneath the animals whose instincts teach them to lay up stores for the season of need. The artificial structure of society, in providing security against existing evils, has too frequently neglected the remote moral influence of its arrangements on the community. Humanity rejoices in the consciousness, that the poorest may obtain the advantages of skilful care in disease, and succour in want; that there are asylums for infirmity, age, and decrepitude; but the *unlimited* extension of benefits, devised by a wise intelligence for the relief of evils which no human prescience could elude, has a direct tendency to encourage, among the poor, apathy concerning present exigencies, and the neglect of a provision for the contingencies of the future. The effect of this will be favoured by every other demoralizing cause, and will therefore operate most powerfully among those who are most debased....

There is no *Common* Slaughter-house in Manchester, and those which exist are chiefly situated in the narrowest and most filthy streets in the town. The drainage from these houses, deeply tinged with blood, and impregnated with other animal matters, frequently flows down the common surface drain of the street, and stagnates in the ruts and pools. Moreover, sometimes in the yards of these houses—from the want of a vigilant circumspection—offal [animal waste] is allowed to accumulate with the grossest neglect of decency and disregard to the health of the surrounding inhabitants. The attention of the commissioners of police cannot be too soon directed to the propriety of obtaining powers to erect a Common Slaughter-house on some vacant space, and to compel the butchers of the town to slaughter all animals killed in the township in the building thus provided.

The districts...are inhabited by a turbulent population, which, rendered reckless by dissipation and want,—misled by the secret intrigues, and excited by the inflammatory harangues of demagogues, has frequently committed daring assaults on the liberty of the more peaceful portions of the working classes, and the most frightful devastations on the property of their masters. Machines have been broken, and factories gutted and burned at mid-day, and the riotous crowd has dispersed ere the insufficient body of police arrived at the scene of disturbance. The civic force of the town is totally inadequate to maintain the peace, and to defend property from the attacks of lawless depredators; and *a more efficient, and more numerous corps ought to be immediately organized*, to give power to the law, so often mocked by the daring front of sedition, and outraged by the frantic violence of an ignorant and deluded rabble. The police form, in fact, so weak a screen against the power of the mob, that popular violence is now, in almost every instance, controlled by the presence of a military force....

The disease of the body politic is not superficial, and cannot be cured, or even temporarily relieved, by any specific:[1] its sources are unfortunately remote, and the measures necessary to the removal of its disorders include serious questions on which great difference of opinion prevails....

The evils affecting the working classes, *so far from being the necessary results of the commercial system, furnish evidence of a disease which impairs its energies, if it does not threaten its vitality.*

The increase of the manufacturing establishments, and the consequent colonization of the district, have been exceedingly more rapid than the growth of its civic institutions.

[Free-trade]: Were an unlimited exchange permitted to commerce, the hours of labour might be reduced, and time afforded for the education and religious and moral instruction of the people. With a virtuous population, engaged in free-trade, the existence of redundant labour would be an evil of brief duration, rarely experienced. The unpopular, but alas, too necessary proposals of emigration would no longer be agitated. Ingenuity and industry would draw from the whole world a tribute more than adequate to supply the ever increasing demands of a civilized nation.

The duties imposed on the introduction of foreign corn were originally intended, by raising the price of grain, to act as a compensation to the landowner for the supposed unequal pressure of taxation upon him. This inequality of the public burdens has, however, been exceedingly exaggerated, and those taxes, which are said to be derived from land on which corn is grown, are also procured from many other descriptions of property which are not protected. The faults of our present financial system[2] are so numerous, that if the principle of relieving the inequality of the pressure of taxation be admitted, we must pay back in bounties one third of what is obtained by taxes. The scarcity and dearness of food certainly bring to the agricultural population no benefit, after the brief demand for labour necessary to bring fresh soils into cultivation is past. The landowner alone receives any advantage from the high price of food, and that much less than has

---

1   Cure or remedy.
2   Sir H. Parnell, on Financial Reform.

generally been supposed. The fluctuating scale by which the duties on corn are at present regulated, has produced the most disastrous effects among the agricultural tenantry: rents have been paid out of capital, and estates have been injured, in consequence of the embarrassments of the cultivators. A tax *on the staple commodity of life* enhances the price of all other food, by increasing the wages of labour, and rent of land; and, as it enters as an element into the cost of every article produced, (and that in a ratio constantly accumulating with the amount of labour employed,) it presses heavily, though indirectly, on the superior classes, and upon all other consumers. Not the least injurious effects of the present Corn-law, are the burden of supporting an unemployed population, which it entails on society at large, and the insecurity of property which results from the near approach to destitution of a large portion of its members. But since this system simultaneously contracts the market of the capitalist, (by excluding one most important object of barter,) and increases the cost of production, its direst effects are felt in the manufacturing districts, which have long been maintaining an unequal struggle with foreign competitors.

[Education]: ....Noxious agencies are abroad, and, while we refuse to sow the germs of truth and virtue, the winds of heaven bring the winged seeds of error and vice. Moreover, as education is delayed, a stubborn barrenness affects the faculties—want of exercise renders them inapt—he that has never been judiciously instructed, has not only to master the first elements of truth, and to unlearn error, but in proportion as the period has been delayed, will be the difficulty of these processes. What wonder then that the teachers of truth should make little impression on an unlettered population, and that the working classes should become the prey of those *who flatter their passions, adopt their prejudices, or even descend to imitate their manners.*

If a period ever existed, when public peace was secured, by refusing knowledge to the population, that epoch has lapsed. The policy of governments may have been little able to bear the scrutiny of the people. This may be the reason why the fountains of English literature have been sealed—and the works of our reformers, our patriots, and our confessors—the exhaustless sources of all that is pure and holy, and of good report, amongst us—*have not been made accessible and familiar to the poor.* Yet, literature of this order is destined to determine the structure of our social constitution, and to become the mould of our national character; and they who would dam up the flood of truth from the lower ground, cannot prevent its silent transudation [infiltration]. A little knowledge is thus inevitable, and it is proverbially a dangerous thing. Alarming disturbances of social order generally commence with a *people only partially instructed.* The preservation of *internal peace*, not less than the improvement of our national institutions, depends on the education of the working classes.

5. **Peter Gaskell, *The Manufacturing Population of England, its Moral, Social and Physical Conditions, and the Changes which have Arisen from the Use of Steam Machinery.* London: Baldwin and Craddock (1833)**

The part of the masters in the great drama, naturally is, and ought to be, the leading one. They are, above all men, interested; and great and almost fearful responsibility rests with them. They have within their power, the capability of doing much either for good or for evil. It is their bounden duty to examine into every thing bearing upon the subject, with the most minute care, with a spirit of strict justice, and with a disposition to ameliorate, as far as is consistent with their own private and indisputable rights. In doing this, they should endeavour so to act, that the confidence of the men may go hand in hand with them, or it will be of no avail. Their name and reputation, like that of Caesar's wife, should be above suspicion; and till they are at pains thus to elevate themselves—thus to establish their reputation upon the pinnacle of fair fame and honourable consideration, they will be looked upon by the world and by their operatives, as the originators and as the keepers up of a system, which is undoubtedly fraught with many things subversive to the morals, health, and individual independence, of all concerned in it.

....The universal application of steam power as an agent for producing motion in machinery, has closely assimilated the condition of all branches, both in their moral and physical relations. In all, it destroys domestic labour; in all, it congregates its victims into towns, or densely peopled neighbourhoods; in all, it separates families; and in all it lessens the demand for human strength, reducing man to a mere watcher or feeder of his mighty antagonist, which toils and labours with a pertinacity and unvarying continuance, requiring constant and sedulous attention.

It is much to be wished that "men in high places" would examine, somewhat more in detail, the existing condition of the manufacturers. The conversion of a great people, in little more than the quarter of a century, from agriculturists to manufacturers, is a phenomenon worthy the attention of any statesman. It is an attention, too, which will be forced upon them, when, from their want of knowledge, they will be liable to take steps which may prove destructive to one or both of the great divisions of national property.

The change, too, which has recently been made in the constitution of the House of Commons, is another important reason why information should be extended widely and generally. The change is one, indeed, characteristic of the times; and the introduction to the House of persons of strictly commercial habits and views, will necessarily operate very powerfully upon the course of legislation, when brought to bear upon its interests. The change will not, however, rest here: the preponderance already acquired by manufactures, is progressing rapidly; and its representatives will, ere long, take the position afforded them by their vantage ground. The riches of a great and wealthy nation, are pouring into the tide of manufactures, and swelling its ascendancy; and it must soon become in appearance, what it is in reality, the directing current of the national prosperity. From the utter absence of information, it is to be feared that crude and badly digested enactments may interfere between the employer and the employed, to the serious injury of both parties, and to the ultimate endangering of the present lofty pre-eminence enjoyed by Great Britain, as the grand focus of manufacturing intelligence,— and may so hamper and obstruct the operations of capital, as to lead, to some extent, to its entire abstraction.

It is, above all things, of importance that the condition of the labourers should be carefully and maturely considered. Though danger may arise from legislative enactments, this is the slumbering volcano, which may at any time shatter the whole fabric to atoms, and involve in one common ruin, themselves, the master, and the manufacture. The struggle carrying on between human power on the one hand, and steam aided by machinery, which is constantly improving in construction, and increasing in applicability, is approaching a crisis, the termination of which it is frightful to contemplate. The contest has hitherto been, between the vast body of hand-loom weavers, who have clung to their ancient habits, till no market is open to their labour; but it is now commencing between another great body and machinery. The adaptation of mechanical contrivances to nearly all the processes which have as yet wanted the delicate tact of the human hand, will soon either do away with the necessity for employing it, or it must be employed at a price that will enable it to compete with mechanism. This cannot be: human power must ever be an expensive power; it cannot be carried beyond a certain point, neither will it permit a depression of payment below what is essential for its existence,—and it is the fixing of this minimum in which lies the difficulty.

One of the most striking revolutions ever produced in the moral and social condition of a moiety[1] of a great nation, is that which has been consequent to the application of steam to machinery. It is one which will be found to possess many points of great interest to every man who considers the happiness, or looks forward to the probable destiny of that large portion of the productive population, connected with manufactures.

The rapidity with which this revolution has been effected, is not the least remarkable circumstance about it; and strikingly illustrates the truth...that wherever men are congregated in large bodies, their morals must be deteriorated. One great effect of the steam-engine has been, to crowd workmen together....[creating] the present depraved and debased condition of the class of manufacturing labourers....

The acquisition of wealth, unfortunately for the interests of all parties, was not attended by a correspondent improvement in their moral and social character; on the contrary, all who had an opportunity of watching its effects, can only deplore and condemn the evil purposes to which, for many years, some portions of it were applied.

....Drink—drink was their only amusement and occupation. Utterly destitute of every thing intellectual, and utterly condemning every thing savouring of refinement, whether in manner or thought, they were in some measure driven to the indulgence of their animal sensations. This was generally sought for in the use of ardent spirits, which roused and maddened them for a time into furious joy, and rendered them unconscious of all that was due to decency or propriety. Thus wallowing in intemperance, little wonder can be excited that other passions were stimulated into active operation; and from their situation, unbounded facilities were offered for their display.

[Promiscuity]: Animal sensations must ever be the predominant occupiers of coarse, uneducated minds. The great advantage of education, when conducted in a way calculated to attain its legitimate end, is—that it makes man less a prey to sense, by giving him other and nobler contemplations, and fixing his regards upon mental exertions, and enjoyments, which are diametrically opposed to the grosser demands of his nature. This is the advantage that education possesses when legitimately conducted; but these purposes are not gained by common education, which is too fundamental, and too exclusively intellectual, and which aims apparently at merely expanding the ideas, without troubling itself as to their proper direction. Hence they are left to wander back to their original tendency, aided in their intensity by the very imperfect development given to

1 Portion, class.

morals.

....The almost entire extinction of sexual decency, which is one of the darkest stains upon the character of the manufacturing population—the laxity in all the moral obligations which ought to exist between the sexes, and the consequent loss of this most important influence in the formation of social manners, may be traced...to this period of their history....The crowding together numbers of the young of both sexes in factories, is a prolific source of moral delinquency. The stimulus of a heated atmosphere [average 70-75 degrees], the contact of opposite sexes, the example of lasciviousness upon the animal passions—all have conspired to produce a very early development of sexual appetencies. Indeed, in this respect, the female population engaged in manufactures, approximates very closely to that found in tropical climates; puberty, or at least sexual propensities, being attained almost coeval with girlhood....

[The nuclear family] preserved in all their vigour the moral obligations of father and mother, brother and sister, son and daughter, and that till a time of life was gained, which had given abundant opportunity for the formation of character—a character most assuredly the best calculated to render the labouring man happy and virtuous, viz., a domestic one; without which, no adventitious aid can ever secure him their possession.

The greatest misfortune—the most unfavourable change which has resulted from factory labour, is the breaking up of these family ties; the consequent abolition of the domestic circle, and the perversion of all the social obligations which should exist between parent and child on the one hand, and between children themselves on the other.

....It is to be feared, that the mischiefs resulting from such an unnatural arrangement, must, in the first instance, be saddled upon the errors of parents—such a dereliction from filial duty being hardly likely to happen spontaneously on the side of the children; and that a plan originally adopted in a few cases, by the family of idle and depraved parents,*—and many such are to be found, who would willingly batten[1] upon the toil of their children—has

---

* Too frequently the father, enjoying perfect health, and ample opportunities of employment, is supported in idleness on the earnings of his oppressed children.—Dr. Kay's pamphlet, p.64. [Gaskell's note; the reference is to James Kay-Shuttleworth, *The Moral and Physical Condition of the Working Classes Employed in the Cotton Manufacture in Manchester* (London: James Ridgway, 1832).]

---

1 Feed, live.

become general, in consequence and affection which ought to exist between parent and child.

....This disruption of all the ties of home, is one of the most fatal consequences of the factory system. The social relations which should distinguish the members of the same family, are destroyed. The domestic virtues—man's natural instincts, and the affections of the heart, are deadened and lost...leaving nothing but attention to the simple wants of nature, in addition to the depraved appetites which are the result of other circumstances connected with their condition;—and in the end reducing them, as a mass, to a heartless assemblage....

[The factory child]: From its birth it sees nothing around it but dissension; its infant cries are hushed, not by maternal tenderness, but by doses of gin or opiates, or it is left to wail itself asleep from exhaustion. In thousands of cases it is abandoned throughout the day by its parents, both of whom are engaged in the mill, and left to the care of a stranger or a mere child—badly used—badly-fed—its little heart hardened by harshness even in the cradle; then badly clothed—unattended during its growth by regular and systematic kindness—constantly hearing execrations, curses, blasphemy, and every thing coarse and obscene in expression—seeing on all sides strife, drunkenness, bestiality, and abominations, and finally sent shivering into the mill, to swell the hordes of children which have been similarly educated, and similarly abandoned to their own resources.....

The social confederacy of the present generation is full of anomalies. Possessing, as the great bulk of the population does, many advantages never known or dreamt of by their forefathers; education rapidly progressing; its wants liberally relieved; its sicknesses carefully tended; religion afforded it, nay, even brought to its doors, and applied to its senses; a practicability of earning something towards a livelihood; continual accessions of political privileges—it is nevertheless filled with immorality, irreligion, improvidence, political discontent, refusal to earn anything, ingratitude, ignorance, and vice, in every conceivable form in which it can develop itself.

Neither are these evils confined to one class of the labouring community, proving very sufficiently that other causes must be at work beyond those dependent upon manufacture, on the one hand, and agriculture on the other. Neither is the excess of the existing demoralization less in the agricultural than in the commercial districts, though the one is a scattered population, and the other is gathered together in towns or crowded localities, circumstances in themselves unfavourable to health and morals; the former of which are

consequently freed from many of those causes of declension[1] which
powerfully influence the latter.

Life, however, though not necessarily shortened by manufacturing occupation, is stripped of a most material portion of that which
can alone render it delightful—the possession of health, and those
who are engaged in it may be said to live a protracted life in death.

6. Robert Macnish, *The Anatomy of Drunkenness.* 5th ed. Glasgow: W.R. McPhun (1834)

Husbands sometimes teach their wives to be drunkards by indulging
them in toddy,[2] and such fluids, every time they themselves sit down
to their libations. Women frequently acquire the vice by drinking
porter and ale while nursing. These stimulants are usually recommended to them from well-meant but mistaken motives, by their
female attendants.[3] Many fine young women are ruined by this pernicious practice. Their persons become gross, their milk unhealthy,
and a foundation is too often laid for future indulgence in
liquor....[Some illnesses] are relieved for a time by the use of spirits;
and what was at first employed as a medicine, soon becomes an
essential requisite.

Some writers allege that unmarried women, especially if somewhat advanced in life, are more given to liquor than those who are
married. This point I am unable from my own observation to
decide. Women who indulge in this way, are *solitary* dram-drinkers,
and so would men be, had not the arbitrary opinions of the world
invested the practice in them with much less moral turpitude than
in the opposite sex. Of the two sexes, there can be no doubt that
men are much the more addicted to all sorts of intemperance.[4]

Drunkenness appears to be in some measure hereditary. We frequently see it descending from parents to their children. This may
undoubtedly often arise from bad example and imitation, but there
can be little question that, in many instances at least, it exists as a
family predisposition....

Women, especially in a low station, who act as nurses, are strongly addicted to the practice of drinking porter and ales, for the

1 Deterioration, decline.
2 A drink combining alcohol, sugar, spice, and hot water.
3 Dark ale was a standard recommendation for pregnant and nursing
   mothers as it was believed to contain blood-strengthening iron.
4 To extend the point, women drinkers were so culturally unacceptable as
   to present a social anomaly, virtually a contradiction in terms.

purpose of augmenting their milk. This very common custom cannot be sufficiently deprecated. It is often pernicious to both parties, and may lay the foundations of a multitude of diseases in the infant. The milk, which ought to be bland and unirritating, acquires certain heating qualities, and becomes deteriorated to a degree of which those unaccustomed to investigate such matters have little conception. The child nursed by a drunkard is hardly ever healthy. It is, in a particular manner, subject to derangements of the digestive organs, and convulsive affections. With regard to the latter, Dr. North[*] remarks, that he has seen them almost instantly removed by the child being transferred to a temperate woman. I have observed the same thing, not only in convulsive cases, but in many others. Nor are liquors the only agents whose properties are communicable to the nursling. It is the same with regard to opium, tobacco, and other narcotics. Purgatives[1] transmit their powers in a similar manner, so much so, that nothing is more common than for the child suckled by a woman who has taken physic, to be affected with bowel complaint. No woman is qualified to be a nurse [to breast-feed an infant], unless strictly sober; and though stout children are sometimes reared by persons who indulge to a considerable extent in liquor, there can be no doubt that they are thereby exposed to risk, and that they would have had a much better chance of doing well, if the same quantity of milk had been furnished by natural means. If a woman cannot afford the necessary supply without these indulgences, she should give over the infant to some one who can, and drop nursing altogether. The only cases in which a moderate portion of malt liquor is justifiable, are when the milk is deficient, and the nurse averse or unable to put another in her place. Here, of two evils, we choose the least, and rather give the infant milk of an inferior quality, than endanger its health, by weaning it prematurely, or stinting it of its accustomed nourishment.

Connected with this subject is the practice of administering stimulating liquors to children. This habit is so common in some parts of Scotland, that infants of a few days old are often forced to swallow raw whisky. In like manner, great injury is often inflicted upon children by the frequent administration of laudanum, paregoric,[2] God-

---

[*] Macnish's note; *Practical Observations on the Convulsions of Infants.* [John North (London: Burgess and Hill, 1826)]

---

1 Cathartic medicines.
2 Paregoric, derived from opium, was used as a sedative and in the treatment of diarrhea.

frey's Cordial, and other preparations of opium. The child in a short time becomes pallid, emaciated, fretful, and is subject to convulsive attacks, and every variety of disorder in the stomach and bowels. Vomiting, diarrhoea, and other affections of the digestive system ensue, and atrophy, followed by death, is too often a consequence....Parents should therefore be careful not to allow their youthful offspring stimulating liquors of any kind, except in cases of disease, and then only under the guidance of a medical attendant. The earlier persons are initiated in the use of liquor, the more completely does it gain dominion over them, and the more difficult is the passion for it to be eradicated.

....Children naturally dislike liquors—a pretty convincing proof that in early life they are totally uncalled for, and that they only become agreeable by habit....This shows that the love of such stimulants is in a great measure acquired, and also points out the necessity of guarding youth as much as possible from the acquisition of so unnatural a taste.

7. W. Cooke Taylor, "Women in Factories." *Factories and the Factory System*. London: Jeremiah How (1844)

It is notorious that females prefer employment in the mill to domestic servitude; and so forcibly was this felt by the Trades-Unionists, that they attempted to get up a clamour on the treatment of female servants, and to bring the domestic economy of private houses within the scope of the Factory Act.[1] These facts are sufficiently notorious; and hence we rarely find the enemies of factories specifying any particular operation as painful or injurious, but limiting themselves to vague declarations respecting "dust," "heat," "toil," and "noise."

....In the great towns the factories have had to contend with all the nuisances which an increase of population beyond the due limits of accommodation must necessarily produce. In fact the few attempts made to support the charges against factories by statistical tables are all based on the supposition that the great-town nuisance is identical or connected with the factory system. Hence visitors to Manchester make the double blunder of believing that all its working-classes belong to the factory population, and that all the health and misconduct they witness among females of the lower rank in that town may be ascribed to the factory system. The question of

---

1   The 1844 Factory Act limited women's work-day to twelve hours.

health in the mills is settled by a reference to the rural factories, and to that of morals we shall devote a separate chapter; but in the mean time we shall show good reason for believing that the worst evils belonging to the sanitary and moral condition of Manchester have arisen from the glaring defects of its domestic accommodations, and the almost total absence of means in several districts for cleanliness, ventilation, and draining.

....In no town in the world probably has population accumulated so rapidly; and the means of accommodation not having increased in anything like the same proportion, the lodgings and dwelling-houses of the poor are about as bad as they possibly can be....There are localities in Manchester which it is a disgrace to have existing in the midst of a civilized community. One street was erected along the course of a filthy ditch for the convenience of excavating cellarage, the cellars being designed, not for lumber, but for the reception of human beings. Many streets are unpaved, with a dunghill or pond in the middle; the houses are built back to back, without ventilation or drainage, and whole families occupy each a corner of a cellar or garret. In these crowded and filthy lodging-houses, delicacy, the great safeguard of chastity, is utterly destroyed, and the young are early initiated into mysteries which prepare them for a life of guilt and suffering. These localities are hot-beds of physical disease and moral pollution; they cannot be visited by any save those who possess the firmest of hearts and the strongest of stomachs; they are a positive disgrace to a Christian land. The visitors to Manchester can see the denizens of these shocking haunts of disease and depravity more commonly in the streets than the sound and healthy portion of the population, and hence, great as the evil is confessedly, it is much exaggerated in appearance by fortuitous circumstances....

About forty thousand strangers arrive weekly in Manchester by railways and other means of conveyance; such an influx must necessarily have a perturbating effect on the tables of crime and mortality, for a very large proportion must become tenants of the low and filthy lodging-houses, where both the sexes are indiscriminately huddled together, and where there can be no doubt that crimes and profligacy of every description are both planned and perpetrated....

There are, indeed, serious evils connected with the employment of women in factories, and indeed, everywhere save in their own homes, which must not be passed over without notice. The girl employed all day in the factory has little opportunity of learning the details of domestic economy and of the management of a household. When she marries she is far from being well qualified to fulfil the duties of a wife and mother, and she often neglects both from not being taught how to set about them....

Ignorance of the commonest things, needlework, cooking, and other matters of domestic economy, is described as universally prevalent; and, when any knowledge of such things is possessed by the wife of a labourer, it is generally to be traced to the circumstance of her having before marriage lived as a servant in a farmhouse or elsewhere. A girl brought up in a cottage until she marries is generally ignorant of nearly everything she ought to be acquainted with for the comfortable and economic management of a cottage. The effects of such ignorance are seen in many ways, but in no one more striking than its hindering girls from going out to service, as they are not capable of doing anything that is required in a family of a better description. The further effect of this is, that, not being able to find a place, a young woman goes into the fields of labour, with which ends all chance of improving her position; she marries and brings up her daughters in the same ignorance, and their lives are a repetition of her own.

The ignorance of domestic economy amongst the operatives is much greater in the towns than in the rural factories....As females may earn from 9s. to 21s. per week in the mills, this rate of wages frequently leads them to continue working in the factory after marriage; many of them do so in an advanced state of pregnancy, and far too early after their recovery from a confinement. Their children are entrusted to the care of a hired servant, generally a little girl not much older than themselves, and are thus exposed to numerous accidents and dangers. The number of lost children found by the police in Manchester, and restored to their parents, during one year, amounted to 2730....

When the mother of young children is absent from home, the whole or the greater part of the day, the mischief to them is very great. They are neglected in every way, morally and physically. Under the most favourable circumstances, they may be left in the care of a grandmother or aunt; but the more common way is to leave them in the custody of the eldest boy or girl, of eight or nine years old, or in that of a girl of the same age, or a little older, hired for the purpose. Sometimes, however, her children are locked up in the cottage, without anybody to take charge of them at all. Where a girl is hired to take care of children, she is paid about 9d. a-week, and has her food besides, which is a serious deduction from the wages of the woman at work.

When children are locked up by themselves, sometimes the most fatal accidents happen, those from fire amongst others....They are left without any control over their conduct the whole day, and without instruction or example of any kind. When left in the care of a child older than themselves, the case is hardly better. No child of eight or ten years can feel the responsibility of such a charge, or be able to attend to children, as far as forming their minds, or keeping them from indulging in mischievous propensities....

To a certain extent, also, the husband is a sufferer from his wife's absence from home. There is not the same order in the cottage, nor the same attention paid to his comforts, as when his wife remains at home all day. On returning from her labour she has to look after her children, and her husband may have to wait for his supper....there is no fire, no supper, no comfort, and he goes to the beer-shop.

When a woman is much employed out of doors, many things in the domestic economy are neglected; particularly such things as require frequent attention. Her own clothes and those of her husband and family are rarely in such cases properly attended to.

Appendix C: Reviews of Illustrations of Political Economy

1. [Josiah Conder] Review of *Illustrations of Political Economy* by Harriet Martineau. *Eclectic Review* 8 (1832): 44–72

....[We turn] to the delightful Political Economy made easy of Professor Harriet Martineau,—the most accomplished and engaging lecturer on abstruse subjects of science....Whether our fair *Dotteressa* be charming or homely, old or young, matron or spinster, we know not; but this we must say, that she has employed to most admirable purpose very extraordinary talents; extraordinary, not because these Tales of hers are in themselves beautifully simple, yet extremely touching, full of character, and at once dramatic and graphic,—for we have many female tale-writers in the present day, who have discovered similar knowledge of human nature and fertility of imagination; nor yet, because her notions indicate a clearness and comprehension of thought in relation to abstruse subjects of inquiry, a masculine faculty of abstraction, with a feminine power of illustration, rarely united; but because the combination of these qualifications for her difficult task *is* a phenomenon. Without pledging ourselves to an entire accordance with every one of the axioms laid down in these publications, we cannot too warmly applaud the design, spirit, and execution of the Parts which have appeared, and rejoice to know that they are already obtaining a wide circulation....

We have very few observations to offer upon the Author's doctrines. Political economy may be generally described as treating of the sources and distribution of wealth; although this does not, and is probably not intended to *define* the range of inquiry which the science embraces. These "Illustrations" sufficiently prove that, with purely economical inquiries, collateral questions of a strictly moral or political nature are indissolubly connected and interwoven. The moment we speak of labour, or at least of the labourer, man, we have got out of pure "catallactics," and have entered upon a mixed subject, which may be said to belong to political ethics; and "national wealth" can no longer be the proper definition of the object of inquiry, unless we understand the term as implying national welfare....We cannot help strongly wishing that Miss Martineau would *exemplify* all this; for we are quite sure that her good sense will enable her to perceive the accordance of our principles with facts; facts too generally overlooked by the framers of axioms and the lovers of abstract principles....

Assuredly, when political economy comes to be better understood, there will be no such thing under a civilized Government, as [industrial] slavery. We cordially thank the Author for her illustration of this truth.

2. Review of "Weal and Woe in Garveloch." *The Spectator* (7 July 1832)

In *Weal and Wo* [sic] *in Garveloch*, Miss Martineau has continued the history of the people with whose characters and condition she had made us so thoroughly well acquainted in the Illustration of last month. We have the heroic Ella, her bold and energetic brethren, the slovenly Murdochs, and the rational and travelled Angus, under new and most trying circumstances. In *Ella of Garveloch*, we learned, by the domestic history of a few families in the poor and sterile Western Islands, how RENT arose, and how exertions meant for private benefit operated on the community. The scene is now changed. Garveloch, under a temporary access of prosperity, becomes a great fishing-station; is taken by a company; and is flocked to by a numerous population, which population is not a little increased by the islanders themselves, under the motives induced by the prospect of wealth and comfort. But the luck changes; the fish take another direction; stormy seasons succeed one another; and ruin falls upon the crowded population of Garveloch: trade fails, supplies cease; in short, there is a famine in the place—the famine succeeded by universal sickness. Here are scenes for the picturesque pen of Miss Martineau: they are painted with a power and quiet self-possession not exceeded in any of her former works; while the didactic conversations that take place amid them are full of practical instruction. *Weal and Wo in Garveloch* is one of the most valuable of Miss Martineau's admirable series. At this moment, no person is doing more good in England than this lady: perhaps no other female ever occupied the same proud position of a national instructress, on the topics of the country's most essential interests.

3. Review of "Manchester Strike." *The Spectator* (4 August 1832)

The praise which we have given to each successive number of this work must be understood as applying to the tale before us; in which the authoress, on wholly fresh ground, and with a totally new set of objects, is as original as ever; and if not quite so attractive, the cause may be found in the dreary and unhappy condition of the class whose history she has taken up.

The theoretical object of the work is to illustrate the nature of Wages, and to show the operation of a movement among the labourers, well known under the name of "a Strike." This is done by going into the domestic history of some of the families of the labourers, of different characters; by depicting the manners, opinions, and conduct of the leaders among the people; and also letting us into a hasty view of the cotton lords themselves—the manufacturers, who, having right on their side, use it as if they were in the wrong. We attend the meetings of the strikers; we become acquainted with the motives of their orators; and we witness, as elsewhere, the fluctuating character of the popularity that depends upon the short-sighted and passionate views of an ignorant populace.

Many of the characters are powerfully conceived. Such is the virtuous and clear-headed William Allen, the gentle yet stern parent of a starving family, and the unwilling Secretary of the Strike. Then comes Clack, the Cleon[1] of the mob—the rater of the masters, and the exciter of the workmen. Bray, the travelling musician, is a fine hearty sketch of another sort, and forms a pleasant relief. The arrogance of the master Mortimer is well hit off, as is also the timid vacillation of his feeble partner Rowe. One master alone condescends to reason with the men,—perhaps because he alone understands the nature of the business. Into his mouth, and that of the Secretary, Allen, are put the principle didactic discussions; and nowhere else can the young political economist collect clearer notions of an important branch of the science....

....Morning breaking upon a Manchester cotton factory would make an affecting picture. It is here depicted by Miss Martineau with the hand and eye of a true artist; and is connected with a touching little incident—the falling asleep of poor, little, declining Martha...over her work....In the early part of the Strike, the children still continue at work. It is not for the interest of the workmen that they should strike too; and the masters permit their continued labour. But after all hope of a compromise declines, and the Strike is likely to prove long and obstinate, the children are turned off, to bring the matter sooner to a crisis. The effect of this unaccustomed

---

1   Cleon (d. 422 BCE), Athenian general who opposed Pericles.

holyday on the poor children, and the additional burden on the funds, is told with true pathos, and as perhaps no other writer but Miss Martineau could tell it.

The authoress thinks it necessary to announce, that she has no acquaintance with any one firm, master, or workman in Manchester; and hopes she will be spared the imputation of personality. This she must scarcely expect: her characters are so strongly drawn, and appear so *true*, that applications will be made in spite of her wishes to the contrary.

If the masters knew their own interest, this little work would be circulated by tens of thousands among their labourers; and the philanthropist who feels for the deplorable state of society in Manchester, could not spend a year better than in devoting himself to the circulation of its ideas and pictures.

4. "Miss Martineau's Illustrations of Political Economy." *Tait's Edinburgh Magazine* (August 1832)

The ladies seem determined to make the science of Political Economy peculiarly their own. Our first instructor in this difficult branch of study was Mrs. Marcet,[*] and a clearer or more judicious teacher we have not since encountered. Miss Edgeworth[1] too has occasional dissertations, which shew what she could have done in that department had she applied her mind to it. And now Miss Martineau comes forward to embody the most abstract, but at the same time most important principles of the science, in narratives which have all the value of truth and all the grace of fiction. After all, we believe that there is something in the female mind which peculiarly fits it for elucidating, in a familiar manner, the intricacies of political economy. The economy of empires is only the economy of families and neighbourhoods on a larger scale. Now woman is eminently the best family manager. Let profane ones sneer if they please—we give it as our deliberate conviction that there never yet was a well-regulated house in which the lady was not the master. Woman alone can exert the strictest economy, unblemished by the harsh heartlessness of

---

[*] Conversations on Political Economy. By a Lady. [Jane Marcet (1769-1858), writer on political economy and chemistry whose work was aimed at young people.]

---

1   Maria Edgeworth (1767-1849), novelist whose narratives often addressed issues of Irish social reform.

avarice—she alone can enforce a martinet [strict] discipline in household affairs, without communicating a sense of oppression. There is a delicate tact about woman which enables her to see at once on what side a recusant [nonconformist] is to be attacked, and an ever ready observation which nothing escapes, and a gentleness which nothing can resist. She lacks the strength to take an active share in the concerns of an empire, but her experience in the business details of her own miniature state enable her to read lessons worthy of serious attention from all who take an interest in public affairs.

This we think is the clue which leads us to the secret source of the excellence of Miss Martineau's works. Her's is, no doubt, even independently of the quality to which we have been alluding, a highly gifted mind. She can put forth, when it suits her purpose, an intense and passionate power, and the next moment whisper an overmastering spell to the gentlest feelings of the heart. She can portray the beauty of heart and mind without degenerating into a sickly sweetness, and the workings of the darker passions without overstepping the modesty of nature. She possesses a quick sense of all the more delicate beauties of animate and inanimate nature. And throughout everything she has written, there breathes a calm undertone of sustained philosophical cheerfulness. The sentiments and opinions contained in her books shew how lovely a thing the mind of woman may become, when allowed fairly to develope [sic] itself. With all man's power of endurance, it has a gentleness and delicacy he never can acquire. It is most fitly typified by the ancient statues of the ideal class to which the Apollo Belvidere belongs, where the artist, by harmoniously blending the proportions of the male with the softer contour of the female, has succeeded in expressing that gentle power which is the truly godlike.

....Narratives, like those constructed by Miss Martineau, by showing how completely the abstract doctrines of Political Economy come home to every man's "business and bosom," how necessary a knowledge of the results of the economist's analysis of society is to the comfort and independence of every individual, will prove more effectual than any means that have yet been proposed, to remove the silly prejudices still entertained against this indispensable branch of knowledge.

....Her characters, and the scenery which surrounds them, are in every new number dashed off with a bolder and more graphic pencil; and the doctrinal discussions are more assimilated to the common conversation of every day life. Some readers may at first think otherwise, seeing that the author has retained all the technical phraseology of the economists; but in doing this we are decidedly of the opinion that she has acted judiciously. If it is of importance that all classes of society should become familiarized with such discussions, it is also of importance that they should be accustomed from the first to conduct them in precise and definite, that is, in technical language....

We look upon Miss Martineau as entitled to rank high among those gifted females whose writings have of late years so eminently benefited their country—the Edgeworths, Marcets, and others. The country is now free; but the just use of that freedom depends upon the moral and intellectual advance of the people. We do not think that the question of emancipation ought, in any case, to be postponed to that of instruction. The slave never can be educated. The freeman *may* act wrong, but the slave *cannot* act right.[1] We struck with our fellow-countrymen for freedom, without stopping to inquire whether they were capable of using it properly, because it was their right, which no man was entitled to withhold from them. Now that the chain has either been removed, or so corroded, that no power on earth can ever again render it effective to rivet us down, a yet nobler task remains— to aid in freeing men from the self-imposed fetters of ignorance and prejudice. Every fellow-labourer shall be received with a hearty welcome; and one so able as Miss Martineau is richly entitled to the most cordial it is in our power to give.

5. Review of "Cousin Marshall." *The Spectator* (8 September 1832)

The first day of each month is marked by no publication of more importance than Miss Martineau's *Illustrations of Political Economy*. Each succeeding Number increases our admiration for the writer's abilities, and our gratitude for the useful direction in which they are exerted. The scene is this time shifted to a city of ordinary population, and the usual institutions; the subject is Parish Charities. It is long since so practical a view has been taken of them, and never did they meet with a sterner or more searching antagonist. Miss Mar-

---

1 The reviewer draws a popular analogy between bond-slaves and the industrial working poor. Education without emancipation is an oxymoron: only when both are present can real and metaphorical slaves become free.

tineau pursues the parish shilling from the pocket of the rate-payer, through the overseer and the workhouse, into the hovel of the indigent and the vagabond; and demonstrates, in various ingenious forms, its invariable tendency to increase the evil it would alleviate. She extends her condemnation even to all those charities that pretend to relieve sufferings that might have been calculated upon and avoided,—such as lying-in hospitals, and schools which supply maintenance, foundling institutions, and the like. It is very difficult indeed to refuse conviction to reasoning supported as hers is, by such a variety of views, such truth of character, such eloquent description, and so intimate a knowledge of the poor, of the nature of their poverty, and their modes of thought and motives to action.

Cousin Marshall is the wife of a steady and respectable working man, who brings up a large family decently and virtuously, by the frugal employment of scanty wages; and when misfortune by fire ruins the family of some poor relatives, is, moreover, able to provide for two of the orphans, and to keep a protecting eye on the others who enter the workhouse. The workhouse is laid open before us, and all its disgusting scenes: the mysteries of mendicancy [begging] are also disclosed; the dishonest tricks of the idle and vagabond to increase the parish allowance are dramatically exhibited, as well as the painful process of degradation, shamelessness, and ultimate vice worked in those who come to look upon the parish as the rightful labour fund. These things are shown in connexion and contrast with the family of Cousin Marshall; which is, however, far from prosperous. In such times as those described, neither hard labour nor the very excess of frugality can keep the heads of a numerous family above water. Wages are too low, and work is too uncertain, for any common operative to look on the future with satisfaction. John Marshall the father dies; the children marry poorly, and have large families; and poor old Cousin Marshall, the mother and grandmother of a numerous progeny, outlives the means of life—nearly; but such is the force of the admirable qualities of industry, frugality, and energy possessed by her, that even in her decrepit days she contrives to scrape up sufficient subsistence to keep life in the body. The picture of her latter days, and the impression conveyed through the whole book, is that of a poor but high-minded creature, worthier of respect than duchesses in their robes or countesses in their coronets and carriages. Miss Martineau is the real painter of the poor: she has all the truth of Crabbe,[1] with more hope and more reason.

---

1   George Crabbe (1754-1832), English poet.

6. [William Maginn], "On National Economy: Review of Miss Martineau's 'Cousin Marshall.'" *Fraser's Magazine for Town and Country* (November 1832): 403-13

The *Westminster* Review, in speaking of one of Miss Martineau's little books, bursts forth into the following exclamation:

"What a country is England! Where a young lady may put forth a book like this, quietly, modestly, and without the apparent consciousness of doing any extraordinary act; and, what is more, where others see as little to be surprised at in the circumstance, and receive the boon with the indifference of any ordinary courtesy!"

This flourish we feel a strong inclination to parody. Our own reflections, after reading *"Cousin Marshall,"* though of a different cast, yet fall into a very similar form. We could not help saying to ourselves—

"What a frightful delusion is this, called, by its admirers, Political Economy, which can lead a young lady to put forth a book like this!—a book written by a *woman* against the *poor*—a book written by a *young woman* against *marriage!* And what is more, where a long tirade against all charity, and an elaborate defence of the closest selfishness, is received with acclamation by those who profess themselves the friends of the people and the advocates of the distressed."

In another point of view, too, we might fairly express amazement at the delight with which Miss Martineau's tracts are received, if we could be surprised at any thing from a *"political economist."*[1] These gentry are ever complimenting each other, and the whole class to which they belong, as the only men who know how to reason logically on the management of a country. The contempt which they uniformly express for the minds and arguments of those who receive not their fancies, is often ludicrous, sometimes irritating. And yet, in the present case, their warmest and most unqualified approbation is unhesitatingly given to a tissue of reasonings, which would disgrace the third class of any ladies' boarding-school of decent character, in these days of improved female education.

What, for instance, would any properly-qualified "English teacher" say to such a specimen of logic as that which forms the main substance and staple of *Cousin Marshall?* The narrative gives us some lively, but rather overdrawn sketches, of workhouse grievances,

---

1 Martineau viewed herself as a popularizer of political and economic theories; she never claimed to be a political economist.

and other mal-administrations of the poor-laws. The conclusion drawn from these sketches, in the doctrinal parts of the book is, that the poor-laws should be *wholly abolished! entirely swept away!!*

....According to Miss Martineau's exquisite logic, it would be better at once *wholly to abolish the Court of Chancery*, and let the lieges, if they will get into disputes about their property, settle those disputes by fisty-cuffs [boxing], or ask for a "writ of helter-skelter."

Or who, again, of higher intellect than some village overseer, grumbling out his weekly complaint, "the more you give, the more you may," would dream of seriously urging the insufficiency of a charity *to do every thing*, as an argument against *doing any thing?* And yet this *"skilful dialectician,"* as one of her admirers calls her, gravely puts this forward, once and again, as a conclusive argument! Lying-in charities are vehemently denounced, as among "the worst in existence" of all public institutions. And what is a chief objection to them?....The *Arabian Nights Entertainments* are dry matter of fact compared with this....Where has this young woman lived all her days?....Her greatest horror is, of course, the perverse folly of the poor in marrying! and nothing can exceed the absurdity of some of the motives she assigns for the marriages of the poor. Lying-in hospitals are denounced as "causing misery," just as much as the distribution of coals and blankets....So that this young lady evidently takes it for granted, that many people marry principally, or solely, in order to have the happiness of lying-in in an hospital!!!

And as alms-houses are not to be built, lest the young folks should marry, so, in another place, the cottage system is condemned, and for the same reason—"Under no system does population increase more rapidly." Now what is meant by the "the cottage system" is merely this, that every poor agricultural labourer should have his own little dwelling; and also, if possible, his own garden. In many districts, it is well known, two or three families are at present crammed into one cottage, and twelve or fourteen persons, grown or growing up, are forced to sleep in two small rooms. This is the system which this young lady would wish to have kept up, because, forsooth, if men were allowed to have cottages, they would soon want wives and children! "Under no system does population increase more rapidly!" Delicate creature!

The truth is, that there is nothing here but a very old story. The feelings of these political economists towards the people, are just the same as those entertained three thousand years ago by Pharaoh towards the children of Israel. The cry is just the same: "Come now, let us deal *wisely* with the people, *lest they multiply upon us.*[1] And there are those among ourselves, who, if they dare, would gladly employ the same means with those adopted by Pharaoh. Dean Swift's plan,[2] however, of making pork of the young ones, was preferable, in many points of view, to the Egyptian method....

In behalf, then, of public morals, we object, with the strongest abhorrence, to all resort to this favourite project of "the preventive check." But we have also shewn that the measure by which this said "preventive check" is proposed to be called into operation,—a repeal of the poor-laws,—would be grossly unjust and oppressive. Also, that it would be impracticable, from its cruelty. Also, that it may be seen in the experience of Scotland and Ireland, that as a check upon human increase, it would be wholly ineffectual. And, further, that the assumption on which it rests, of poverty being a check upon the growth of a population, is entirely and grossly unphilosophical.

7. [George Poulett Scrope]. Review of *Illustrations of Political Economy*. *The Quarterly Review* 49 (1833): 137-52

Here we have a monthly series of novels on Political Economy—Malthus, M'Culloch, Senior, and Mill, dramatised by a clever female hand. The authoress has, moreover, the high recommendation of being an Unitarian. How could such a series fail to be considered as an important ally of the Society for the Diffusion of Useful Knowledge?[3] What wonder that...there should be a general chorus of exultation over the Sibylline[4] leaves of Norwich?

There is, we admit, much which it is impossible not to admire in Miss Martineau's productions—the praiseworthy intention and benevolent spirit in which they are written,—and the varied knowledge of nature and society, the acute discrimination of character, and remarkable power of entering into, and describing the feelings of the poorer classes, which several of her narratives evince. But it is

---

1 Exodus 1:10: Come on; let us deal wisely with them; lest they multiply, and it come to pass that, when there falleth out any war, they join also unto our enemies, and fight against us, and so get them up out of the land.

2 Jonathan Swift (1667-1745), Irish satirist and writer, author of *Gulliver's Travels* (1726). Swift's "A Modest Proposal" (1729) proposes that Ireland's poverty and overpopulation can both be resolved by turning Irish babies into commodities and serving them up as an epicurean delicacy.

3 Unitarians are a dissenting sect focusing on social reform rather than religious dogma or elaborate ritual. The Society for the Diffusion of Useful Knowledge published various social reform tracts, including Martineau's *Illustrations of Taxation* and *Poor Laws and Paupers Illustrated*.

4 A sibyl is a female prophet.

equally impossible not to laugh at the absurd trash which is seriously propounded by some of her characters, in dull didactic dialogues, introduced here and there in the most clumsy manner; and what is worst of all, it is quite impossible not to be shocked, nay disgusted, with many of the unfeminine and mischievous doctrines on the principles of social welfare, of which these tales are made the vehicle.

This young lady's work consists of the several chapters of the 'Principles of Political Economy,' according to the doctors we have named, rendered into popular stories. Each tale has attached to it the 'principle' it is intended to illustrate; and the readers of each little volume are expected, we suppose, by the time they arrive at the end, to have duly imbibed and digested the substance of these 'principles.' We can only say, if any individual has accomplished this feat, his powers of deglutition [swallowing] and digestion are such as an ostrich might envy....

"Ella of Garveloch," the fifth tale, is improbable, but amusing,— that is to say, if we skip the political economy in it, which consists of sundry long and doleful dialogues on the nature of *rent*....The sixth tale ["Weal and Woe in Garveloch"] takes up the history of Garveloch (a rocky islet among the Hebrides) at a later period....A considerable population had settled there from the neighbouring islands, and was rapidly increasing....This is a state of things to alarm a Malthusian; and Ella, the Martineau of Garveloch, begins, even when the island is at the zenith of its prosperity, to quake at the anticipation of its over-population. She sees the cultivation of the islands so rapidly improving, that their produce had more than doubled in the last ten years, but she is impressed with the idea that "all this time the consumers are increasing at a much quicker rate."....

This is rare logic and arithmetic, and not a little curious as natural history....But these are the discoveries of genius! Why does Miss Martineau write, except to correct our mistaken notions, and expound to us the mysteries of the "principle of population?"...By the admission of the author,...it would be necessary,...that every female should marry at three months old, and have twenty children at a birth! We believe *the herrings* multiply at some such rate; and it seems Miss Martineau thinks herring-fisherwomen must be equally prolific. A little ignorance on these ticklish topics is perhaps not unbecoming a young unmarried lady. But before such a person undertook to write books in favour of "the preventive check," she should have informed herself somewhat more accurately upon the laws of human propagation. Poor innocent! She has been puzzling over Mr. Malthus's arithmetical and geometrical ratios, for knowledge which she should have obtained by a simple question or two of her mamma....

It has always appeared to us one of the strangest inconsistencies of which the anti-populationists are guilty, that they, of all economists, are ever the loudest in crying up the advantages of every increase of inanimate machinery—in spite of its *immediate* effect in throwing labourers out of employment—at the same time that they decry every increase of the human machine, as a cause of immitigable want and woe.

....The "Manchester Strike" contains some well-drawn pictures of the state of the operatives in our manufacturing towns—and some useful lessons to that class, on the mischief and inutility of their "strikes and turn-outs"—but has its moral marred entirely by the constant reference of the distress that arises from a temporary and local redundancy of hands, to the sinfulness of those weavers who marry without having previously ascertained that there cannot for a generation occur a stagnation of business in the cotton-trade! What?—when masters occasionally advertise throughout the kingdom for 'several thousand fresh hands wanted' at Macclesfield or Manchester—when hordes of Irish are pouring in daily to supply the demand for labour in our great manufacturing districts—are the *natives* of those very districts to be told that it is *their* fault if labour is ever in excess; that *they* have the remedy in their own hands, by refraining from matrimony; and that they neglect their duty to society by taking wives under such circumstances? When it is notorious that in these districts the relative supply and demand for labour often oscillates from one extreme to the other within a year or two—we are to be informed by Miss Martineau, in delicate phrase, that the labourers have the power, and they alone, by more or less of continence, to adjust the supply of labour exactly at all times to the demand! Are the interests, the existence of millions, to be thus trifled with? Is the destiny of our industrious population to remain in the hands of men who have the imbecility to listen with reverence to such "principles" as these—or the quackery to pretend to do so?

In another story, "Cousin Marshall," Miss Martineau follows up her grand "principle" to its legitimate inference, the grievous abomination of poor-laws; and not of poor-laws only, but of charity in every shape,—of anything, in short, which can stand for an instant of time between the poor and that utter destitution,—which this gentle philosopher expects to teach them to keep their numbers within the demand for their labour,—and which, at all events, would *kill them off* down to the desirable limit. If the subject were not too sadly serious, the monomania of these misogamists[1] would be amusing....Lying-in hospitals are denounced as "causing great misery"....Nay, the very dispensaries are accused of increasing the number of sick patients—the poor falling ill, of course, on purpose to have the pleasure of being physicked gratuitously; just as they marry with the express view of being brought to bed in an hospital, and dying in an alms-house!

....We all remember Moore's[2] "She Politician": "'Tis my fortune to know a lean Benthamite spinster,/A maid who her faith in old Jeremy puts"...Did Miss Martineau sit for the picture? But no;—such a character is nothing to a *female Malthusian*. A *woman* who thinks child-bearing a *crime against society!* An *unmarried woman* who declaims against *marriage!!* A *young woman* who deprecates charity and a provision for the *poor!!!*

Miss Martineau has, we are most willing to acknowledge, talents which might make her an useful and an agreeable writer. But the best advice we can give her is, to burn all the little books she has as yet written....

8. [Anon.] "On the Review Entitled, 'Miss Martineau's Monthly Novels,' in the last *Quarterly.*" *The Monthly Repository* 7 (1833): 314-23

In the last number of the 'Quarterly Review,' there is an article entitled 'Miss Martineau's Monthly Novels,' reported to be the work of an ex-official....[who] might perhaps be worse employed than in offering insults to the womanhood of England. We will not transcribe the peroration [at length] of this review, in which he insults a lady whose delightful and instructive volumes have already dispelled much of the ignorance and prejudice in which he breathes most freely. We shall only refer the reader to this precious passage, sure that every man and every woman,—for those who offer and those who countenance such language are not to be reckoned,—will have no doubt on whom the disgrace of this unmanly attempt really falls.

---

1 Misogamists are anti-marriage. Although she remained single, Martineau did not denigrate the institution of marriage; she did, however, criticize the "political invisibility" of married women and their lack of legal protection and political representation.
2 Thomas Moore (1779-1852), Irish poet.

It is as well, perhaps, that the most flagitious [heinous, shameful] attack of this description by which Miss Martineau has been assailed, should be made from such a quarter. It tends to unveil the foul reality of things which have long been gilded over. Talk of the *gentlemen* of England, indeed! where are they to be found? If their own organ is to be credited, less among the Tory Aristocracy and the Church,[1] for these are the parties on whose behalf the 'Quarterly Review' speaks, than in any other class of society whatever. We know not where to look for the mechanic, however uneducated his mind or coarse his habits, who would not shrink in utter disgust from the language and insinuations which this Reviewer has not scrupled to employ; nay, over which he seems to have gloated as the best arrow in his quiver. And with contemptible hypocrisy this foulest of all passages that have been penned in recent times, is introduced with a profession of unwillingness 'to bring a blush unnecessarily upon the cheek of any woman.'...Having spit his venom, he sinks into the following silliness:—

'Did Miss Martineau sit for the picture? But no;—such a character is nothing to a *female Malthusian*. A *woman* who thinks childbearing a *crime against society!* An *unmarried woman* who declaims against *marriage!!* A *young woman* who deprecates charity and a provision for the *poor!!!*'

Have we exceeded our warrant in saying that the article...is an unmanly insult? It remains to show that it is sophistry,[2] and bigoted sophistry to boot....Will, we repeat, this Tory sophist tell us that his unmanly attack on Miss Martineau, for affirming the expediency of prudential checks on population, is not sophistical as well as unmanly?....We retort the sneer of the Quarterly Reviewer as most applicable to himself. 'Poor innocent! *he* has been puzzling over Mr. Malthus's arithmetical and geometrical ratios, for knowledge which he should have obtained by a simple question or two of his mamma.'

...We cannot think that delicacy....forbids a lady noticing truths, on which the science she is allowed to treat is principally based. Miss Martineau could not have illustrated even the leading truths of political economy, without noticing the doctrine of population; nor could she have spoken of that doctrine in terms less calculated to offend real delicacy, than those she has employed. For that over-del-

---

1 Tories are Britain's conservative, Royalist political party; the Church refers to the Church of England.
2 Sophistry is an argument based on seemingly plausible but in fact fallacious reasoning.

icacy, which is plainly in this, as in every other case, under-delicacy, we trust she will continue to hold it in deserved contempt, and that she will proceed in her task with the glorious freedom with which science and benevolence have made her free, leaving it to her reviewers...to arrange their plain duties with their fine feelings as they can or will.

....Aided by a large knowledge of the records of this experience, *a woman*, it must be confessed of no ordinary talents, is able in these latter days to write political lessons, full of the most important truths, set forth in a very striking manner, for the reverend seigniors [lords], who, as appears by the bitterness of the Quarterly Review, are still not only too bigoted in principle and too sophistical in reasoning to profit by these pearls of precious price, but will turn again and rend the hand which offers them....Let Miss Martineau be assured that no testimony we could bear to the ability of the writer, or the importance of the writings should be half as flattering to her feelings, or would be half as useful to her interests, identified as these have been, and we feel confident ever will be, with *the cause of truth*, as the testimony which has been borne to her talents and principles by the unmanly and sophistical article in the Quarterly Review.

9. Edward Bulwer Lytton, "On Moral Fictions. Miss Martineau's Illustrations of Political Economy." *The New Monthly Magazine and Literary Journal* 37 (1833): 146-51

....In the heaven of philosophical fiction there are many mansions. There may be often truths known to the few which it is almost originality to popularize to the many. For next to inventing a truth, is the merit of making it generally known. This is peculiarly the case with political truths. So few have analyzed them,—and, while so necessary to the public, they have been for the most part treated in so dry a manner,—that to drag them from their retreats,—to gift them with familiar language,—to send them into the world preaching and converting as living disciples, is only a less proof of the inspiration of genius than the primary power of creation. It is to perform to political morals the same task as Addison[1] fulfilled with domestic. Miss Martineau, in the excellent fictions she has given to the world, has performed this noble undertaking, and accomplished this lesser

---

1   Joseph Addison (1672-1719), English essayist and co-founder of *The Spectator*.

species of inspiration. She has taken the facts of Political Economy, woven a series of tales, of great and familiar interest, illustrative of the broader and more useful of its doctrines. It is as a writer of fiction, however that we only regard her....As a political economist, then, we do not consider Miss Martineau entitled to high estimation: as a writer of moral fiction, we think she is entitled to a considerable station....

The style of Miss Martineau, though not the order of her talents, resembles rather that of Richardson than of Marmontel:[1] the rapid, condensed, antithetical analysis, is perfectly unknown to her—she writes with purity and elegance, but with that style which requires expatiation [elaboration] to do justice to her own conceptions. She is subject, moreover, to another fault—which is the consequence of her choice of subject;—her dialogue offends verisimilitude [believ-ability]—she writes more simply when she narrates, than when she causes her labourers and her fishermen to speak in their own persons. It is easy to see her benevolent and wise purpose in making the poor themselves speculate on truths, rather than be lectured by others into instruction. It opens to them what may be called "Intellectual Independence," and teaches, on a large scale, the Lancaster system, that the best schoolmaster is the pupil himself. But while this purpose is a full excuse for her practice in drawing philosophical fishermen and Socratical cottagers, the practice cannot but interfere with the effect of the fiction, and the artist-like delineation of the characters....

This want of keeping between the truth and its propounder, is yet more unpleasantly glaring in the tale called "Weal and Woe in Garveloch," where, in the most barbarous spot of earth, half-starved fishermen take the most astonishing views on the theory of population; and in this instance of inconsistency, there is a grosser want of truth than in the other tales. The language of the fisherman is never beneath his wisdom; he talks simply indeed, but it is with the simplicity of a scholar....

Now, without this being fine language, it is not natural, it is not conceivable, language in the mouth of a fisherman of Islay. True we are told he is of a superior mind, and in his course of trade has seen a little of the world. But a superior fisherman is a fisherman still; nor

---

1   Samuel Richardson (1689-1761), English novelist; author of *Pamela* and *Clarissa*. Jean-François Marmontel (1723-99), French philosophical writer.

does he utter the intricate doctrines of a Malthus in the elegant simplicity of a Hume....[1]

We come to the more pleasing part of our critical duty, and speak of the counterbalancing merits of Miss Martineau's performances. And in the first place we must beg the reader to observe that it is but fair to attribute the greater part of the defects we have spoken of, not to a want of capacity in the writer, but to the nature of the work—to the limited space of each tale, and to Miss Martineau's evident desire of making everything subordinate to the illustration of certain valuable truths. It is just therefore, in this, as in all works, to consider first, the author's design; secondly, to see if the design be accomplished; if so, we ought to look leniently on many of the faults inseparable, perhaps, from the accomplishment of the design itself. Putting aside the fact that the dialogues are not appropriate to the speakers, nothing can be more clear, succinct, and luminous than the manner in which the reasonings conveyed in the dialogues are expressed and detailed. A remarkable excellence in Miss Martineau, is the beauty of her descriptions—not exaggerated—not prolix—but fresh, nervous, graphic, and full of homeliness or of poetry as the subject may require. And this power of description extends not only to the delineation of scenery, but also to that of circumstances and of persons....

Another great excellence of Miss Martineau, and the most irrefragable [indisputable] proof of her talents, is in that nameless and undefinable power of exciting and sustaining interest in the progress of her tale,—which is the first requisite of prose fiction, and without which all other requisites become wearisome and vain....Miss Martineau's talents, and the value of her works, are indisputable. She has arrived at that point of excellence where we begin to estimate the value and adjudge the station of the writer. The greatest and most consummate order of perfect intellect, is that in which the imaginative and the reasoning faculties are combined,—each carried to its height:—the one inspired, the other regulated, by its companion; and though we cannot of course attribute to Miss Martineau these faculties in their greatest extent, we can yet congratulate her on no inconsiderable portion of them united with no common felicity.

---

1   David Hume (1711-76), Scottish philosopher and historian.

10. [J. S. Mill] "On Miss Martineau's Summary of Political Economy." *The Monthly Repository* 8 (1834): 318-22

Besides subjoining to each of her Political Economy Tales a brief summary of the doctrines which it was intended to illustrate, Miss Martineau has concluded the Series by a similar compendium of the whole science.* We should rather say, not of the Science, but of its leading doctrines and most important applications, as taught by the highest contemporary authorities. For a science is a connected *body* of truth; the *entire* philosophy of some distinctly definable portion of the field of nature: and when it is taught as Science, that is, with a view to the perfection of speculative knowledge rather than to the readiness of practical application, the teacher aims at making such a selection of its truths, and at presenting them in such an order, as will best exhibit the connectedness of the whole, and the completeness with which it solves all the questions which a contemplation of the subject-matter suggests to the speculative inquirer. But this was not the task which Miss Martineau set before herself, nor had it been left for her to perform. Her object was, not to exhibit the science as a whole, but to illustrate such parts of it as lead directly to important practical results. Having accomplished this, she has now brought together in one series, the principles which she had separately exemplified, and by hanging them each in its place, upon a logical framework originally constructed for the entire science, has given to the "Moral" of her "many Fables," some semblance of an elementary treatise. It would be unjust to weigh this little work in a balance in which most of the elaborate treatises on the subject would be found wanting. To all of them, perhaps, it may be objected, that they attempt to construct a permanent fabric out of transitory materials; that they take for granted the immutability of arrangements of society, many of which are in their nature fluctuating or progressive; and enunciate with as little qualification as if they were universal and absolute truths, propositions which are perhaps applicable to no state of society except the particular one in which the writer happened to live. Thus, for instance, English political economists presuppose, in every one of their speculations, that the produce of industry is shared among three classes, altogether distinct from one another—namely, labourers, capitalists, and landlord; and that all these are free agents, permitted in law and fact to set upon their labour, their capital, and

---

* Illustrations of Political Economy, No. XXV. "The Moral of Many Fables," by Harriet Martineau.

their land, whatever price they are able to get for it. The conclusions of the science being all adapted to a society thus constituted, require to be revised whenever they are applied to any other....Though many of its conclusions are only locally true, its method of investigation is applicable universally; and as he who has solved a certain number of algebraic equations, can without difficulty solve all others, so he who knows the political economy of England, or even of Yorkshire, knows that of all nations actual or possible: provided he have sense enough not to expect the same conclusion to issue from varying premises....

Miss Martineau's little work is not more subject to the above criticism than works of far greater pretension; but on the contrary, less. And as an exposition of the leading principles of what now constitutes the science, it possesses considerable merit.

There is but one point of importance on which we are obliged to differ from her. We cannot concur in her unqualified condemnation of the principle of the poor-laws. In this she is decidedly behind the present state of the science; political economists having mostly abandoned this among other exaggerated conclusions to which naturally enough they had pushed the principle of population, when they first became acquainted with it. The recent investigations of the poor-law commission, with which Miss Martineau is familiar, seem to us as conclusive in support of the *principle* of a poor-rate, as they are in condemnation of the existing practice....

But even these small blemishes are rare, and do not materially impair the value of the work: for which we may safely venture to bespeak numerous readers and a favourable reception.

Further Reading

Harriet Martineau

Arbuckle, Elisabeth Sanders, ed. *Harriet Martineau in London's Daily News*. New York and London: Garland Publishing, 1994.

__, ed. *Harriet Martineau's Letters to Fanny Wedgwood*. Stanford, CA: Stanford UP, 1983.

Bosanquet, Theodora. *Harriet Martineau: An Essay in Comprehension*. London: F. Etchells and H. Macdonald, 1927.

Burchell, R.A., ed. *Harriet Martineau in America: Selected Letters from the Reinhard S. Speck Collection*. Berkeley: Friends of the Bancroft Library, 1995.

Courtney, Janet. *Freethinkers of the Nineteenth Century*. London: Chapman and Hall, 1920.

David, Deirdre. *Intellectual Women and Victorian Patriarchy*. Ithaca, NY: Cornell UP, 1987.

Frawley, Maria. "Harriet Martineau in America: Gender and the Discourse of Sociology." *Victorian Newsletter* (Spring 1992): 13-20.

__, ed. Harriet Martineau, *Life in the Sickroom*. Peterborough, ON: Broadview Press, 2003.

Frost, Cy. "Autocracy and the Matrix of Power: Issues of Propriety and Economics in the Work of Mary Wollstonecraft, Jane Austen, and Harriet Martineau." *Tulsa Studies in Women's Literature* 10:2 (Fall 1991): 253-71.

Greg, W.R. "Harriet Martineau." *Nineteenth Century* 2 (August 1877).

Hill, Michael. Introduction to *How to Observe Morals and Manners by Harriet Martineau*. New Brunswick, NJ: Transaction Publishers, 1989.

Hill, Michael and Susan Hoecker-Drysdale, eds. *Harriet Martineau. Theoretical and Methodological Perspectives*. New York & London: Routledge, 2001.

Hoecker-Drysdale, Susan. *Harriet Martineau. First Woman Sociologist*. Oxford and New York: Berg Publishers, 1992.

Lipset, Seymour. Introduction to *Society in America by Harriet Martineau*. New York: Anchor Books, 1962.

Logan, Deborah, ed., *Harriet Martineau's Writing on the British Empire*, 5 vols, London: Pickering & Chatto, 2004.

__. *The Hour and the Woman. Harriet Martineau's 'somewhat remarkable' Life*. DeKalb, IL: Northern Illinois UP, 2002.

___, ed., *Writings on Slavery and the American Civil War by Harriet Martineau.* DeKalb, IL: Northern Illinois UP, 2002.

Martineau, Harriet. "Some Autobiographical Particulars of Miss Harriet Martineau." *Monthly Repository* 7 (1833): 612-15.

Miller, Florence Fenwick. *The Lessons of a Life: Harriet Martineau.* London: Sunday Lecture Society, 1877.

Nevill, John Cranstoun. *Harriet Martineau.* London: Frederick Muller, 1943.

Payne, James. *Some Literary Recollections.* New York: Harper Brothers, 1884.

Polkinghorn, Bette. "Jane Marcet and Harriet Martineau." *Women of Value. Feminist Essays on the History of Women in Economics.* Ed. Mary Ann Dimand, et. al. Aldershot & Brookfield: Edward Elgar, 1995: 71-81.

Sanders, Valerie, ed. *Harriet Martineau: Selected Letters.* London: Clarendon P, 1990.

___. *Reason over Passion: Harriet Martineau and the Victorian Novel.* New York: St. Martin's Press, 1986.

Shackleton, J.R. "Two Early Female Economists: Jane Marcet and Harriet Martineau." London: Polytechnic of Central London, October 1988.

Webb, R.K. *A Handlist of Contributions to the Daily News by Harriet Martineau, 1852-1866.* U of Birmingham, Special Collections, 1959.

Wheatley, Vera. *The Life and Work of Harriet Martineau.* London: Secker and Warburg, 1957.

Yates, Gayle Graham, ed. *Harriet Martineau on Women.* New Brunswick, NJ: Rutgers UP, 1985.

Illustrations of Political Economy

Conder, Josiah. "Illustrations of Political Economy." *Eclectic Review* 8 (1832): 328-49.

[Empson, William]. "Miss Marcet—Miss Martineau." *Edinburgh Review* 57 (April 1833): 1-39.

Freedgood, Elaine. "Banishing Panic: Harriet Martineau and the Popularization of Political Economy." *Victorian Studies* (Autumn 1995): 33-53.

Hobart, Ann. "Harriet Martineau's Political Economy of Everyday Life." *Victorian Studies* (Winter 1994): 223-51.

Marks, Patricia. "Harriet Martineau: *Fraser's* 'Maid of Dishonour'." *Victorian Periodicals Review* 19 (1986): 28-34.

Mill, John Stuart. "On Miss Martineau's Summary of Political Economy." *The Monthly Repository* 8 (1834): 318-22.

Review of "The Farrers of Budge Row." *The Spectator* (11 January 1834): 13-14.

Shattock, Joanne. *Politics and Reviewers: the 'Edinburgh' and the 'Quarterly.'* London, Leicester, and New York: Leicester UP, 1982.

Weal and Woe in Garveloch

Review of "Ella of Garveloch." *The Spectator* (9 June 1832): 540-41.

Review of "Weal and Woe in Garveloch." *The Spectator* (7 July 1832): 639.

Ricardo, David. *On the Principles of Political Economy and Taxation*. Ed. Piero Sraffa and M.H. Dobb. Cambridge: Cambridge UP, 1951.

Senior, Nassau. *Two Essays on Population, Delivered Before the University of Oxford in Easter Term 1828. To Which is Added, a Correspondence between the Author and the Rev. T.R. Malthus.* London: Saunders and Otley, 1829.

Smith, Kenneth. *The Malthusian Controversy*. London: Routledge & Kegan Paul, 1951.

A Manchester Strike

Barrett Browning, Elizabeth. "The Cry of the Children." *Poems Before Congress*. London: Chapman and Hall, 1860.

Brantlinger, Patrick. "The Case Against Trade Unions in Early Victorian Fiction." *Victorian Studies* 13 (September 1969): 37-52.

Hammond, J.L. and Barbara Hammond. *The Age of the Chartists 1832-1854. A Study of Discontent*. Hamden CT: Archon Books, 1962.

Horner, Leonard. *The Factories Regulation Act Explained, with some Remarks on its Origin, Nature, and Tendency*. Glasgow: David Robertson, 1834.

Martineau, Harriet. *The Factory Controversy; a Warning Against Meddling Legislation*. Manchester: A. Ireland and Co., 1855.

___. *The Rioters; or, a Tale of Bad Times*. Wellington, Salop: Houlston and Son, 1827.

___. "The Scholars of Arneside." *Illustrations of Taxation*. London: Charles Fox, 1834.

___. *The Tendency of Strikes and Sticks to Produce Low Wages, and of Union Between Masters and Men to Ensure Good Wages*. Durham: J. H. Veitch, 1834.

___. *The Turn-Out; or, Patience the Best Policy.* Wellington, Salop: Houlston and Son, 1829.

Review of "Manchester Strike." *The Spectator* (4 August 1832): 733-35.

Review of "'The Rioters' by Harriet Martineau." *The Athenaem* (29 October 1842): 930-31.

Tonna, Charlotte Elizabeth. *Combination.* New York: M.W. Dodd, 1832.

Cousin Marshall

Blaug, Mark. "The Myth of the Old Poor Law and the Making of the New." *Journal of Economic History* 23 (June 1963).

Brundage, Anthony. *The Making of the New Poor Law: The Politics of Inquiry, Enactment, and Implementation, 1832-1839.* New Brunswick, NJ: Rutgers UP, 1978.

Chalmers, Thomas. *On Political Economy in connexion with the Moral State and Moral Prospects of Society.* 2nd ed. Glasgow: William Collins, 1832.

Checkland, S.G. and E.O.A., eds. *The Poor Law Report of 1834.* London and New York: Penguin Books, 1974.

Cowherd, Raymond G. *Political Economists and the English Poor Laws. A Historical Study of the Influence of Classical Economics on the Formation of Social Welfare Policy.* Athens: Ohio UP, 1977.

Extracts from the Information Received by His Majesty's Commissioners, as to the Administration and Operation of the Poor-Laws. Published by Authority, 1833.

Jones, Kathleen. *The Making of Social Policy in Britain. From the Poor Law to New Labour,* 3rd ed. London and New Brunswick, NJ: Athelone Press, 2000.

Nicholls, Sir George. *A History of the English Poor Law in Connection with the State of the Country and the Condition of the People.* Vol. 2 (1714-1853). London: P.S. King & Son, 1904.

"On National Economy: Miss Martineau's "Cousin Marshall." *Fraser's Magazine* (November 1832): 403-13.

Review of "Cousin Marshall." *The Spectator* (8 September 1832): 853-55.

Review of *Poor Laws and Paupers, Illustrated. The Spectator* (29 March 1834): 300.

Sowers not Reapers

"An Address to the Labourers, on the Subject of Destroying Machinery." Society for the Diffusion of Useful Knowledge. London: Charles Knight, 1830.

Harrison, Brian. *Drink and the Victorians. The Temperance Question in England 1815-1872.* 2nd ed. Staffordshire: Keele UP, 1994.

Kadish, Alon, ed. *The Corn Laws. The Formation of Popular Economics in Britain.* Vol. 6. London: William Pickering, 1996.

McCord, Norman. *The Anti-Corn Law League 1838-1846.* London: George Allen & Unwin Ltd., 1958.

Of related interest

Bentham, Jeremy. *Fragment on Government.* London: T. Payne, 1776.

___. *Introduction to Principles of Morals and Legislation.* London: T. Payne, 1789.

Blaug, Mark. *Economic Theory in Retrospect.* Homewood: Richard D. Irwin Inc., 1962.

___. "Political Economy to be Read as Literature." *Ricardian Economics: A Historical Study.* New Haven: Yale UP, 1958.

Brantlinger, Patrick. *The Spirit of Reform: British Literature and Politics, 1832-1867.* Cambridge, MA and London: Harvard UP 1977.

Chadwick, Edwin. *Report on the Sanitary Condition of the Labouring Population of Great Britain.* Edinburgh: Edinburgh UP, 1842.

Checkland, S.G. *The Rise of Industrial Society in England 1815-1885.* New York: St. Martin's Press, 1964.

Cunningham, Valentine. *Everywhere Spoken Against. Dissent in the Victorian Novel.* Oxford: Clarendon P, 1975.

Fielding, K.J. and Anne Smith. "*Hard Times* and the Factory Controversy: Dickens vs. Harriet Martineau." *Nineteenth-Century Fiction* 24:4 (March 1970): 404-27.

Gallagher, Catherine. *The Industrial Reformation of English Fiction. Social Discourse and Narrative Form 1832-1867.* Chicago and London: U of Chicago P, 1985.

Godwin, William. *Caleb Williams.* London: B. Crosby, 1794.

Harrison, J.F.C. *Early Victorian Britain 1832-51.* London: Fontana P, 1971.

Himmelfarb, Gertrude. *The Idea of Poverty. England in the Early Industrial Age.* New York: Alfred A. Knopf, 1984.

Hobsbawm, E. J. *Industry and Empire*. Vol. 3 *The Pelican Economic History of Britain*. New York and London: Penguin Books, 1969.

Hollis, Patricia. *The Pauper Press: a study of working class radicalism of the 1830s*. Oxford: Oxford UP, 1970.

Llewellyn, Alexander. *The Decade of Reform. The 1830s*. New York: St. Martin's Press, 1971.

Marcet, Jane. *Conversations on Political Economy: In Which the Elements of that Science are Familiarly Explained*. London: Longman, 1806.

Matthew, Colin, ed. *The Nineteenth Century. The British Isles: 1815-1901*. Oxford: Oxford UP, 2000.

McCulloch, John Ramsay. *A Discourse on the Rise, Progress, Peculiar Objects, and Importance, of Political Economy*. Edinburgh: Archibald Constable & Co., 1825.

___. *The Literature of Political Economy*. London: Longman, Brown, Green, and Longmans, 1845.

___. *The Principles of Political Economy*. London & Edinburgh: William Tait, 1830.

___. *A Statistical Account of the British Empire: Exhibiting its extent, physical capacities, population, industry, and civil and religious institutions*. 2 vols. London: Charles Knight and Co., 1837.

Mill, James. *Elements of Political Economy*. London: Baldwin, Cradock, and Joy, 1821.

Mill, John Stuart. *Principles of Political Economy*, 2 vols. London: John W. Parker, 1848.

More, Hannah. *Stories for the Middle Ranks of Society; and Tales for the Common People*, 2 vols. London: T. Cadell and W. Davies, 1818.

Morris, R.J. *Cholera 1832. The Social Response to an Epidemic*. New York: Holmes & Meier, 1976.

Owen, Robert. *A New View of Society*. London: Cadell & Davies, 1813.

Paine, Tom. *Rights of Man*. London: J.S. Jordan, 1791.

Pike, E. Royston. *Human Documents of the Industrial Revolution in Britain*. London: George Allen & Unwin Ltd., 1966.

Seeley, Robert B. *The Perils of the Nation. An appeal to the legislature, the clergy, and the higher and middle classes*. London: Seeley, Burnside and Seeley, 1843.

Smith, Adam. *An Inquiry into the Nature and Causes of the Wealth of Nations*. London, 1776.

Tillotson, Kathleen. *Novels of the Eighteen-Forties*. New York and London: Oxford UP, 1962.

Webb, R.K. *The British Working Class Reader. 1790-1848. Literacy and Social Tension.* London: George Allen & Unwin Ltd., 1955.

Wood, Anthony. *Nineteenth Century Britain 1815-1914*, 2nd ed. Harlow: Longman, 1982.